CUT THE CLUTTER

AND STOW THE STUFF

THE Q.U.I.C.K.
WAY TO BRING
LASTING ORDER
TO HOUSEHOLD
CHAOS

CUT THE CLUTTER

AND STOW THE STUFF

EDITED BY LORI BAIRD

RODALE

© 2002 by Yankee Publishing Inc.
Illustrations © Molly Borman-Babich
Cover photograph © Zeitgeist/ZEFA/Photonica

Printed in the United States of America
Rodale Inc. makes every effort to use acid-free ♾, recycled paper ♺.

Interior design by Eugenie S. Delaney
Cover design by Tara Long

Library of Congress Cataloging-in-Publication Data

Cut the clutter and stow the stuff : the Q.U.I.C.K. way to bring lasting order to household chaos / edited by Lori Baird.
    p.   cm.
Includes index.
ISBN 1–57954–493–2 hardcover
ISBN 1–57954–512–2 paperback
1. Storage in the home.   2. House cleaning.   I. Baird, Lori.
TX309 .C88   2002
68'.8—dc21   2002004953

Distributed to the book trade by St. Martin's Press

  4   6   8   10   9   7   5   hardcover

FOR MORE OF OUR PRODUCTS
WWW.RODALESTORE.COM
(800) 848-4735

WE INSPIRE AND ENABLE PEOPLE TO IMPROVE
THEIR LIVES AND THE WORLD AROUND THEM

Cut the Clutter and Stow the Stuff Staff

PROJECT EDITORS: Ellen Phillips, Kathy Everleth

BOOK EDITOR: Lori Baird

WRITERS: Linda Buchanan Allen, Larry Bean, Tom Cavalieri, Christine Halvorson, Connie Hatch, Matthew Hoffman, Bill Keller, Rose Kennedy, Arden Moore, Lynn Naliboff, Michelle Seaton, Ken Sheldon, Cheryl Winters Tetreau

INTERIOR DESIGNER: Eugenie S. Delaney

COVER DESIGNER: Tara Long

PHOTO EDITOR: Robin Hepler

ILLUSTRATOR: Molly Borman-Babich

FACT CHECKERS: Mary Johnson, Trish Johnson, Marina Maina

COPY EDITOR: Kathy Dvorsky

PROOFREADER: Eileen Fitzmaurice

EDITORIAL PRODUCTION MANAGER: Marilyn Hauptly

LAYOUT DESIGNER: Jennifer H. Giandomenico

PRODUCT SPECIALIST: Jodi Schaffer

Rodale Women's Health Books Group

VICE PRESIDENT, EDITORIAL DIRECTOR: Elizabeth Crow

VICE PRESIDENT, EDITOR-IN-CHIEF: Tammerly Booth

SENIOR MANAGING EDITOR: Madeleine Adams

RESEARCH DIRECTOR: Ann Gossy Yermish

ART DIRECTOR: Darlene Schneck

OFFICE STAFF: Dawn Fiore, Cathy Fraschilla

Contents

You <u>Can</u> Conquer Clutter!

My husband laughed out loud when I told him my next book project would be about cutting clutter and getting organized. "You'd better hope they don't come here to take pictures," he said.

I admit it: I'm a slob. When I come home from work, I fling my clothes onto the floor, where they stay until some unidentified laundry day in the future. A day without my whining, "Honey, have you seen my cell phone?" is like a day without sunshine. And the refrigerator? It's bad—and that's as specific as I'll get in print.

In fact, I'd given up hope of ever clearing out the mess and finding anything in less than an hour's frantic searching when the manuscript for this book landed on my desk (where it promptly disappeared beneath an old American Express bill and a recipe for Spicy Roast Beef). Once I dug it out and began reading, I found that I couldn't just edit. I *had* to give some of the techniques our legion of clutter-busting experts recommended a try. And you know what? They worked.

Of course, decluttering doesn't happen overnight. Getting organized means changing long-held habits, like saving used batteries or holding on to pens that haven't worked since Jimmy Carter took office. It was with that in mind that our experts devised their ingenious clutter-cutting system.

It starts in chapter 1, with a fun quiz that will help you determine what kind of clutterer you are. That's important information, because once you know your Clutter Type, you'll know which organizing tactics will work for you—and which won't. (I'm an Accumulator-Tosser, which means that stuff piles up around my apartment until I get fed up. Then, in a frenzy, I indiscriminately throw it all out.)

In chapters 2 through 6 you'll learn about the Q.U.I.C.K. organizing system, a five-step process for conquering clutter once and for all. The steps are simple: 1. *Quantify* or inventory your clutter; 2. *Unload* what you don't want or don't need; 3. *Isolate* the rest into categories that make sense to you; 4. *Contain* it with appropriate storage systems; and then 5. *Keep it up*. These five steps will guide you through the process of letting go of clutter in your life—hey, it's working for me.

Don't be intimidated. The beauty of the Q.U.I.C.K. system is that it allows you to start small. You can start with the silverware drawer, the stamp collection, your sewing supplies, or your sweaters. Later, as your confidence builds, you can move on to bigger projects like your home office files or (gulp) the garage.

I started with my address book. I gathered all the addresses and phone numbers that were scattered throughout the apartment. Some were in old address books, some were scrawled on old Post-it notes that had fallen behind my desk, others were stuck in old files. Once I had them in front of me, I looked through all the names and numbers and got rid of the ones I didn't need. Next, I organized the addresses that were left in a way that was meaningful for me. Then I entered all the information into my PDA (personal digital assistant—the best known is the Palm Pilot, a terrific tool that makes adding, deleting, and organizing information quick and easy). And that—*finally!*—was that.

As you work your way through the Q.U.I.C.K. system, you'll have the expert advice of our organizing pros at your disposal. In chapters 7 through 16, our experts offer nearly 1,000 ways to help you declutter every room in the house. You'll learn how to get junk off your kitchen countertop (on page 97), how to keep your home office files under control (on pages 223–229), and how to organize pesky pieces of small hardware (on page 254). There are loads more, too!

Every month or so, I use the Q.U.I.C.K. system and those wonderful hints and tips to organize the next small part of my life. I'm still not perfectly organized, but I don't know if I even *want* to be perfectly organized. I'm kind of attached to my untidy self, and it's just not my style to care whether or not the bed gets made every morning. What I *do* want is to be able to find my keys when I leave the house, put my hands on my receipts at tax time, find a clean pair of jeans when I need them, and not be crushed by a falling stack of catalogs. You know what? I'm getting there. And with this book, you can get there, too. Happy organizing!

Lori Baird

Editor, *Cut the Clutter and Stow the Stuff*

PART

Your Unique Clutter Style

It's bad enough to have to go through your clutter, without having to fight yourself every step of the way. To avoid that (literally) self-defeating battle, take the Clutter Type quiz in this section. You'll discover your own clutter style—and the best ways to beat your clutter habits without beating yourself up. If your spouse and kids take our clutter quiz, too, you can see if your clutter styles are compatible, and—if not—how you can clear out your clutter without starting a family feud. The quiz is fast and fun. Go to it!

CHAPTER

What's Your Clutter Style?

lutter is like the tide: It comes in every day, whether you want it to or not. It slows down sometimes, but it never really stops. And unless you find a way to deal with it as quickly as it flows in, pretty soon you'll be drowning in clutter.

Has anyone ever visited your home and asked, "Gee, when's your rummage sale?" (when, in fact, you recently tidied up)? Have you disagreed with someone you love about keeping or tossing a certain item? Perhaps you even have an ongoing clutter conflict with other family members. Maybe you've avoided answering the door when neighbors came calling, simply because you couldn't face letting them see the accumulated clutter.

Make no mistake—getting rid of clutter is a challenge. Many of us seem to have a relationship with our inanimate objects. We don't know what to do with them all. They weigh heavily on our hearts and countertops. We long for simpler lives and less dust, but we seem unable to part with anything—at least not for long.

Rest assured, you're not alone in your clutter conundrum. Consider the cases of these four families. Can you identify?

- A wife confesses to throwing things out without telling her husband. He confesses to sorting through the trash when she's not looking.
- A high school drama teacher owns up to the fact that a new staff member had to lead her through the painful process of throwing out 25 years' worth of old costumes, backdrops, and props—not to mention the lumber she'd accumulated "just in case" it all could be used in future productions.
- A successful, well-respected prosecutor in New York City admits that he and his wife had to buy a larger home and are now renting even more space to store their growing mound of "collectibles."
- A wife and mother of three says that she would forgo a new kitchen, which she sorely needs, in exchange for a door to her husband's office. She wants to hide his clutter.

What's to be done? Here's where our "everyday experts" come in. They're here to help you declutter your life—and your home. We begin by gently prodding you to recognize your clutter style, then to take small steps toward leading a

Old-Time WISDOM

Neatness is a point in minor morals that deserves much more attention than it receives. There is such a comfort in order and tidy habits, that as a source of refined pleasure they should be taught, encouraged, and persisted in.
—*The Old Farmer's Almanac, 1879*

A brief history of clutter

PART I

Clutter has been with us since the dawn of history, when primitive man stood at the opening to his cave and grunted, "Oog-oog, mooga-goog," which translates roughly to, "Honey, have you seen my good mastodon knife?" Primitive woman eventually got sick of keeping track of primitive man's stuff ("I don't use your mastodon knife! How should I know where it is?!"), so she wove some reeds into a "junk basket," tossed everything in it, and told him to "Ooga-kooga" for the things himself (or words to that effect).

Following the dawn of history—say, around the coffee break of history—nomadic peoples began storing important items in chests so they could carry them from place to place. God told Moses to place the Ten Commandments inside such a chest. That was the Ark of the Covenant, and originally, the Ten Commandments were all that was in it. Later, Moses put in some of the manna God gave the people in the desert, then he added his brother Aaron's staff. You can see where this was leading. Eventually Moses probably had to ask Mrs. Moses, "Honey, have you seen the Ten Commandments?"

less cluttered life. Along the way, we'll show you hundreds of ingenious ways to cope with clutter. Our aim is not to judge, but to help you get a handle on the clutter in your life. Hope—and help—are on the way!

What's Your Type?

Over the years, scientists have studied human personalities, dividing them into types according to a variety of schemes: sanguine versus melancholy, introverted versus extroverted, left-brained versus right-brained. To our knowledge, however, no scientist has ever conducted a serious study of personality types and their relationship to clutter management. Until now.

Based on our exhaustive research, we have identified four primary Clutter Types: the Collector, the Concealer, the Accumulator, and the Tosser. Knowing your type helps you to tackle the clutter in your life by tailoring your approach to your style.

The following quiz will help you identify your Clutter Type, learn some general strategies for dealing with clutter based on that type, and discover ways to get along with other Clutter Types. After taking the quiz, refer to the sections that follow for an explanation of your type and discussions about how the various types function in relationships at home and at work.

It's important to answer the questions truthfully, not the way you *think* you should answer them or the way your mother would want you to answer them. Also, your responses should be based on your actual behavior, not the way you wish you behaved or how you plan to behave at some mythical time in the future such as "when I get my act together," "when I have the perfect house," or "after the children are gone" (the latter being mythical because, although your children may leave, they hardly ever take their stuff with them—and besides, they just might come back!).

A brief history of clutter

PART II

Throughout history, great conquerors have exhibited traits that we now associate with the main Clutter Types. Alexander the Great was an Accumulator, annexing so many countries that he eventually couldn't keep track of them. The Egyptians were classic Concealers. In fact, they were so good at hiding their treasures that we're still finding them today. Centuries later, the English established themselves as Collectors, building an empire that was the envy of their neighbors, who tried unsuccessfully to keep up with the Tudors.

Try as they might to build an empire, the French have always been Tossers, which could explain why they have had a hard time holding onto colonies.

A number of great individuals have contributed to the development of clutter, among them Johannes Gutenberg, inventor of the printing press. After printing his famous Bible, Gutenberg had reams of paper left over, so he decided to create junk mail. Thanks a lot, Johannes.

(For more famous Clutterers, see "A Brief History of Clutter, Part III" on page 15.)

The Clutter Type Quiz

PART 1: CLUTTER AS LIFESTYLE

For each of the following questions, circle the answer that best describes you and your behavior. If you can't decide on a single answer, you may circle more than one—although that in itself probably tells you something about your Clutter Type.

1. A friend asks to see your high school yearbook photo. You:

Ⓐ have every yearbook from every year of school, but aren't certain about where any of them are;

Ⓑ can quickly retrieve the yearbook from the bookshelf where all your yearbooks are chronologically arranged;

Ⓒ climb into the attic and are never seen again;

Ⓓ threw away your high school yearbook years ago.

2. You've just received a get well card from Aunt Edna. You:

Ⓐ read it and drop it on the dining room table, never giving it another thought;

Ⓑ read it and file it away under Cards, Get Well;

Ⓒ put it on display and find it 3 years from now, right next to the Easter greetings from Cousin Bert, who died 2 years ago;

Ⓓ read it and throw it away.

3. The local recycling center has a swap shop where folks can drop off unwanted items and pick up others free of charge. You:

Ⓐ occasionally find objects of value there and bring them home;

Ⓑ rearrange the items on the shelves as you're looking them over;

Ⓒ are the first in line to check out the good stuff on Saturday mornings, and rarely leave without something;

Ⓓ occasionally drop items off and never bring anything home.

4. You have a two-car garage. You:

Ⓐ can fit only one car in it, because the other side contains 10 lawn chairs, three ladders, two lawnmowers, and a dozen boxes of canning jars;

Ⓑ have the same items as in *a*, but they are all neatly arranged;

Ⓒ aren't sure, but you think there may be a car in there somewhere;

Ⓓ sold your husband's car because it was taking up too much space.

5. You've just knocked down a wall in your home and have a pile of used lumber. You:

Ⓐ pull out the nails and save the boards;

Ⓑ save the boards and the unbent nails, placing them in little jars, separated by size;

C save the boards and *all* the nails;

D throw away the boards, the nails, and the hammer, since it's broken.

6. At a yard sale, you:

A hope to find that missing collectible you've been searching for;

B move quickly, since you have a long list of yard sales that you plan to hit before noon and very specific items you're looking for;

C buy something you're not sure you need, but can't pass up;

D wouldn't be caught dead.

7. For you, a clutter crisis would be:

A misplacing that valuable, unopened can of Billy Beer;

B running out of storage containers;

C a daily event;

D finding anything out of place.

8. How many collections (seashells, rocks, baseball cards) do you have in your house?

A More than 10

B A few, all neatly arranged

C Who knows? They're all here somewhere.

D None.

9. The collection you had as a child is:

A more than twice the size it was then;

B on display in a tasteful, well-lit display cabinet;

C at the bottom of a box, beneath a stack of other boxes, in the back of the attic behind other stacks of boxes, but, by golly, you could find it if you had to;

D long gone.

10. The clothes in your closet:

A were borrowed by the local community theater troupe for its production of *My Fair Lady*;

B are neatly arranged by style and color;

C were moved out to make room for other stuff;

D actually fit in your closet.

11. When your eyeglass prescription changes, you:

A keep the old pair "just in case";

B immediately donate the old pair to charity;

C plan to donate the old pair to charity, and therefore carry them in your car's glove compartment for many years until they are too bent up and scratched to be used by anybody;

D throw the old pair away immediately.

12. In your house, magazines are:

A kept only if you think they'll be valuable someday;

B placed in specially designed holders in chronological order;

(continued)

C often lost before you get around to reading them;

D thrown away immediately after reading.

13. The old saw "a place for everything and everything in its place" is:

A something to be aimed for but not necessarily achieved;

B the motto you live by;

C a joke, right?

D true; and more often than not, that place is in the trash.

14. Your child has been assigned a craft project for school. You:

A warn him not to touch certain items that, while appearing to be junk, are actually valuable;

B direct him to the craft corner, where he'll find an ample supply of neatly organized materials;

C can't find the craft materials, though you're sure you have them around here somewhere;

D advise him to pick up his mess afterward or he'll risk having the project discarded along with the craft materials.

15. For you, the perfect storage container is:

A already filled with your prized mollusk collection;

B color coded, labeled, and stackable;

C one of those mini storage units you rent by the month;

D the wastebasket.

16. The main bathroom in your house:

A contains several antique grooming items (such as a shaving brush and dish);

B has a place for each person to store his or her personal items;

C would probably be condemned by the health department if you ever let them near it;

D is neat enough to be used as a surgical suite.

17. You misplace something of value or importance in your house:

A occasionally;

B rarely;

C daily;

D never.

18. Cleanliness is next to:

A resale value, when it comes to flea-market purchases;

B clayware, in the dictionary;

C impossible;

D godliness.

19. You videotape a television program. You:

Ⓐ add it to the other tapes of that program, hoping to complete the set;

Ⓑ label it and file it alphabetically with the others in your video cabinet;

Ⓒ put it in the enormous stack of videos you intend to watch someday and never get around to;

Ⓓ erase the tape after watching it and use it again.

20. Your children are in college. Their baby clothes are:

Ⓐ packed away, accumulating value.

Ⓑ neatly packed away, awaiting your grandchildren.

Ⓒ somewhere in the house, along with their baby toys, their baby teeth, and their baby blankets.

Ⓓ long gone.

Note the letters you circled (*a*, *b*, *c*, or *d*) at the beginning of each response. Add up the total number of *a* responses and write the number in the appropriate column of the score sheet on page 13. Do the same for *b*, *c*, and *d* responses.

PART 2: YOUR CLUTTER INVENTORY

Place a check next to any of the following items that you have (or, in a couple of cases, don't have) in your home, office, or garage. Check as many as apply.

☐ A Peg-Board with tool outlines indicating where tools belong, *and the tools are actually hanging there* (b)

☐ A dining room table with only a centerpiece on it (d)

☐ A piece of furniture you bought specifically to hold or display collectibles (a)

☐ Any item of clothing you haven't worn in 10 years (c)

☐ Boxes of dishes that you have no intention of eating from (c)

☐ Items you have collected but not looked at in more than a year (a)

☐ Labeled file cabinets, drawers, shelves, boxes, and other storage containers that actually contain the item(s) listed on the labels (b)

☐ Magazines or newspapers more than 2 months old that you're keeping until you get a chance to read them (c)

☐ No boxes of loose photographs that you're going to put into albums someday (d)

☐ No item of clothing that you don't wear, for whatever reason (d)

☐ School papers that are more than a year old. Check twice if you have school papers more than 10 years old (c)

(continued)

☐ Storage bins that are prettier than your actual furniture (b)

☐ Strictly enforced rules about what goes where (d)

Note the letter at the end of each response you checked (*a*, *b*, *c*, or *d*). Add up the total number of *a*, *b*, *c*, and *d* responses and write the number in the appropriate column of the score sheet on page 13.

PART 3: CLUTTER BEHAVIOR GUIDE

Place a check beside any statement that describes something you've ever done. Check all that apply.

☐ Bought a storage container before you knew what you were going to put in it (b)

☐ Purchased something you didn't like because it was part of a set (a)

☐ Bought something you didn't need because it was a bargain (c)

☐ Established no-clutter zones and warned household members that anything left there would be discarded (d)

☐ Kept something because it might be useful someday (c)

☐ Gone to auctions, flea markets, or yard sales looking for items to match others you already have (a)

☐ Argued with someone who wanted to keep something you intended to throw away (d)

☐ Kept something because you didn't know what else to do with it (c)

☐ Moved or built an addition because you needed more space for your collectibles (a)

☐ Rescued something from the trash that your spouse threw away (c)

☐ Sacrificed a room to clutter to keep the rest of the house clean (b)

☐ Spent an entire day organizing your files, kitchen cupboards, or medicine cabinet, based on a scheme only you understand (b)

☐ Kept something because you didn't want to hurt the feelings of the person who gave it to you (c)

☐ Thrown away an item you could not identify (d)

☐ Thrown away something that belonged to someone else without asking that person (d)

As in parts 1 and 2, add up the total number of *a* responses and write the number in the appropriate column of the score sheet on page 13. Do the same for *b*, *c*, and *d* responses.

SCORING THE QUIZ

Once you've completed the clutter quiz, add up the number of responses in each column on the score sheet on page 13 and put the total at the bottom. This is your clutter score. Below each total is a Clutter Type. The column with the highest score is your primary clutter type. So if your score is 1-3-0-10, you are a Tosser. A score that peaks in the second column indicates a Concealer, and so on.

Once you've identified your Clutter Type, you can turn to the discussion of Clutter Types below to read more about yourself—and try to identify your friends' and family members' types! We've also included a number of special Clutter Types that are combinations or subcategories of the main types.

IDENTIFY YOUR CLUTTER TYPE

	Number of *a* responses	Number of *b* responses	Number of *c* responses	Number of *d* responses
Part 1				
Part 2				
Part 3				
Total				
	Collector	**Concealer**	**Accumulator**	**Tosser**

The Primary Clutter Types

Before we discuss Clutter Types, it's important to state that no type is inherently good or bad—they're just different. Remember: One person's disaster area is another person's creative personal space. Here, then, are the primary Clutter Types.

THE COLLECTOR

Collectors, well, collect things. Whether it's 18th-century candle snuffers or the latest memorial coin series from the Franklin Mint, a collector's just gotta have it. There is a certain obsessiveness about Collectors' accumulation of clutter. Their collecting *appears* to have a method or goal, which differentiates them from Accumulators (see page 16). A Collector's collections are always incomplete, a situation that provides structure to her life as she strives, above all else, to complete the collection. The very process of looking for the one piece that will complete her set leads, inevitably, to finding more things to collect. Eventually, a Collector has a collection of collections.

Collectors are easy to spot early on: A child becomes one the moment she succumbs to the latest marketing craze. "Collect all 58 Dippy Dingbats, then buy the handy Dippy Dingbat display unit!" It's one short step from a childhood collection of Dippy Dingbats to an adult obsession with the Cherished Memories figurine collection or the latest in the Elvis commemorative plate series.

A Collector who wants to get organized must at some point honestly examine his or her collections and ask, "Why am I collecting this? Will it become valuable or just dusty? When it becomes valuable, will I sell it or keep it forever, never actually realizing any return on my investment? Will my children wonder what in the world I was thinking?"

The truly committed Collector will probably have to become a junk dealer, flea market operator, or auctioneer. His or her passion for finding that missing collectible could also lead to a lucrative career as a private detective.

THE FIVE STAGES OF DECLUTTERING

Decluttering can be emotionally challenging, particularly if it's not your own idea. Clutterers (that is, every Clutter Type except Tossers) are attached to their stuff and don't let go willingly. Most clutterers undergo five distinct stages of Clutter Separation: denial, anger, bargaining, depression, and finally, acceptance.

When first approached with the decluttering task by, say, a persistent spouse, it's not uncommon for the cluttered one to deny the problem. After that, he or she may get angry. The clutterer will then try to bargain with the Tosser ("I'll put it in the garage. You'll never know it's there," or "Okay, you can toss the newspapers, but I'm keeping the copies of *Crustacean Quarterly*."). When decluttering becomes inevitable, the clutterer becomes depressed. Eventually, though, he gets over it. After all, there's always more clutter where that came from.

One approach to dealing with this clutter separation anxiety is to affirm the clutterer's feelings and to remove the stuff gradually. At first, that box of place mats from around the world may have to move from the middle of the den to the back of the hall closet. Later, it can move to the top shelf in the garage, then to the trash can.

Even the most emotionally attached clutterer can let go. Every day is a new, clutter-free beginning. Although one day the clutterer will swear he could never part with his doorknob collection, at some other time he may wonder what he ever saw in it. This is why we recommend periodic sifting through the stuff.

When a clutterer gives the sign that he's ready to declutter, a clutter coach may be necessary. A supportive spouse, for instance, can stand by when the Accumulator asks, "Is there a reason to keep this key from my roller skates from when I was 10, even though I don't have the skates anymore?" The clutter coach can lovingly and gently say, "No, dear. You have the memory of the key. The key will live in your heart forever. Now chuck it."

THE CONCEALER

The Concealer is similar to the Accumulator (see page 16), but his stuff is neatly packed away or hidden so that an outsider won't catch on to the fact that he has clutter, too. The Concealer loves storage containers of all types: boxes, baskets, bins, canisters, containers, file cabinets, and crates. His items are often neatly stacked and carefully labeled, maybe even color coded. When he was a child, the Concealer's bedroom and school desk were neat. He meticulously arranged his pencils in pencil holders. When they visited his home, non-Concealers wondered where this kid kept all his "stuff." (It may be that his mother was a Tosser, so in fact the family owned no "stuff.")

Despite what he tells you, the Concealer's lifestyle has inherent clutter dangers. A Concealer's habitual storing and labeling of items could be masking a tendency toward indecisiveness. Concealers may find it easier to organize than to make the tough decisions about what to keep and what to toss. A woman we know confessed her obsession with clear plastic storage bins of all types. However, she noted, "I buy no more than two at a time, so my husband doesn't get too suspicious. I believe the bins will save us." But there's a problem with this mind-set: Simply sweeping things into a bin or box doesn't *reduce* clutter. It merely organizes and rearranges it. At some point, Concealers may start stacking those plastic bins in their living

A brief history of clutter

Famous clutterers in history include P.T. Barnum (a classic Collector who started a circus to show off his stuff), R.L. Ripley (believe it or not), and Imelda Marcos (she of the thousands of shoes). However, the champion clutterers of all time may have been Homer and Langley Collyer, wealthy brothers who lived like hermits in a Fifth Avenue mansion in New York.

In 1947, the police were tipped off that someone had passed away in the Collyer mansion. The police forced their way in but found themselves barricaded by walls and booby traps made of old newspapers, folding beds, and tons of other junk that the reclusive Collyers had constructed to keep outsiders away.

By the time authorities located the deceased brothers, they had removed more than 130 tons of rubbish from the mansion. The stash included the top of a horse-drawn carriage, a primitive X-ray machine, an automobile engine and chassis, 14,000 books, old medical equipment, dressmakers' dummies, and 14 grand pianos (that is *not* a typo).

In an interview before his death, Langley Collyer was asked why he and his brother had saved tons of newspapers dating back to 1918. In a statement sure to endear him to Accumulators everywhere, Langley said he was saving the newspapers for his brother (who was blind) "so that when he regains his sight he can catch up on the news."

The Dropper feels that the best place for anything is right where he's standing. A wrapper from a candy bar? Drop it on the counter. Shoes and socks? Right next to the chair where they were taken off. For the Dropper, the presence of a nearby clothes hamper, closet, or other storage device is insufficient reason to actually place the item there. Apparently, the act of removing clothing so weakens the Dropper that he or she can't possibly move that additional 2 feet to dispose of the item(s) in question.

Our research indicates that husbands and children are most likely to be Droppers, but anybody can become a Dropper. Often, Droppers are the children of Tosser parents. A child reared by a Tosser probably never learned to pick up her toys, because the Tosser parent was right there behind her doing it for her. Droppers, as adults, frequently marry Tossers, who are sometimes responsible for enabling the Droppers' behavior.

rooms, right next to the Louis XVI armoire. That's when a Concealer needs a Tosser around (see "Clutter Types and Relationships" on page 19).

THE ACCUMULATOR

The Accumulator is your basic pack rat, the person who keeps everything. Stuff just keeps coming into her life (and house, and garage, and toolshed, and cellar) and never goes out. Some Accumulators imagine the things they keep have value—or will have value someday. Others are just indecisive: They simply can't decide what to do with the tide of clutter, so they set it aside for some later time that never arrives.

As with all Clutter Types, there may be an emotional basis for becoming an Accumulator. Experiencing a loss may create a desire to accumulate material possessions to provide a sense of stability and security. People who have moved frequently sometimes amass belongings as a way of taking their home along with them. Perhaps one or both of the Accumulator's parents were Tossers who threw away her belongings indiscriminately, causing her to now hold on tightly to "her stuff."

Whatever the root cause, a typical Accumulator no longer has space for her clutter, but she doesn't see that as a problem. The Accumulator doesn't think that she needs less stuff, only more space.

For the Accumulator, there are two general approaches to clutter management: containment and reform. If you're a committed Accumulator and are unable or unwilling to change, you may need to learn some methods of organizing and arranging just to keep things under control. If you're an Accumulator who *wants* to change, you can adopt some new principles. The first is recognizing that the act of hoarding

When you don't have time to take the systematic approach to decluttering outlined in the rest of this book, try playing these tricks on yourself as a motivational tool. Imagine one of the following scenarios.

1. Someone has offered to buy your house at three times its value, but only if he can move in tomorrow. Start packing.

2. Your mother-in-law has called from the mall around the corner and is stopping by for tea.

3. The Queen of England is stopping by for tea.

4. Your doctor has just diagnosed your allergy to dust and advised you to remove all dust-collecting knickknacks from your shelves.

5. The recycling center is offering prizes to the family that can bring in the most stuff.

6. Your boss is coming for dinner.

stuff of questionable value is costly, in that it can steal your life. Second, recognize that you're not responsible for the clutter other people bring into your life. Just because your dentist sent you a calendar doesn't mean that you have to keep it. Similarly, Aunt Edna may have meant well when she gave you that ceramic statue of Ye Olde Fisherman, but you don't have to keep it, and it doesn't mean you don't love her if you get rid of it. Flex those tossing muscles!

THE TOSSER

The Tosser doesn't let anything lie around for long. Yesterday's newspaper? Outta here. A mateless glove? Gone. Tossers see no relevance in things that are only partly there—parts of

For many of us, old clothes are a primary source of clutter. Sweaters shrink, we expand, styles change, yet we keep the clothing anyway since we expect to lose weight, give the clothes to someone smaller, or wait until the fashion pendulum swings back their way again. The number of pieces of clothing you actually wear ("active" clothing) compared to the number you no longer wear ("retired" clothing) can provide an indication of your Clutter Type. It's called the active/retired or A/R ratio. Here's how to calculate yours.

1. Count the number of shirts (or skirts, or suits, or other items of clothing) you own that are appropriate for this season.

2. Count the shirts (or skirts, or suits, and so on) that you've actually worn this season.

3. Divide the second number by the first number. This is your A/R ratio.

An A/R ratio of 25 percent means you really wear only 1 in 4 of your shirts—time to clean out that closet. The ideal A/R ratio is 100 percent (that is, you don't own anything you don't wear regularly), but only the most committed Tossers ever achieve this.

lamps, pens without ink, and the like. Tossers are not sentimental. They do not own dolls from their childhood, their children's first pair of shoes, or the plastic figures from the top of their wedding cake.

Tossers who live alone have few problems with clutter, while Tossers who live with others are in a constant state of battle. You see, clutter not of their own creation offends the Tosser's sense of order and neatness. (See "Clutter Types and Relationships" on page 19.) The emotional background of Tossers is not well understood. They may have come from large families where it was easy for things to get out of hand. They may be attempting to control their space or reclaim something lost in their youth. They may just be ruthless dictators (of course, we mean that in a nonjudgmental way).

Ideally, a Tosser should always ask the offending clutterer before throwing something out. One friend tells of a beloved grandfather clock his parents had given him. When he and his wife moved, the movers placed the pendulum in a special box. Later, he found the pendulum out on the sidewalk with the trash because his wife "didn't know what it was." It may be hard for a Tosser to accept, but sometimes—just sometimes—there is a reason to keep something.

If it's not feasible to check with everyone else in the household before tossing items, a Tosser should at least make sure everyone is clear about the household tossing rules so they can't say they weren't warned. (If you leave it on the kitchen table, it gets tossed. When a new newspaper or magazine arrives, the previous edition gets discarded.)

COMBINATION CLUTTER TYPES

Most people will show a strong inclination toward one of the four main Clutter Types, though combination types are common. See if you're one of these three:

Accumulator-Tosser. As unlikely as it seems, some people combine the seemingly opposite Accumulator and Tosser traits. A person

MORE CLUTTER TYPES: THE DECORATOR

The Decorator is a combination of the Collector, the Accumulator, and the Concealer Types. Decorators feel unworthy unless their homes look like the advertisements in Better Mansions and Castles. The Decorator believes that if a little is good, a whole houseful is better. When she loves a style, she really loves it, filling every nook and cranny with lacy pillows, ornate picture frames, matching lampshades, and dried-flower arrangements. She is the Queen of Tchotchkes (pronounced "chotch-kas," a Yiddish word for knickknacks). A visitor to the Decorator's home may develop stimulation overload. A Tosser would simply feel faint.

The Compromiser is a Tosser who lives with a Collector or Accumulator and who has made some concessions to the clutter that those types generate. The Compromiser sacrifices certain areas of the house to clutter in an attempt to contain it. She has designated clutter-free zones throughout the home, while clutter reigns in other places.

Don't look in the Compromiser's spare room: While her living room is a pristine showcase, her kitchen is so spotless it appears unused, and the only thing on her dining room table is the shine from the furniture polish, her back room is a veritable warehouse of all the items she's removed from those other areas. Once the spare room was a guest room. Now the bed is hidden under mountains of clothing that needs to be repaired, laundered, given away, or hung up.

The children's bedrooms in a Compromiser's home may look like toxic waste sites, but the guests she's entertaining in the dining room will never know. The Compromiser is the Neville Chamberlain of housekeepers, sacrificing some territory in the vain hope that clutter won't take over the rest of the house.

with this hybrid Clutter Type generally lets clutter build up until it's no longer tolerable, then jettisons it in a frenzy of tossing. Periods of clutter-buildup and clutter-tossing alternate in an endless repeating pattern.

Collector-Concealer. A Collector with Concealer tendencies has a massive quantity of stuff firmly under control, perhaps displayed in custom-made cabinets with good lighting.

Concealer-Tosser. This fairly common combination type results when a Concealer realizes that the organizing process is made easier by first tossing out nonessentials. Eventually, the Concealer-Tosser may discard so many things that there's nothing left to organize.

Clutter Types and Relationships

Ideally, a person would determine his or her Clutter Type before taking major life steps such as choosing a mate, sharing an apartment, or clearing out the junk in the cellar that's been building up for years. As one of our survey respondents said, "I've found that one of the few elements that contribute to a peaceful marriage is finding someone who feels the same about religion and clutter as you do."

In the following sections, we'll examine some typical Clutter Type combinations. Although we focus on couples, the information may be applied to roommates and parent-child relationships, too.

The Crafter is a subset of the Collector and Accumulator Clutter Types. The Crafter has a propensity for collecting things—often otherwise useless things—to use in future craft projects. Crafters are often Scout leaders, kindergarten teachers, or vacation Bible school organizers. Old clothes are never thrown away—they become costumes, or quilts, or picture-frame covers. Popsicle sticks present endless possibilities to the Crafter's mind. Even empty cereal boxes are kept and put to use for a child's game of "Let's Go Grocery Shopping." The Crafter has never met a margarine tub she didn't keep. A Crafter may also be a Concealer, keeping all the scraps of felt in one bin and all the craft plans torn from parenting magazines hidden in a box.

MATCHING AND OPPOSING CLUTTER TYPES IN RELATIONSHIPS

The smoothest path to harmony at home may be to marry someone of your Clutter Type—at least you'll be able to sympathize with each other's weaknesses. Of course, that doesn't mean that equally matched Clutter Types don't have specific challenges: When two Tossers share one house, the result will probably be lost pet vaccination records. Two Collectors living together will tend to encourage one another and end up having to buy a bigger house to hold all their stuff. A pair of Accumulators will have to buy two houses. Finally, a Concealer married to another Concealer simply has to make sure that both have the same organization scheme. (Imagine a library in which two librarians shelve books based on two completely different systems.) Check out these six "mixed marriage" Clutter Types.

Tossers and Accumulators. This is, unfortunately, an all-too-common combination among married couples. Ideally, the Tosser should ask the Accumulator before throwing anything out, to make sure it isn't something important or valuable. The problem is that, for the Accumulator, *everything* is important or valuable and if the Tosser asks for permission every time she goes to throw anything out, she can *never* discard anything.

For this reason, Tossers in relationships often engage in "stealth tossing," removing old, unworn clothes from the Accumulator's closet, discarding papers when the Accumulator isn't around, and so on. A variation is "delayed stealth tossing," also known as the "Out of Sight, Out of Mind, Out of the House" technique. That's where the Tosser gathers the Accumulator's clutter in a box and hides it. If the Accumulator notices anything missing, the Tosser can always retrieve it. If—as often happens—the Accumulator doesn't even *notice* anything missing, after a suitable length of time the Tosser quietly removes the box and its contents from the house. (This technique is also a favorite of parents whose kids tend to hang on to shredded stuffed animals and dog-eared books from when they were 1 year old.)

To live together in peace, Tossers and Accumulators must declare détente early on. The Tosser should assign the Accumulator his own room (or attic, garage, or basement) and never go in there. One man we know bought an extra house to hold all the things he had bought at yard sales, but which his wife refused to allow into their regular home. People who rented this guy's "fully furnished" extra home were often surprised to find that the full furnishings included a bust of Lenin, several stuffed wild animal heads, a giant plush pink dinosaur, and a statue made entirely of beer bottle caps, among other treasures.

Tossers and Collectors. Tossers married to Collectors may have a challenge similar to the

---

CLUTTER: IT'S ALL IN YOUR HEAD

Our clutter psychologists have identified four syndromes related to clutter. Being able to spot these patterns is one of the first steps to leading a clutter-free life.

1. VICARIOUS CLUTTERING. Folks who suffer from this syndrome tend to buy items for people that those people (a) didn't ask for; (b) may not need; and (c) won't know what to do with, as a way of fulfilling their own need to accumulate things. Grandparents often engage in vicarious cluttering by buying too many presents for their grandchildren.

2. COMFORT ACCUMULATION. This is the gathering of objects to make up for something else missing in your life. The single guy with 500 videotapes in his collection, the single woman with a dozen cats, and people who crowd their lawns with ornaments all suffer from comfort accumulation syndrome.

3. HUNTER-GATHERER SYNDROME. This syndrome is often found in Collectors, who collect for the thrill of the hunt. To the true Collector, finding a rare bargain or filling in a gap in a collection is better than actually owning the items.

4. SENTIMENTAL KEEPER COMPLEX. This syndrome lies at the root of many an Accumulator's battles. People with this condition hang on to every drawing their children bring home from school, clothing that belonged to departed family members, and memorabilia from every vacation ever taken. One woman, whose son gets a T-shirt every time he plays in a hockey tournament, told us that she has saved them all, neatly folded, though she isn't sure what to do with them. Another hockey mom suggested that her collection could be made into a quilt, though she estimates that at this point, the quilt would be roughly the size of Connecticut.

Tosser-Accumulator couple's, perhaps exacerbated by the Collector's knowledge that the box of old beer bottles in the cellar really *does* have some value to someone, somewhere. For harmony to reign in this relationship, the Collector must convince the Tosser that what he's collecting is of value. Also, the Collector will have to contain the collections in a specified collection area as designated by the Tosser.

Tossers and Droppers. For a Tosser, the only Clutter Type more challenging to live with than the Accumulator is the Dropper (see "More Clutter Types: The Dropper," page 16). Ironically, the Tosser may actually exacerbate the Dropper's behavior by enabling it: The Dropper deposits newspapers in the den, from whence they automatically migrate to the trash. Similarly, the Dropper married to a Tosser leaves his shoes in the middle of the living room. Later, he finds they've been magically transported to his closet. Why bother putting things in the right place when your home appears to be inhabited by invisible cleaning elves who do the work for you?

Occasionally, then, the Dropper-mate may need to resort to an intervention. One friend, tired of finding her husband's shoes and dirty socks everywhere except where they belonged, put them on his pillow. He got the point.

Tossers and Concealers. Although this might seem like a good match, the Tosser-Concealer couple could encounter clutter conflicts. For a Tosser, the mere fact that the Concealer

has neatly arranged her stuff isn't reason enough to keep it. Meanwhile, the Concealer may resent the Tosser's interference with her carefully arranged system.

Collectors and Accumulators. Despite their surface similarities, Collectors and Accumulators may have a hard time living together, since the Accumulator may not recognize the subtle distinctions that separate junk from collectibles. A Collector may resent the Accumulator's lack of discrimination (a mayonnaise jar is not the same as a Coke bottle), while the Accumulator thinks the Collector is just too fussy. Even if the Collector-Accumulator couple works out their problems, they are in danger of needing to have separate garages, one labeled "Collections" and the other "Stuff."

Collectors and Concealers. This could be a good combination, as long as the Collector doesn't bring things into the house faster than the Concealer can manage them. If the Concealer is not particularly concerned with the quantity of things needing organization, it could in fact be a Concealer's dream come true, for a Collector will always need something to be organized—by height, size, year, or number of broken parts.

Accumulators and Concealers. Of all the potential clutter combinations, this one is fraught with the most potential difficulties. The Accumulator will resent the Concealer's messing with his or her stuff, while the Con-

Here's a fun game to play with your family. (All right, maybe "fun" is too strong a word. Let's say "less boring than a meeting of the planning and zoning commission.") Give every player a copy of the following list, along with a grocery bag. (If you don't have any grocery bags, stop now. You don't need to play this game.) Choose a time limit. Within that time limit, each player tries to collect as many of the following items as he or she can from anywhere inside the house. At the end of the game, collect the bags and throw them in the trash. Everyone wins!

☐ Bent paper clips

☐ Bottle caps

☐ Broken earrings

☐ Broken stapler

☐ Corners of envelopes bearing the return addresses of people you don't remember

☐ Dead batteries

☐ Desiccated rubber bands that break at the first stretching

☐ Dried-up pens

☐ Half-used birthday cake candles

☐ Handy sewing kit you got free from a hotel

☐ Keys to unknown locks

☐ Membership cards that expired more than a year ago

☐ Necklace completely in knots

☐ Negatives without photographs

☐ Paper umbrellas from a tropical drink

☐ Power cords to unknown appliances

☐ Rolls of tape that have fused into a solid crystalline doughnut with no perceivable beginning

☐ Spare buttons for unidentified shirts

☐ Stamps no longer used by the post office

☐ Unidentified audio cassettes

☐ Unused greeting cards without envelopes

☐ Tie tacks you haven't worn in years

☐ Used twist ties

cealer's continuing attempts to bring order to the chaos is like shoveling the tide with a pitchfork. Separate housing may be the only solution.

Clutter Types at Work

When we head off to the office, we don't leave our Clutter Types behind. Understanding the various Clutter Types in your organization may help you get along with workmates whose styles are different from yours. It may also explain why you haven't gotten the big promotion you've been angling for.

Tossers often make good managers, as they can cut through nonessentials to get to the heart of a matter quickly. They can also be ruthless when it comes to slackers, so watch out if a Tosser becomes your boss. And when the

Although not necessarily a Collector or Accumulator, a Paper Piler is a special Clutter case. Paper Pilers are physiologically incapable of dealing with the periodicals in their lives. The Paper Piler simply can't throw out a magazine or newspaper unless he's read it—and there's never enough time to read it. The Paper Piler is terrified of missing some terribly important information in those periodicals. If he doesn't read an issue of Personalities on Parade, he might miss the crucial news of Madonna's latest breakup. That issue of Big Money may have the key to successful investing in shoe leather futures. The Paper Piler loves subscriptions, picks magazines out of recycling bins, and takes home the newspapers from the lunch table at work. Special subsets of the Paper Piler include the Magazine Magnet, the Journal Junkie, and the Catalog Collector.

refrigerator in the lunchroom is in danger of being shut down by the public health service, it is usually a Tosser who cleans it out.

Another useful type to have around the office is the Concealer, even though he or she may drive the rest of the staff nuts. Concealers often gravitate to positions as office managers or executive secretaries, simply because they're the only ones who know where the manila folders are. Of course, Concealers may spend so much time creating files, setting up systems, and establishing committees that no actual work ever gets done.

As at home, the workplace nemesis to the Tosser and Concealer is the Accumulator, whose office is a no-person's-land of books, memos, reports, coffee cups, and pens that may or may not work. These days, Accumulators even manage to gather stuff around them electronically. The paperless office? Hah! Thanks to computers, an Accumulator can keep *every* draft of that important memo about the holiday gift exchange. An Accumulator's computer desktop is usually just as cluttered as his real desktop. ("Delete that old program? Are you kidding? I might need it some day!")

If Collectors can apply the same zeal to work that they bring to collecting, they will soon be president of the company. John D. Rockefeller was a Collector of such magnitude that it took the federal government to break up his collection. On the other hand, Collectors may simply do their jobs and have the best collection of free coffee mugs, pens, tote bags, and T-shirts from trade shows.

Where Do I Go from Here?

Now you know who you are—in terms of clutter, anyway. So what good does that do you?

Well, that's where the rest of this book comes in. In the next 300 or so pages, we offer all sorts of ingenious ways to clear your life of clutter, based on your Clutter Type—and the Clutter Types of your loved ones.

First things first. In Part II, we introduce you to our simple five-step decluttering process. It's called the Q.U.I.C.K. system, and it stands for Quantify, Unload, Isolate, Contain, and Keep It Up. But don't worry—we'll take it one step at a time.

Old-Time WISDOM

I have made it a rule in my housekeeping arrangements to have a set place—nail, box, bag, nook, or closet—for everything from a clothes-pole to a darning-needle. I have made it a set rule, never to be departed from, always to put a thing away in its exact place as soon as I have used it.

—*The Old Farmer's Almanac, 1883*

PART

The Q.U.I.C.K. System

In part 1, you learned about your unique Clutter Type—what kind of clutterer you (and your spouse and family) are. Now, it's time to take action, and follow our quick—or rather, Q.U.I.C.K.—plan to get that clutter out of your house and out of your life. In just five steps— Quantify, Unload, Isolate, Contain, and Keep It Up—you can conquer clutter for good. We'll show you how! And by playing to the strengths of your individual clutter style (and avoiding your unique clutter temptations), you can make it a painless process. So come on—let's get started!

CHAPTER

Step One:
Quantify Your Clutter

You've discovered your clutter style. And you've admitted that, yes, you actually *do* have clutter, and need to do something about it. Now it's time to get started. In the next five chapters, you'll learn how to use our Q.U.I.C.K. decluttering system, the first step of which is Quantifying. It's easy—and sometimes even fun! (That's why we call it Q.U.I.C.K.)

But here's an irony for you. The first phase of Quantifying is talking about clutter—and why you haven't done anything about it. That's because when you sum up where your clutter-cutting efforts have fallen short in the past, you reveal how you should proceed in the future. "If you've consistently resisted dealing with the clutter in your home, you probably just haven't been able to make the connection between cutting clutter and what is most valuable in your life," says longtime therapist and personal coach Melanie McGhee of Maryville, Tennessee. "Most people who can't get started are tapped into someone else's value system, telling themselves, 'I should get rid of this junk because junk is bad by definition.' But that won't help you see it through. You need to find out why controlling clutter is important to you."

For some folks, the reason to get rid of clutter will be the visual appeal: The house will just look better. For others, "it's more about creating ease in their lives, a less hectic pace, more comfort, less stress," says Melanie, who also happens to be a longtime meditator who helps people identify what's important in their lives.

Quantifying why this matters is the "soft" component of the quantifying step. After that, you'll move on to the hard-nosed, pragmatic quantifying—actually looking at the stuff and the space in your home. After all, you need to know exactly what you have before you can decide which of those items don't fit into your life anymore. (In fact, sometimes it's easier to get started by telling yourself that all you're committing to is finding out what you have. It's kind of like telling yourself that all you're doing is climbing a ladder—who said anything about diving?) So take stock of your stuff, measure your spaces, create a log, then talk about what could be done with the stuff you have.

Don't start making decisions about the fate of any objects just yet—are you listening, Tossers?—that's jumping ahead to step two. You see, just like smart midseason coaching replacements, the wisest clutter managers figure out what's been done in the past—and *why*—before they rush in with big changes. That way, the changes are more likely to take hold and less likely to make people mad. In other words, finish quantifying before you start qualifying. (Remember: What you *don't* do is just as important as what you do when it comes to quantifying.)

Okay, while you're at it, remember not to give life to sacred cows, either. Nothing is exempt from scrutiny in the Quantify stage. At this point, you're not deciding what stays and what goes—you're simply taking account of what you have. Maybe later, when you're deciding what to get rid of, you can put some items on a "Not to Be Tampered With for Any Reason" list. But not yet. So unpack that trunk in the attic—even though "every woman saves her wedding dress for her daughter." List all the publications you receive—even though "our family could never do without *TV Guide*." Eye that gargantuan mahogany bedroom suite that weighs 2 tons—even though you'd "never give away furniture that's worth more than our car!" Examine everything. Why? Because your life changes, your space changes, your taste changes, and your needs change. Constantly.

Knowing how much *stuff* you own is one important component of the quantifying step. Knowing how much *space* you have is another. So as you tally your objects, start assessing your space, too. Define your future needs and goals.

CLUTTER CRUSADERS

Timing Things Right

"WE LIVE IN A COLLEGE TOWN, so I do all my best clutter-cutting the second and third week of August," says Amy Witsil of Chapel Hill, North Carolina. "The last week of August is when school starts, and our family always participates in a multifamily garage sale for the students. Several neighbors pitch in to pay for the ads and the signs, then each family sells its own stuff. I'm really motivated to sort through the household items that students might need then, like sheets and towels or castoff dishes. The other great part about timing my work that way is that I know that local junk shops also accept stuff that week because of the returning students. So I know that I can get rid of whatever doesn't sell and not have to drag lots of stuff back into the house."

Then you can match them all up. And that will put you well on the way to combating clutter.

So let's start quantifying. Don't worry! We're not going to throw you right into the soup—we'll take it slowly. To start, we offer a few ways to help you get motivated. Next comes some advice for getting (and keeping) the whole family involved. We'll also discuss ways to make time for your quantifying project, how to actually get started, and—of course!—tips and techniques to help you keep up the fight. Let the quantifying begin!

What's My Motivation?

As they say, every journey begins with a single step. And for the wonderful, difficult, irritating, and inspiring journey of organizing your home, getting motivated to quantify your clutter is that all-important first step. The good news is that there are dozens of ways to get motivated (though some of them seem to contradict each other). The bad news is that lots of them won't work for you. But the *best* news is that if you keep trying options, you'll find a motivator that works for you. The same way a smoker increases his odds of quitting with each attempt, you'll increase your odds of success if you keep trying new ways to get started. Here are five to consider.

Put on your thinking cap. Brainstorm the specific long-term benefits of having less clutter in your life. Obviously, if you've been living with clutter for a long time, having less clutter is not in and of itself enough motivation. So identify exactly what you'd like to have happen when you're done. "We'd have a better social life because we won't be embarrassed to have people over," could be one. "I could find my keys when I need them," might be another. Or "I'll finally be able to see the stairs." Dig deep, because these benefits may have to keep you going for a long time. For example, a clutter-free household might help you avoid late charges on bills, because you'll be able to find the paperwork easily. A well-ordered kitchen

So why, when it's crystal clear that we'd be better off without all this junk, do we refuse to lift a finger to do away with it? "It's human nature to prefer the devil you know to the devil you don't," says Knoxville, Tennessee, family counselor Steve Brown. "The unknown is so scary that people will go to extraordinary lengths to stay with the known, no matter how dysfunctional or draining it is." The concept may have evolved back in the days when the safety of the clan was at risk if new elements were introduced, but more important than understanding it is combating it. "What works best for most people is to model after the Alcoholics Anonymous motto and take it one day at a time," says Steve. "Inch yourself into new ways by breaking down tasks into manageable parts—one room, one desk. If you focus on all the huge changes that might come about, it's too daunting and can keep you from getting started at all."

Of course, pack rats and collectors may resist altering their overstuffed lives for another reason. "For them, possessions may be a way of holding on to a fleeting past, so they might not want to change regardless of the benefits," says Steve. Others aren't resisting change as much as they're feeling too tired or helpless to change anything. But Steve has one rule of thumb for everyone: "Make the connection between the outer clutter and what's going on inside you, and the direction you need to take to start cutting clutter will become clear."

might improve your diet (and therefore your health) or even help you lose weight, because you'll be able to cook at home more often. Write your primary goal on a note card and post it where you'll see it often. Commit the benefits of meeting that goal to paper, too, and review them every few days while you're quantifying to keep you on track.

Don't forget the benefits along the way. Next, brainstorm the benefits of the clutter-quantifying process itself. We admit, this may sound like advice from Pollyanna. But you really will reap benefits just from quantifying your clutter—we promise. You'll get exercise and gain muscle tone, for example, as you walk boxes up and down the stairs. You'll have the opportunity to talk with family members about meaningful topics. Consider your clutter-quantifying day as the perfect excuse to pay someone to mow the lawn or a chance to get to know that nice lady at the thrift store.

Go for good timing. Sometimes you can get out of the quantifying gate just by timing it right. For example, find out when the local food bank has its Thanksgiving food drive—that can motivate you to clean out the pantry for donations. For larger jobs, consider when, for example, a friend with a truck might be visiting or when someone who could thwart your efforts (like the household pack rat) might be out of town. But don't make the mistake of waiting for a rainy day—unless you're a farmer and that's the only time you're free. It's difficult to move stuff out of the house or to transport it when it's raining! And even when you're just moving stuff from room to room, it's nice to be able to get rid of the piles of trash at the end of the day.

Lock yourself in. If you're a procrastinator who works well under pressure, consider arranging ahead of time for the Goodwill workers to pick up a large piece of furniture at a particular time or date. That will probably get you moving in a hurry! Or, if you're particularly frugal (and justifiably proud of it!), lock yourself into an arrangement that will cause you to lose a little money if you don't follow through. For example, take out a classified ad for a garage sale on the day you'd like to reach a clutter goal. If you don't perform, you've wasted the ad money. One lawyer we know invites friends over for a happy hour every Saturday night. That gives him all day Saturday to purge the living room of magazines and the kitchen of other debris. And on Sunday, he takes out the discards from cleaning and empties the trash from the party. Of course, such techniques are not for the faint of heart. If it will truly stress you out to have no choice but to cut clutter, use another motivator.

Beware of backfires. Some motivating techniques are self-defeating for certain clutter types. Accumulators and Collectors, for example, might reward themselves for starting to quantify their clutter by buying something. But that's like rewarding yourself for going a whole day without a cigarette by chewing tobacco. Instead, those types should promise themselves an activity to reward their positive behavior: a massage, for example, or a trip to the classic movie house, where they can see someone else's beautiful vintage possessions with no danger of bringing anything home. (Accumulators and Collectors, do *not* reward yourselves with food instead of purchases, though, or you may soon find yourself fighting to lose weight as well as clutter!)

Letting Decorators or Crafters reward themselves is also like letting the cat guard the canary. When these types see an empty space, their first thought is, "How could I fill this space?" Decorators and Crafters need a compromise solution: List your decorations as part of the quantifying process, then finish organizing and decision-making *before* you commence any new decorating projects. That will be your motivation to get the other work done quickly and well. And remember, you can always reward yourself by making something for someone else.

Of course, Tossers don't have to motivate themselves to get started. Instead, their challenge is to find ways to slow down and take stock thoughtfully instead of tossing items indiscriminately.

It would be too easy to let getting ready to figure out how much stuff you have take the place of actually quantifying your clutter. That said, there are some things you should gather before you begin, and that won't give yourself and your family and help you persevere.

going into the project may be triggered in some time someone develops allergic reactions. Either way, a dust mask or respirator (the type used by painters—available in hardware and DIY stores—not by hospital patients) will come in handy.

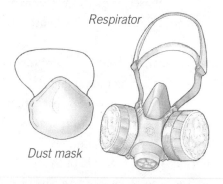

Respirator

Dust mask

2. PUT ON SOME GLOVES. Dishwashing gloves are fine if you'll just be dealing with dirt,

but choose the heavy-duty kind if you'll be picking up boards that might have nails, or other sharp, bulky, or contaminated clutter.

3. TAKE A MEASURED APPROACH. Keep a measuring tape on your belt so that you can instantly and accurately measure storage spaces, rooms, windows, large pieces of furniture, doorways, and the like. If you're just estimating, it's a lot harder to make decisions about what will fit in a room or storage area and which space-consuming pieces of furniture could actually be moved elsewhere.

4. TAPE IT TO THE LIMIT. Keep a tape gun or packing-tape dispenser handy so that you can tape up all your boxes.

5. LEAVE AN INDELIBLE MARK. Use permanent markers to label items immediately, so you don't have to identify them more than once.

6. GET A CLEAR PICTURE. If there's a Tosser in your household, clear plastic trash bags are a must. They allow everyone to get a good look at what's been designated for the trash pile. Of course, the bags come in handy in any household organizing efforts, since they protect against a momentary lapse of memory.

Get Everybody in on the Act

Everybody in your home needs to know about your plan to start quantifying. Yes, even the ones who are going to bite, kick, and scream so loudly that they may convince you not to get started. After all, you can't say you've truly

taken care of clutter if you've left out people who need to have input into the decision-making. They should (and *should*, not might) offer input and, down the road, prevent problems. To solve by thinking and acting everybody in on the what, when, and how of your plan, including how you envision their roles. Set goals together for your home, for your clutter, for the time you'll spend, for the money you can spare. Of course, a good starting point is the Clutter Type quiz in chapter 1. Take it together and compare your answers.

Stakeholders who don't live with you are a different story. Show no mercy. You know—the nephew who left his motorcycle in your shed, what was it, 8, 10 years ago? Or your grown children, whose lunch boxes molder in your attic and team pennants still hang on your guest room walls? Maybe it's your siblings, who promise to collect their share of your parents' estate next time they're in from California; *if* it will fit in their carry-on bags. Deal firmly with the folks who clutter your spaces from afar. Drop them a line explaining that you'll soon assess the "stuff" in your home. (It's worth the extra money to send the letter registered mail.) Ask the long-distance clutterers if they want to be involved in the process, or if there's some-

thing that you should ship to them. Don't be shy about asking for postage! Make it clear that their "stuff" moves out when the quantifying process ends—whether it's to their home or the local children's home is *their* decision.

Finding Time, Making Time

You're going to need to guard your clutter-quantifying time. Protect it as you would a hair appointment or time with a loved one. Write it down on your calendar. And above all, don't deviate—at least not for the first four or five scheduled appointments. It's all too easy to say, "Let's check out the attic sometime this weekend," then forget all about it until Sunday evening, when you're bushed. Much better: "Saturday after breakfast and before the matinee we're going to look over those tax record boxes in the attic. If we finish early, we'll try the wrapping paper tub next to them."

If there are two of you and you plan to work at the same time, make sure that each of you schedules half of the quantifying appointments. That way, you'll both be invested in the process. Otherwise, one of you will be stuck begging the other to show up—and that will put you in a nagging, subservient position in what's supposed to be a joint effort.

Let's backtrack for a moment. Before you can protect your quantifying time, you have to find it first, right? Well, we have a solution, and it doesn't involve waking up 15 minutes earlier every morning to work on it. No, quantifying is

---

CONCEALERS TAKE NOTE

Asking a Concealer to prepare to quantify clutter is like asking a dog to monitor the supply of dog treats. Do not, dear Concealer, use this occasion as an excuse to buy lots of storage containers. In fact, don't buy any. And resolve to halve your current stock, reducing your hoards of stuff enough so you can empty two containers into one.

important enough to work into your regular schedule. Only a few spartan souls would welcome the idea of missing sleep for the pleasure of going through piles of household objects. Remember, you're fighting inertia to get to the clutter at all—don't add resentment to the mix by missing a favorite activity or some much-treasured downtime.

In fact, even though it will probably turn out to be kind of fun, start this journey with the idea that clutter-quantifying is going to be a strenuous, time-consuming chore. Instead of depriving yourself by scheduling it in lieu of something enjoyable, like sleeping or watching your favorite television show, schedule it for times when you'd be doing an odious task, like cleaning the litter box. But what about the poor cats, or trash day or whatever?

Here's a suggestion, but be warned: Some of you will have to fight every fiber of your being to employ it. If you plan to skip cleaning the cat litter box (or mowing the lawn, or folding the laundry, or shopping for the groceries) to embark on a clutter-quantifying project, find someone else to do those chores for you. Some family members might welcome the opportunity to get out of the particular clutter chore you're doing instead. (When faced with cleaning the attic, suddenly mowing the lawn might start to look really appealing.)

Another alternative is to (gasp!) hire a teenage neighbor to do it. To convince yourself that it'll be money well spent, revisit your long-term benefits list to recall why making time to get started is an absolute necessity. Remember: The clutter-clearing payoffs will be far greater than the little you'd spend to hire someone to do those small chores.

So what about the really big, time-consuming quantifying jobs? For instance, what if you want to do the whole house, or need to settle an estate, or have a 2,000-book library to contend with? How on earth do you find time for those? One suggestion: Use some of your vacation time. Now we know that taking a week's worth of vacation time to quantify your clutter may not sound as much fun as a vacation. But maybe this will help. We know a woman who took several weeks off from work to have some plastic surgery done. She told everyone that she was going on a cruise, but all the while she was at home with a face bruised beyond belief. The surgery was no fun, but for it she got the face she wanted, and that was a vacation for her soul. It's the same with decluttering a room or home—only it costs a lot less than a vacation and may give you many more hours of pleasure.

Make sure to plan your schedule if you do give yourself an entire week or two to get started on your decluttering project. Otherwise, that time might melt into afternoons spent lazing on the porch watching the scenery—while the piles of clutter grow even larger.

If you just can't justify spending your vacation time dealing with clutter, consider the remodeling mentality. When you have your kitchen or bathroom remodeled, you know you'll have to live without that room for a period of time, but you also insist that the con-

We know a man who quit smoking a pack a day, but didn't tell anyone for years. In fact, when people asked him whether he had quit, he denied it. You see, he just didn't want the pressure of being scrutinized to see if he succeeded—or ridiculed if he failed.

On the one hand, you certainly would be justified in taking a similar approach to telling your colleagues, relatives, and others about your clutter-cutting efforts. Accumulators and Collectors in particular may be better off not risking the ridicule. Remarks such as "Not again" or "It's about time" can really wound. Concealers, too, might do better to keep the news under their hats. People would exclaim, "But you don't have any clutter!" and—though you know better—you might be tempted to believe them.

On the other hand, if you want sympathy and support while you quantify clutter, by all means let a few people know what you're up to. If you're an avowed Accumulator, tell your friends, "No jokes, please," and keep repeating your request even if they won't honor it at first.

How to tell whether your friends and acquaintances are ready to encourage and support you? Think back to how they reacted when you tried to diet, start a new career, kick smoking, or even got a divorce or broke up with a partner. Some people just naturally feel competitive when a friend tries to make a change for the better and may resort to put-downs. Others are uncomfortable when faced with someone who admits to (and tries to right) a real or perceived shortcoming, or confesses that he or she is under duress, and they may pull away or joke to cover their discomfort. But fortunately, most people will go out of their way to applaud your efforts and—even more important—check on your progress. That keeps the decluttering pressure on you—in a really good way.

tractor stick to a schedule. In this instance, you're both contractor *and* displaced homeowner, so come up with a schedule that the family can live with, and stay with it.

Ready, Set . . .

Yes, we told you to make sure you spend *some* time preparing for your big day (or week or month). But don't let the preparations get so involved that they take all the time and energy you need for quantifying! These steps strike a happy medium.

Invite the gang. If you need to deal with heavy furniture (and who doesn't?), line up a few friends, relatives, or neighborhood high-school boys to move things around. Not for the whole time—maybe just for an hour or two on one of the quantifying days. You won't believe how much more progress you'll make evaluating furniture when you can actually move it around. Otherwise, you'll just think, "too hard," and there that mahogany wardrobe will stay for the rest of its cluttery, oppressive days. (Note: Make sure you provide pizza or other refreshments for the helpful hordes. People tend to be more motivated to work when there's food involved!)

Ready your recyclables. Call the recycling center and the town or county's hazardous waste disposal office to find out what it will and won't accept. That'll help you make decisions about what you can readily get rid of in the paper, cleaning supply, and paint departments.

Do your research. Check out the local classifieds, national publications like the *Antique Trader*, and a few local garage sales. No, *not* so you can buy more stuff, but so you'll have a rough idea of what type of stuff sells (you'll

---

WHEN COUPLES QUANTIFY

Starting to quantify your clutter is the first test of your clutter-control partnership. Rest assured, you will have some rocky moments. A Tosser, for example, might ride roughshod over previous agreements and proceed to toss first and ask questions later. The Accumulator or Collector, on the other hand, may feel so threatened by the impending loss of his or her security-blanket possessions that he or she picks a fight so no one can get anything done—both parties are too busy shouting and nursing hurt feelings. After such behavior, all bets are off, right? Wrong. That would just grant the instigator his or her unconscious wish to halt progress. Instead, follow these steps so you don't let a spat sabotage your efforts.

1. Before you start, both partners should bone up on the pitfalls of working together to declutter your home. Recognize that simply looking over your joint possessions implies future change, and that even positive change almost always threatens people and makes them defensive. In other words, expect some emotional behavior.

After all, like a bird pretending to have a broken wing to distract a predator from the nest, both parties may be (subconsciously or with full awareness) trying their best to distract the other so they can keep their own clutter style.

2. Write down your joint goals concerning clutter in the house and the benefits you expect to reap. This isn't so you'll have a legal document or anything, but it does give you something to refer back to when one of you gets agitated. (This is, of course, after the storm has passed: No waving a paper under the nose of the person in a snit!)

3. Agree ahead of time that when tempers flare you'll take a timeout and resume again—same tasks, same goals, same cooperative efforts—after a set period of time. Preferably an hour or so, even if you've taken off the whole week to get something done. In later days, you can apologize and whatnot, but don't go there now. What's important right now is not to let emotions keep you from proceeding with the clutter-quantifying.

probably be amazed) and for how much. That will help you see your household objects in a new, more profitable, light.

Close the kitchen. Even if you're not going to tackle the kitchen, make things easy on yourself. Stock up on home-cooked, frozen meals—or splurge on takeout for the duration—and buy plenty of refueling beverages like soda, sport drinks, and orange juice. Plan to use disposable dishes and utensils while you're in the thick of quantifying your clutter, whether it's for a day or a few weeks. Unplug the phone so that so you can concentrate on your work without interruption (and enjoy avoiding telemarketers—that ought to counterbalance the agony of unearthing things like mildewy books and chipped china!).

Let's Get Started Already!

You have your quantifying strategies in place, your essentials in hand, and it's time to stop getting ready and just pitch in. But where do you start? Well, that depends on you. Here are five ways to begin. They all work. So choose the one that gets you excited about tackling your clutter. And then get going!

- Tackle an area of your home where you can make an immediate change. That'll boost your confidence.
- Start by taking on a really tough area first— the attic or basement, for instance. Everything is bound to be easier after that.

- Begin with a category of items and collect those from all over the house. Deal with all the artwork and houseplants, for example, or all the household change.
- Take out the trash. Do you have old bags of pet food, or piles of plastic bags or empty egg cartons, or other trash that you've been

CLUTTER CRUSADERS

Ease Into It

"I usually start trying to get cleaned up and organized when my husband Dan's mother is coming to visit," says Cathy Steever of Medfield, Massachusetts. "It's not that she would ever say anything, it's just that I try to look at things with her eyes so she'll be comfortable here. I find that the easiest place to start emotionally is the refrigerator. After all, it's just food, and it's mostly real obvious what needs to go. My husband and I do the job together, because it's gross and awful, and it takes two people.

"Even though he's much more likely to want to hold on to things than I am, we don't get into too many disagreements, because we're only discussing 2-year-old exotic mustard, nothing really close to our souls like sheet music or golf clubs. And I get one of my teenage daughters to reorganize the pantry at the same time. That appeals to them because they like to be in charge of something entirely. It's not as much fun as decorating, but arranging stuff is sort of in the same vein. I find that once we've done the refrigerator, it's easier psychologically to tackle something else, like the living room."

saving for that proverbial rainy day? Just clearing out some heaps of throwaways can give you a real sense of accomplishment—especially when you see just how much space all that trash was taking up!

• Make a donation. By taking a few bags of old clothes or linens to the Goodwill, or cans and cartons of food to the soup kitchen or homeless shelter, you can start your decluttering efforts by helping others. And that's a great feeling.

Try whatever feels right. If it doesn't work, try something else. Keep trying until you hit on an idea that will help you get moving in the right direction—by *your* definition, of course.

SET YOURSELF UP FOR SUCCESS

At the end of each day, Ann M. Martin, the famous and prolific author of the *Baby-Sitters Club* series for kids, stops her work in midsentence. The next day, when she comes back to work, finishing that sentence is usually enough to get her back into the flow of writing without disruption.

Try a similar approach when it comes to quantifying your clutter. Leave yourself a fairly simple task to finish the next day: unloading the last half of a box of books, for example, or sorting through that last stack of towels in the linen closet. Then, once you're off and running, remind yourself of your successes. Note your progress at the end of each day, for example, and haul out your list of long-term benefits to see how far you've come.

Treat yourself while you're embarking on this life-improving task. Indulge in a hot bath with candles at the end of the day, for example, or a pricey cup of gourmet coffee and a muffin from the shop on the corner, before you start a particularly demanding day of quantifying. If the job carries on longer than you thought (or longer than you'd like!) and the chaos is stressing you out, do what you'd do if your water main broke or if you were remodeling a fixer-upper: Stay with relatives or friends, or—luxury of luxuries—at a hotel for a few nights. Spend a little money on the small luxuries that encourage you to keep moving forward, because it's worth it. After all, the changes you're making will improve your whole life!

Motivated? Ready to jump in and quantify? Great! Now, let's move on to the next step—and the next chapter. It's time to Unload!

Step Two: Unload

Y ou've made it through the Quantifying step of the Q.U.I.C.K. process—and we'd bet that you might not want to do it again. So don't! Plunge right into the second step and Unload while you still have momentum and your dust mask is on! Get rid of the items that you've decided you can do without while you can still remember what you've sorted—and before it dons another disguise and starts cluttering a different part of your home. "If you've found ample motivation to get rid of clutter, keep moving forward—it's torment to go through the preliminaries more than once," says family counselor Steve Brown of Knoxville, Tennessee.

Which brings up another point. Now that you've finished with the preliminaries, you're going to need a different set of strategies to actually rid yourself of the clutter. After all, part of Quantifying includes convincing yourself that you don't *have* to part with anything, that you're just taking stock of what you have. But Unloading requires that you commit to physically removing objects. If you told yourself you were just climbing the diving board ladder before, now you'll have to hold your nose and jump. This is no time to get psyched out,

Here's a clever idea to help you get motivated: Make a video or take pictures of your home in its ultracluttered state, and view it (or them) every couple of days to remind you what you're trying to escape—and how far you've come.

though. Unloading is entirely possible if you find good homes for your discards, deal with the trash, and keep your clutter personality from chapter 1 in mind. So let's move along—and take out the clutter as we go.

Getting Started

You must let go of old objects to let new things into your life. That sounds like a mystic's advice (and it probably is), but that's the mind-set to adopt as you make decisions about what to unload from your cluttered household. Give up as much as you can, not out of any sense of martyrdom, but to have the space and the visual calm you need to give yourself a higher standard of living. Of course, this lofty goal might fade from consciousness the second you're faced with an 18-year accumulation of children's clothes or informing Aunt May that you gave away her sister's collection of Franklin Mint plates and figurines. But keep the final results in mind as you make choices about what stays and what goes. If this doesn't occur naturally, write down some affirmative goals and review them with everyone at the beginning of the clutter-unloading session.

Once you're in the proper state of mind, there are lots of ways to get down to the dirty work of deciding what to get rid of. Keep your clutter personality in mind, and just as with therapy, budgets, or diets, keep trying methods until you find one that works for you. Here are two of our favorites:

Take five (away). There are five things in your home right now that you don't need. In fact, there are five things in your house you *know* you don't need because you just finished

"When I met my husband," says Nancy Byrd of Indianapolis, Indiana, "he was in his early forties, but he still had socks from high school with holes in them! We can't even recycle together. As my 6-year-old daughter and I took newspapers to the bin, he pulled them back out! That's why the unloading of junk around here really has to be a one-person show. My husband can't be around when we get rid of things, and he's accepted that. It's just too hard on him to participate. If I sort items and get rid of them, he never misses them. Part of that, though, is that he does have one cabinet full of anything he wants to keep. I do sort that, but I never give away anything from that cabinet. That's what works for us."

quantifying at least one room filled with family possessions, didn't you? Use those items to start unloading. Just get rid of five items at a time, every day, until you can purge no more. This is particularly recommended for Collectors and Accumulators as a way to ease into unloading, because it's nonconfrontational and you can make it a game. Also, this five-a-day method keeps you from fretting about the big picture and getting so overwhelmed that you don't get rid of anything at all.

Take it 30 minutes at a time. For some people it's more difficult to make the time to consider all their "stuff" than it is to deal with it emotionally. If that describes you, try chipping away at clutter 30 minutes each day. Like the approach described previously, this method keeps the fretters among us from getting overwhelmed by the long-range implications of dealing with the whole house. All you've committed to is a half-hour today and another tomorrow. Chart a course for your first half-hour. "First we'll declutter the downstairs bathroom, then, if there's time, I'll hit the garage, the refrigerator and pantry, then my jewelry box." That way you'll always know what's next and won't spin your wheels. Another important part of this method is being decisive so that you don't have to repeat your efforts. So, for instance, instead of sorting your candles into two stacks, then moving on to another task, sort them into two stacks, then immediately put away the stack that belongs in the buffet and

---

SEE WHAT YOUR SPACE COULD BE

Decorators, Concealers, here's an unloading procedure designed just for you. With this decision-making tool, you decide what you want to keep instead of deciding what you want to get rid of. First, empty virtually everything from an area you're unloading. It can be a large space (say, the attic) or something more manageable—an afternoon's work, such as a linen closet.

Next, one item at a time, move the large pieces you would like to keep back into the space. Each time you place a piece of furniture (or similar-size item), pause and let it rest for at least 30 minutes before you add the next piece. This allows you, perhaps for the first time ever, to contemplate the effect of that item alone.

Don't rush through this project! Take the whole day. Even when you get to the smaller items or collections of items—the spice rack, a coaster, the remote control—give yourself 5 or 10 minutes to make sure it's worthy of the space it's taking up, and really adding something to the look you're seeking.

This is an ideal technique if you crave comfort or have an aesthetic bent. It can even convert Accumulators and Concealers, because those two types can see how the room (or the junk drawer or the pantry) will look without as much stuff in it or without as many storage containers. And this is the ideal method for Decorators, because isn't that your main motivation—making the house look great?

take the discard candles to the thrift store, give them away, or toss them.

CONSIDER THE REWARDS

By now, you may be feeling a bit of muscle strain, and your motivation may be weakening. So recognize human nature as you start to unload objects, and haul out that list of benefits of less clutter once more if you need some good reasons to stay motivated during this stage of heavy moving and lifting. Add to the list by contemplating the benefits of the unloading itself. You may actually pick up some extra cash, for example, or delight some worthy charities with your castoffs.

List the advantages of unloading clutter in order of their appeal to you. That might help you determine the unloading method that will work best for you—a garage sale if you could always use a little cash, for example, or a big donation to a women's shelter if it's most important to you to know someone else will really use your castoffs. Still not sure what it would take to push you to action on that pile of semiused paint cans? Read on for some ideas that will have you scrambling for cardboard boxes and a dolly.

Get sick and tired. If you're absolutely, positively sick of your junk, you are in the very best position to unload. That's because you probably don't need anything more than the satisfaction of no longer seeing those ancient flour canisters on the cluttered counter or the rafts blocking the lawn mower or the men's suits clogging up the entrance to the attic. This doesn't mean you have to be a Tosser, who indiscriminately gets rid of everything. (Most Tossers are probably busy right now explaining to their spouses why the household no longer possesses the Mickey Mantle baseball cards that were going to pay for at least one college tuition. They don't need much help with unloading!) Your main motivation in moving stuff out of your home is to have fewer things draining your mental energy.

We have a friend who fits in this category. She's gone so far as to leave valuable castoffs on the curb on trash day. Some of the objects that

---

DON'T GET EVEN, GET MAD!

This sounds crazy. Isn't emotional well-being the whole reason you're trying to declutter your home? Yes, but during the unloading step a healthy dose of agitation doesn't hurt anything. "I always try to get rid of things while I'm frustrated with my lot in life," says Amy Witsil, a working mom in Chapel Hill, North Carolina, who has moved three times in the past three years. "I'm much more likely to give away things that I'll never use—magazines, unrealistic craft projects—when I'm facing up to my lack of time. And I can ruthlessly sort through much more stuff—I guess the agitation gives me more energy. But most important, when I'm done, I feel more in control of my life, and I've done something positive with my frustration."

have found their way to her curb include three almost-new oak bookcases, a recliner, and a nearly new area rug. It's the local custom for scavengers to pick up the objects before the trash guys arrive. But our friend knows that she deeply needs to be rid of the stuff, so she doesn't worry about those junk dealers retrieving and reselling the valuables—they're welcome to whatever they want. That's because she'd rather get rid of what she can, while she can, than pressure herself to host a garage sale.

If this mind-set appeals to you but you're not quite there yet, try unloading a few small, inconsequential objects with no thought about whether they'll do anyone any good or yield a profit. You may find that it's so satisfying to be rid of those items that you're able to move on to more and bigger objects using the same standards.

Move out high-maintenance stuff. Another way to get into the unloading mood is to first focus on objects that are difficult or bothersome to maintain. For instance, if you unload those miniblinds, you won't have to clean them anymore. Or if you get rid of that pesky outdoor water garden, you won't have to worry about algae, leaks, or safety issues. Use this as your motivation and you may be able to do without any monetary reward.

Make some money. Some folks hold on to stuff because they think it might save them money down the road. If that describes you, take that frugality one step further and let your clutter *make* you some money by selling it. Once you realize that some of your treasures translate into filthy lucre, you may dig deeper and find bigger and more valuable objects that you can do without. But be forewarned: Making money as you unload unwanted items takes some planning, waiting, and work. For items to fetch their full value at a garage sale, for example, they must be in good repair. You also must have the patience and the energy to amass enough stuff to host a sale that's worth attending. This probably isn't a good idea for a

JUST FOR ACCUMULATORS

Uh-oh. How are you Accumulators supposed to host a garage sale, even if you're bent on making extra cash? After all, isn't that where you got most of your stuff in the first place? There *is* one way to make sure that accumulating stuff to sell at a garage sale doesn't become just another excuse for keeping piles of junk around.

Make arrangements ahead of time for someone to come around at the end of your sale, at an appointed time, and pick up anything that didn't sell. For low-level stuff that would be the local thrift store. And since you know you'll be giving away whatever doesn't sell, you'll be more likely to negotiate prices throughout the day. If you're settling an estate and have higher-value items, see whether you can interest a local flea-market vendor or even an antiques dealer in setting a flat price for the remains of the day.

long-established Accumulator, at least not without the help of a veteran Tosser.

There are several less complicated—but no less profitable—unloading methods. A consignment store might take your old formals or cast-off jewelry, for example, or all your baby things. You also might tap into one of those multi-family garage sales, where it won't matter much if you have only one table or big bag of stuff.

In any case, make sure to have a stern talk with yourself to decide how much money an object would have to be worth before you'll try to sell it. For lots of objects, from romance paperbacks to coffee filters, terra-cotta pots, and muffin tins, the wait and the space are simply not worth the paltry return. Instead, cart them off to someone who can use them or to a charity thrift store.

SEVEN WAYS TO HOST A BETTER GARAGE SALE

Hosting a garage sale is not for the faint of heart. Not only do you need to be prepared to part with treasured items, you must be ready to watch complete strangers paw through and belittle them—and offer $3 for a rug you bought for $99 six months ago. If you're up for the challenge, though, go all the way with these clever tactics.

1. Paint footprints or draw big chalk arrows on the sidewalk or road leading up to your sale.

2. Stock plenty of Polaroid film to take pictures of high-priced items for anyone who wants to go home and "talk it over with the wife."

3. Set out an extension cord so people can immediately make sure that electric lamps and appliances work.

4. Concoct brown paper grab bags stuffed with several small items suitable for children or teens and charge a low price so that kids can buy them, contents unseen. Start with stuff that you probably need to get rid of anyhow—costume jewelry, convention giveaways, hotel soap and shampoo freebies, Easter Seals holiday stamps, shells—and consider picking up a few other inexpensive items, like bubbles or pencils. The mystery will draw more young buyers.

5. Provide some free amusement or refreshment that might draw people to the sale. Ideas include a "guess your weight, guess your age" table (charge a nominal fee, give a gift certificate to the sale if you're wrong by 5 pounds or 2 years), sidewalk chalk for the young kids, or the old standby: free lemonade and cookies.

6. Borrow an idea from the estate sale market and leave large items in the house and in their natural setting for a tag sale. Put an oversize price tag on the item. Seeing it in your home might inspire people to realize it would be perfect in their own home—and if that trunk or bedstead doesn't sell, you won't have to tote it back into the house. Just make sure a family member or someone else you trust is in the house to make sure nothing "walks off."

7. In the last hours or on the last day of the sale, slash prices with a catchy gimmick. A "buy one, get one free" table is one idea, or try a "bring a friend and you buy for half-price" tactic.

Give yourself a (tax) break. The only certainties in life are clutter and taxes, or something like that. But did you realize that the two are related? That's because unloading clutter may offer you some tax breaks. That is, if you plan the donations correctly. So listen up, then consult your personal tax expert if you think any of this might apply to you.

Itemized charitable donations are tax deductible. You can claim the fair market value of a donation to a tax-exempt charitable organization, which adds an interesting wrinkle to the equation. You see, in some cases, the tax deduction might be worth more than your item would fetch if you were to sell it yourself. Take expensive china, for example. If you take a deduction for its fair market value (supported by an independent appraisal) after donating it to a local charity, the taxes you avoid might exceed the price someone would pay for it at a yard sale.

Another tax planning note: If you intend to get rid of a whole house worth of clutter or replace lots of furniture, consider itemizing this year even if you don't ordinarily. If you do decide to itemize, make sure to unload everything you can (or everything that merits a charitable deduction) in the year you decide to itemize.

Just Tell Me Where to Send It All

You've culled all the stuff you can sell, and now you're stuck with a whole lot of other clutter.

You could truck it to the dump, but that would be a waste. Here are a whole host of ways to get rid of that stuff without throwing it away.

DO A GOOD DEED

For many of us, even more compelling than having extra cash or extra space is realizing that the stuff we can't use anymore might be treasured by someone else—or at the very least put to good use. There's a two-part benefit here. First, you'll feel better about giving things away (or even selling them) if you know that someone else can use them. Second, an organization that truly needs your extras may make the unloading process easy for you: by sending a truck to collect your stuff, for example, or even just by organizing an event for which you can donate items. To uncover people and groups that would consider your "trash" as treasure, follow these steps.

Find a clearinghouse for charities. Start by visiting the local library and ask the librarian. Or call your local or state Department of Health and Human Services, listed in the blue government pages in your phone book. They'll know of charities in your area and may even know what sort of donations they're looking for.

Call on the garbage men. This may sound illogical, but bear with us. Call your local government (county or city) office of solid waste. It—or the recycling office, if your city is large enough to support one—frequently knows of organizations that accept certain types of items, from usable building supplies to unwanted boxes of letterhead. (Close your eyes, Accumulators. The upcoming advice is for people who have things to get rid of and is *not* recommending a new treasure trove for people who want more stuff.) The same offices will probably know whether your city has a waste exchange, where people meet online or in a group to exchange unwanted items with others who can use them. Someone might have several doghouses, for example, or an overabundance of padded envelopes or canning jars.

Contact a local school. Consult your local school system (usually the main office or elementary school office is the best bet) to see whether it hosts an annual clothing or coat drive. Often, the school is also the repository for clothing for needy children. Elementary schools in particular also need clothes for indigent kids who show up without suitable clothing or kids who have accidents or make messes during the school day and need to change into something. Often, children in fourth or fifth grade are already able to wear adult-size castoffs.

Watch some television. Tune in to the local news or local access cable channel. They, along with local radio stations, frequently broadcast community announcements and local school "wish lists."

Donate to homes away from home. Since you're probably trying to get rid of still-useful household items, contact national or local organizations that provide housing. A few suggestions include the YMCA and YWCA, which may provide low-cost, short-term rooms for individuals who need them; the local battered women's shelter; foster homes or orphanages; or Habitat for Humanity, which frequently operates a thrift store, too.

Reprogram phones for women at risk. Call the local women's shelter. They'll know the

JUST FOR COLLECTORS

Unloading can be particularly difficult for Collectors, because different collections peak in value at different times. To avoid all the research and perfect timing involved in selling a collection, donate it, then let the recipient either display the collection or do the legwork involved in selling it . . . while you earn the goodwill, tax deductions, and added space in your home.

Consider donating a collection to an auction for a worthy cause or to a local library for display. If young collectors are involved in your hobby, consider making the collection a prize for a school- or library-sponsored essay contest. Or you can always consider donating the collection to a suitable hobby group, since they'll be able to enjoy it and you'll still have visiting rights.

So no one is going to want your dog's used chew toys: There are still plenty of places that need the sort of castoffs you accumulate if you're a veteran pet owner. Find out whether the local chapter of the Humane Society needs some of your stuff. Food that Fido or Fluffy has turned up her nose at; newspapers for bedding; leashes, runs, and collars; flea medicine; doghouses; stuffed animals; and new toys are just a few possibilities of things that you don't need—but they do. Veterinarians or animal hospitals may also appreciate donations of soft rags, towels, or blankets for patients or animals who are being boarded.

Another possible recipient: the local zoo. Zoos often have petting zoos with more ordinary animals or young critters that need "baby stuff." One of our favorite calls for donations came from the Knoxville, Tennessee, zoo, which requested castoff Christmas trees to use to keep the elephants from getting bored. (They push and carry them with their trunks for entertainment!)

---

nearest organization that accepts deprogrammed cell phones to reprogram for victims of domestic violence.

Get rid of those glasses. Contact a local optometrist to find out who collects castoff eyeglasses to send to remote areas in the United States or overseas. Local Lions Clubs often collect old eyeglasses.

Find fixer-uppers. Keep up with the names of organizations that are willing to fix up or repair toys and bikes for Christmas giveaways, so you'll have an outlet for used items. The Boy Scouts and Toys for Tots (a U.S. Marine Corps Reserve program) are two possibilities, and if the chapter in your area doesn't accept used toys, it may know who will. Frequently, a large local industry will spearhead such an effort, which you can find out about by calling their corporate communications arm. Or, as a fallback, call the local paper's features editor as the holidays draw near. He or she may remember a suitable local effort or have articles about previous years' efforts.

Don't wait around. Follow up immediately when you see a plea for donations; otherwise, you might misplace the number, and it can be quite difficult to reestablish contact before the donation drive is over or the volunteer staff changes hands again.

Plan for next year. If you aren't prepared for a donation drive this year, mark it down on next year's calendar, along with the organization's phone number. That way, you can call the organization ahead of time the next year and see if they're hosting the same or a similar event.

One other thing to remember. Just because a

you work through the Unloading portion of the Q.U.I.C.K. process, give that old saw careful consideration.

For just about any usable item, there's a potential recipient. So says Bob Grimac, a veritable recycling guru in Knoxville, Tennessee, who has initiated a school system–wide recycling program and worked for the Peace Corps. "Just because some items wouldn't be suitable for members of your community doesn't mean they can't be shipped to Africa or Honduras or somewhere else. In some of those countries, children in particular don't own even one shirt, and any shoes are welcome." Here are some of Bob's suggestions for unloading items that might not make it at the suburban garage sale, but could make a real difference in many people's lives.

group doesn't already run a donation drive doesn't mean it can't use the things you have. Call and suggest that the organization take your donations! Lots of the smaller homeless shelters and programs for underprivileged children in particular don't have enough staff or time to solicit donations and might just love to receive a set of encyclopedias, first aid or beauty supplies, magazines, linens, or sporting goods.

GETTING RID OF STUFF YOU THINK IS JUNK

"One man's trash is another man's treasure." How many times have you heard that? But as

Pack 'em up for overseas. Local chapters of the national organization Goodwill often warehouse items that won't sell in American stores and ship them to Africa or other needy nations. Call ahead to find out what items might fit in that category, from worn towels and sheets to socks and stuffed animals.

Go to church. Many congregations seek everything from crayons to small toys to old clothes to bats and balls. They may mail them to help communities in seriously underserved nations, such as Honduras. In some cases, missionaries from the church deliver the items in person. There are also similar needs in American regions such as Appalachia. To find out about churches in your area that are involved in these efforts, check the local Council of Churches. Its number should be listed in the business section of the phone book.

Let computers stay after school. Even the dreamiest accumulator knows that computers lose value quicker than day-old bread. But you can still find someone who might need an old PC. The best places to try are local homeless shelters that cater to families and after-school programs for low-income kids. Even if the machine is pretty old, it may have enough memory to sustain a couple of computer games or a word-processing program, and that should be enough to allow a computer to earn its keep at its new location. Make sure to call ahead to make the offer.

If you itemize on your taxes, also ask for a receipt so that you can deduct the fair market value of the computer, which, trust us, will be negligible. More important, ask a techie friend to help you strip the hard drive of anything the kids won't need. That'll increase the available memory and make the computer easier to use. If you can, add value to your donation by volunteering some time to show someone at the organization how to play solitaire or type poetry on your old machine. (For specific advice about tossing your home computer, see "Recycle Software and Hardware, Too.")

Peddle that metal. Contact a local foundry or scrap metal dealer to see whether it accepts

---

RECYCLE SOFTWARE AND HARDWARE, TOO

While you'll never get rich on the proceeds, you can always earn space by getting rid of old computers that you no longer use. Just can't envision anyone wanting your 1980s vintage PC with the XyWrite word processor and the plug-in modem the size of a toaster? Don't try to pawn it off on unsuspecting Aunt Agnes. Instead, donate the whole kit and caboodle to a computer recycling outfit. Find out who will take your model by contacting the folks who sold it to you in the first place or who have most recently serviced it. If you can't find them, use the search engine on the computer you plan to keep to find another recycling venue. Search by the computer brand and the keywords Computer Recycling.

Even we have to admit that there are a few of your discards no one can make use of, namely, hazardous wastes. You may not think of it, because of course you don't have subatomic particles sitting around, but lots of the items in your garage or workshop can be hazardous to the environment, including motor oil, paint, insecticides, and batteries.

What makes this part of the Unload step even trickier is that the local dump or trash collector might reject this waste, too. So check with your town hall or sanitation department (usually listed in the blue pages of the phone book) to find out who will dispose of this stuff properly, and at what cost. Usually whoever sells motor oil must accept used oil for recycling. With car batteries,

a local auto store may offer a trade-in value.

Often a local "green" organization will collect batteries or other hazardous waste that can be recycled. Or you may have to resort to paying the local hazardous waste outfit to get rid of, say, your paint and varnish cans. But pay the price! You don't want hazardous materials hanging around your yard, getting wet and leaching into the soil. And of course you don't want to pay a stiff fine for illegally disposing of hazardous waste! If you're in doubt over what's forbidden for local trash collection, trash collectors will happily provide you with a list. One other idea: Find out if the local hazardous waste center ever offers freebie days. If it does, plan to clean up a few days ahead of time.

metal box springs, broken or useless metal furniture, or metal plumbing materials or hardware. They do profit from the recycling, but you probably reap the larger benefit when you don't have to look at that rusting heap of kitchen chairs on the back porch.

Recycle that tire. Increasingly, says recycling guru Bob Grimac, there are regulations and laws about sending tires to landfills. But that's just as well, because the power industry is developing ways to burn old tires as fuel. Any business that sells tires must accept them back, but in most states they'll also charge you a nominal fee.

Help the kindergarten have a ball. Schools are the place to offload old tennis balls. They put little slits in them with a knife and slip the balls over metal chair and table legs to keep them from scraping the floor and driving the teacher to early retirement. If they haven't caught on to this practice in your area, suggest it.

Unload It Already!

Let's see. You've figured out what to get rid of along with the benefits of unloading it, and who might need it or wish to pay you for it. That's a lot of progress (congratulate yourself), but it seems as though we're forgetting something. Oh, yes. Now it's time to get the stuff out of your home. You'd think this would be the downhill slope, but it's actually where many clutter-cutting projects founder on the rocks. That's because you got tired, or you missed the Junior League's donation deadline so what's the point, or the guy with the truck went to tow his buddy's bass boat to the lake the same Saturday he promised to come move your old fridge to Goodwill. Don't let this happen to you! Instead, make sure you convey at least one object that you've quantified to its new destination the *very first day* of the Unload process.

Of course, you know the best time for you to unload clutter. After all, you've been around your household long enough to know what doesn't work, and probably could pinpoint the precise moment at which those carefully organized boxes somehow make their way back into the household mainstream. The trick, of course, is making yourself unload items before

it gets to that point. Here are some tips that will help.

Hire a Dumpster. One of the things that make unloading junk such a chore is that there can be so many stages: Pack up the trash bags, lug them to the garage, get them out to the curb on trash day, then hope the trash man takes them all. If not, you'll need to repeat the routine for the next pickup date. Well, there's a way to get rid of trash all at once. Just check in your Yellow Pages under Garbage and Rubbish Removal (or a related category). That's where you'll find companies that rent Dumpsters. The company will bring one to your home, then make it disappear once you've filled it up. Don't worry that your job is too small—Dumpsters come in all sizes, and the cost is well worth it when you want to get rid of the trash right now.

Deep-six the detractors. If you really want to get clutter out of the house, don't rely on someone who really *doesn't* want to get clutter out of the house. That sounds obvious, but so many of us wait for Uncle Walt to make the truck available for the afternoon, when Uncle Walt's own home is bursting at the seams. He'll never be able to make time for you. Same thing if the pro-clutter attitude resides in your own house. Forget about fair, forget about division of labor, forget about "his" stuff and "your" stuff. If the two of you have agreed on what you can get rid of and you

---

GIVE TOSSERS A TRY

Tossers are an energetic bunch, and the unloading stage is the perfect time to use their skills. Carefully set aside all the items that you're sure that you're going to give away or sell. Then cut the Tosser loose only in that area. She can finally toss to her heart's delight!

Before you unload lots of valuable used books, do some homework, says book reviewer Rose Kennedy of Knoxville, Tennessee. She's reviewed kids' books for more than a decade, and during that time she estimates she's given away more than 1,000 "extras" that publishers have sent her. "Unless you live in a small town, you'll probably want to bypass the public library," she says. "Believe it or not, they have restrictions on which books they can circulate, which may include Golden Books, which generally don't wear well and sometimes aren't considered high quality, or books that haven't received a positive review in a top-notch national review publication, like *Kirkus Reviews*. They may turn down books with even infinitesimal tears, writing, or wear." Instead, says Rose, see if you can thrill one of the following places with your used books.

FOR KIDS' BOOKS

1. School libraries (call ahead to find out content restrictions)
2. Elementary school reading improvement programs (it's very important for poor readers to own their own books)
3. Local day care centers
4. The local health clinic
5. Foster parents (donate through the local Human Services Department)
6. Shelters for homeless families
7. The nearest hospital's emergency waiting room, especially children's hospital's waiting rooms
8. Local groups or churches that provide emergency food or shelter for families
9. Church nurseries
10. Friends who are new grandparents or new stepgrandparents

FOR RECENT NONFICTION OR REFERENCE BOOKS

11. Local women's shelter
12. Nearby state-sponsored job training center
13. The local homeschooling association or acquaintances who homeschool their kids
14. After-school care programs (check the Yellow Pages)

FOR MODERN PAPERBACKS, PARTICULARLY MYSTERIES, ROMANCES, OR WESTERNS

15. Local veterans hospital
16. Friends who own vacation homes
17. Local senior citizens center
18. Some remote-branch public libraries (which typically circulate them without penalty for late or nonreturns)

IF ALL ELSE FAILS

19. Thrift stores (they seldom sell many books, but better them than the trash)
20. The giveaway bin at the local used-book store

want it gone, take it out and away yourself. Don't stand on ceremony about who should do what. It's more important to get the clutter out of the house before you have to re-sort it. So do what you can by yourself—no guilting the other party!—and hire out what you have to.

We know one woman who made her grumpy husband drive her 20 miles in the family truck on a Sunday evening just to drop off an oversize polyester quilt and one pair of pants at the

Catholic Charities clothing-drive box. Oh, the woman—who wishes to remain anonymous—had somewhere around 500 similar giveaway items back at the house. But she felt like she had to start somewhere. "And you know, neither one of those items ever showed up back at the house, which was a revelation to me," she says. "I had really started thinking that nothing would ever leave this house. After that, I went on a 'bag a day' program, taking one brown paper bag of stuff to another destination every day for 23 days! I'm not done yet, but if we hadn't inconvenienced ourselves to make that first silly trip, I don't think I would have made any progress at all."

And that's the best part about Unloading. The process becomes self-propelling once you tote that first load to the thrift store or that first wide-lapeled suit to the consignment shop. Because with that initial transaction, you realize clutter is not an immovable force. You might see how happy others are to have your donations, and you return home to just a little empty space where there once was none. And from there, you should catch the bug: less clutter, more space. Just tell yourself, "I can do it!"

Step Three: Isolate

ver make the mistake of whacking a weed off at its base? Not only does it grow back, it gets bigger and stronger than ever. Clutter can be like that. Just as you're feeling safe because you've eradicated the "stuff" that's cluttering your home, you realize that other piles of junk are growing like, well, weeds. And that's when you're ready for the last three steps of the Q.U.I.C.K. system: Isolating, Containing, and Keeping It Up. All three steps help you organize your household in ways that keep clutter from taking root.

Isolating, the first step of your clutter-prevention regimen, is working with what's left after you've unloaded all the clutter you can. You isolate groups of objects, just as you would keep peas and mashed potatoes away from each other on a picky child's plate. This allows you to see what you have, what function it serves, and where it needs to go. As you group and evaluate objects, you'll also isolate your storage spaces and decide whether you can make them work more effectively for the groups you've created. Isolating is essential if you're going to be effective in step four of the Q.U.I.C.K. system, Containing (i.e., storing) your stuff.

Isolating can be one of the most enjoyable steps of the Q.U.I.C.K. process, because you're handling objects that you have actively decided to keep around (during the Quantifying and Unloading steps)—there's no pressure to part with anything. It's kind of fun to sort and arrange, like so many kids trading Halloween candy after a big haul. You can chip away at the Isolating step on rainy days, by yourself, when you're feeling a little sentimental.

Isolating also gives you another chance to review and eliminate any excess clutter you may have missed on the first pass through. But, though you probably *will* find more items to give away, that's not the gist of the step, so you won't need to be prepared to head off to the dump at a moment's notice. And there's a certain amount of humor connected to the whole exercise. One man we know, a wealthy but absent-minded executive, found no fewer than 17 brand-new Chap Sticks when he started grouping like objects at his house! Another woman, the wife of a chef, unearthed seven jars of plain yellow mustard as she started to round up the contents of her pantry.

So try to find enjoyment in the isolating process, not just its end result. And prepare to use your creative powers, because once you've grouped your things, you'll need to start looking for a place for everything and start putting everything in its place, however quirky. Cat-box litter in the bathroom hamper, anyone? How about storing slippers in the newspaper delivery box?

Isolating Your Stuff

Here goes. Step three. Ready? Then use this step-by-step process to work through Isolating.

Prepare mentally. Just as you did before launching into the previous two steps of the Q.U.I.C.K. system, take a few moments to remind yourself of the benefits of Isolating before you start. Need a hint? Well, there will be less clutter and fewer worries that you'll undo the accomplishments you made Quantifying and Unloading. Don't forget that the end results will be well worth the distraction and havoc you'll create while sorting through every object you own. And it's also satisfying to really know what you own—you just may be pleasantly surprised!

Put together a staging area. It's hard to relax and group objects when they're in the middle of the kitchen floor and everyone wants dinner, or when every drawer in the house is dumped out and your mother-in-law will be over any second. So plan a place to do your sorting. For small objects, a broad, flat table in a well-lit area is best because it allows you to see what you're doing. But if the items are too large, too delicate, or too numerous to move to another area, sort on the spot. Just be sure to make other plans so that your household can run smoothly in the meantime. If you don't arrange another place for people to, say, shower while you do the bathroom, or a spot to work on the computer while you sort the home office

objects, chances are someone will get upset and run you off before you've accomplished your isolating. It also helps to have a collection of clear bins or shallow boxes on hand so you can move stuff around as you group it. These are separate from any boxes you might use to store the goods; they're "sorting" boxes.

Separate the "someday" stuff. When it comes to isolating, all objects are not created equal. First, there are the "someday" items—those that you want to hold on to for the next generation. If you do it right, you'll have to isolate "someday" objects only once or only once every few years. Group them on a day or during a week when you have time to savor the decisions and revel in unabashed sentimentality (also it's a good idea to choose a time when it's okay to get teary or feel sad and miss those who have gone before).

CLUTTER: PASS IT ON

"I have a method to organize and to pass precious finds to young relatives," says Evelyn Abbott of Albuquerque, New Mexico. "Over the years, I have created collections for my grandchildren and my sister's grandchildren, and now I'm starting for the next generation. I call them 'I Feel Like Being Someone Else Today' boxes, and I'll put everything in there that a child might need to become someone else for a time. I'll include an extra flashlight or magnifying glass I might find, in case they want to be explorers. I may put in one of my daughter's old stethoscopes, an Ace bandage, a cheap fire hat, some beads, an old pair of high heels, or some lacy tulle scraps. This is close to a dress-up box, but I include just the suggestion of other personalities, not costumes. If the little things I have around the house don't fit into the scheme of one of these boxes, I'll know it's time to take them to a rummage store I'm fond of. I keep the whole conglomeration in a plastic tub or a hatbox near the back door until it's ready to deliver to the child. I've also kept one here at the house in the guest room, for when the children come here."

Unearth keepsakes from all over the house, basement, and attic, then carefully consider: For whom am I keeping these? Will they really want these items? What is the best way to store them so they won't be destroyed by varmints, the elements, or the passage of time? Then, if at all possible, store all these objects in one place, where you can get them out occasionally to share with the future heirs. Store a copy of your will next to them, so you can always remember what goes to whom, or just jot down an informal list of your wishes. This really helps Accumulators, in particular, face whether they're saving objects for posterity—or just for themselves. If your mate is a Tosser, it will also help him or her understand why you're hanging on to these objects.

Say "same time, next year." The next grouping session should involve all your seasonal objects. Cast a wide net—check out everything from Christmas lights to canoe paddles, flip-flops to sweaters. And here's the hard part: Actually open all the boxes with holiday labels and make sure there's something inside besides bent wire ribbons and packing peanuts. Then start the sorting. Isolate everything needed for Halloween, from carving implements to candy dishes; everything that's good only in spring, from bulbs to egg dye; and so forth. In general, if possible, plan to store items from the same season near one another.

This isn't just to be orderly. It's also so you'll remember to rescue all the rest of the season's accessories if you remember even one. In fact,

you may want to stash a really crucial item, such as your softest winter jammies, among the less memorable stuff so that you'll be sure to head into the back bedroom closet before the season starts. And by all means make a list of what's in the box and where it is, and paste the list into the upcoming year's calendar in the appropriate season. This combats one of the easiest ways to create clutter, which is forgetting what you have stored away somewhere, then buying more over and over again. Oh, and about those boxes labeled "Holiday Stuff": Should you find things in there that aren't being used, it's off to the thrift store with them.

Study motion like an expert. Once you're done with the "somedays" and the "same time, next years," you're left with the "stuff for everyday living." These objects, because they must fit into your everyday life, warrant careful consideration. So before you get down to the heavy gazing, play motion-study expert, kind of like the father in *Cheaper by the Dozen*. He studied how quickly his kids, say, ate their eggs, then trained them to shave seconds off their meals. Here, you're not interested in increasing efficiency. Rather, you want to uncover how and where your family goes about its daily routines. This will help you figure out which groups of objects should go where—and which activity hubs within the household attract junk. Here's how:

Use "The Way You Are" on page 62 to describe your family's activities, then indicate why they happen in the places they do. Do you sort

As you group objects, make sure you also identify how those objects fit into the way you live. Mapping out household activities will help you decide where to store items. Use this chart to identify how you use your living spaces and why.

COLUMN A (LIST ALL THAT APPLY)

Where household members:

1. Apply makeup
2. Bathe
3. Cook
4. Dress
5. Eat
6. Entertain guests
7. Feed pets
8. Listen to music
9. Pay bills or do paperwork
10. Play with pets
11. Repair household items
12. Sleep
13. Sort and fold laundry
14. Watch television
15. Work on hobbies
16. Work on the computer

COLUMN B

Why the activity occurs in that space (list all that apply, including comfort, light, space, household rules, habit, other)

---

laundry in the living room because that's the only place with enough space, for example, or because you started the habit when you had a tiny apartment? Once you've outlined current practices, you can either sort objects accordingly, or, if needed, try to change your work and play habits to make it easier to store things in a way that will reduce clutter.

HAUL IT ALL OUT

Now for the fun. It's time to group your everyday living objects! Start by pulling out all the items in one category. For example, look on your motion-study list under "sleeping." Then pull out all the sleeping stuff, from linens and sleeping bags to pajamas and night-lights. Be sure to unpack all boxes, yours and the manufacturers', and open multicomponent kits and collections.

Is that groaning we hear? Being reluctant to drag stuff out is a dead giveaway that you need to—you haven't been through that blanket trunk in years, have you? If you need to, work with a really narrow category first, something you can find easily, such as gardening tools or playing cards. Work your way up to the more extensive categories, such as "Eating" or "Tax Records and Paperwork."

Separate the groups. Now that everything from one area of your everyday life is staring you in the face, start grouping *within* that category. There are, of course, many ways to do this, but two emerge as the most effective. First, you can group objects that essentially do the same job—all the household writing implements, for example, or all the rolls of duct tape. If you isolate that way, you should then compare the group to the appropriate motion-study activities on your sheet. Then you'll know, for example, whether you have enough rolls of duct tape for the places you use them—home office, garage, workshop, kitchen, and bathroom, for example. Of course, you may also realize that your family uses duct tape in entirely too many places, and then decide to omit duct-taping sites and several rolls of the stuff. These decisions are easy to make if you filled out a comprehensive motion-study list, but if you didn't, use common sense. See whether you have too many (or not enough) of the same object (AA batteries come to mind), then move along with your clutter-storage planning.

The second way to group objects is by the tasks for which you use them: Instead of grouping similar objects, you could pull to-gether all the objects you need for a particular task or activity. A chef friend of ours, for example, always keeps the ingredients for chili together in the same place. Another guy we know keeps all the tools and supplies for changing the car oil in a single bin in the garage, which works for him, since that's the only time he pulls out any car maintenance tools at all.

This grouping method can get tricky when one item is necessary for unrelated tasks. For instance, you might need a roll of tape in your holiday wrapping kit and in your bill-paying kit for sealing recalcitrant envelopes. In that case, it makes sense to buy more than one roll of tape—but don't let that become an excuse for acquiring more clutter.

Go forth and divide. Before you start finding homes for all these groups of items, consider whether there might be ways to sim-

---

A SECOND CHANCE TO GET A LOAD OFF THAT CHEST

As you Isolate, continue to get rid of things you don't need. Sure, you could tell yourself you're done with the Unloading step, and you are. You'll never need to make such a strenuous sweep of your home again. But the Isolate, Contain, and Keep It Up steps of the Q.U.I.C.K. process each demand their own brand of Unloading.

As you examine, organize, and store household objects, you will naturally discover duplicates and items that don't merit the space they occupy. Everyone, but Accumulators in particular, should make every attempt to deal swiftly and conclusively with these "extras" as they emerge. Don't kid yourself that you've already "Been there, done that!" Timely unloading during the Isolate step gives you fewer things to organize and store—and provides all the same advantages that the full-blown Unload step does, just on a smaller scale.

"**M**y daughter and I love to camp and have lots of supplies," says Judy Van Wyk of Providence, Rhode Island. "But we never have to go through the basement and shed looking for them when it's time to go. Instead, we wash and mend everything we used at the end of one camping trip and pack it up perfectly for the next one. And I mean everything—fuel, dehydrated and canned food, hiking socks, ground cover, ponchos. . . . We just do it automatically. While it's fresh in my mind, I replace anything we used up on that trip. We never have to make a huge mess looking high and low for something that we're pretty sure we have somewhere. I store the camping stuff over the rafters in the garage until the next trip. This keeps sleeping bags and canteens and so on from taking over several areas of the house. The best part about the whole system, besides that it's neat and tidy, is that if someone extends a last-minute offer to go to the lake, we're ready in a flash."

plify or reduce their ranks. When you finished the Unload step, you were probably convinced that you'd purged every useless object. It's almost embarrassing, but the detailed comparing and organizing of the Isolate step will help you identify more things you don't need because they're all right in front of you, vying for space. So while you have everything at your fingertips, take the opportunity once more to scale back groups with lots of objects in them, unload duplicate items, and eliminate multiple sites for the same household activity. Here are some ways to do that.

• **Give each item one home.** Eliminate obvious duplicates by finding a logical storage place for the item you keep. For instance, if you attach the nail clippers to the vanity-drawer handle with a pretty ribbon, you'll *always* know where to find them. That way, you'll need only one pair, not one in your purse, one in the junk drawer, one in the bathroom, and so forth. You'll cut down on unnecessary objects and save wear and tear on your nerves, since there will only be one place to look when you need that particular object.

• **Break up sets.** There's no law against it! So feel free, when you see how many of something you have, to cherry-pick. If you use only part of a tool set, for example, by all means get rid of the odd drill bits and glue gun that you never touch. If you use only the nail clippers, don't keep the manicure scissors and emery boards just because they match.

• **Rub out some activity hubs.** Consider reducing the number of household activity centers and the clutter that goes with them. If your family watches three different televisions, for example, each one probably has its own flotilla of videos, remotes, magazines, and so forth. If you (heresy of heresies) limit the household to one television, you may be able to cut back on a number of the objects you've isolated in your "TV viewing" group. Also consider reducing the number of places you snack, work on the computer, read, play with pets. . . . The list is nearly endless.

Keep items that do more than one job. There's such a thing as being *too* specialized. When you examine your groups of everyday objects, see whether some are pulling more weight than others, then get rid of the ones that aren't as useful. If you've amassed a huge pile of cleaning supplies during the isolating step, for example, consider whether you could keep only the glass cleaner and vinegar and do away with the rest. How many of the other products really do the specific job you need? This mentality could apply just about anywhere. For example, could a good sharp paring knife allow you to get rid of the vegetable peeler, six dull steak knives, SaladShooter, and lemon zester?

• **Don't keep two when one will do.** It's too easy to fall into the habit of keeping several of an object when you need only one. So ask yourself the really hard questions. For example, does every member of the house need a portable CD player, or could you share on the rare occasions that you need to take music out of the house? Or cameras: Do you and your husband each need your own, or could you get rid of one and save the space from its many attachments, too? Medicine cabinets are another example. It's probably easier to maintain one complete set, or even a transportable first-aid kit, than to float from bathroom to bathroom trying to find the tweezers or the cough syrup.

This is not, repeat, not, about trying to get rid of everything you have. (Are you reading this, Tossers?) It *is* all about matching the ob-

---

JUST A SMALL PIECE FOR ME, PLEASE

In clutter terms, the parts can be greater than the whole. In other words, you can save just a portion of a treasured group, instead of the whole thing—and sometimes save your sanity in the bargain. Decorator types in particular can benefit from this mentality. Rather than saving a rarely used drape and comforter set, if you really love it, keep a swatch of fabric from it and make a tiny throw pillow to remember the set by. Or follow the lead of a designer friend of ours. She kept only the changing table from a cherished set of her grown daughter's baby furniture. She decoupaged some of the baby's artwork and wallpaper on the outside and lined the drawers with swatches of baby blanket. So instead of holding on to (and having to store) a whole room's worth of baby furniture and accessories, she has one manageable piece. This idea can work for many sets, including china.

jects you have to the functions they serve, then finding suitable, accessible space for the groups you've created. When you don't have so much stuff, you won't need as much accessible, clutter-free storage space.

SET YOUR PLACE

After you've fine-tuned your holdings, it's time to decide where each group will go. Take it slow. The same place they've always been might be fine, but somewhere new might be better. Here are factors to consider.

• **Proximity.** It's almost always more convenient to put away items when they're near the activity they support. Sheets might be better stored under the bed than in a linen closet down the hall, for example. Or you might want to improve the chances that a group of objects will stay stored by putting them near the place where they're cleaned or repaired. By that token, the sheets would do just as well stored in the laundry room.

• **Access.** This is key. You must be able to get to anything you store when you need it. And we mean without wedging the door open 6 inches with one knee while you snake blankets out until you reach the one you want, or lifting 75 pounds of dog food off the cooler in the garage every time you need it. You've gone a long way by grouping items that function together in the same place; that means you need to create just a few access routes, not a million.

GIVE IN EVERY NOW AND THEN

Sometimes you can protest too much. That's what happens if you keep trying to store an isolated group in one area, and, despite incessant nagging, it keeps showing up somewhere else. Every once in a great while, you should bow to the inevitable when you're trying to decide where to store things, particularly if you and your mate turned out to be considerably different Clutter Types when you took the test in chapter 1. Take shoes, for example. If everyone insists on taking them off in the living room, why not set up a shoe shelf there? A woman we know realized she was getting absolutely nowhere begging her kids to take their backpacks out of the car and up to their rooms when they got home. Her husband wouldn't ever clear out his briefcase, either. So she decided to go with the flow and made a rule that backpacks and briefcases *stay* in the car, and lunches and papers and schoolbooks make the trip back and forth to the house on an as-needed basis. If you do implement similar ideas, though, it's essential that you exchange one storage place for another. For instance, once shoes belong in the living room, family members don't get to also have big stacks of them in the kitchen and on their bedroom floors.

- **Frequency of use.** If you use a group of objects a lot—and to determine this you should hark back to your motion-study list—make sure you can reach the whole kit and kaboodle with ease. It's much more acceptable to have to stack a crate on a chair and stand on tiptoe to get the once-a-year fruitcake pan than to have to do the same to get your toothbrush. Not only do you want to make it easy on yourself to get to the things you need, you want to avoid clutter—and knocking over things to reach other things is probably Clutter Enemy No. 2.

- **Space.** If you have to keep it and it's big and bulky, you have to find an ample storage space—somewhere it will fit, where you don't have to cram it in or leap tall buildings to haul it out. Never mind if the space seems weird to other people. One of the best-organized, most visually appealing homes we know has sleeping bags in the top of the entertainment center, a stuffed animal collection in the shoe organizer, and the newspaper recycling bin completely hidden by the drop leaves of the dining room table.

- **Defy logic when it makes sense.** Don't get too bogged down by the rules about isolating objects. Just about the time everything seems to make sense in its place, you'll realize that some place just won't work. Take cooking oil, for example. The proximity clause indicates that it should be above the stove on a shelf. But safety says it could ignite there, so you should store it in a cool, dark pantry or the refrigerator instead. Car wax is another case in point. If you create a big car-care kit and leave it out in the garage, the wax will freeze and go bad in the winter. So keep your eyes and your mind open while isolating objects and choosing storage spaces for the groups you create—there may be a better way or a blockade right around the next corner.

That open mind will also come in handy as we move to the next step of the Q.U.I.C.K. process, Containing. This is when you'll consider everything from ammunition boxes to plastic ice cube trays to house your carefully sorted and selected household objects. Read on for hundreds of ways to contain everything—except your excitement that the clutter is finally coming under control!

CHAPTER 5

Step Four: Contain

Time—or should we say timing—is of the essence during the Contain step of the Q.U.I.C.K. process. Now that you've fought the war to unload all your unneeded stuff and categorize the rest, you need to store the victor's spoils. You'll want to move on quickly, while everything's out and in order. Still, you don't want to move too fast or you'll accomplish little more than "hiding" your stuff again, and miss lots of opportunities to thwart clutter. So proceed at a pace that allows you to identify suitable storage areas and containers for the items you've just finished Isolating.

Even though the timing is tricky, the work of the Contain step is fairly straightforward. You figure out what type of storage works and why, then punt anything that doesn't work and try something else. There is the occasional land mine within the Contain process. Old storage habits die hard, for one thing. A couple we know who lived in the husband's childhood home comes to mind. One day, after she requested—rather sharply—that he take the boot blacking out of the kitchen, he looked her in the eye and said earnestly, "I've been polishing shoes in the kitchen for 37 years, and putting the polish in the drawer next to the stove just that long, and I don't suppose I'm going to stop now."

Along with accommodating practices that simply aren't going to change, you'll have to work extra hard to smooth over your differences if you're part of a couple with different clutter personalities. Envision the Concealer awash in a sea of Rubbermaid containers, her horrified spouse looking on. Or a frantic Accumulator stocking shelves with stacks of World War II newspapers just as quickly as his Tosser spouse empties them to house tools and tennis rackets. This step requires lots of talk ahead of time. If you and your spouse can't agree on, say, where to store the camera and film, you'll have to at least be able to agree on whose way you'll try first.

You'll have ample motivation to work through the struggles, though, because Contain is also the most rewarding step of the Q.U.I.C.K. process. At last, you can see the results—a whole lot less clutter—of all your hard work. All the items you've decided to keep find homes that are effective and accessible, and maybe even attractive. So sketch out a battle plan for the Contain step, starting by considering the many suggested storage containers and storage spaces outlined in this chapter. (Hey, we didn't say you *had* to start storing your

HOW COUPLES CAN CONTAIN TOGETHER

When a mother walks into her daughter's kitchen, chances are she can find anything she needs, because the two probably store things in approximately the same places. If you're part of a couple, keep this example in mind as you work through the Contain step. Both halves of a couple will probably bring their familial storage ideas to bear as they decide where to contain their stuff. And however silly or outdated your mate's ideas seem, you're much more likely to succeed at clutter containing if you follow these suggestions.

MAKE A LIST AND CHECK IT TWICE. OR THREE TIMES. Together, list your storage needs and opportunities, and refer to that list during disagreements—not like lawyers whipping out briefs, but like two friends pulling out a grocery list. This will put the decisions on a more practical, less emotional footing.

LET THE PERSON WITH THE HIGHEST STAKE MAKE THE MOST DECISIONS IN A GIVEN AREA. For example, if you're not the family golfer, you probably shouldn't have much say about where the clubs get stored, unless your mate is envisioning the very spot where you keep all the gardening tools.

ATTEMPT REFORM ONLY WHERE YOU'RE LIKELY TO SUCCEED. If your husband has always stored clean coffee cups on the counter next to the coffeepot, for example, he's unlikely to remember to put them in the cabinet at this late date, even if he wants to. If you push the issue, he'll soon feel doomed to failure (or just plain annoyed), a feeling that might extend to *all* the new clutter-containing ideas. So concentrate your efforts in an area where he's less entrenched, such as requesting that all car keys be stored in a dish on the sideboard.

potato chips in a laundry basket—it was just a suggestion!) Ten hut, and remember, where clutter is concerned, take no prisoners!

Take a Magical History Tour

Those who don't study history are doomed to repeat it. Of course, where clutter containment is concerned, there are some historical patterns you'll want to repeat and some that you most definitely will not. So to kick off the Contain step, observe your current containment practices and note any that seem to work particu-larly well. Here's a sample of the type of questions you should ask yourself.

- Are the papers in my file cabinet usually up to date, or does it just serve as a hiding place for old mail-order catalogs and the service agreement for the Mustang you sold in the 1980s?
- Are we more likely to put away videos in a cabinet, or in a basket near the VCR?
- Are the family's toothbrushes usually lying on the countertop, or are they stored snug in their individual holes in the toothbrush rack?
- Are garden rakes more likely to be stored properly in an oversize trash can or mounted on a Peg-Board?

SEVEN WAYS TO USE BASKETS

There are really good reasons to use baskets to contain clutter. First, they make collections of even the most utilitarian items more attractive. Second, baskets with handles make transporting a group of items a cinch. And third, since you probably have lots of empty gift baskets, Easter baskets, and so forth taking up valuable storage space, you might as well get some use from them. Not sure where a basket would fit in with your clutter-containing plan? Consider stashing these seven items in baskets.

1. Extra rolls of toilet paper in a basket on the bathroom floor or on a shelf.

2. Mittens and scarves in an Easter basket (with a long handle) hanging from a peg near the back door.

3. The remote and reading glasses in a small basket on an end table in the family room.

4. In a basket on the pantry shelf, stash staple ingredients for the "house specialty," such as chili or lasagna, so you'll always be prepared for unexpected guests.

5. In a deep, large basket, arrange several houseplants in inexpensive plastic pots. Cover the tops of the pots with sheet moss so it looks like one planter. (Line the inside of the basket bottom with heavy plastic first.) Not only will you save bucks on several more expensive pots, but you can also rotate plants in and out more easily than you can in a multiplant container.

6. Hand towel and guest soaps in a basket on the guest room nightstand. Not only will you always be prepared for guests, you save space in the bathroom cabinet or linen closet.

7. Library books or rental videos in a sturdy basket near the door (or near where you keep car keys).

Don't just glance around, either. Perform a room-by-room inspection and commit your analysis to paper. Try to identify whether you or your family does particularly well or has a problem with the following container options:

- Chests with hinged tops
- Clear containers that let people see what's inside
- Closets with doors
- Containers with lids
- Countertop containers
- Drawers
- Flat trays or baskets
- Open containers, such as pencil holders
- Out-of-sight storage options such as the attic or blanket chests
- Pegs or other visible wall storage
- Shelves
- Under-the-bed drawers or containers

If you know what type of storage works well for you, try it first (but probably not exclusively) when you're attempting to contain the stuff that always seems to end up cluttering the house. An example: One man we know figured out that he never got around to putting away his clean laundry if he was expected to pull drawers in and out of a dresser. So he converted all the bedroom closets in his house to shallow shelves, and now he quickly and willingly sorts laundry just as soon as it's clean and folded.

After you have an idea of the containment methods that are most appealing to you and the other cluttermongers at your house based on your history and preferences, follow these steps to complete the Contain process.

List what needs to be stored. Working from the decisions (and the notes) you made in the Isolation step, record what you need to contain. Specify whether you plan to put everything of one type in one area (like flashlights) or all the related items for one activity or project in one place (like the camping equipment, which might include a flashlight). If you have time, put the items that really need to remain out of sight (like toilet plungers and underwear) at the top of your list, in case you run out of spaces that aren't visible to guests or to easily embarrassed teenagers.

Determine how often you'll need the stuff. Once a day? Once a month? Every Thanksgiving? This will help you decide what to relegate to the attic, what can be stored at the bottom of a barrel, and what, like toothbrushes and plastic drinking glasses, needs to be readily accessible at a moment's notice. Examine each object to determine its unique storage needs. Is it flammable, so you need to store it far from heat sources? Does it need to be stored in a cool, dry place? Out of the sunlight? Away from children? Keep notes right on the list of stuff to be stored.

Consider the container. Even if a storage container is clearly marketed for a certain purpose, it may not fit your needs. "A good example is those empty paint cans that most home stores sell and that lots of home improvement shows recommend for storing kid stuff," says Tom Russell, who designs the program guide for a house

Unless you're almost saintly in your clutter habits, don't plan to store items in a container with lots of other items stacked on top, says antiques dealer Ollie Belcher of Corbin, Kentucky. For example, if you use a blanket chest as a coffee table, don't display your collection of china teapots on top unless you never want to see those blankets again. Human nature being what it is, most of us are never going to clear off items to get at what's underneath. You lose use of the stored objects, and, horror of horrors, gradually forget what's in there and inadvertently replace it, which means more clutter to get rid of one fine day. Ollie's rule: Place one or two items at most atop a storage container—a lamp on the foot locker that serves as a nightstand, for example, or a single afghan on the toy chest.

- Does it have sharp edges that will make it difficult to pull down from high shelves without injuring someone?
- Does its lid go on and come off easily? This is particularly important for airtight food storage.
- Is it breakable? Could a child or pet break it easily?
- Is it fire resistant or fireproof?
- Is it moisture resistant if I plan to put it in the refrigerator, freezer, or outdoors?
- Is it waterproof?
- Is the container so heavy it will be difficult to move with other items inside?
- Will it fit under the bed?

Once you've decided what type of storage an item requires, match it with the most appropriate of the different containers you have readily available.

and garden cable network based in Knoxville, Tennessee. "I've found that the lids are hard to get on and off, and they're fairly heavy. They could give a kid a good knock on the head if one fell off a high shelf. Plus the handles dig into your skin when you carry them around." No matter what expert finds a container useful, evaluate it by your own criteria, whether it's something you have on hand or an impending purchase. Ask yourself these questions:

- Can it hold heavy items?
- Do its drawers slide in and out easily?
- Does it have a flat top that will make it easy to stack?

Choose a starter project. You won't be intimidated by the sheer magnitude of the changes if you start with just a few objects or groups to contain first. If you're feeling particularly overwhelmed, do a small project in a room that's already almost completely organized. If you're full of energy and strong will, start with the highest-priority storage project— kitchen stuff, for example, so you can actually resume cooking family meals, or the valuable china that risks being broken each day it's out in the open. Once those storage ideas have taken hold, move on to a couple of others until you've contained the whole house (or everything you've managed to Isolate).

Some of the trickiest items to store are soft or soft sided, such as stuffed animals, bags of chips or pasta, throw pillows, sleeping bags, or empty padded envelopes. They defy laws of efficiency, because they don't stack, you don't want to crush them, and they can instigate an avalanche if someone mistakenly places another item on top.

To corral these items effectively, look no farther than the laundry room. No, don't destroy the stuff with an extra-long spin cycle. Instead, consider acquiring a few more of those rolling laundry-sorting contraptions with the three spacious net compartments (they look like open sacks) held up by folding metal legs. They provide fine permanent storage for soft, bulky items, without wasting space—and there's no way an object will come toppling out.

Less than $20 at a home or discount department store, these mobile hampers fit nicely on the floor of a closet or in a more informal room, such as the basement or a teen's bedroom. One woman we know, starved for kitchen storage, stashes Tupperware, pasta, and chips in the compartments and just wheels the contraption to a new place in the kitchen if it's blocking an appliance she needs to use. The off-white mesh sides are fairly attractive, but you can always use fabric paint to pep them up if you like. If you know you're the type who will overflow the pockets with too many things, consider hunting down a tablecloth to cover the top.

A mobile laundry hamper can corral a lot of clutter.

Try before you buy. Once you know enough about what you're storing to reasonably choose a container for it, try the concept for a while before you commit. For example, if you've decided on shelves for the television and videos, experiment with cinder block and two-by-four shelves first (or another reasonable facsimile) before you buy the expensive entertainment center. If you plan to use open plastic bins for recycling or children's toys, put cardboard boxes out where you envision the bins going later. Should an under-the-bed blanket chest appeal to you, try a drawer from the dresser in that space before you make any purchases. The low-cost tryout has two benefits: If it fails, you haven't wasted money on storage containers that wouldn't have worked in the long run; if it succeeds, it serves as a training period for the new storage habit.

Evaluate and regroup. A few weeks after you start using new containers (or old containers in a new way), evaluate how well they're working. Are the toys still strewn everywhere

A Concealer in the Contain step is like a kid in a candy factory. You feel entitled to splurge on dozens of brand-new containers, because that's what this step is all about, right? Well, not exactly. Even the trendiest new container system being peddled by storage solution companies won't work if you haven't made the necessary decisions about where items need to go in your household. To keep yourself from concentrating on form over function, put a moratorium on any purchases until you've placed items in the area where you want them for at least two weeks. If they need some sort of container to stay in place, use clear plastic trash bags, jars, and cardboard boxes.

while the pristine toy chest sits empty nearby? Is everyone really using that new shelf for books? Add your analysis to the list you prepared at the beginning of the Contain step, then refine what's not working. For example, you might take the lid off the toy chest and try that for a while, or move the bookshelf closer to the chair where everyone reads. After a few more weeks, evaluate once again. If you keep modifying as necessary, sooner or later you'll hit on the storage containers that will work for you.

Containment Dos and Don'ts

As you make decisions about where to store your stuff, and in what containers, listen to yourself. Do you sound like a whiny teen trying to get permission for a tattoo or the car keys? "But everyone else. . . ." Forget, we repeat, forget, everyone else. If everybody else jumped off a bridge, would you, too?

Look. You and your household members are absolutely the only ones who can make decisions about where to store your stuff. That's because you and you alone have to live with your decisions—not that smiling salesman who sold you the hundreds of dollars of plastic containers to repackage your pantry items; not your mother-in-law, who would never dream of putting sheets anywhere but in a sachet-satu-

C ontainer preferences are unique and completely up to you, but you must not ignore these safety guidelines for storage.

1. Never store flammable objects such as dry paper or oily rags in the attic, where heat may cause them to combust.

2. Never store aerosol cans with "contents under pressure" near a stove or other source of heat.

3. Never reuse a gasoline, motor oil, or paint container to store something else.

rated linen closet; not your meticulous neighbor who always has room for the car and the lawn mower in his garage. You. You must figure out which storage ideas will work at your house. Of course, no one said you should do that without some input from other people. Read on for advice that you can take or leave.

Tamper with tradition. Some of the most clutter-provoking storage containers survive in the name of tradition. Take canisters on the counter, for example. Do you really need a flour canister when you bake once a year? Is your coffee in the coffee canister? Do you even own tea?

A storage container that has been in your family for generations (or even one like it) is immediately suspect. Just a few other examples include tissue box covers (when you typically use a bit of toilet paper to blow your nose); medicine cabinets (when all your bathroom supplies are in plain view on the counter); and shoe racks in the closet when the shoes are strewn about the room. What's the message here? Question all containers as skeptically as you would a potential son-in-law. Just because most homes have one, or your home always has, doesn't mean they're doing the job they claim to do, or that you need them.

Think outside the box, literally. We know one woman, a psychologist no less, who stores all her shoes in a rack by the door, since that's the only place she's been reliably known to take them off and put them up. Another friend has stashed

THREE OVERRATED CONTAINERS

Just because storage ideas have been around for years doesn't automatically make them effective. Here are four containers that really don't warrant space in your household.

1. Thin plastic "sweater caddies." These look like clear plastic storage for hanging clothes, only they have cardboard separators that act like shelves for individual sweaters. Problem is, the cardboard shifts around unless the entire caddie is perfectly full of folded sweaters. And it's hard to unzip the 2- or 3-yard zipper just to get one sweater out of the bottom. In its place, try an inexpensive cardboard dresser or shoe rack with lots of drawers or cubbyholes.

2. Cookie jars. The loose-fitting lids let air in, so they keep thin, crisp cookies such as gingersnaps fresh, but let gooey, chewy chocolate chip–type cookies get hard quickly. Better to use an empty plastic ice cream pail with an airtight lid.

3. Shampoo holders for the shower. These are never big enough for all the brands you have on hand, and most of them let water pool in the bottom, which eventually causes mildew. Better to place rubber coasters on the lip of the tub if you have one, and place an individual shampoo or conditioner on each. If they get mildewed, send them through the dishwasher. If you have an enclosed shower with no tub, hook a cylinder-shaped plastic sand pail to the neck of the shower fixture with holes drilled in the bottom for drainage.

a four-drawer file cabinet on her covered back porch, because that's where it fits, and she rarely needs to cross-reference a tax record. (Her three pet chickens also lay eggs between it and the wall, but that's another story.) We offer these examples just to remind you that there are no bad storage solutions . . . just some that take a little longer to get used to than others. There's no point in having unusual containers just to be unusual, though. You're much more likely to succeed if you go with the flow. For example, you notice that you've always left your shoes in one place, so you decided to install a shoe tree for them there. The bagels are way too wide for the container marked as a bagel keeper, but the plastic Kool-Aid pitcher is sitting right there and they'll obviously fit. You get the idea. So go for it.

Stamp out or shorten stacks. Not much creates clutter faster than a stack of objects, be-

SAME CONTAINER, DIFFERENT NAME, LOWER PRICE

Go ahead and buy into the marketing hype: Purchase the latest "cool" containers for everything from beads and jewelry to children's toys. But do yourself a favor and shop in the "un-cool" departments of the store, where you can save as much as 50 percent on items nearly identical to the trendy ones being peddled. Here are six examples.

Instead of this	Buy this
Plastic children's toy chests from the kids' furniture department	Sturdy covered plastic boxes from the automotive department
"Bead" sorting boxes from the craft store	Clear tackle boxes from the sports section of the discount department store
Sewing boxes from the craft or sewing store	Metal or plastic tool boxes with a top tray from the hardware or home store
Office supply sorting trays from the office store	Plastic silverware trays from the dollar store
Cardboard pencil or art supply boxes	Free empty cigar boxes from the store, with rubber bands to keep them shut
Clear glass canisters	Large glass jars from the local school cafeteria or diner, lids covered with gingham fabric

cause someone's just bound to want the one at the bottom and end up toppling the whole pile, says hard-core neatnik Nancy Byrd of Indianapolis, Indiana. That's why she hangs up all her clothes, even T-shirts, instead of stacking them on shelves. While that may be a little too radical for most, the basic advice is sound: A tall stack is a toppling stack. So strive to store piles or stacks in containers or on shelves where only a few items will be on top of each other. That may mean installing a few extra shelves in the armoire or entertainment center to avoid a stack of videos or board games, or putting casual clothes and the like in a cardboard dresser with lots of tiny drawers. Then you have one T-shirt per drawer instead of top-heavy stacks in a larger dresser. If you go with Nancy's method, you may want to fix your closet up with two rods in one section, to double the space for hanging shirts.

Don't let stuff reach the ground. Another Nancy Byrd recommendation: Don't let anything touch the floor. She's not talking about dusting off fallen toast and eating it anyway. "Anything I'm going to store on the floor—under the bed, in the garage, on the porch—goes in a container first," she says. Not only does it keep the items clean, but it makes it easier to pull out the collection without leaving part of it behind, and also keeps piles of stuff from degenerating into tangles of junk. No one will step on a big plastic trunk with sleeping bags inside, for example, but they'll happily trample the same sleeping bags if they're on the floor. Nancy's favorite under-the-bed freebie container? Empty

plastic ice cream pails, which she uses to store Lego blocks and other small objects. She hauls them out individually, but says if you had more than four or five, you might want to set them all on a throw rug, so you could pull them out and shove them back under the bed easily.

If you can, make it look nice. We do know a man who tried to mount his electric drill in the master bedroom, where it would be handy for hanging pictures and bathroom repairs. That's just one example of taking the idea of accessibility and convenience a little too far, with no concern for appearance. It won't do to go too far the other way, either—those delicate shell-covered boxes, for example, won't last a day on most makeup tables, and most households can't maintain silk storage bags or velvet-covered photo albums.

Tom Russell manages to balance form and function. He wants storage containers that fit in with his carefully decorated rooms. His idea of the least expensive, handiest solution? Hatboxes. "You can find the real article at thrift stores or never-used cardboard or plywood versions at a craft store," he says. "They sell almost any size you could think of, in the traditional round shape or in ovals or rectangles." Tom uses large or medium hatboxes to stash everything from light bulbs and candles to balls of yarn; he uses the tinier versions to hide away paper clips, cat toys, cuff links, and the like. They're light, they stack easily, and they're attractive in plain view. The best thing about the hatboxes? "You can customize them to match your decor, using wallpaper, paint, or decoupage," Tom says.

Other attractive storage options include decorative screens that obscure loads of boxes, curtains attached with Velcro to disguise unsightly shelves, pretty fabric pouches, baskets, and bins. But more important than any artistic touch is just the work of completing the Contain step. With the clutter out of the way, your home will be beautiful . . . in the eye of any beholder.

Call in the pros. Sometimes you just want to tell someone, "Here, fix this for me." Luckily, there are a lot of companies that are happy to take your money to solve your storage problems. Some send a consultant to your home who helps you determine your exact containment needs. From those discussions and measurements, the company constructs a custom-made storage system and installs it in your home. If you have the cash, this is a wonderful solution. California Closets is one company that offers this service, but many home improvement centers offer the service, too. To find a local California Closets branch, check the Yellow Pages under Closets and Closet Accessories or Closet Design and Accessories.

CHAPTER

Step Five: Keep It Up

With everything safely stowed in snug containers—or at least tucked on shelves—you can put your feet up and just enjoy your uncluttered house, right? Absolutely. And at the same time, not exactly. The sole reason you clear clutter is so you can enjoy your home more, so you *should* take every opportunity to revel in the space you've created, the visual ease, the uncomplicated comfort. But you can't just kick back once you've completed the Contain step, or eventually your home will revert to its old ways. That's why the fifth step of the Q.U.I.C.K. process, Keep It Up, is an ongoing process.

But it isn't very time consuming. The Keep It Up step is more of a maintenance thing, requiring some occasional tweaking, a few refreshers on the many changes you made during the Quantify, Unload, Isolate, and Contain steps. Lots of it really falls under the category of simple "cleaning." And the clutter control just gets easier as you go along, because the strategies that were once entirely foreign are now habits.

This step does involve action, and much of it will seem familiar—recycling

Before wading into the Keep It Up step, please pause to pat yourself on the back. Go back and review those "before" snapshots you took during the Quantify step and marvel at how far you've come. Take time out to thank anyone who helped you Isolate or Unload, and let them know how great everything looks. Go out for a movie or a picnic if you haven't taken much time for anything but decluttering lately. Why all this hoopla? When you remind yourself what a great job you're doing, you rejuvenate your interest in keeping up the good work. It's all too easy to rush off to the next thing without enjoying what you've already accomplished.

Which brings us to another point. Spend at least one day without allowing any negative thoughts to intrude. You'll only sap your energy for the Keep It Up step if you keep beating yourself up over the tasks you weren't able to accomplish. Instead, after your day of positive thoughts, record those "yet-to-do" items on a short list and see if you can't work them in over the long haul.

weekly, for example, or holding an annual garage sale. But most of Keep It Up is mental, remembering how your life has changed, remembering why you want to keep it that way, and seeing ways to prevent clutter from creeping back into your home. Most important, Keep It Up involves remembering that you are no impostor. That is *your* decluttered home. Tosser, Accumulator, Concealer, no matter— you were able to conquer the clutter. And now you're more than ready to Keep It Up!

Lifelong Clutter-Control Habits

Although it may seem that your home can get cluttered all on its own, it can't stay decluttered by itself. Happily, lots of the approaches that worked in the earlier steps of the Q.U.I.C.K. process can be modified to work here, too. You can, for example, occasionally take five unnecessary objects from your home (see page 44). But since you've done the bulk of unloading, you may want to "take five" once a week, or even once a month. Here are some other ways to keep clutter under control.

Reconsider carefully. Especially if you completed Q.U.I.C.K. steps one through four in one blitz, there will be some unexpected fallout from your earlier decluttering decisions. Suddenly the hatboxes that seemed so cute look messy with video-camera cords spilling out. So you decide they're better suited for storage in your bedroom. Or Aunt Edna's armoire looks silly in the middle of the dining room, now that Cousin Ned mentions it. How to cope? Let the new organization stay put for at least 2 months, then consider a few changes. But don't doubt yourself. Some ideas work for some folks, other ideas work best for other people. That doesn't mean you should change everything back to the way it was. At the most, take on two revisions at a time. Otherwise, you'll get bogged down and depressed and feel like your earlier efforts were for naught—and you might give up on clutter control altogether.

Rotate the stock. Ollie Belcher of Corbin, Kentucky, has learned a valuable lesson as an antiques dealer and avid collector: "Rotate your stock," she says. "If you want to keep your home from getting cluttered, pack some things up and store them with a big sign on the side of the box that says what they are, then put some other items out." This approach works best with artwork and knickknacks, and it yields two benefits: You can really enjoy and appreciate the newly unpacked items with a fresh eye, and while you're unpacking replacement items, you can evaluate whether you've outgrown what's in the box.

Borrow and swap. If you've never had a sister, you probably don't know the principles involved in constantly borrowing stuff from other people. But it pays to get comfortable with the concept, because borrowing is an essential long-term clutter-control device. When you borrow games, movies, and library books, you have more room for other stuff that you'd prefer to keep permanently. Of course, you must loan objects as often as you borrow them. And don't expect, say, your aunt to maintain all the folding chairs for family gatherings when she lives in a one-room walkup and you have a house with seven closets.

You can also get much more creative and so-

BETTER BUYING HABITS, LESS CLUTTER

You can't bring new objects home if you don't buy them first. Here are ways to cut back on purchases, particularly on the discretionary items that are so likely to cause more clutter.

• **CUT BACK TO ONE CREDIT CARD.** If possible, make it one that isn't accepted everywhere, such as Discover. That way, even if you have plenty of money, you don't have plenty of credit limit for spur-of-the-moment discretionary shopping or Internet and mail-order purchases. When you have to use a check or cash, you'll probably spend more judiciously.

• **GET THREE PRICES FROM COMPETING** STORES, EVEN FOR INTERNET AND MAIL-ORDER SALES. Comparison shopping will slow you down and make you immune to slick sales pleas.

• **DON'T SHOP AT MALLS.** There, one store leads right to another. Instead, buy from freestanding stores that don't provide as much temptation.

• **WAIT 3 DAYS.** Between the time you find an item that you can't live without and the time you finalize the purchase, wait 3 days. Maybe you'll change your mind or won't have time to go back to the store.

---

phisticated with borrowing by planning ahead to share with another family or person. Go halvsies on anything from Crock-Pots to beach floats to videotapes to expensive statuary to maternity clothes. You can even pay for a portion of something a friend already owns so you can use it more often, subsidizing part of a leaf blower or video camera, for example. Just remember, every time you incur a bit of inconvenience by sharing an item, you save money . . . and prevent a lot of clutter.

Keep storage areas operative. Letting your attic or basement get crammed full is one of the worst things you can do to your freshly decluttered home. "If you can't store the extra things that you don't need right now, you can't keep the house organized. It's that simple," says Jim Slate, a retired electrician in Winnsboro, South Carolina. Gradually, even in those household areas where you ruthlessly unloaded all the reject items, things will need to be stored or they'll become clutter. If you know they can't move on because the attic is packed, you're much more likely to leave them in place. So keep your storage spaces clean and organized, and also easy to reach with a sturdy ladder or steps and handrails, says Jim. That way, when you decide you're tired of the record player that's blocking the fireplace, or that you're now ready to stash the Nancy Drews that were "must-have display items" just 6 months ago, you'll have somewhere to move them.

Retire old items. There's an old management adage: If someone isn't performing at

ANNUAL ACTIVITY CHECKLIST

If you schedule certain clutter-control chores once a year, they'll take only minutes. You may want to start some clutter-control traditions. Always check the shed for outdated gardening products on Memorial Day, for example. Sort through clothes each year on your birthday. Cull hobby and exercise equipment on January 1, after you've made your resolutions. And decide on a day (mark it on your calendar) that you'll remove the following items from your household:

- ☐ Damaged Christmas lights and decorations, tattered gift wrap and ribbons

- ☐ Hobby, sport, or exercise equipment that no longer matches your interests (or is broken or unusable)
- ☐ Partly used car products such as brake fluid or gasoline
- ☐ Seeds that no longer germinate
- ☐ Tax and bookkeeping records you're no longer legally required to keep
- ☐ Too-worn or too-small bathing suits and beach and pool stuff
- ☐ Too-worn or too-small winter coats and boots
- ☐ Worn out or mismatched socks and underwear

Look around your home. How many of the objects that you'd rather do without were gifts from other people? How about the stuff occupying at least a third of that donation box heading for Goodwill? Other people give you lots of clutter, and they'll probably keep doing so even if you just reorganized your home. Drawing names for a gift exchange is one way to steer clear of misguided gifts. With a gift drawing, you only have to buy gifts for one person or family, not the whole crew. You'll cut down on clutter and save money, too. Just follow these guidelines:

• **GET STARTED.** While you might anticipate resistance, everyone else may very well be waiting for you to make the first move toward turning the gift mayhem into something more manageable.

• **MAKE IT A RANDOM DRAWING.** Otherwise, people may feel as though you're trying to cut them out of the gift giving, not trying to cut clutter and unwanted gifts.

• **EMPHASIZE THE BENEFITS.** Remind people that they'll save time and money, and also be able to select more meaningful gifts since they'll focus on just one person.

• **PUBLICIZE THE PLAN BEFORE YOU PUT IT INTO ACTION.** This is not a covert operation and shouldn't be perceived as such.

• **HAVE A TRIAL PERIOD.** Tell anyone who's worried that it can be an experiment, "just for this year."

• **EXPAND THE IDEA.** Extend the grab-bag idea to all groups you exchange with. What works for family members will work for your book group, coworkers, and neighbors—or vice versa.

• **UP THE DOLLAR AMOUNT.** Since you're giving fewer gifts, you can afford a little more, and upping the ante increases the odds that you won't get something that's entirely useless to anyone.

---

his job, you don't hire an extra person—you hire a replacement or you'll be paying two people to do one job. That goes double for household items. It's all too easy, especially for Concealers, to buy something new to solve a problem but then to never get rid of the problematic possession. So don't be passive with an item that has stopped working or that you've decided you no longer like. If, for example, you purchase new golf shoes because the old ones weren't comfortable, don't keep the old models around "just in case you need them."

Ongoing Clutter-Control Chores

Nice as it would be to finish with clutter once and for all, there are small maintenance tasks that won't take care of themselves. Here's how to make sure clutter control becomes a seamless part of the household operation.

Link clutter control to other automatic activities. Ever notice how you never seem to be able to organize an outing with certain beloved friends, but wouldn't dream of skipping

The Keep It Up step of the Q.U.I.C.K. process can be tough for Concealers, because it's your style to hide away stuff without evaluating it. To avoid a return to the Quantify, Unload, and Contain steps, skim through your "decluttered" possessions often, maybe one room once a month. Open all those boxes, closets, and containers, and relocate anything that doesn't belong—or that belongs at the dump or the Salvation Army. While you may never change your clutter personality, if you reevaluate often, you may not need to conceal as much because your stuff will be neatly organized out in the open.

your Thursday night bridge (or book or bowling) club? That's because the one activity is organized and occurs automatically. Do the same for your ongoing clutter-control chores. Instead of starting from ground zero to schedule each time you inspect the bathroom for empty shampoo bottles, for example, do it when you replace laundered towels or just before you get out of the shower. Purge magazines each Sunday evening as you watch your favorite television program. Clean old food out of the refrigerator each week before you go food shopping, and so on. Just so you (and anyone else who does chores at your home) are clear about your new approach, make out a chore list with the additions until the habit takes hold.

Find someone who cares. When you know someone is relying on your vigilant clutter-maintenance efforts, you'll be more likely to keep them up. So link your chores to someone else's welfare. Find a quilting group that would really like to have your old rags, for example, so you're more motivated to frequently evaluate your old clothes and dish towels. Or tap a church or the local Health and Human Services department to find out whether there's a poor family you can "adopt." Then send them regular donations of outgrown clothes, little-used dishes, discarded furniture, or even canned goods. If that's too personal for you, find out the high-need times at a homeless shelter or low-income day care, and note them on the calendar so you'll be more likely to take up a collection at your home at those times.

Think Like a Clutter-Control Genius

Somehow we keep envisioning a woman in a rocker on the porch with a shotgun over her knees, ready to keep clutter out with force, if necessary. But where bullets don't work, mind power does. Think before you bring stuff that you don't really need or want into the house. Remind yourself how you want to live and how you want things to look. Think before you buy.

People who are naturally good at clutter control automatically think in a particular way. Instead of feeling cheated that they don't have every object they ever admired, instead of worrying that everyone will hate them if they don't keep the 300-piece china set that's been in the family since 1937, they're comfortable with their simplified lives and the decisions they've made. Here are six attitudes that clutter-control geniuses share—and that you can cultivate if you keep at it.

Number one: "I can share." When you see something you like, it's natural to envision it in your own household. But for the sake of clutter control, start sharing. That is, enjoy the great stuff in other people's homes or at the museum store where you saw it or in the park. Tell yourself, "I can always visit my beloved water garden when I walk the dog," or "I can always enjoy my sister's collection of figurines when I visit her."

One woman we know drove by a neighbor's house daily, always coveting the family's decorative flags, one of which featured the cartoon character Snoopy, her favorite. When she found out how many hundreds of dollars the "flag of the month" club cost, though, she started changing her tune. She considered what a pain it would be to store the 20 flags and climb up on the porch roof to change them once a month. Finally, she realized that she would get much more enjoyment from "her" flags if she just continued to admire them as she rode in the carpool each morning.

Number two: "That will only be wasted on me." More than 30 years ago, Joanne Kennedy of Toano, Virginia, was at a big-deal church lunch with a friend. When the priest urged a second helping of a rich entrée on her friend, she declined. "But it will go to waste!" said the priest. "It would only be wasted on me," said the friend. This was the first time it ever occurred to her that you could turn down something luxurious and expensive on the grounds that you really couldn't use it, says Joanne, who grew up during the Depression.

She has since applied her friend's motto to furniture offerings and other "stuff" as well as food. If it's not something she needs or wants, she doesn't worry about how much it costs or whether it will go bad or languish in a basement if she doesn't take it. That would be a waste, she reasons, but it would also be a waste if the same object sapped her mental energy, blocked a nice view, or languished in *her* basement. Joanne's mind-set, and her polite turn-down phrase, "That would only be wasted on me," are great to remember when you're tempted by bargains and family heirlooms that really won't fit in with your simplified lifestyle.

Instead of worrying about how valuable items are, concentrate on whether they'd be valuable to you—or just potential clutter. Too often, especially if you're an Accumulator, you worry too much about the waste if no one snaps up that violin that's selling for $200 less than book value, or what will happen to that salvage cabinet set if no one buys it—will it end up at the dump? Instead, focus on whether you could use an item to its full potential at your home, or whether it would just be "wasted" there.

Number three: "Objects don't have feelings." This is probably the toughest thing for Accumulators in particular to say. Because it seems as though that sad, worn teddy bear or Grandpa's tool set probably *do* have feelings that we can injure. But they don't. They're inanimate objects that will never know whether they're at the animal shelter or a Habitat for Humanity office or upstairs in your attic. And you'll feel good about doing a good deed for someone else.

Number four: "It's moderation, not deprivation." People who are naturally good at controlling clutter view it as a lifestyle choice, not a death sentence. Part of the balance means

---

ADVICE FOR . . . COUPLES

A simplified, more beautiful, uncluttered home is an odd thing to blame your partner for. But it's all too easy to do. When people start questioning why you no longer have that ratty old dartboard they like to play with once a year in your basement, or how come you don't want their old living-room carpet, you tell them, "My wife got this crazy idea that we have too much stuff!" That's no good. Just as you had to agree that you both wanted the benefits of a simpler lifestyle, now you have to back each other up when the questions start flying. "We decided we had too much stuff and we're trying to cut back," you say. "I didn't think to offer you the dartboard!" The note to strike is proud but not smug and above all, united. As you refuse to sell your mate down the river, you'll refresh your memory about why you're committed to a simpler lifestyle, and positively reinforce your clutter-control partnership, too.

It's so natural. You've found this great, reduced-clutter lifestyle, and now you think everyone should discover it, too. But if you nag people who haven't expressed any interest in your transformation, you'll soon learn that it's a bad idea. Of course you're going to irritate them, and that's bad, but that's not what we're worried about. When you start preaching, you may get some argument, and it may sway you back to the other side. Or, worse, you may alienate so many friends that it seems that friendship and a low-clutter house are mutually exclusive! So keep your thoughts to yourself. And if you have friends with particularly cluttered homes, visit them often so you'll remember what you're *not* missing.

being able to splurge on occasion, to acquire something that doesn't absolutely fit into the plan. As art professor Sam Yates of Knoxville, Tennessee, says: "If you get a really good deal on a Mercedes, you can figure out where to park it." He uses the analogy to include art acquisitions, but his attitude applies to all sorts of stuff. If you don't give yourself a little room to get the things you really love, the ones that make your spirit soar, you may rebel against your new, simplified life entirely.

Number five: "Lots of people are just like me, and I don't need to apologize for my choices." When you've first earned your clutter-cutting wings, you may feel tentative explaining the "new you" to other people. "Um, you, uh, might not want to store your bike, in, uh, my pantry anymore," you stutter to your nephew, "but, uh, I guess it's okay for today." Hold it right there. You have every right to lead a more simplified life, and there's no reason to apologize for it. Nor do you need to call a lot of attention to yourself. A simple "Bob and I are trying to do without so much stuff because it just saps our energy. One way you can help is to keep your bike out of our pantry" will suffice. And this is an important thing to remember: Even if your friends and family can't imagine you as a low-clutter soul, every person alive knows at least one neat and organized adult. So they've had practice acting well in a simplified, organized home, and can be expected to do the same for you.

Number six: "My definition of clutter can change." People who seem to have clutter under control never blindly assume that all clutter is bad. Instead, they realize that people must continually consider what works for them. Each piece of furniture, each collection of teacups, each worn blanket, must be taken on its own merits—and never evaluated by the standards of the outside world. And you can't ever let your definition of clutter stop growing. Any major life change—death, divorce, retirement,

Part of the Accumulator mind-set is the idea that you can provide for those who will follow, the old "Some day this will all be yours." That's why you pick up that ham radio set when you don't know how to use one, or keep your wife from tossing that salt and pepper shaker collection that may have been Uncle Billy's in the '80s, or even why you might hang on to the daily newspaper. This is a hard habit to break, because you're not selfishly motivated: You're trying to preserve the past for future generations.

But you know what? Your heirs will probably feel more burdened than enlightened by a bunch of stuff, particularly before they settle down and have families of their own. And they can probably learn more about the '60s and even the local community in books and local exhibits. Instead of acquiring things they may not want and definitely won't need, why not spend your time *talking* with the next generation? Take the time while your nieces and nephews are young and you're still around to have an evening of family reminiscing. If you like, write some great family stories down in a notebook for the next generation. They'll treasure those moments and the (brief) written records far more than any object—unless you have a perfectly preserved Picasso or a '65 Mustang!

empty nest, to name a few—will affect your needs for "stuff." So will the passage of time, because the longer you're on this earth, the more your lifestyle and hobbies will evolve. In response, revise your clutter expectations and attitudes. The best way we've found is to have an annual soul-searching session, alone or with your mate, for an hour or a weekend. Jot down where you think your life is headed. Then list five current big-ticket items that you will and won't need on the journey. After you compare lists, tour the house and chat about the smaller objects.

And while you're on the topic, bring the Keep It Up step full circle by reviewing the many benefits that reduced clutter has brought to your lives, from money saved to space earned to hassles averted. Being able to voice those benefits will tell you that while you'll always need to Keep Up with clutter around your home, you have absorbed the essential lesson of the Q.U.I.C.K. process: Life is better with less clutter.

PART

Q.U.I.C.K. Strategies for Every Room in the House

Sometimes it may feel like clutter's taken over your whole life—or it may have just taken over one room. In this section, we provide specific clutter-cutting strategies for every room in your house. So whether your garage is too stuffed to squeeze in the kids' bikes (let alone a car!), the bathroom is boiling over with half-used bottles, or your home office has become the "home junk room," you can put a stop to the mess just by looking inside. Let our clutter-busting experts show you what's worked for them—and how to make it work for you and your home.

CHAPTER 7

Kitchen and Pantry

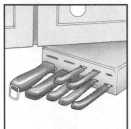

The kitchen is the center of family activity—and focal point for family clutter. And your pantry isn't much better. Sure, it started out neatly organized—spices in a rack on this shelf, seldom-used pots and pans on that shelf—but was quickly taken over by the odds and ends that had nowhere else to go: grocery bags, extra cleaning supplies, batteries, and lightbulbs. Now, when you look for the paprika—yikes!

If any of this sounds familiar, rest assured that you are not alone. Although the kitchen and pantry are universal clutter magnets, they're also easy to get back under control. Our experts will show you how to cut the clutter in the kitchen, organize a jumbled mess of a pantry, and bring peace and harmony to every family meal. (Okay, maybe that last bit is an exaggeration, but you get our drift.)

Holey Counters!

A RESOURCEFUL elderly gentleman we heard about hit upon a rather unusual method for getting his trash from the kitchen to the basement. Since he suffered with arthritic knees, the walk down the basement stairs was painful and, considering his advanced age, quite dangerous when he was carrying trash bags. His solution: He cut a hole in one of the kitchen countertops and another the same size in the floor directly below. That allowed him to drop his trash bags right down to the basement.

Practical? Yes. But also unsightly, and the gaping hole (even though it was covered with a matching circle of laminate countertop) was a real turnoff to prospective buyers when his house went on the market a few years later.

This may be one idea that you *don't* want to try at home!

Corralling Kitchen Clutter

If you often find yourself clearing the papers off your kitchen counters just to make room to prepare a meal, you're all too familiar with how quickly a kitchen gets buried in clutter. Fortunately, there are lots of ways to corral the clutter and keep your kitchen an inviting place for family and friends.

GETTING STARTED

A cluttered kitchen can be overwhelming, especially when you need to store the stuff that's cluttering up the countertops but your cupboards are too jammed to take on any more. Take a few deep breaths, grab a garbage bag and a few cardboard boxes, and take it one step at a time.

The garbage bag is, of course, for garbage. Your goal should be to fill it up. The boxes are for stuff that belongs elsewhere in the house. You should have one box for items that belong in the kitchen, one for items that belong in other living areas, a box for recyclables, and a box for each family member. As you clear off the counters, make quick decisions. Are you really going to read a 3-week-old newsmagazine? Probably not, so put it in the recycling box. A magazine that just arrived yesterday, though, can go in the "other rooms" box so you can place it in the family room next to your reading chair.

Continue this way, collecting T-shirts, shoes, sunglasses, dog or cat toys—anything that anyone's left lying around in the kitchen. Put it in its appropriate box and move on. Be ruthless when it comes to old newspapers and magazines, broken toys, scraps of paper, or ribbon—toss them. Once you've begun to make a dent in the piles, read on for even more ways to get out of the starting gate.

Categorize the clutter. One way to start tackling kitchen clutter is to choose one type of clutter—dishes, or kids' toys—and focus only on that category to start with. So if you choose paper, for example, ignore the dirty dishes piled up on the counter, the toys under the kitchen table, and the sweatshirt hanging over the back of the chair, and just home in on the paper. Sort, toss, and file until every last bit of paper is under control. If it takes you most of the day, fine. You can start with a new category the next morning. When you turn your attention to the next category, maybe dishes, don't even think about clearing up anything else in the kitchen until all the dishes are in their place. (See chapter 16 for even more ways to put the kibosh on paper piles.) Continue categorizing and working in just one category over the next few days and your kitchen will soon be clutter-free.

Work on your workstations. Sometimes it's easier to organize your kitchen when you think in terms of workstations—those areas where you cook, clean up, store food, do paperwork, and the like. Look at your kitchen layout with a critical eye. Could you move some of your appliances to make your kitchen work better or to create a better flow of traffic? Perhaps you could move your refrigerator closer to the sink or stove. Or maybe it's the stove that can move.

Even if you have no choice about where your refrigerator or stove resides, think about how you can use the space in your kitchen better. For example, if your main meal preparation consists of heating something in the microwave, then keep all your microwaveable plates, bowls, and other containers near the appliance itself. If you spend lots of time baking and use your island or one section of countertop as your prep area, then use the cabinets nearby to store all your bakeware.

Use space wisely. Are there areas in your kitchen that go unused or could be put to better use if only you had _____? Go ahead, fill in the blank. Maybe a kitchen desk has become a holding area for stray paper. If you had a chair, you'd probably want to spend more time at the desk, so you'd be motivated to clean it off and make it usable.

Or perhaps you have several feet of empty space with no counter or cabinets, or a roomy corner that stands empty. Why not buy a baker's rack, wood cart on wheels, or table, so you can use that area and give yourself some extra storage space?

SET THE TIMER

The key to staying focused and on task when organizing kitchen clutter is to limit the time you spend on the process. Try this technique: Set a timer for 15 minutes. As soon as the clock starts, tackle the first decluttering task, like clearing out one drawer or cabinet. If you finish the task before the clock runs out, move on to the next one. But when the timer goes off, stop what you're doing, whether or not you've completed the job. Don't keep going for "just a few more minutes." The idea here is to break up the huge job of clearing the clutter into many smaller tasks. You defeat the purpose if you ignore the timer.

When time is up, take a break. Get yourself a cool drink or sit down and read the newspaper for 5 minutes. Then set the timer for another 15-minute interval and dig in.

When was the last time you actually *moved* one of your kitchen cabinet shelves? Go ahead, take a look inside your cabinets—most have movable shelving, though few of us ever take the time to make adjustments.

The usual scenario is this: When we first move into a house and are busy cutting and installing shelf liners, we adjust the shelf heights for large items, like a pitcher or flower vase. Or maybe we don't even realize that the shelf can be moved and we lay the item on its side because it can't stand up in the space. That's the start of cluttered cabinets!

By adjusting shelf heights, you'll be able to make better use of your cabinets' interior space. For example, if you lower the shelf above the coffee mugs, you eliminate that "dead" space above the mugs, while at the same time opening up more space above the shelf.

Experiment with moving your cabinet shelves up or down to get the most from the space you have. You may be surprised by how much "extra" room you can make!

Take a look around your kitchen and see whether there are unused areas that you can turn into productive places with a minimum of expense.

Get a little help from your friends. Sometimes it can be overwhelming to confront the clutter that seems to be overtaking your kitchen. You've lived with it for so long, it's almost a comfort. But you know you'll be more efficient if you become better organized. So how do you get over that hump and get down to business? Some folks have found that having help from a friend or relative makes the job a lot easier. For example, your friend can point out how ridiculous it is to hang on to 60 paper bags when you get a half-dozen more each time you go to the grocery store.

A friend is particularly helpful to have around if you're a Collector. Once you've cleaned out your kitchen, your friend can take the trash bags home with her to dispose of. That way, you're not tempted to break into them later on and retrieve tossed items.

Put it in writing. As you empty out and sort through your kitchen cabinets and drawers, you're going to find plenty of items that are in good condition, maybe even some that are brand new and never used. Don't be too quick to toss these out. Instead, set them aside and jot down on a piece of paper the items you've found and where you can donate them so that they can be put to good use. For example, extra pots and pans can go to a soup kitchen; plastic cups can go to a day-care center; unopened or barely used cleaning supplies can go to a homeless shelter.

After you've finished decluttering, take your list and get on the phone with various charitable organizations. Tell them what you have and find out who can use your unwanted items.

CONQUERING COUNTER MESS

When was the last time you actually saw the countertops in your kitchen? And not just a clean spot or two, but a nice, clear expanse of gleaming, uncluttered counter? If you can't remember what color your countertop is, read on for tips about clearing your counter clutter.

Clear the decks. Take a cold, hard look at your countertops. Is your 10-year-old food processor in the exact same place you put it on the day you bought it, collecting dust all the while? Is your mixer in full view, even though you use it only a few times a year? What about that waffle iron? Do you *really* make waffles every day?

Cut down on kitchen clutter by putting away those seldom-used appliances, and you'll be amazed at how much counter space you've freed up. Keep out only those appliances—such as the coffee machine and toaster oven—that you use every day.

Stick 'em up. Keep your countertops clear by wall-mounting as much as you can. Your telephone and answering machine can easily be hung on the wall. And when you're in the market for a kitchen radio or small television, look for those models that install under the cabinet.

Garage your appliances. Appliance garages are all the rage in space-conscious kitchens. These built-in countertop storage areas hide—but also give easy access to—small appliances such as toasters, blenders, or coffeemakers. The garage can be recessed into the wall—and that means that your appliances won't take up *any* counter space.

An appliance garage keeps all those indispensable kitchen gadgets neat—and out of sight.

MORE WAYS TO SAVE SPACE

Here's a handy kitchen accessory that can save you tons of counter space: an over-the-sink shelf that holds soaps and sponges, and that has a paper towel holder and a slide-out cutting board. The wooden shelf stands on four legs and spans the width of a double sink. This ingenious shelf is available from Home Focus by calling (800) 221-6771; or visit its Web site at www.HomeFocusCatalog.com.

Home Focus offers a variety of space-saving kitchen supplies, such as tiered shelving, that organize spices, tea boxes or tins, decorative jam and jelly jars, or any other items you use frequently and want to keep close at hand.

Stand up your spoons. Sometimes it's worth giving up a bit of counter space to save your sanity. If you're constantly digging around in drawers searching for wooden spoons, spatulas, and other frequently used kitchen utensils, do yourself a favor and get them out into the light of day. An attractive crock, oversize mug, or other ceramic container can hold a half-dozen or more spoons, whisks, and other utensils. Keep it near the stove so you can easily reach out and grab what you need. A bonus: When you wash out plastic storage bags for reuse, you can place them over the utensils to dry.

Hang your cutting boards. Ever wonder why most cutting boards have an opening at one end? That's so you can hang them up! If your cutting boards are presentable, keep them from cluttering up your cabinet shelves by hanging them on a kitchen wall or exterior cabinet wall near the stove or sink. If your cutting boards don't look that great anymore, or you don't have handy wall space, no problem. Simply hang them on the *insides* of your cabinet doors.

These days, for safety's sake, many people are using different cutting boards for different foods, such as meat and vegetables. An easy way to keep track of which is which is to buy a different color for each food—white for meat and green for vegetables, for example.

Can the canisters. Do you have a set of canisters just sitting on your countertop, unfilled and unused? Or do you have a sugar canister that contains a half-inch of hard-as-rock,

2-year-old sugar? Unless you're really in love with the look of your canisters, get rid of them. Not only do they clutter up the countertop, they really aren't the best place to store your kitchen staples. Flour, sugar, salt, and other staples will stay fresher longer if they're sealed tightly in plastic zip-top bags and stored in a cool, dry place (see "Change the Container" on page 110).

Roll 'em, roll 'em, roll 'em. If your microwave or toaster oven takes up valuable countertop space, consider buying a microwave cart to house it. Not only will you free up counter space, but you'll also gain additional storage from the shelves and/or cabinets on the cart.

And don't worry about giving up too much floor space to the cart. Standard microwave carts measure about 36 inches wide and 18 inches deep; you can even find compact carts measuring about 24 inches wide and 18 inches deep.

Utility carts, with butcher-block tops and open shelves below, can hold a microwave or toaster oven and are a tidy 20 inches wide. For super-tight spaces, there are corner carts. All of these carts have wheels so you can move them where you need them, then roll them out of the way when you're through.

Empty the dishwasher in the morning. What does running your dishwasher at night have to do with countertop clutter? Plenty. You may know that running the dishwasher at night saves energy costs (check with your utility company to find out when reduced residential rates go into effect). But when you run it at night and empty it first thing in the morning, you can scoop up the breakfast dishes and load them right into the dishwasher before you head out the door, keeping your counters clear and clutter-free.

Soak it to 'em. You probably learned this one back in home economics class, but it still holds true. Whenever you cook or bake, fill the sink with warm, soapy water. Then, as you prepare your meal, drop in the mixing bowls, cutting boards, used utensils, and the like, and let them soak. Once the food is in the oven, wash what's in the sink or put the items in the dishwasher. If you let the dishes soak, you don't have to scrub them, and your counters aren't cluttered with dirty dishes. It's a good idea to wash and dry knives right away, rather than dropping them in the soapy water. That way, you don't risk getting a nasty cut.

DON'T MAKE IT A STRETCH

If you want your children to help with the chores (and who doesn't?), you need to think about how to make it easy for them. You can't expect your children to, say, set the table, when you're putting plates on shelves that are beyond their reach. So keep dishes, utensils, and nonbreakable cups on shelves with kid-friendly heights. That way, everyone can pitch in at table-setting time and can put the clean dishes away, too.

COORDINATING CABINETS AND DRAWERS

Just because your kitchen cabinets are fixed in place doesn't mean you have to live with whatever arbitrary shelving arrangement the manufacturer supplied. Here's how to make the most of the cabinet and drawer space you have.

Scrutinize your cupboards. Go ahead, take a look inside your cupboards. You can skip the ones that hold your everyday dishes and glassware. Those are probably full and fairly organized. But what about that messy cupboard filled with plastic containers, mismatched lids, and dozens of sports-drink bottles?

With a garbage bag in hand, put it all on the countertop. Now, pick and choose carefully. You don't really need more than a half-dozen plastic containers in assorted sizes, so recycle the rest. And make sure to keep only those lids that fit on the containers you've saved. Get rid of the other 40. As for those sports-drink bottles, keep one for each member of the family and one or two extras. Clear out any split, stained, half-melted plastic containers, bottle lids with no bottles, and so forth.

Now return the plastics you're keeping to the cupboard. Voilà! You've just freed up two-thirds of the space, giving you room to store items that actually belong in your kitchen.

Continue purging cabinets in this way, keeping only what you truly need and use regularly and getting rid of the rest. Don't expect to do it all in one day. Take your time and make a goal of, say, cleaning out one or two cupboards a day.

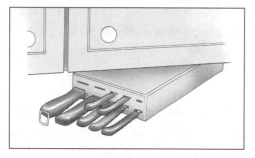
By the end of the week, your cupboards will be organized and clutter-free.

Keep it all in the family. When you're returning items to your cupboards, think about keeping like items together. For instance, store mixing bowls and beaters, measuring cups, and measuring spoons together. Put the coffee scoop with the filters, and if you don't have your coffee machine out on the countertop, store all the coffeemaking paraphernalia with the machine. It will save you lots of time when you need to cook or bake.

Organize by activity. Beth Hudson, a Philadelphia-based professional organizer, recommends that you examine your kitchen cupboards not only with an eye for what will fit in them, but for what activity will occur nearby. For example, put glasses in a cupboard near the refrigerator and dishwasher, for ease of use and washing. Store pots and pans near the stove, and keep plastic wrap and waxed paper near the microwave. By doing so, you have the materials you need close at hand for whatever job has to be done.

Take a head count. How many people are in your family? Four? Six? Then why the heck do you have 28 mugs cluttering up your kitchen cupboard? And we're not talking about the matching ones that go with your dinnerware. We mean all the other drinking vessels you have. You know, the chipped mugs from your last trip to Sea World (back in '92); the dozens of plastic water bottles with sports-drink logos on them; the assortment of plastic drinkware from restaurants and vacation spots.

Now ask yourself, how many of them do you actually use? How many of them did you not even remember having? Allow each family member to keep one item, no matter how old, if it has sentimental value, but toss the rest. Unless you're never going to set foot outside your town again, you'll soon be collecting a whole new batch from your future travels.

Hang 'em high. If you have decent-looking pots and pans, a collection of woven baskets, or attractive stemware, clear space in your cabinets

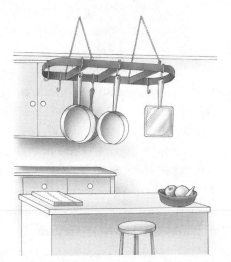

Get your pots and pans out in the open where you can see and use them with a ceiling rack. Frees up cabinet space, too.

by getting them out of the way and out in the open—hang them from the ceiling. Baskets can be hung from ceiling hooks or arranged right on top of your wall cabinets if you don't have soffits. Pots and pans can be hung from a rack suspended from the ceiling, and stemware can be hung upside down in wood grids that are suspended from the ceiling.

See 'em next year! There's no reason to clog up your kitchen cabinets and drawers with items you use only once a year. So take those Christmas cookie cutters, the huge Thanksgiving turkey platter, and the carving knife you use at holiday time, and store them in a less convenient place. Since you need to use them only once or twice a year, there's no point in having them cluttering up that precious space you need to store items you use year-round.

Use your oven. If you're short on cabinet or pantry space for storing large bakeware items like cookie sheets, muffin tins, jelly-roll pans, and so forth, use your oven for storage. The sheets stack up nicely, and they won't be damaged if the oven is turned on before you realize the pans are still inside.

Dejunk the junk drawer. We'd bet that just about every kitchen in America has a junk drawer. (If yours doesn't, you deserve a medal!) Sometimes the junk drawer actually holds a few useful items, such as a bottle opener, a nutcracker, or a cheese slicer. But what's all that other stuff in there? If you spend minutes digging through the junk drawer for one useful item, it's time to clear it out. Pull out the drawer and take it to the kitchen table. Pour yourself a cool drink, grab a plastic garbage bag, and dig in.

Throw away anything you haven't used in the last year. Don't fool yourself into thinking you might need it someday. If you haven't used it in at least a year, you're never going to use it. (This should be your mantra for clearing any kitchen clutter.) Throw away anything you can't identify or any tool that's missing a part. If you don't know what it is or what it's used for, why are you hanging on to it? When you find something useful, set it aside.

Once you get all the junk out of the drawer and into the trash, congratulate yourself—you've just freed up an entire kitchen drawer. Now, that wasn't so bad, was it?

Save the day with trays. Cutlery trays that fit inside kitchen drawers don't have to be limited to just storing forks, spoons, and knives. Throw one inside your junk drawer and use it to sort pencils, paper clips, and anything else you need to keep handy. Then take a look around your kitchen for other areas where small items need to be corralled. One place might be near the phone. If you don't have a desk in your kitchen, use a cutlery tray inside a drawer to hold pens, pencils, a letter opener, paper clips, scissors, and the like.

FREEING UP THE FRIDGE

As you go about decluttering your kitchen, don't overlook the one place that accumulates *lots* of stuff—the refrigerator. When was the last time you took everything out of there and gave your fridge a good cleaning? Have you put it off because you think it's overwhelming? Just follow these tips and you'll have it all under control in no time.

Shrink your containers. Ever notice that even after the leftover lasagna (or pasta salad or beef stew) has been whittled away by hungry munchers, the remains still sit in the original huge baking pan (or storage bowl), taking up lots and lots of refrigerator space? Make it a habit to reduce the container size of your leftovers as they get eaten. Sure, it takes more work and means you have a few extra containers to wash, but it frees up needed space in the fridge. Plus, it keeps the leftovers fresher, because when a container is sized right for the quantity of food that's in it, there's little room for air, and air circulating around food in a closed container speeds up food spoilage.

Cut your leftover losses. It's tempting to save one leftover pork chop, or one sliver of uneaten steak, or a lone baked potato, but ask yourself, is anyone *really* going to reheat it and eat it within the next few days? Probably not. So save yourself the time and effort of wrapping up small amounts of leftovers and using up space in your fridge. You know you're only going to toss the food out a week later. If you just can't bear to throw food away, feed it to the dog.

Keep your cool. Your refrigerator's cool, that is. While you're clearing the clutter from the fridge, take a moment to take its temperature. Refrigerators should stay at 41°F or lower. This slows the growth of most bacteria, decreasing the chances of food spoilage. While you're at it, take a peek in the freezer. That compartment should be chilling at a cool 0°F.

Give it a good cleaning. Once in a while, you're going to have to completely clear out the fridge and make sure it's *really* clean. Here's how to make that as painless as possible.

- First off, keep in mind that the best time to clean out your refrigerator is just before you go grocery shopping, when it has the least amount of food in it. And when you start, have a plastic garbage bag with you—you're going to need it when you discover the moldy bread and unidentifiable something-or-other way, way in the back!
- Next, get out your cooler and put a few ice packs inside. Now start on the top shelf and work your way down, then move to the door shelves.

DECLUTTER THE DOOR

In many kitchens, the outside of the refrigerator looks as cluttered and messy as the inside. Why? Because the refrigerator door seems to be the one place where everyone is sure to want to hang something—school or vacation photos, a calendar, the grocery list, the phone numbers for take-out pizza and Chinese food, and so on. Does your fridge door have some (or all) of these items, hanging on for dear life by magnets and clips? If so, take it all down. Give the door a good cleaning with warm, soapy water and towel it dry.

Now take a look at all the stuff you removed from the door. Are there better places to store some of it? If so, set it aside. Can some of it be thrown away because it's outdated? Then put it in the trash. Pare down until you have as little as possible left to put back up on the fridge. Then arrange the items in a pleasing (and logical) order on the door.

Take out every item and check its expiration date. If it's overdue, toss it. If it's still fresh, and needs to be refrigerated, put it in your cooler.

- Be on the lookout for those once-in-a-lifetime buys that are still hanging around. You know, like the red currant jelly that you bought to use as filling in Christmas tarts 2 years ago. You used about 3 tablespoons, and the jar has been in the fridge ever since. Time to go!
- Are there other food items that no one likes? Keep in mind that even if they're still fresh,

they may not get eaten. Take those and put them in a grocery bag to give to one of your neighbors. Why let good food sit in your fridge, taking up space until it goes to waste?

• Now take a peek in the produce bins. Pretty nasty, right? Toss the wilted celery and the brown, mushy lettuce. Set aside anything that's still fresh.

• When the refrigerator is bare, wash the interior with warm, sudsy water and a sponge. Then sponge it down with clear water. Remove the produce and meat bins and give them a good soak in warm, sudsy water. Then clean them out, rinse, dry, and return them to the fridge.

• Return only those items to the refrigerator that you know your family will use. Put foods with earlier expiration dates in the front rows of the shelves, with later-expiring foods in the back.

• Now step back and admire your work. Isn't it great to see those shelves sparkling? And now

you can quickly find everything in your fridge. Repeat this clean-out every month and you'll never waste food.

MISCELLANEOUS KITCHEN-CLEARING IDEAS

Clearing out kitchen clutter doesn't just mean focusing on the big tasks. It also involves the little chores, such as taking a peek under the kitchen sink (yikes!), dealing with that cache of plastic bags, and doing the simple pickups, such as keeping the kitchen table clear.

Bag those bags. If you like to have plastic bags in assorted sizes on hand, but don't know what to do with them all, here's one solution: Stuff all those bags inside a large plastic lawn/trash bag, then set that large bag on the floor in a closet. Anyone who needs a plastic bag can just reach in and grab one.

CLUTTER BUSTERS

The nice thing about clearing up kitchen clutter is that a little bit of effort can go a long way. Here are some quick and easy ways to keep the kitchen in tip-top shape.

☐ Put a tablecloth and centerpiece on the kitchen table. A bowl of fresh fruit or a vase of fresh or dried flowers is a good choice. When family members see how nice the table looks, they may be less likely to clutter it up.

☐ Set a decorative bowl or tray on the counter to

hold car and house keys. If you put them in the same place every day, you'll never waste time hunting for them. The bowl is also a good place to hold laundry receipts, the day's outgoing mail, or any other paper or item that needs to be visible so you remember to do the task.

☐ When shopping for food or other storage containers, look for square containers instead of round ones. They stack more easily and can fit snugly into corners.

Downsize to free up space. You know that the more clutter-free your countertops are, the cleaner and tidier the kitchen looks. Well, the same is true of the floor. So if space is at a premium in your kitchen, don't clutter up the floor with an oversize trash container. Instead, mount a smaller one on a sliding rack under your kitchen sink. (You'll have plenty of room there after you clean it out! See "Declutter Kitchen Cleaning Supplies" on page 114.) On one hand, you'll be making more trips to the garage (or wherever you keep your large garbage cans) to get rid of your kitchen trash, but on the other hand, you'll be freeing up space in the kitchen.

Use sit-on storage. Do you have bench seating at your kitchen table? If so, you may want to replace one or both benches with a storage bench. These attractive benches have hinged seats that conceal a storage space that runs the length and width of the bench. These benches come in a variety of styles, and their storage capacity is a real bonus, especially in a small kitchen. You can also find storage chairs that function in the same way but take up less space.

CLEARING OUT THOSE COOKBOOKS

For some, cookbooks are a necessary evil, the reference book you need to have on hand to make the daily bread—or at least the daily hamburger casserole. For others, like Rose Kennedy of Knoxville, Tennessee, who owns more than 100 of them, cookbooks offer diversion. "I can read them, even while eating cold spaghetti

from the can, and get a glimpse of exotic worlds, a promise of fabulous meals, reminders of times past." To be able to enjoy her hobby without destroying her clean kitchen, Rose has come up with a recipe for keeping cookbook and recipe clutter to a minimum. Here are her instructions. (For help sorting through all the other books in your life, turn to chapter 16.)

Keep the cookbooks out of the kitchen. The only cookbook that really needs to reside in the kitchen is the one with the recipe you're cooking right that minute, says Rose. "The others should go on a shelf in another room, preferably near a comfortable reading chair or the place where you make out the grocery list." Staying away from the food prep areas keeps cookbooks out of the tomato sauce and pancake syrup, but it also protects them from undue heat or moisture—both of which are damaging. "Cookbooks are like any other household object," says Rose. "The better shape they're in, the more pleasant they are to have around—and the more likely you'll be to use them." And, of course, if you're a cookbook collector, the better their condition, the more valuable they are.

Use a backpack for the basics. If you feel you simply *must* have a few cookbooks in the kitchen, keep them out of harm's way in one of those inexpensive clear backpacks kids use for school. They'll easily bear the weight and protect the pages from spattering grease and other kitchen mishaps, plus you can always see what you have inside. If you're short on space, sling

confessions of . . .
a Collector

LINDA CAVAZZINI of Greenville, New York, loves to cook. And she loves to collect recipes. In fact, Linda figures she's accumulated hundreds of recipes, and that's not counting the ones in her cookbooks! "When I sit down with the newspaper, I almost always see a recipe that looks interesting," Linda explains, "so I always have scissors in hand to cut out recipes whenever I read newspapers or magazines. And now that I have Internet access, I find recipes there, too, and print them out."

While there's nothing wrong with collecting recipes, Linda's problem was that she didn't know what to do with them all. "I started out putting them inside the covers of my cookbooks, but then there got to be too many of them, and before I knew it, I had clippings and torn magazine pages piling up all over the kitchen. I knew that I had to get things under control. I thought about just putting them in a shoebox, but I knew it would be hard to find a specific recipe without digging down to the bottom of the box. Then I realized I could organize my recipes and view them easily if I put them into plastic sleeves in a three-ring binder. That did the trick!"

the bag over the back of a chair, or put a peg for it on the wall or in the pantry.

Rotate the stock. "Cookbooks are my toys," says Rose. "And just as I've learned to keep a few toys hidden away so the kids will enjoy them more later, I've started storing most of my cookbooks. I just get a few out at a time so they're new and surprising." Rose uses copier-paper boxes she collects at the office to store her cookbooks. "Paper manufacturers spend a lot of money on boxes made especially to protect paper from the elements," Rose says, so she feels comfortable using them to store her treasures.

Get it at the library. You may not realize that cookbooks are just books as far as the local library is concerned—meaning that they circulate them just as they do *Little Women* and the latest Stephen King thriller. So consider relying on the library's collection instead of maintaining one of your own, and check out what you want when you need it. Or spend an afternoon browsing the cookbooks, then use the library's photocopier to copy the recipes you're interested in. When you're on a frozen-food binge or simply lose interest in cooking (after the holidays or in sweltering weather), you'll have no worries about cookbooks taking up space.

Give it to the library. If you have lots of hardback cookbooks in good shape, consider donating some to the library to free up some space at your place. "I would never part with my one-of-a-kind Junior League cookbooks or anything like that, but I feel good giving the library more modern cookbooks that cost lots of money, but I just can't use that often," says Rose Kennedy. "In particular, I give them the really specific, one-topic cookbooks, like a book on Mediterranean cooking or a waffle and pancake cookbook. Once

I've read them, I don't need to keep the books around any more, and I feel good knowing other people might want to check them out." And don't forget—*you* can check the books out, too!

ORGANIZING THE RECIPE FILE

If your recipes aren't in books, they're probably on note cards, newspaper clippings, computer printouts, and well-worn scraps of paper. Even more than the cookbooks, these recipes can get out of hand. Here are some ways to rein them in.

Weed out the undesirables. The first step in organizing your recipes is to gather every one you can find and then sort the whole batch into three piles: the recipes you've tried and like, those you've tried and found to be dogs, and those you've never tried. First, get rid of the dogs. Now, with a cold eye, look through every single recipe in the "never tried" pile and banish the ones you know in your heart you will never make—the cold aspic and tripe salad, for instance. If it makes you feel better, record the titles of all those recipes neatly in a notebook, throw the recipes out, then rest assured that you'll be able to get the same (or similar) recipe online anytime you might want it.

Turn the scraps into books. Once you get rid of the recipes you don't want, you have several options for organizing the rest. One is to spend an afternoon (or several afternoons) typing those recipes on the computer, printing them out on 8½- by 11-inch paper, and then putting them in a three-ring binder. (See "Confessions of a Collector" on page 106.) But if you don't want to spend all that time at the keyboard, you could simply tape or glue the scraps of recipes to 8½- by 11-inch paper, slip them into plastic sleeves, and file them away in the binder. If you want to get *really* fancy, take a picture of each dish when you've finished cooking it and slip it in the sleeve next to the recipe.

Use virtual file folders. Once you've entered all your recipes into your computer, there's still the matter of organizing them on your hard drive. One way to do that is to create folders for each kind of recipe: Chicken and Poultry, Fish, Meat,

RECIPE FILES—BIGGER IS BETTER

A little file box of recipe cards is a sentimental favorite, but this kind of sentiment leads to lots of clutter. That's because only about one in three recipes would actually fit on a 3- by 5-inch card. And who wants to read that tiny type? Soon you're stuffing clippings in there, too, or stapling two cards together, or giving up and just letting the cute little box sit around collecting dust. If you're wedded to using recipe cards, buy a bigger box, one designed to house 5- by 8-inch cards—even if it's an ugly slate-gray one from the office supply store (though we daresay you'll be able to find something a lot prettier!). Tape any 3- by 5-inch cards from the old set to the larger cards, and then start anew.

Pasta Dishes, Desserts, and the like. Place each recipe in the appropriate folder, and then move all the folders into a main folder called Recipes. Or you can buy one of the many programs on the market that will organize your recipes for you. Some of the more popular programs include MasterCook, Recipe Organizer, and AccuChef.

Transfer your cookbooks to the computer, too. If you're really hell-bent on getting rid of your cookbooks but not the recipes therein, you could invest in a scanner and spend some time scanning the recipes you want and storing them on your computer. Depending on how many recipes and books you have, this could be a time-consuming endeavor, but it would certainly eliminate cookbook clutter!

Go the paperless route. If you have an Internet connection at home, then you have a terrific recipe storage device—one that won't take up any space in your kitchen. Many cooking Web sites—www.allrecipes.com, www.epicurious.com, and www.cookingvillage.com among them—offer a recipe box function. That is, the site allows you to choose recipes from its database and save them to your own file on the site. Later, when you want to make that chicken cacciatore, all you do is return to the site and look up the recipe in your file. Then you can print the recipe out and use it while you're making the dish. When you've finished, you can recycle the paper instead of storing it, because you'll always know exactly where to get the recipe again.

Picking Up the Pantry

Whether your pantry is a large walk-in area, a small closet, or just a cabinet or two, it is the warehouse that holds your kitchen "stock." So if it's always a mess, you'll learn that you're out

---

DON'T MAKE IT A SHOE-IN

If you find yourself tripping over your kids' (and maybe even your spouse's!) shoes every time you trek through the kitchen, here's a solution that doesn't involve threatening to burn everyone's sneakers in a giant backyard bonfire.

Place a shoe rack—the freestanding kind that sits on the floor—either directly inside the entry that gets used the most, or outside the door if it's an entry from an attached garage. Put down a doormat so everyone has a place to stand while they work off their shoes and put them in the rack.

There are three big advantages to this shoe-storage system: First, there'll be no more shoes cluttering up the kitchen floor. Second, you won't be washing grit and grime off the floor every few days, because everyone's coming inside in stocking feet. Third, no more frantic searches for Johnny's shoes or Susie's sandals—they're always right where they were placed, in the shoe rack by the door.

---

of tomato soup or pasta only when you need it. Don't be caught short because of a disorganized pantry. Follow the tips below to make your pantry shipshape and functional.

Make the most of what you have. You don't need a dedicated closet to have a pantry. Kitty Mace, a graphic designer who lives in the Philadelphia suburbs, doesn't have much cabinet space in her kitchen, and her house doesn't have a pantry, but it does have a first-floor laundry room. So Kitty put shelving along one wall of the laundry room and she now uses it as her pantry area.

Because her kitchen-cabinet space is at a premium, the amount of food that she keeps in the kitchen is minimal. Kitty says that if you open up her cabinet doors, you'll find just one box of cereal, rice, or pasta in the cabinet. When she has to pull a replacement off the pantry shelf, she puts that item on her grocery list. This helps her keep her small kitchen well-organized and keeps her on top of her grocery needs.

Use these space savers. Whether your pantry is large or small, space-saving closet systems can maximize your storage space. Here are the favorites of organizing pro Ellyn Gellar-Elstein, president of Creative Closets, Ltd., in Allentown, Pennsylvania.

• Tiered shelves. Even if your pantry has limited wall space, you can fit in more than one shelf if you use shelving in different lengths. This allows you to fit shelves into tight spaces, such as under stairs.

CLUTTER CRUSADERS

Avoiding Pantry Pitfalls

ELLYN GELLAR-ELSTEIN, president of Creative Closets, Ltd., in Allentown, Pennsylvania, has seen her share of pantry disasters. Here are her tips for making the most of your pantry space and avoiding common pantry pitfalls.

• **Keep shelves narrow.** "A lot of people think pantry shelves should be really deep, to hold lots of goods," Ellyn explains, "but the reality is that deep shelves decrease access and visibility. If, say, soup cans are in rows that are three or four cans deep, you'll never see what's way in the back, and you'll end up going to the store to purchase what you already have."

• **Keep nonfood items separate from food items.** "Ideally, pantries should hold only food, the way clothing closets should hold only clothes," notes Ellyn. "But pantry space often has to accommodate nonfood items. I work with my clients to keep those items in a separate pantry area, away from the food. We may put the items on their own shelf, or in a drawer or bin; anything that keeps them separate from the foods."

• **Use door space.** "Most people overlook the door as a storage unit," says Ellyn. Not only can you use the back of the door for hanging items, but you can also install a rack on the back of the door to hold rolls of paper towels, canned goods, and more.

• Pull-out bins. These coated wire mesh or plastic-sided bins on wheels are perfect for storing onions and potatoes. They fit right under the bottom shelf of your pantry and roll out for easy access.

• Drawers. Most people don't think of adding drawers to their pantry, but they come in handy for holding extra utensils, like barbecue tools, that don't get used regularly. Deep drawers can hold little-used kitchen appliances, like pasta machines. They can also "hide" tools or other nonfood items.

• Wine rack. If your pantry temperature is cool enough, you can store wine there in a built-in wine rack.

• StoreWALL. This modern-day version of old-fashioned Peg-Board is great for hanging pots and pans, aprons—anything that you can put on a hook. The beauty of the storeWALL brand storage system is that instead of containing small holes in which to put the hooks, it's slatted, so you can slide the hooks around and change the configuration to meet your needs. It's also more durable than Peg-Board, with a more attractive and resilient finish. StoreWALL is avail-able through closet companies, office furnishing companies, architects, and building contractors.

Put your items in order. Your pantry should function just like the stockroom in a grocery store, office, or other business. That means items should be shelved by category. For example, you can put all the pasta, rice, and other grains in one place. Then put all the soups in one area, the cereal boxes in another, and so forth. Then you can see at a glance what's getting depleted so you can put it on your shopping list and restock your pantry before you've completely run out of an item.

Change the container. If your pantry space is really limited, you can still buy more than a week's worth of goods. The key is to repackage the products to fit your space. Take dry goods such as sugar, rice, flour, and beans out of their bulky boxes and pour them into heavy-duty zip-top plastic freezer bags. Now you can flatten out each product and stack the bags one atop the other, using a minimum of shelf space.

Sort your spices. Is your pantry stuffed with spices and herbs that you purchased sometime during the Ford administration? Or can't you tell because everything's such a mess? Don't worry; use these three tips to get things under control.

1. Know your ABCs. You probably don't give this a second thought, but when you go to buy spices in your grocery store, guess what? The bottles and tins are arranged alphabetically. "Of course they are," you may be thinking.

SAFETY FIRST

There's one item that absolutely belongs in every kitchen: a fire extinguisher. But it doesn't have to contribute to clutter. You can mount most any model to the wall, and that keeps it out of the way. Be sure to mount your fire extinguisher as close to the stove as the directions allow.

"Otherwise, how else would shoppers be able to quickly find what they need?" Aha! Now take a look at your spice shelf. Is everything in alphabetical order? Or are jars tossed willy-nilly on a pantry shelf, the basil here and the oregano there, with cinnamon sticks in between? Take 5 minutes right now to get your spices in order, and you won't spend 10 minutes searching the shelves the next time you need some coriander!

2. Rack 'em up. Don't overlook the old standbys: If you have the wall space, mount a spice rack to keep your spice containers neat and orderly.

3. Check it out. While you're organizing your herbs and spices, take a minute to open each jar, take a pinch, and sniff it. Dried herbs lose their potency after about 6 months; spices after about a year. Once they lose their fragrance, it's time to toss them.

Lose the bomb-shelter mentality. Some folks think that a jar of peanut butter or a can of tuna sitting unopened in the pantry will last just about forever. Well, that's not quite the case. Although many unopened items will last more than a year or two, there are plenty of others that need to be replaced annually or even more frequently. The "Shelf Life of Foods" chart on page 112 lists some of the most common pantry items and their shelf lives. Use this chart as a guide when you do your semiannual pantry clean-out.

Keep 'em high and dry. To prolong the shelf life of pantry items, seal their containers

CLUTTER CRUSADERS

A Pantry Primer

Beth Hudson, a professional organizer with 20 years' experience, owns the Philadelphia-based Right@Home. Beth says that the pantry can really clutter up if you don't have an organizational plan. Here are her suggestions.

• Group spices that you use frequently up front where they will be easy to grab. "I put all the Indian spices together, all the Italian spices together, and so on."

• Keep ingredients together for recipes that you prepare often. "It really streamlines the cooking process."

• Group items by category in your pantry. "It not only helps you see your inventory at a glance, it also makes putting away the groceries a lot easier on shopping day."

• "Once you have things organized in the pantry, even younger children can help put groceries away because they can easily see where the cereal boxes go, where the tuna and soup cans go, where the pasta goes, and the like."

tight and store them in a dry place away from light and heat. If you live in a hot, moist climate, your packaged foods can be attacked by insects and molds, so keep an eye out for signs of spoilage or holes in the packaging, and throw away any affected packages.

Let's make a date. Most packaged foods contain some type of product dating, even though federal regulations require product dating only for infant formula and baby food.

SHELF LIFE OF FOODS

Food Item, Unopened	Shelf Life	Food Item, Unopened	Shelf Life
Baking chocolate, chocolate chips	1 year	Parmesan cheese, grated	4 months
		Peanut butter	6 months
Bread crumbs	6 months	Pickles	1 year
Cake mix	1 year	Pie-crust mix	8 months
Cereal	3 to 4 months	Potatoes	2 weeks in the dark
Coffee, canned	1 year	Pudding mix	1 year
Coffee, instant	6 months	Soft drinks	3 months
Crackers	3 to 4 months	Soup, canned	1 year
Evaporated milk	1 year	Soup, dried mix	6 months
Fish, canned	2 to 5 years	Spices, dried, ground	6 months to 1 year
Flour	1 year	Spices, whole	1 year
Frosting, canned or dry mix	8 months	Steak sauces	2 years
Fruits, canned	12 to 18 months	Sugar, granulated	2 years
Gelatin	18 months	Sweetened condensed milk	1 year
Gravy, canned	1 year	Syrup, pancake	1 year
Herbs, dried	6 months	Tabasco sauce	2 years
Honey	1 year	Tea bags	6 months
Jams and jellies	1 year	Tea, instant	1 year
Meat, canned	2 to 5 years	Tea, loose	6 months
Nonfat dry milk	6 months	Tomatoes, canned	12 to 18 months
Nuts, shelled	1 month	Tomato sauce	1 year
Olive oil	3 months	Vegetable oil	3 months
Olives	1 year	Vegetables, canned	2 to 5 years
Onions	2 weeks in the dark		
Pasta	1 year		
Pancake or baking mix	6 months		

Note: You can use these foods past their optimal time frame, but their flavors will fade or textures may be affected.

Once you have your kitchen under control, how do you keep it from becoming a cluttered mess again? The best way is to create task lists that keep you and your family on track for cleaning up and clearing the clutter. Make a daily list, a weekly list, a monthly list, and a yearly list. Here are some ideas to get you started.

A daily list may include the following.

☐ Clear off the kitchen table after every meal/snack.

☐ Load or unload the dishwasher and put away the dishes.

☐ Put bills in their allotted space.

☐ Put school papers and messages in appropriate areas.

☐ Read the mail and file or toss.

☐ Take personal belongings out of the kitchen and put them away.

☐ Wash the dishes and put them away.

☐ Wipe down all countertops, the stove, and the sink.

A weekly list might include these tasks.

☐ Clean the microwave/toaster oven/toaster.

☐ Dispose of catalogs.

☐ Pay bills.

☐ Take out the recycling and trash.

☐ Vacuum and wash the kitchen floor.

Monthly and yearly lists might include those major "spring cleaning" type projects, such as taking down the curtains and washing them; culling the baskets that contain mail-order catalogs and other saved reading materials; washing the windows; wiping down walls; cleaning the oven; and so forth. If you have any portable furniture in your kitchen, like a rolling cart for your microwave, it's a good idea to move it away from the wall each month and do a thorough cleaning of the cart and wall/floor area on which it resides.

Here's how to decipher the dates on the products you buy.

• Sell by. These dates tell the store how long to display the product before disposing of it. Sell-by dates are found primarily on perishable foods such as dairy products, eggs, meat, and poultry. You should buy these products before their expiration dates.

• Best if used by or Best if used before. These dates are manufacturer recommendations for best flavor or quality. They aren't the same as expiration dates in that they aren't related to the product's safety. In fact, a product can be used safely after the "Best if used by/before" date if it has been stored at 40°F or below in the refrigerator or freezer (see "Keep Your Cool" on page 103). Once you do open up the product, use it quickly—within a week or so.

• Use by. These dates are the last dates recommended by the manufacturer for use of products while they are at their peak quality.

Tool time in the pantry. Pantries often do double duty as a storage spot for batteries, lightbulbs, and small tools, in addition to their primary job of storing food. But you don't want to reach for the cinnamon sticks and come up with a screwdriver instead! If your pantry is home to nonfood items, keep them well-organized and away from the edibles. Here's how.

- Designate one shelf or part of one shelf (the bottom one is practical) for nonfood items.
- Put batteries in a bucket on the shelf, or buy one of those battery racks that you can hang on the back of the pantry door.
- Use a shoebox or plastic container with a lid to store lightbulbs on the shelf. Keep the bulbs in their original packaging so they stack neatly and are cushioned in the box.
- Put any tools that you need to have on hand—a few different sizes of screwdrivers, a pair of pliers, a tack hammer, and some nails—in a small toolbox that you can keep on the bottom shelf or on the floor. If you have only a few small tools, you can keep them in a cutlery tray on the shelf. Store any other tools that are floating around in the basement or garage.
- Hang mops, brooms, even the ironing board and iron on a pantry wall or on the back of the pantry door.

KEEP THINGS MOVING

A University of Illinois business professor found that nearly 12 percent of all grocery items remain on the pantry shelf year after year. Why? Most of the homemakers he surveyed said that they bought the items for a specific reason, such as making a special dessert or holiday meal.

Take a look in your pantry. Are there food items in there that you don't even remember buying? If so, throw them out. Then make it a habit to regularly check the contents of your pantry and keep moving the items from back to front as you use them. For example, when you buy more soup, move the older soup cans to the front and put the newly purchased ones in the back. Do the same for all of your pantry items, and be sure to use them by their expiration dates.

Declutter Kitchen Cleaning Supplies

Great expectations are fine in a Dickens novel, but they're the main thing that keeps the kitchen cleaning-supply area completely overrun with clutter. How many times have you purchased a barrage of gleaming supplies, each bottle, can, or gadget purporting to tackle a kitchen cleanup headache? And how many of those have taken up permanent residence in the cabinet under the sink, while the microwave sports an inch of crud, the counter continues to collect crumbs, and there's a line of mildew along the rim of the refrigerator door? Oh yes, there's the other kind of "great expectation" bogging down the kitchen cleaning supplies,

So few kitchen gadgets live up to their manufacturers' claims, but there is a little $2 or $3 scrub brush that doesn't just clean, but also cuts clutter. Here's how it works: The bottom portion is a sturdy scrub brush, the top a container of dishwashing liquid that you refill as needed. When you scrub pots and pans, you can squirt a little soap out for the tough jobs. This takes away your need for scouring pads, which means no box under the sink and no rusting steel wool on the edge of the sink. But, as they say on the infomercials, that's not all! The scrubber allows you to store the big bottle of dishwashing liquid out of sight. If you want a sink full of suds, all you need is a few squirts from the coffee-cup–size brush. And it cuts down on dishwashing time, too, because unlike ordinary scrub brushes, it constantly has a bit of soap on the bristles. So washing just one bowl and spoon is done in a jiff, and all you do is rinse the brush under the faucet when you've finished scrubbing.

too. That's the idea that the half-used Brillo pad, the three-bristle bottle brush, and the petrified mop head are somehow supposed to find new life when someone (you?) cleans the kitchen one fine day. So consider this: If you cut back to fewer—but better—cleaning supplies, you'll save space, you'll be more likely to tackle cleaning jobs, and you'll be halfway to keeping your kitchen clutter-free. Expect great results if you follow these steps!

Get down. Whether you keep cleaning supplies in a pantry, closet, or cabinet under the sink—or on the back porch—before you can declutter, you first need to inventory everything you've accumulated. But instead of crouching down for a quick second as if you're putting away scouring powder, or slipping the door open just long enough to cram the broom in, settle yourself in a comfortable position. Bring a chair to sit on for unloading a closet, or position a doubled-over towel (or one of those foam garden kneeling pads) so your knees won't bother you while you're kneeling down to work under the sink. Once you're comfortable, remove every single item, no matter how icky or appalling. And speaking of icky, make sure to put out some old newspapers or a drop cloth if lots of muck is lurking in the cleaning-supply area.

Forget about that rainy day. After you have everything in plain view, start tossing things you haven't used in months or will probably never use. Some of the things that fall into the "toss" category include any granulated products that are now solidified, such as dishwasher detergent or scouring powder; any natural-fiber tools that should be soft but are petrified, such as dishcloths or mop heads; any brushes or brooms with bristles in clumps or sticking out at an angle; and any brush or cloth with unidentifiable cleaner, mildew, or gunk on it.

Add an extra shelf. While you were cleaning out, you probably found sponges, dishcloths, and other soft cleaning aids that you do use on a regular basis. Keep them convenient by installing small wire bins on the inside of the undersink cabinet doors. Use the bins to hold dishcloths, towels, potholders, sponges, and the like. They'll be right where you need them.

Spray, don't say "someday." As you go through your kitchen cleaning supplies, be on the lookout for faulty spray bottles. You know, the one that takes 15 pumps to yield a little squirt of glass cleaner, or the one that dribbles at least as much down your wrist as it sprays? These bottles don't earn their keep, but it's hard to throw them away when they're still practically full. In fact, if you're like most people, you might have several look-alike bottles—one that *really* sprays and two imposters that spray air every time you clean the cabinets. Curse poor manufacturing if you like. But then go out to the dollar store and buy four or five sturdy spray bottles, the ones they sell for cleaning and hair-care products. Transfer each product into a sturdier bottle, and toss what doesn't work. You can probably

DISCARD WITH CARE

If you've finally gotten around to getting rid of all those cleaning supplies that have outlived their usefulness, congratulations! But be sure you don't create an environmental problem far worse than clutter under the sink. Follow these guidelines when disposing of cleaning chemicals.

☐ **Down the drain.** Municipal sewage treatment and household septic systems can ordinarily handle water-soluble products, so pour them down the drain unless the label says not to. A few products you can pour down the drain are all-purpose cleaner, bleach, dishwashing liquid, and water-based metal polish. But for gosh sakes, read the labels first. Rinse the discarded liquid down with plenty of water, and never drain two products at once—they could have a reaction.

☐ **Take special care with solvent-based products:** Any cleaning product that's labeled flammable, anything that includes turpentine, and some metal and furniture cleaners should be treated like household hazardous waste—because that's what they are. Call your local sanitation department to find out how you should handle this waste—and *never* dump it down the storm drain, flush it down the toilet, or throw it out with the other trash.

☐ **Check before you recycle:** Some communities don't take empty bleach bottles or containers that held oven cleaner for recycling. Check to see if you need to send these containers to the household hazardous waste collection site.

A constantly clogged drain creates clutter two ways: You never catch up on the dishes, because you can't use the sink, and you have to keep all manner of snakes and plungers on hand, and maybe even (shudder) resort to chemical decloggers. Avoid the muss and fuss by keeping your drain free-flowing. Follow these safe steps:

1. Never pour used cooking grease down the kitchen sink drain.

2. Keep the sink strainer operative by cleaning it every time you finish washing dishes or loading the dishwasher.

3. Peel vegetables over the trash or compost bin, not the sink. Vegetable parings and grease are the top causes of clogged kitchen drains!

4. Give your drain a weekly dose of boiling water. Heat about a gallon of water (or strain it from a vat of pasta) and pour it directly down the drain, half a gallon at a time.

---

even combine the contents of a few faulty bottles into one good one (as long as you're combining the same brand!). Here's the rule: Anything that doesn't warrant being transferred to a new bottle doesn't warrant space in your decluttered cabinet.

Hang up the spray bottles. If you mostly use sprays to keep the kitchen tidy, install a towel rod on the side of your cleaning-supply cabinet or on the wall under the sink. Then you can suspend the spray bottles from the rack by their triggers. You'll be able to see what you have, and there will be no need to shuffle every bottle around each time you want one. Heck, you'll probably stop accidentally buying duplicates at the store, too, because you can see that you still have some of that glass spray you love, right here—they've just changed the color of the label since you last looked.

Double up on buckets. A plastic bucket is quite a handy way to keep, say, all the mopping supplies in one place, or all the stuff you need to clean the oven. But two are truly better than one. Slip a same-size bucket (just a dollar or two at a discount department store) under the one you have, and you'll have one bucket to work from and one to tote your supplies in. It takes a lot of time and makes a lot of mess to move everything out of the bucket each time you start a cleaning project.

Downsize your broom. Check out the inexpensive collapsible-handle brooms on the market nowadays. When the at-rest broom is only a yard long, you can save a bit of space in your cleaning-supply closet. You may even want to consider moving the whole cleaning-supply operation to a shorter cabinet or wide shelf if your broom was the only tall item you were storing before.

CHAPTER 8

Living, Dining, and Family Rooms

The best way to keep clutter out of your dining, family, and living rooms is to be self-centered. It's okay! "Our homes need to be a refuge from the very busy world, and the key is comfort," says Trudye Connolly, president of Coco Connolly Company, a public relations firm in Chicago that represents numerous design and home furnishing clients. "So stop and ask yourself how you want to use your living spaces and what will make you most comfortable. That will help you decide what you need to keep or acquire—and what you can do without."

To get the most from your space, make sure you don't fall back on the "musts" and "shoulds" that you picked up in childhood. For example, who says that you *must* have a china service for 20, or that your living room *should* be on the first floor? Free yourself of traditional notions, and you just might lose some clutter in the bargain.

Read on for dozens of ways to rearrange your available space—and to adjust your thinking about the spaces where you do most of your living. You'll learn how to pretend your home's a museum, and discover the pitfalls of setting decorating time limits. You'll also discover practical methods for addressing common clutter bugaboos of the living room, dining room, and family room, including a prickly technique for keeping junk off windowsills, a way to keep the remote in plain sight, and an idea for a tabletop that makes a room seem bigger. And along with clever ways to do away with clutter, you'll find ideas for making a room *look* less cluttered, such as painting your window shades the same color as the walls and hanging artwork at eye level.

But don't put too much pressure on yourself to try all these techniques at once, says Trudye. "Adopt one or two tactics to begin with, if they suit your lifestyle," she says. Then add others as you find the time and opportunity.

A Storage Benchmark

EVERY SUMMER, Adrian Algañaraz boards his 36-foot sailboat, *Whistler*, which he docks in East Hampton, New York. For the next 3 or 4 months, he spends most of his time on board, sailing along the East Coast. The quarters may be a bit cramped, but they're impeccably designed to avoid any trace of clutter—and not an ounce of space is wasted. One on-board innovation that moves effortlessly from the water to your living area is the storage bench.

Nearly all the benches on board Adrian's boat have flip-up seats. Inside go life jackets and other necessary equipment. You can use more decorative (but no less utilitarian) benches as a great way to add storage to your dining room, living room, or family room. They can become a repository for toys, blankets, books, linens, shoes—almost anything!

Entrance Tactics

When Ollie Belcher lived in Minnesota, each of the homes in her neighborhood had a small mudroom just off the entryway. That's where family members stashed their snowy boots, hung their coats, and paused with groceries. Modern homes rarely have a space like that, but if you want to stop clutter before it makes its way to your living room, den, or dining room, create a similar effect with shelves, hooks, and cubbies. "Just remember that people will always set things down in the first spot they come to when they walk through the door," says Ollie, an antiques dealer who works from her home in Corbin, Kentucky. So walk through your front door and see which dumping ground you reach first—the living room coffee table? Your favorite armchair? A desk in the den?

Next, create a more obvious spot to park the items, one that a person will come to before they reach your precious living spaces. For instance, if the living room is the nearest room to the front door, place a wardrobe—

angled away from the living room—in the hall near the entrance. It can serve as a transition station, keeping the day's junk out of sight of the peaceful living room. A solid-backed bookcase facing the door can serve the same function.

Hold it right there. Homemaker Barbara Wilhoit meets clutter right at the front door—and lets it get no further than the foyer. "We're always in a big hurry to dump things when we come in, and it would be really easy to drop them in any of the first-floor rooms to junk up the place," says Barbara, who is the mother of four teenagers in Farragut, Tennessee. "That's why I have a hall tree in the foyer. The kids can hang their backpacks there, and their coats, and put their shoes on the shelf on the bottom. Plus, at night they can pack their backpacks and then put them out in the hall for the next morning . . . not on the couch or the coffee table." Barbara also has a second hall tree in the laundry room, which is only a step away from the back door. That keeps people from wandering in and sticking their things in the dining room, she says.

Make a mini mudroom. Melanie McGhee, a therapist who employs meditation in her practice in Maryville, Tennessee, propped a metal shoe rack on a low bookshelf. That's where she and her husband and two daughters hang their shoes and other "stuff" before they enter the living room. Not only does the rack keep shoes off the floor, but it makes it easy to locate foot-

confessions of . . . a Collector

JOEY X (he asked to remain anonymous) has been collecting stuff—toys, magazines, radios, books, comics—since he was a kid. Granted, as an editor for a large comic book publisher, he probably needs to keep *some* comic books at home—but 15,000 of them? The halls of the New York City apartment he shares with his wife, Connie, were lined with bookshelves groaning under the weight of his collections, and his home office was a veritable Collyers' mansion.

When Connie (an avowed Tosser) had had enough of the creeping clutter, she came up with an ingenious solution that satisfied her Tossing urges while respecting Joey's Collecting instinct. She found a document storage company in nearby New Jersey. But this was no ordinary storage facility. For a fee, the company would not only pick up boxes of documents from Connie and Joey's apartment, it would also deliver a specific box back to them, too. (It's Joey's responsibility to know which comics are in which boxes.) So if Joey wakes up one morning and decides that he just *has* to have *Metamorpho* number 12, all he'd have to do is pick up the phone and the box with that particular comic book would be delivered in a day or so. Problem solved.

wear on busy school and work mornings, too. Along the top of the bookcase, she displays one or two family photos in neutral frames, to create a pleasant view for anyone who enters the room.

Digging Out the Dining Room

The traditionally arranged and furnished dining room is usually fraught with clutter. That's because it's home to heavy pieces of furniture—as well as heavy expectations about the fine, formal meals we should be eating there on our fine china under our fine chandelier. Whew. Want to lighten the room, the expectations, and the clutter in one fell swoop? Then pull up a chair and read on!

Get up against the wall. Yes, the table is the center of the dining room, but that doesn't mean it has to be *in* the center of the dining room. In fact, sending yours to the sidelines just might make your dining area look larger and less cluttered.

"To get the table out of the middle of a small dining room, put a pew or bench against the wall for seating," says Trudye Connolly. "Then you can push the table to that wall and free up some space." When you hear "bench," don't think "uncomfortable," says Trudye. "I mean a bench with a back, similar to a church pew. You can buy one at any unfinished furniture store and stain it to match your furniture." Sometimes you'll find one at a salvage store. Heck, you could even use a wrought-iron bench. And you can make any bench more comfortable with cushions.

Bring out the benches. Maybe you're the family entertainer. Folks pile into your dining room on all the big holidays for a good meal and a few laughs. It's wonderful to be able to play hostess, but it does have its clutter-related consequences. For one thing, you have to keep lots of extra chairs on hand—chairs that need to be stored somewhere in the house. That's when benches come to the rescue. You can replace four chairs with one good-size bench. Two benches will seat eight. The best part? After dinner, you can simply tuck the benches under the table—no chairs to find homes for.

Go through the looking glass. Here's another trick of the trade that can make your dining room seem larger without knocking down any walls. Use a glass tabletop. It will give the illusion of more space, and glass is compatible with a variety of furniture styles.

Shelve the buffet idea. If your dining room is small and you have other storage options throughout the house, think about booting your buffet (also known as a sideboard). Buffets take up more space than their storage is worth, cramping diners when you could store tablecloths in an upstairs closet, instead. For the function a buffet provides, a thin shelf is just as good. "You can provide an extra serving spot that uses a lot less space with a narrow, wall-mounted shelf of glass or wood," says Trudye. "Support it with brackets. You can put creamers or hot dishes on it or use it any way you'd use the top of a buffet."

Dress(er) up your dining room. When you're looking for a practical storage piece that can hold its own in even the most formal setting, head to the bedroom. "Wooden dressers are great in the dining room, because they have flat tops and wide drawers for storing table linens, but they don't take up as much space as the traditional buffet," says Ollie Belcher. Also, you can find lots of dressers in most thrift and antiques stores, in designs and colors to match just about any decor. "That's because even families who couldn't afford fancy dining room sets usually owned a dresser of some sort," Ollie explains.

One caveat: "Don't use a dresser with an attached vanity mirror in your living room or dining room," says Ollie. "You won't be able to place the dresser under a window, and the mirror takes up a lot of space on the wall."

Put your table to work. Wouldn't it be nice to have an extra drawer or two in the dining room for storing napkins, placemats, and the like? Look no further than your dining room table—actually, look *under* your dining room table. If you're the handy type, you can attach one or more shallow drawers to the underside of the table and keep your table linens inside. You'll find simple drawer hardware at most home and DIY stores.

Take the stack tack. There's a character in the book *The Accidental Tourist* whose wife leaves him to fend for himself. He hits on the idea of putting all the bottom sheets on the bed, and then taking off the top one when he wants a clean sheet. You can adapt this literary idea to your tablecloths. Instead of storing them, which takes up space and usually involves reironing one when you actually want to use it, put them all

out—one on top of the other. Then, when you host a formal meal, take off all but the one on the bottom or the top. If you have a nice-looking vinyl tablecloth, put it on or toward the top so that spills don't soak through and ruin all cloths below. Keep in mind that you won't want to put more than four tablecloths on your table at one time—after that the tabletop gets too cushiony for everyday use, because things tip over.

Let it shine—but not too brightly. Want to discourage people from using the dining room table for, say, science fair projects or paying the bills? Think romance. That chandelier over the table, the one with the dimmer switch? Set it to one of the dimmest settings possible and keep the light low when people are in the dining room, even in the morning. Then family members are less likely to think of that area when they're looking for a place to work on junk-producing projects. Sure, they could reach up and brighten the light, but if you habitually keep it low, no one will think of it. And who knows, you might get in a few more romantic dinners than usual, too!

Finding Space in the Family Room

Remember Jimmy Stewart's line in *It's a Wonderful Life*? "We used to have such a great family," he says. "Why did we have to go and have all these kids?" That's the story with family rooms. They'd be perfectly organized, neat, and simple, if only family members would stay out. But they don't. Not only that, but they bring in all their stuff and leave it lying around, all the while claiming that you're messing up their stuff if you try to straighten it up.

Breaking up your family is not the answer! Our ingenious clutter-cutting tips are.

Take it from the top. Want to make your family room look larger? Go for floor-to-ceiling storage. "And carry it all the way up to the ceiling," says Trudye Connolly. "That makes the whole room look pulled together, not crowded." Trudye recommends a storage system with cupboards across the top for storing items that you don't use very often—Christmas ornaments, luggage, or perhaps a folding card table and chairs. Add more cupboards at the bottom of the wall, with storage shelves in between for books, games, televisions . . . you get the picture. "Many home stores sell the pieces, which you can customize for your space," says Trudye.

Avoid clutter *and* late fees. A place for everything and everything in its place, right? Why not make a home for library books, rental videos, permission slips, and so forth right by the television—on the console shelf or in a basket next to the cable box, for example. That way, unless you're one of the few Americans who isn't plugged in, you'll see those items daily and increase your odds of turning them back in on time. That means fewer fines, and fewer days that the stuff clutters up your house.

DO A DOUBLE TAKE

If you don't have much room in your living spaces, don't use two pieces of furniture where one will do, says Trudye Connolly, president of Coco Connolly Company, a public relations firm in Chicago that represents numerous design and home furnishing clients. Here are five of Trudye's favorite ways to make one piece of furniture do double duty.

1. TAKE ADVANTAGE OF TRUNK SPACE. Turn a trunk into a coffee table, with storage for books, table linens, blankets, or sweaters.

2. CHOOSE A TALL COFFEE TABLE. Find a coffee table that sits at least 2 feet off the ground. Store oversize pillows underneath, and use it for Japanese-style dining—or take-out pizza night.

3. ARM YOURSELF WITH AN ARMOIRE. An armoire, also known as a wardrobe, works well in place of a separate toy chest and bookcase. Store books in the top and toys in the bottom drawers or cabinet.

4. BUY A LONG SOFA. If you're in the market for a new sofa, choose one that's at least 75 inches long. That way, you can also use it as an extra bed—an average-size adult can sleep there comfortably. That means you can eliminate a cot.

5. TRY THIS UNIQUE END TABLE. You won't need an extra bookcase if you use a small chest of drawers as an end table in your family room. Store the phone book, games, and magazines inside.

MAKE A CLUTTER-FREE FAMILY GAME SET

It's amazing how much space board games can take up. It's also amazing how a piece is always missing when you want to play. Solve both problems with an idea from game manufacturers, and create your own family game set. ("Eight games in one!") Don't include your great-grandfather's domino set or the original edition of Monopoly you've been hoarding. But for other games, follow these steps.

1. Take each game board out of its box and refold it. Label the back of each board by writing the game name on a strip of masking tape or right on the board. Arrange the boards alphabetically. Put the boxes aside for your next trip to the recycling center.

2. Insert the game direction sheets into acid-free, clear plastic three-ring binder sheets. Label the sheets, arrange them alphabetically, and place them in a binder. For any games whose directions are on the box, cut them out and place them in the plastic sheet.

3. Place the game pieces and any play money from each game into resealable plastic storage bags. Stow the bags in one large tin or a plastic tub with a tight-fitting, flat top.

4. Add a kit to the tin that includes an egg timer, a deck of cards, poker chips or pennies, small objects that can be used for game pieces (small thread spools, pebbles, thimbles, or seashells), six die, score sheets and loose-leaf papers, and several stubby pencils (which you can swipe during your next golf game).

5. Stack the boards flat on the shelves, then put the binder and tin or tub on top.

Stack, don't rack, your magazines. Whoever invented those wooden and wicker magazine holders was certainly optimistic to think they'd help anyone organize periodicals. You know the kind: You slip your magazines down into the rack (where you can't see their covers) until no more will fit. Then you start heaping them in slippery stacks on the coffee table, where you never look at them. Instead of buying those expensive baskets and boxes built specifically for magazines, get yourself a shallow flat-bottomed basket. Stacking your magazines and catalogs there has numerous benefits. First, you'll be able to see the magazine on top and get tantalizing peeks at the ones below, especially if you fan them out. Second, it's easy to shuffle through the basket and throw away the magazines you've already read. Third, you can tote the basket from room to room until you find a cozy spot to read. And last, since the basket sides are only a couple of inches deep, you can hang on to only so many magazines before they start cascading over the sides, creating a mess.

Oh, and one more thing that a music lover can certainly appreciate: You don't have to throw away your "real" magazine holder. Use it to store old record albums, which are tall enough to extend over the walls of the magazine holder so you can read the spine titles.

Slide into easy storage. Get full clutter-containing use from storage pieces by keeping their drawers in good working order. When you can't open and shut drawers easily, you're much less likely to sort through the clutter in them. And family members will be less inclined to put away items such as clean table-cloths or the playing cards if they first have to wrestle with the proper drawer for five minutes. But don't try that old trick of using soap to make a drawer slide more easily. High humidity will dissolve the soap, which is water-soluble. Instead, rub candle wax over the runners.

Build your own bookshelves. One San Diego bookstore owner we know jokes that the only way to keep a burgeoning book collection organized and tidy is to keep moving to larger and larger houses. But there's a more practical way to create more space for books (even if you know you'll just buy more books to fill it): Build your own shelves.

With store-bought bookcases, particularly those made of particleboard, you lose several inches on each shelf because the sides are so wide. Plus, the shelves are usually so deep and tall that you have quite a bit of wasted space above and in front of the books. Or, horror of

CALL IN THE BIG GUNS

If you've taken lots of small steps to cut the clutter in your living room, dining room, and den and still need more space, it's time to consider big changes. Taking one of these three major steps could offer you more space, a better use of the space you have, or better-organized space. Try them!

1. Combine space, conquer clutter. Do you really need a separate living room and den? If your living room acts as your formal entertainment setting, ask yourself just how much formal entertaining you do. Is it sit-down dinners for eight, or ball games and Chinese food on the couch? If you really don't need a formal room, go for the combination and don't let your valuable living space go unused.

2. Do away with the dumping ground. Do you eat most of your meals at the kitchen table? And is your dining room table nothing more than a high-rent dumping ground for coats, books, and transitional stuff? Why not get yourself a trunk or shelving system to store those things and transform your dining room into a more usable space? Turn it into a crafts room, a reading room, a sewing room, or a home office. Keep the large table in there as a work surface. That way, if you *do* need to host a large meal, you can transform it back into a dining table for the evening.

3. Kick your den upstairs. Hey, who says that the den has to be on the first floor of your home? Especially if the only action going on there is couch sitting and TV watching, consider moving it upstairs to a small bedroom. That way you can use the larger first-floor room as a library, home office, breakfast nook, or even a master bedroom.

horrors, you cave in and start putting rows of books in front of other books—that causes the shelves to warp from all the weight and keeps you from ever seeing half of your library.

Bookshelf plans are widely available at home-supply and DIY stores, and materials are usually around half the price of a prefab bookcase. The best space-savers are those you build across an entire room, using the walls of the room as side walls for the shelves. Buy boards that are at the most an inch deeper than most of your hardbacks, and space the shelves just far enough apart to accommodate most of your books. (Rest oversize books on their sides—it's better for their spines, anyhow.) If you don't have the confidence to build your own shelves, hire a handyman (no need for a bona fide carpenter) to do it for you. Even if you break even versus the price of store-bought shelves, the space saved will put you way ahead of the game.

Phone your remote control. If you've never had to search for the remote control, there's a special spot for you in the Clutter-Cutters Hall of Fame. For the rest of us, here's a handy idea— if you're willing to spend four or five dollars for the enjoyment of having the remote by your side (or at least being able to reel it in quickly).

First, if your den telephone isn't already on an end table near the comfy couch or recliner, move it there. Next, invest in a dual-line phone jack and a short phone cord (no more than a couple of yards long). Plug your phone into one of the empty spots on the jack and plug one end of the short cord into the other. Now attach the

free end of the short cord to your remote with electrical tape. Now you can put the remote on the table right next to the phone. No one will be able to carry off the remote, and the hookup is no more unsightly than another phone cord.

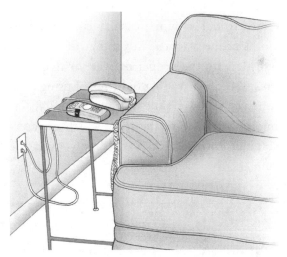

Try this quick cord trick, and you'll never lose your remote control again!

Find more door space. Tired of corralling your kids' toys? If your family room has a door, you have a solution. That's because wherever you find a door, you'll find dead (but potentially usable) space behind it. Here's how to take advantage of that space: Attach a hook (a cup hook or the kind you use to hang plants) to the ceiling just behind the door, then hang a plastic chain, one that's just a few inches shy of reaching the floor, from the hook. Use twist ties, Velcro strips, or colorful yarn to attach small stuffed animals and other toys to the chain every few inches. You'll get those toys off the floor—and out of sight.

Play the giveaway game. It's ever so tempting to simply bag up every toy and craft project that lingers in the family room, take it to the trash, and hope nobody notices. But that won't help your children learn to work with their clutter-cutting personalities, or make the important decisions about what to keep and what to give away. One way to make a game out of giveaways is to hold an auction. First, amass all the toys in the family room. If you have, say, 25 per child and want to cut that number to 20, assign each toy a price of $5, then give each child $100 in play money. Next, with you acting as the auctioneer, let your kids bid on the toys they want to keep. Once their money is gone, the kids help you decide which thrift store or charity will receive the castoffs. If your child (or one of them) is an unshakable pack rat, this is probably not the game for him. If he does participate, make sure to hold the discarded toys for a few days after the auction in case he decides that he can't live without them.

Lightening Up the Living Room

It's enough to make you wonder how the living room ever got its name. Half of us keep the place so tidy and formal that no one dares to breathe, much less *live* in there. And for the other folks, the living room is really the place we eat, read, watch television . . . and should probably have the more realistic name of the

CLUTTER CRUSADERS
Put It Away or Give It Away

LEAVING STUFF ALL OVER THE HOUSE is part of your child's job description. But that doesn't mean you have to like it or live with it. Antiques dealer Ollie Belcher of Corbin, Kentucky, found a way to break that habit in her kids when they were small.

At the time, she and her husband, a medical student, had four young children. "We didn't have much space in the places we lived, and the kids always threw their stuff everywhere," she remembers. "I kept nagging. Then one day I got fed up and said, 'If you don't care enough about these things to put them away, I'm going to give them to someone who wants them.' The first time I just packed the things up and locked them in a closet. I let them think that their stuff was gone for good, and that really made an impression. But after I gave those things back, the kids gradually fell back into their old habits. So the next time, I really gave away the things that were lying around. The kids couldn't believe it. I gave away a brand new pair of tennis shoes, and it nearly killed me because I didn't have much money at the time. But it helped a lot. We didn't have many problems with picking things up after that."

lounging room. Whether your living room challenge involves creating a more functional design or wrestling all the family's everyday stuff into submission, here are ideas you have *got* to try.

The living room and dining room are fraught with temptation if you're a pack rat. At every yard sale and on every trash day, you see loads of perfectly good furniture that just needs a little fixing up. That can lead to a living room with four end tables where one would do, or a den with two broken bookshelves—but no books. Here's one way to let go of some of those larger items with a little less angst. The key is to weigh your need for that item against someone else's.

First, remember that the reason you first took those pieces in was that they were still usable. Second, find someone who can use those finds now, not at some undefined point in the future. Call the nearest Habitat for Humanity office, whose number you'll find in the Yellow Pages under Associations, Societies, and Foundations or Social Service and Welfare Organizations. Ask if any of the working poor for whom the organization builds homes could also use tables, chairs, or whatever you have. Or contact your local YMCA, church group, or Department of Health and Human Services to find out about others who might appreciate some decent, usable furniture.

It's a lot easier to part with that extra sleeper sofa when you know that it's going to a family who otherwise would be sleeping on the floor, or to give up an unused table to a group of teens in a shelter. Of course, this doesn't have to be a heartrending experience, either—it may be easier, for example, to part with an extra television knowing that the local 4-H club could really use it to show animal-care videos to young animal owners.

Paint the floor red, or blue, or . . . Here's a clutter-cutting idea for folks who love rugs but prefer easy-to-sweep bare floors. Paint a design right on the floor. All you need are stencils in the shapes you want (you can make them or purchase them from a craft store), acrylic paint in the colors you want, and polyurethane. Once you've painted the basic rug shape and stenciled on the border(s) and/or overall pattern(s), apply a couple of coats of polyurethane after the paint dries to seal the design.

Fight fireplace clutter. If you have a fireplace, you already know that it's a major source of clutter and what can only politely be called dirt. Here are two ways to give up the chaos—without giving up the charm.

1. It's a gas. Wood-burning fireplaces are a constant source of dust and grime, but if there's a natural gas line running to your house, help is on the way. That's because for a few hundred dollars, you can replace the wood fireplace with a gas fireplace insert. Not only will it produce less dust, but it will save you money to boot, says retired electrician Jim Slate of Winnsboro, South Carolina. "Any models made in this century are a real source of heat, especially since they don't have chimneys to bring in cold air.

No matter what your clutter-cutting personality, it can be hard to part with living room furniture if it has sentimental attachments. "It was Mom and Dad's couch when they were starting out," you say. Or, "Remember the time we found a savings bond in this drawer and paid the milkman?" Suddenly this piece of furniture you can do without is hard to give away.

If you live in a college town, you have a superb opportunity to combat that sentimentality. Just make all your furniture giveaway decisions the week before school starts, then advertise the free goods in the first edition of the student newspaper or the classified section of the local paper. Students clamoring for used furniture and *really* appreciating that musty sofa bed or wobbly kitchen table will remind you of where you were when *you* really needed this furniture—and how far you've come since then.

That cuts down on the other heat sources you'll need. In fact, they can get so hot they'll run you right out of the room. If you're like us, and mostly hang out in one room of the house, you can save even more by just heating it, instead of turning on the central heat." The positives in the clutter-cutting department? Gas fireplaces eliminate ashes, kindling splinters, and bark and dirt from logs. But here's the best part: Unlike those electric fake fireplaces, gas fireplaces create real flame, so they still provide the primeval fire experience—without the soot.

2. So long, mantel mailbag. The mantel above the fireplace doesn't generate clutter, but it sure seems to collect it. Even in the face of what are obviously laboriously created mantel decorations, people seem compelled to stow incoming mail, stopwatches, bunches of wax grapes, hard candies, and the like on the mantel. One way to stop that pesky habit is to remove everything from the mantel and apply a thick coat of paste wax. But don't buff it off, not for

several weeks or until everyone in the house realizes that setting items on the mantel is a sticky proposition.

Windows and Window Coverings

Windows let light and air into your home, but the accessories that go with them can make a room feel cluttered, crowded, or cramped. Here are three ways to let the sunshine in and let go of the clutter.

Stick it to 'em. Discourage family members (and anyone else, for that matter) from casually dropping tidbits on your windowsills by placing live cacti there. A few accidental brushes with the stickers, and even your messiest loved one will find a new spot to park his soda bottles, car keys, and matches, without sustaining any long-lasting bodily harm.

CLUTTER CRUSADERS

Empty the Nest Now

THERE'S NO NEED TO WAIT 20 or 30 years to pass along heirloom family furniture if it no longer fits the space you have or the lifestyle you aspire to, says Joanne Kennedy of Toano, Virginia. If your grown children or relatives can enjoy the things, why not do it now? Joanne and her husband Bob, longtime antiques collectors, recently passed several valuable pieces of furniture—including a vintage jukebox—to their eight grown children. "Each of those pieces was hard to dust or lift," Joanne says. She gave her children heirlooms they would love and simplified her own home with these three tactics.

1. Ask, don't assume. Joanne and Bob identified which child they wanted to give each piece to. "But we asked first, gave the child a time limit to make up his or her mind, and had a runner-up in mind if someone said no. That way, you're not just passing along a problem for the child to deal with."

2. Take it to them. "The furniture will be around forever if you wait for your relative to come haul it away, which defeats the whole purpose," says Joanne. She and Bob were willing to spend time and money to deliver the furniture to its new owners, renting a U-Haul and driving heavy pieces to their new destinations.

3. No strings attached. "We didn't have any conditions for getting the furniture, because that would have put too much pressure on the kids—and probably would have taken a lot of enjoyment out of it for both of us," says Joanne. "It's tempting, but we don't inquire about the fate of the furniture."

Make it in the shade. Do your windowsills collect clutter the way Imelda Marcos collects shoes? Then matchstick blinds just might be the answer to your troubles. Those inexpensive, neutral-colored wooden blinds look beautiful with virtually any decor from formal to Victorian to modern. They're translucent during the day, which means that clutter you stash on the windowsill will be in plain view. (Maybe that'll embarrass your housemates into moving their gym socks or fingernail clipper to a less obvious spot.) At night, though, the shades do their job by blocking light and keeping nosy neighbors from looking in.

Lighten up. Heavy draperies can make a small room look even smaller—not to mention hot and crowded. To make almost any room seem more airy, an interior decorator would tell you to choose lightweight fabric shades and eliminate the drapes altogether. You can get shades in the same color you painted the walls, and many manufacturers sell shades in the exact same patterns as their wallpaper. Matching colors or patterns will make your room seem larger and less busy.

Creating the Grand Illusion of Space

Removing unneeded items and staying organized is only half of the clutter-cutting equation. The other half is using techniques that make a room *appear* larger or more spacious when you decorate, paint, or arrange furniture. Here are a few suggestions.

Find your focus. Every room needs a focal point—a spot to which your eye goes immediately when you enter a room. If everything in a room has the same visual impact, the effect can be confusing. Aim for only one focal point per room or you start creating visual clutter. Some objects, like fireplaces or armoires, are obvious focal points. If there's nothing that prominent in the room, you can create a focal point. For instance, if one of the walls has two windows, place a chest between them and a painting above it. Or, on a wall with no windows, arrange two small bookcases with a chest or small table between them, and place a piece of art above the chest or table.

There's an added benefit to having a focal point: When clutter is a problem, a focal point directs your eye to a pleasing object (an arrangement of photographs) rather than a not-so-pleasing one (that pile of laundry in the corner).

Declare neutrality. Rooms painted in neutral colors, or rooms with neutral-colored accessories, create an aura of simplicity and lack of clutter. "Neutral" means any color that isn't based on the primary colors red, yellow, or blue. "Benjamin Moore Cameo White and Linen White are outstanding neutrals—and so is your favorite shade of sage green," says Trudye Connolly, who has picked up lots of tricks of the de-

sign trade while representing design and home furnishing clients. "Any of the paints with a pearlized finish will also give the neutral look you're looking for."

Pepper them with patterns. This might seem contradictory, and—to tell the truth—it is. But bear with us. Instead of covering your room with neutral colors, you can also pull it together, making it seem cozy and simple, with pattern. For example, you can use lots and lots of toile, the French fabric with hunting scenes and such, on the walls, sofa and chairs, pillow covers, and the like. Toile is a "loner" pattern—you would want to use only one type of it in a room, and pair it with a simple, small check or stripe. But other patterns, such as florals and stripes, can be mixed up in one room. For either, though, don't go halfway: Inundate the room with pattern, or stick with neutrals.

Displaying Art and Collectibles

It's the little things that make a house a home: a sepia-toned photograph of Grandpa fishing on the dock; the clay pot your daughter made with her own little hands at summer camp; your prized Honus Wagner baseball card.

Of course, it's not for nothing that mementos are also called dust collectors—poorly arranged, they can quickly overtake a space,

To keep your walls from looking cluttered when you hang your prized collections, hang artwork and pictures at eye level. That's the advice from Catherine Thimmesh, a children's book author and former art gallery owner from Minneapolis.

"Most people tend to hang pictures too high, which makes them difficult to view and makes the room feel chaotic because there's no obvious focal point," she says. Another tip from Catherine: If you're hanging more than one piece of art or photography in a room, make sure that the center of each work is at the same level—regardless of the differing sizes of the pieces. "That helps people view the art comfortably, and the pieces don't have to fight each other for attention."

making it look junky and cluttered. But before you sell off that Honus Wagner baseball card and give away that clay pot, consider these clever tips.

Don't hurry, be happy. The best advice Ollie Belcher can give anyone who's trying to achieve a lovely decorator look without cluttering up the place with too much decoration is: Don't rush. "Men in particular will go out and find something, even a ready-made collection from a home store, to hang up so that they don't have to look at empty space. Keep in mind that the items you select reflect who you are, so choose items that you like," she says. "If you don't have something that's really special to you, leave the wall empty, even for a really long time. Eventually, you'll find the special item that belongs there."

Close the door on collectibles. To keep your collections neat and pretty, display them on shelves or in cabinets with glass doors. "That way, they won't get dusty, and no one can lay items on top of them," says Ollie, who has displayed thousands of items in booths for antiques shows and Native American pow-wows.

Don't play the match game. It's a natural inclination, like making sure you're wearing matching socks: People want to pick artwork that matches the colors in their living room. "But that's a mistake," says Catherine Thimmesh, a children's book author and former art gallery owner from Minneapolis. When you match colors, hanging a dark blue museum poster in a room with a dark blue rug and sofa, for instance, the look you think will be unified is actually too busy. "The eye just doesn't know where to go," says Catherine. "Instead, when you choose fine art, consider only the space, not the colors in the piece." To give each piece visual appeal and avoid crowding the space or overwhelming a small piece, place large artwork in large spaces and smaller pieces in small spaces.

Arrange an audition. Art history professor Amy Neff of Knoxville, Tennessee, jokes that the best way to avoid cluttering your walls with artwork is to marry a man who's phobic about wall repair—he'll be so afraid of punching holes in the wall that he'll never hang up anything. Luckily, there is a way to make fewer holes in the wall and get the look you like when you hang artwork, says Amy. She recommends arranging the pieces on the floor before getting out the picture hooks. "Lay out what you have and balance colors and shapes," she says. "It's a lot easier to change something that looks cluttered while it's on the floor. Once the stuff is already on the wall, you're much less likely to rearrange it."

More can be less. So much of displaying art relies on personal aesthetics, says Sam Yates, director of the Ewing Gallery at the University of Tennessee. Nobody likes visual clutter, but not everyone appreciates the minimalist look: a single bud in a vase or the solitary image on a wall. "The art salons in France hang pieces bumper to bumper," says Sam. "You can have 20 pieces on the wall and still not be cluttered, if you take some design concepts into consideration." Here are six of Sam's best suggestions:

1. Let special pieces shine. "If you have something that really needs attention, don't overwhelm it with other stuff," says Sam. "When there are lots of pieces on a wall, it takes the focus away from the individual pieces."

2. Hang the great wall of pictures. If you have lots of pictures or photos but not much space, consider turning over one entire wall—

OPEN A HOUSE MUSEUM

As long as you really want everything you have, you never have to feel as though you have too much art or too many decorative items, says former gallery director Catherine Thimmesh. But to keep your acquisitions from overwhelming your display space, "think of your home as a museum, and rotate your collection," she says. "That way you won't crowd the items and lose the visual appeal of the pieces you've taken such care to acquire."

To increase the chances that your museum will succeed, make sure your "inactive items"—which is to say, the ones you're not currently displaying—have a designated storage space. Then, plan specific dates to rotate the "exhibits"—Labor Day and Memorial Day are good choices—and mark them on the calendar. Another possibility: If you and your mate have different decorating styles and collections, alternate whose display goes up every 6 months.

from floor to ceiling—to a multi-image display.

3. Get into uniform. "When you display lots of pieces, strive for a uniform presentation. Space them evenly and make sure they're level," says Sam.

4. Make the mat big. "If you have a lot of little pieces, think about using big mats," says Sam. "I've seen postage stamp-size photographs framed in huge mats, and it really works."

5. Great frames look alike. If you're going to hang lots of framed artwork, make sure that the frames aren't fighting each other for attention. "They shouldn't take away from what's in them, either," says Sam. If you don't want to display exactly the same frames, make sure they're all in the same family—all metallic, all wood, all modern, or all the same color, for example. The sides of the frames should be about the same width. And even if you choose different-size frames, they should all be similar shapes. "Crafty frames, like the kind that are made to look like logs, detract from the other artwork if you hang them in a multipiece arrangement," Sam points out.

6. Mats shouldn't attract attention. "Avoid too many contrasting patterns or colors in your mats," says Sam. "One way to showcase your framed artwork is to choose mats of neutral colors. Ideally, they should all be the same color, and not too many different textures."

Let there be no light. Do you know those little museum lights, also known as picture lights, that illuminate one special piece of art? Skip them, says Sam. Unless you're building

your home and can plan ahead, the light cords will dangle down and make the wall look junky.

Organizing Needlecraft Supplies

Maybe you're one of the many folks who, after a hard day, settles down in the living room or family room to relax with your craft of choice. But that relaxation can quickly turn to frustration when you reach for a crochet hook and come up with a broken knitting needle or when, to your horror, you see the kids cutting cardboard with your expensive fabric shears. When disorganization rules, crafting is the last thing you want to do. Well, now you can relax again, because we've gathered a bevy of clever ways to contain your needlecraft clutter!

SORTING THROUGH SEWING SUPPLIES

Sewing is one of those gear-intensive hobbies. Bobbins, spools, patterns, needles (hand and machine)—it never ends! But organizing all this gear isn't an impossible task. It simply requires a bit of diligence.

Cut clutter from the floor up. Of course, there's more to cleaning up after a sewing session than just stowing the project and its supplies into your sewing bag or craft drawer. You also have to deal with all the dropped pins and tiny scraps of trimmed fabric and snippets of thread. But there's a simple way to clean up that messy floor—or rather, keep it from getting messy in the first place. Before you start sewing, lay an old sheet or a large towel at your feet, under your craft table or sewing machine. When you've finished working, use a magnet to pick up all the dropped pins. Then pick up the sheet or towel—and all the scraps with it—and shake them right into the trash.

Keep track of your *good* scissors. Crafters are fiercely protective of their good shears—and with good reason. Those tools can be quite expensive, and using them to cut paper or cardboard dulls the blades and forces them out of alignment. Keep track of your scissors and prevent someone from accidentally walking off with them by tying a short length of a light-weight ribbon around one of the handles. When someone spies the ribbon, they'll know to search for another pair of scissors.

Finagle fabric storage. Folks who enjoy crafts that involve fabrics know how their collection can grow, threatening to overtake all efforts to keep it contained. Here are three ways to keep your fabric collection under control.

1. Try the legal approach. One of the challenges associated with storing fabric is keeping it organized so that you're able to see what you have. One storage device that works for many folks is a lawyer's or barrister's bookcase—a bookcase that has a glass door that lifts up and slides back on each shelf.

These bookcases allow you to see your neatly folded and organized fabric while keeping it free of dust. The only tricky part about using these bookcases is that, since the doors are made of glass, sunlight can fade the fabric stored inside. So if you store your fabric in a room with direct sunlight, turn the bookcase so that the doors face *away* from direct light.

2. Devote a dresser. If your sewing area lies in full view in your family or living room, you

---

SORT YOUR FABRIC STASH

Before you store your fabric collection—no matter how big or small it is—you should organize it into groups for efficiency. Here are six ideas to get you started. Group your collection in any of these ways.

☐ **BY COLOR.** Reds with reds, blues with blues, greens with greens, and so forth.

☐ **BY FIBER CONTENT.** Cotton, wool, silk, fleece, blends.

☐ **BY MANUFACTURER.** If you have lots of designer fabrics, this might be a good option for you.

☐ **BY PATTERN.** Solids, plaids, stripes, small prints, large prints.

☐ **BY PROJECT.** Millie's birthday dress, the pillow covers you're making for next spring.

☐ **BY QUANTITY.** Large pieces, small pieces, scraps.

---

may not want your fabric on display, no matter how organized it is. In that case, consider moving a bedroom dresser into the area. The right dresser can blend in with your decor and at the same time hold lots of fabric.

3. Keep a running list. No matter how you store your fabric, it's a good idea to keep an inventory of it. With a detailed list of what you own, you won't need to sort through several boxes and bins to find what you want—a real bonus if your space or taste dictates that your fabric gets stored on high shelves or in an out-of-the-way part of your home.

Get yourself a small three-ring binder with some heavy paper, a pair of fabric scissors, and some white household glue. Then go through your whole fabric stash and clip a swatch from each piece. Glue the piece onto a sheet of paper in your binder and beside it note how much of the fabric you have, what the fiber content is, where and when you got it, and where you stored it.

Plan your pattern storage. If you make clothing, you know that keeping the patterns in some kind of order can be a challenge. And trying to refold and stuff them back into their original envelope is no picnic either. Here are three better ideas.

1. That's a wrap. Collect a few empty wrapping paper rolls, wrap your ironed patterns around them, and secure them with a few glass-head pins (which will be easier to remove than the usual sewing pins). Rolling the patterns will keep them smooth and wrinkle-free, and the

PREPARE FOR PATCHES

You know kids are tough on clothes, and you also know that you'll probably have to make a repair to those duds at some point. The trouble comes when you try to find the matching fabric for an outfit you made a year ago.

Next time you make any piece of clothing for kids, fold up a small (¼ yard at most) piece of the original fabric and store it in the envelope or bag with the pattern. It's also a good idea to save an extra button or two, as well as the thread color number, so you can always make a perfect match. Then, when you need to make a repair, just go back to the pattern and you'll find everything you need.

cardboard rolls don't take up much space tucked in the corner of a closet.

2. Use transparent storage. If keeping your pattern pieces free of folds and wrinkles seems impossible, try this technique. Fold the pattern and its original envelope and store both in a 1-gallon resealable plastic bag, which is a lot roomier than the paper envelope. Then file the whole thing away in your pattern box or a filing cabinet.

3. Keep a notebook. To keep track of your pattern collection, make a copy of the front of each envelope, then jot down on it where the actual pattern is stored. Punch holes in the copies and store them in a binder. With your binder in hand, you won't have to search through your whole collection to find a pattern you squirreled away last season.

Rack your spools and bobbins. If your sewing box is a tangle of thread spools and half-full bobbins, it's time to think outside the sewing box. Sewing shops are full of clever gadgets designed to organize those pesky notions. Our favorite is the hanging bobbin and spool rack. Some models hold more than 100 bobbins and spools, keeping them off your work space, out of the way, and neatly organized. If you don't have a dedicated crafting area, attach the rack to the back of a door to keep it out of sight. These racks are available at most sewing shops.

KNITTING AND CROCHETING

For many of us, the coziest feeling in the world comes from curling up on the sofa and knitting a woolly sweater or crocheting a snuggly afghan. But keeping the accoutrements of these hobbies organized can be a chore, especially when you don't have the luxury of a dedicated craft room. But don't fret, because we've come up with some simply splendid ideas to help you get things shipshape.

Keep your needle collection under control. Does this sound familiar? You're at the yarn store, where you find a pattern you want to make. You get the yarn the pattern calls for and then you check the needle sizes. "Wait a minute," you think. "Do I have a pair of number-eight needles?" You decide that the safest course of action is to go ahead and buy them, because if you don't have the right needles at home, you'll just have to make another trip to the store. Of course, once you do get home, you realize that you already own not one, but two, pairs of number-eight needles.

Put an end to the madness! Get out all your needles, make sure every one has a match, then

---

IT'S A WRAP!

Needlepoint and cross-stitchery fans take heed: Avoid storing your finished pieces or works-in-progress in plastic bags. The static electricity created by the bags attracts dust and dirt, which will then get transferred to your canvas or fabric. In addition, plastic keeps the canvas or fabric from breathing, and that creates an ideal environment for mildew.

Storing your treasures in regular old paper bags isn't the solution. Over time, acids in the paper can discolor or weaken the fibers in your piece. Instead, store your work wrapped in un-buffered, acid-free tissue paper, which is specially made to protect fabric and keep it from degrading. You can find the paper at crafts or better art-supply stores.

If your needlework pieces are small, lay them flat between layers of tissue paper. If they're large, roll them on an acid-free cardboard tube (which you'll also find at crafts and art-supply stores) first, and then roll a layer of the tissue paper over them. Finally, place your whole collection in clean fabric bags and store them in a dark, dry spot.

organize them by size. Now, make a list of what you have and stash it in your wallet. With that list, you'll never buy a clutter-causing duplicate again! And to keep the needles you do have organized, try these two tips.

1. Have a drink, then store your needles. Many brands of liquor are sold in cylindrical cardboard boxes, and those boxes are terrific for knitting-needle storage. Place a thin sponge or even a folded paper towel in the bottom of the box to protect the needle points, then place the needles inside, points down. If you like, use rubber bands to keep needles of the same size together in the box.

2. Use cardboard tubes. You can also use empty paper-towel and toilet-paper tubes to store knitting needles and crochet hooks. Close off one end with tape, and then lay several of the tubes on a shelf. Slip your needles and hooks, sorted by size, into the tubes.

Rein in your yarn. No ifs, ands, or buts: Yarn takes up a lot of room, and whether it's in balls or skeins, it's tricky to keep the stringy stuff organized. Here are two approaches to this ageless clutter issue.

1. Keep only current projects at hand. Make things easy on yourself—keep out only the yarn for the project you're working on right now. And don't try to tell us that you're working on several projects at once! That may be the case, but you can have only *one* of those projects on your lap at any one time. Stow the rest of the yarn in clear plastic bins and store them out of the way. Luckily, yarn doesn't weigh much, making it a good candidate for high-shelf storage.

Crafty Ideas for Prescription Bottles

PRESCRIPTION BOTTLES just might be the next wave of ingenious storage containers, especially for crafters. Here's a sampling of the items they can help you sort and store.

• **BEADS.** The bottles are handy for storing beads and beadmaking supplies. The bottles aren't clear, so to know what's inside, hot-glue one of the items you're storing inside onto the lid.

• **BENT AND BROKEN NEEDLES.** As you accumulate broken and bent needles, just store them in a prescription bottle. Hold on to the bottle until it's full—which will probably be quite some time—then throw it away. The bottles keep needles from poking through garbage bags and hurting someone.

• **BOBBINS.** Toss your bobbins in the bottles, then store them on a shelf or in a drawer.

• **NEEDLES.** Use separate bottles for different sizes and different varieties of hand and machine needles.

• **FLOSS.** Stash small amounts of embroidery floss for take-along projects.

• **THIMBLES.** Sort them by size, style, or project.

2. Sort yarn in hanging baskets. If you've eked out a separate area of your family room to call a crafting area, make use of the ceiling space with three-tier hanging baskets—the kind you might use in your kitchen to store fruit or vegetables. Use the baskets to store yarn out of the way, but easily accessible.

Lose the Shoes, Gain the Storage

WE'VE RECOMMENDED over-the-door shoe caddies in other chapters as an ingenious tool for cutting non-shoe clutter, and we're at it again. Hung on the inside of a closet door, these caddies can hold skeins and balls of yarn, embroidery floss, packages of pins and needles, scissors, measuring tapes, patterns—almost any crafting accessory you can think of. The best part? The caddies are inexpensive, starting at around $20 for a good-quality model.

QUILTING

Making a quilt, whether by hand or by machine, can take many months. And the more time a project takes, the easier it is for the supplies to get scattered to the ends of the earth. But with just a little of our clutter-cutting advice, you'll never lose track of your gear again!

String your pieces along. A single quilt, depending on its size and style, can be made up of more than 1,000 pieces. And after cutting out that many pieces of fabric, the last thing you want to do is have to cut *more* because you lost track of some of them. Here's a truly ingenious way to keep all those pieces together. First, stack the pieces by type. Next, thread a needle with a piece of thread about 8 inches longer than the stack is tall, and then knot it well. Thread each stack onto separate threads, but don't knot the other end of the thread. When you need one of the pieces, just slip it off the thread—the rest will stay neatly in their stack.

Bag your blocks. Here's an easy way to keep track of quilt blocks as you make them. You'll need one 1-gallon resealable plastic bag for each kind of block your quilt requires. On each bag, use a permanent felt-tip marker to note the total number of blocks you need to make in that style. As you finish each block, place it in its bag and make a tick on the bag. You'll always know how many blocks you have completed and how many more you need to make, and the bags keep the blocks neatly organized.

Scrap your scraps. We know some folks who save 1-inch pieces for miniature quilts, and others who consider any pieces smaller than a 5-inch square needless clutter. The point is to get rid of scraps that are too small for you to use—however you define "small." If you do decide to chuck small scraps, find out whether there's a quilting guild near you (www.quiltguilds.com is a good place to begin your search). Members may want even your tiniest scraps.

The Eyes Have It

HERE'S AN ingenious way to keep your scissors and quilting rotary cutters organized, clean, and protected: Store them in soft eyeglass cases.

CHAPTER 9

Bedrooms

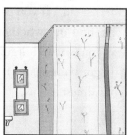

You've heard the statistic: We spend one-third of our lives sleeping. But most of us probably spend a lot more time than that in our bedrooms. Even if you don't get the standard 8 hours of shut-eye each night, think about what else goes on there: You dress and undress, put on your jewelry or tie your necktie, read a book or a newspaper, maybe even watch a little television in your bedroom. When you're sick, you crawl into bed and pull the covers over your head. When you're feeling blue, you hide with a pint of ice cream and a romance novel. If you're a workaholic, you prop up the pillows with your laptop on your knees. If you have kids or grandkids, your bed is often the house's designated wrestling ring (use of pillows encouraged).

Your bedroom reflects much of what happens during

your day. It's also the room in which most of your personal belongings get stored. So it's not surprising that it can attract the detritus and clutter of your life. Are stray socks strewn across the floor? Not sure whether that pile of laundry in the corner is dirty or clean? Haven't read that tower of novels on your nightstand?

If you're ready to dive under the quilt because you can't face the junk that's taking over your room, our experts will help you turn your dump into the cozy haven that it should be. You'll meet interior designers who offer ways to increase storage space, an antiques dealer who shares creative ideas for making the most of your furniture, a condominium dweller who tackles the special problems of tiny bedrooms, and two nurses who will help you organize a sickroom. We'll even give you tips on how to conquer the clutter in your kids' rooms.

Where do you start? "Take everything out of your bedroom, including all small pieces of furniture," advises Diane O'Halloran, an interior designer from East Kingston, New Hampshire. If that sounds radical, remember that clutter control sometimes demands drastic measures. Removing everything is the best way to determine what you need and what you don't, and to get organized.

By now you know that "less is more" is the credo of our clutter captains. And that applies not only to the number of knickknacks on your nightstand, but also to the way you furnish and decorate your bedroom. So when you start putting objects back into your empty, clean room, think minimal. "The ideal bedroom would have as few pieces of furniture as possible," says Diane. This means that the furniture and accessories you *do* include should

FOUR WAYS TO BEAT BEDROOM CLUTTER—FAST

Let's say that company is coming, or you're about to tear your hair out because you can't see the carpet for the clutter in your bedroom—or any room, for that matter. Here are four fast ways to clean up and feel better.

1. EMPTY THE WASTEBASKET. Just emptying the wastebasket will reduce that trashy, unkempt atmosphere in your room.

2. STRAIGHTEN THAT PILE OF BOOKS OR MAGAZINES. Don't have time to weed through those unread paperbacks and old magazines on your bedroom floor? Collect them in a neat stack and they'll look a whole lot better.

3. TOSS EVERYTHING INTO A BASKET. Have hair doodads, earrings, and loose change in a jumble on your dresser or nightstand? Drop them all in a small basket or ceramic dish for now. When your company goes home (or when you have a few extra minutes), you'll be able to sort through your items and store them properly. At least they won't be scattered all over the place.

4. MAKE THE BED. Even if the rest of your room is sparkling, rumpled bedcovers make everything else look messy. So pull up the bedspread and fluff the pillows—and you'll notice a real difference in the appearance of your bedroom.

probably serve more than one function. Read on for more tips about transforming your bedroom from the stuff of nightmares to a storehouse of sweet dreams.

Shazam! Conjuring More Storage Space

Storage isn't a panacea for clutter, but it certainly helps to have a place to put the things you've decided you really need to keep. "This is where the art of disguise and storage comes into play," Diane says.

Norman MacLean, owner of The Wingate Collection, an antiques shop in Stratham, New Hampshire, agrees. When he and his wife Allison travel to antiques shows to buy furniture and accessories for their shop, "We look for things that hold stuff," he says. Norman and Allison know from experience how important it is to find imaginative ways to store possessions: They and their daughter live in a 1,000-square-foot apartment above their shop, which is in an old farmhouse. Norman, Diane, and other experts will show you how to hide your treasures in plain sight (or at least within easy reach) so that your bedroom or guest room appears as neat and serene as you want it to be.

Think vertical. If you live in a house with no closets—or your spouse seems to think that clothes belong on the floor—here's a way to keep those socks and boxer shorts in their proper places. "Choose tall men's bureaus for a bedroom instead of the longer, lower chests that are typically associated with women's clothing," recommends Diane. Because they're vertical, tall chests hold more than the horizontal dressers hold without taking up as much floor space. And tall dressers have more drawers, which allows you to separate items and keep them organized. Of course, you don't have to be a guy to use a tall chest!

Acquire an apothecary chest. Next time you spot an inexpensive old apothecary chest at a yard sale or flea market (or in your grandparents' attic or basement), consider grabbing it for your bedroom, suggests interior designer Linda Stone, of Paul Stone Interiors in Hampton Falls, New Hampshire. The multiple drawers hold tons of stuff—from pens and markers to hair clips to loose change—all compartmentalized, all organized, and all in the same piece of furniture. What a bargain!

Stick with two-for-one storage options. One of the smartest ways to save and create space in your bedroom is to choose furniture that can do double duty. Here are three easy-to-find pieces that do just that.

• An old piano bench. The kind with the flip-top lid makes a perfect nightstand and provides extra bedside seating to boot. Just slide your favorite magazine, facial tissues, and eyeglasses out of sight inside the storage bin, and leave the top free for additional seating or your bedside lamp.

STREAMLINE YOUR BEDROOM

Streamlining—reducing the number of items, shapes, colors, and textures—in your bedroom goes a long way toward cracking down on clutter. When you decorate, choose colors, accessories, and other decorations that blend well. "Similar objects are restful for the eyes," explains interior designer Diane O'Halloran, of East Kingston, New Hampshire. "When you have jumbles of color and shape, your eyes don't know where to go." Here are six ways to streamline.

1. STAY ALL IN THE FAMILY. Choose colors from the same family for your walls, windows, and bedding. By giving your room a cohesive color palate, you require fewer decorative elements to make the room feel complete.

2. KEEP IT SIMPLE. If you select a busy pattern for your bedspread, go with something simple for your curtains, and vice versa. Busy patterns add to visual clutter.

3. TRANSFER YOUR TCHOTCHKES. Display your collectibles somewhere other than your bedroom. Move those tiny porcelain animals to a curio cabinet in the den instead of scattering them across the top of your dresser.

4. DEACCESSORIZE. Limit the number of decorative pillows, stuffed animals, or dolls perched on your bed. Sure, you see this trend in home magazines. But the reality is that they jumble up the look of your bed, and end up on the floor once you turn in for the night. (And of course, that means you need to pick them all up and rearrange them again each morning.) Instead, pick a few favorites. They'll stand out more anyway and won't be in the way.

5. NIX THE BOOB TUBE. Do you need a television in your bedroom? If so, store it in a cabinet with closing doors.

6. CHOOSE A FULL-LENGTH MIRROR. Trade in the mirror hanging over your dresser for a full-length mirror attached to the back of your bedroom door. Chances are, the mirror over the dresser is reflecting not only everything on your dresser top, but other objects around the room as well, doubling the number of objects you see in the room. A full-length mirror does a better job of reflecting your entire outfit, and when attached to the back of your door, it stays out of sight most of the time.

• A blanket chest, steamer trunk, or gardening bench. Slide any of these up against the foot of your bed and fill the storage compartment with blankets, bed linens, bath towels, sweaters, jeans, or whatever fills the bill. Shut the lid and you have the perfect place to sit and tie your shoes.

• A barrel. Turn an old wooden barrel into a table—and a place to put off-season jackets, bed linens, beach towels, or whatever your heart desires, suggests Diane O'Halloran. Make sure the interior of the barrel is clean, and then decorate the outside or leave it as is. If the barrel doesn't have a lid, it's easy to cut a piece of finished plywood to fit. Use veneer tape to finish the edges. Fill your barrel with whatever you want, and slide the lid across the top. Add a tablecloth if you like, a lamp, and a vase of fresh flowers, and no one will ever know what lurks inside the barrel.

Add a tablecloth, add storage. Need a little more space to shove a few things from plain view? Throw an old tablecloth or fancy bedsheet over a table in the corner of your bedroom as an instant table skirt. Store your sewing machine, a basket of magazines, your hat collection—whatever—under the table. You'll have spent nary a penny, but will have added a whole new place to hide—we mean, store—your stuff.

Nix your nightstand. Would you believe that a nightstand takes up more space than a simple wall shelf? It does, according to Diane O'Halloran. So streamline your bedroom—but still give yourself a place to put your hand cream and eyeglasses—by hanging a shelf on the wall beside your bed.

Make use of underbed storage. You know you want to—shove stuff under your bed, that is. Well, here's the good news: There are ways to take advantage of the potential storage space under your bed without guilt. Here are two.

1. Add a bed skirt. If you're planning to use the space under your bed as storage, you can create a cleaner look by adding a bed skirt. Of course, if your bedspread already reaches the floor, you don't need a bed skirt! The skirts are readily available at discount home furnishing stores in all the conventional sizes, and fit between the mattress and box spring. Yours will work like a magic curtain behind which all kinds of surprises are hidden!

UNCLUTTER WITH COLOR

Some colors are better for clearing out the cluttered atmosphere in your bedroom than others, says interior designer Linda Stone of Paul Stone Interiors in Hampton Falls, New Hampshire. She and her husband Paul have been helping clients choose the right colors for their rooms for more than 20 years. They've fulfilled all kinds of requests, including one from a client who asked that they match a color scheme to a 3-day-old mushroom she produced from a paper bag during a consultation. In general, says Linda,

stay away from jarring colors: bright or neon hues or dark paints that make you feel claustrophobic. As long as you're cleaning out the jumble in your bedroom, consider wielding a paintbrush while you're at it. Paint is cheap, and a soothing color can go a long way toward making your haven feel clean and orderly.

Uncluttered colors include soft blues, soft greens (such as sage or celery), soft yellow, taupe, and other beiges. Colors to stay away from include bright or deep red, orange, plum, and purple.

UNDERBED STASHING STRATEGIES

Of course, you can cut the clutter in your bedroom by stashing some items under the bed—but if you aren't careful, all that stuff can disappear into the black hole under there. So be sure to choose items wisely, and don't shove more beneath the bed than you can reach. Place delicate items such as clothing and bed linens in clear plastic containers with lids to deter dust and allow easy access. Decide whether you want to push off-season items out of sight or whether you want to keep items you use a lot within ready reach. (Don't mix them, or you'll have a pile of dusty junk that you'll have to paw through to find the things you want.) Here are some suggestions.

OFF-SEASON ITEMS

- Beach towels
- Holiday decorations
- Off-season clothing
- Rugs
- Shoes
- Sleds, skis, and other sporting gear
- Winter blankets and quilts

QUICK-REACH ITEMS

- Bath towels
- Bed linens
- Gift-wrapping supplies
- In-season clothing
- In-season sporting gear

2. Add rolling storage. You can organize your underbed storage better by building your own rolling storage device with a sheet of plywood on casters (available at discount home stores, lumberyards, or hardware stores), suggests Diane. Measure the width of your bed and cut the plywood to fit underneath, then screw a caster to the bottom of each corner. Attach a rope or piece of webbing to each end of the plywood so you can pull the rolling platform out from under the bed. Now you'll be able to store off-season clothing, suitcases, bed linens, and other items in an organized manner—instead of a jumble—under the bed. If you don't like the look or texture of the bare plywood, buy finished plywood, sand it lightly, and give it a coat or two of polyurethane.

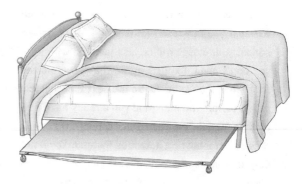

Make a rolling underbed platform to add hideaway storage with easy access.

ORGANIZING THE SMALL STUFF

If you're like most of us, your bedroom is cluttered with bits of paper, doodads, toiletries, and other smallish items. That's why "we need to have organization; otherwise, we feel like we're losing control," says Linda Stone. Linda and her husband, Paul, live in an antique farmhouse, where they've come up with clever solutions for storage for themselves as well as their clients.

Banish loose change. What do you do with loose change from your pocket at the end of the day? Here's an idea: Toss it in an antique lunch pail or tin, which decorates the top of an armoire or dresser and solves the storage problem. (You can find all kinds of unusual—and decorative—storage containers like this at flea markets.)

Drop change in the fishbowl. If loose change is running amok across your dresser top, empty the contents of your pocket or purse at the end of each day into a small glass fishbowl on your dresser. You'll be able to see how fast the change adds up in the bowl instead of cluttering your bureau. When the bowl is full, empty it and take your sweetheart out for dinner.

Box up your clutter. Decorative hatboxes make wonderful places to store everything from gloves to gadgets. Pick up a few at a yard sale, flea market, or discount craft store; even if you buy them new, they cost only a couple of dollars each. Fill each one with related items—knitting supplies, grooming items, stationery, whatever—and stack them in a corner or under a table. The boxes add a colorful, cozy touch to your bedroom—and provide neat, dust-free storage for all sorts of things.

10 THINGS TO DO INSTEAD OF SHOPPING

It doesn't take a rocket scientist to figure out that if you buy less clothing and fewer accessories, your closet will be less jammed with stuff you don't need. Experts agree that people often shop when they're bored. So the next time you feel pulled toward the mall (and you already have new clothes for your vacation or for school), try one of these clutter-busting activities instead. You'll not only save yourself a bundle, but you'll also accomplish some streamlining at the same time.

1. Make a scrapbook from a trip, Christmas cards, your kids' school photos, or the like.
2. Organize and label old photographs.
3. Organize wrapping paper, ribbons, gift bags, and so forth.
4. Polish or condition shoes and handbags; you'll use or wear them more often.
5. Roll loose change.
6. Spend 1 hour getting rid of clutter in the basement, garage, or attic.
7. Throw away old makeup and other cosmetics.
8. Throw out expired coupons.
9. Update your address book.
10. Weed out catalogs and magazines.

Toss it in a bucket. Old metal sap buckets are stylish containers for all kinds of items, says Norman MacLean. Mittens, socks, toys, and grooming supplies all fit well. The buckets also make excellent bedroom wastebaskets. They're cheap, too. You're most apt to find these at flea markets and junk shops in New England, where the buckets were once used for maple sugaring.

Look for locker baskets. Remember those old wire locker baskets that you used to find in the school gym's locker room? Now you can find them at flea markets and rummage sales—for practically nothing, says Norman. If you see a few, nab them and bring them home for clutter control in your bedroom. Each one is the perfect size for stacks of magazines, newspapers, books, towels, athletic shoes, CDs, and so forth. They'll help you keep your bedroom organized, and even spark a little nostalgia.

Tuck your toiletries in a wine case. What can you do with tall bottles of grooming supplies—shampoo, hair mousse, facial cleanser, and the like—when you have a small bathroom or share a space with someone else? Stash them in a wooden or metal wine case, set it on your dresser top or nightstand, close the top, and no one will know what's in there, suggests Linda Stone. You can find the cases at a flea market or any of the discount home furnishing shops for very little money, and they help you accomplish three things: collecting your grooming supplies in one place, keeping them within easy reach, and adding a decorative touch to your room.

CLUTTER CRUSADERS

Case Closed

"WE LIVE IN A TINY HOUSE, and when our boys were young, space was really tight," recalls Sue Morrill, who works at The Hayloft, a women's clothing shop in Hampton Falls, New Hampshire. With two small children, clutter was a constant battle. So Sue stored the family's off-season clothing, including shoes and boots, in empty suitcases that weren't currently in use and slid the full suitcases under everyone's beds. "That way, I had a single storage place for off-season clothes and for the suitcases at the same time," says Sue.

Organize with pottery. Pottery bowls are popular collectible and decorative items; you'll find all sizes at craft shops, yard sales, flea markets, discount home stores—just about anywhere, including your own kitchen cabinets. So why not use those collector's items to collect clutter? Choose a few of your favorite bowls and distribute them around your bedroom at key spots—on a table, your dresser, or nightstand, on a wall shelf, even atop a pile of magazines on the floor—then toss renegade hair clips, buttons, safety pins, loose change, and so forth in them. Here's the key to avoiding piles of clutter in the bowls themselves: Designate each bowl for a specific type of object. That way, when you need one of these items, you'll be able to find it right away.

Turn to a lazy Susan. If you're plagued by a pile of grooming supplies and other bits and pieces that are taking over the top of your dresser, head to the kitchen—not for a snack, but for a lazy Susan. Collect all your gewgaws, arrange them on the lazy Susan, and place it on top of your dresser.

Sweet (Doggie) Dreams

ADDY ESHBACH, an attorney who lives in a small condominium (about 650 square feet) in Boston, has become expert at using every inch of space in her tiny but charming abode. Keeping clutter to a minimum is a constant challenge, so she's always searching for alternative but efficient ways to store things. When she brought home her new companion—a cairn terrier named Charlotte—she needed to figure out where her new friend could sleep without occupying too many square inches. As Addy looked around her bedroom (which is actually an alcove), she found a solution. She shoved Charlotte's dog crate next to the bed where a nightstand would usually be. Now, every night Charlotte slips into her cozy crate for a long nap. The best part? "On top of the dog crate I can put books, magazines, tissues, anything else I would normally put on a nightstand," says Addy. "The crate not only serves as Charlotte's bed, it organizes all those necessities I like to have nearby."

Ban photographs. Not really—but if your dresser, nightstand, and other furniture surfaces are covered with photographs of your favorite cousins, friends, and pets, you probably don't have room for much else. So hang those photos on the wall, instead. Choose frames that are similar for a unified look, and group them in a way that is appealing to the eye. You'll not only reduce the number of objects sitting around your bedroom, you'll add a new decoration to your bedroom walls (for free). And you can see your friends and family any time you want!

Transfer your lights to the wall. Wall lamps occupy less space than table lamps, says Diane O'Halloran. So do away with your nightstand light and hang a few wall lamps around your bedroom. They'll light the room more efficiently and reduce the number of objects competing for attention on your nightstand or dresser top.

Get Your Clothes Off the Floor

No matter how old you are, you can probably still hear your mother saying, "Get your clothes off the floor!" Maybe you've made the same entreaty to your own spouse or kids. Or perhaps you're guilty of dropping your duds and leaving them where gravity puts them. So if you want to clean up your (or your family's) act without sounding like a drill sergeant, try a few of these hints from our experts.

Fold your laundry. Want to encourage someone in your family to put away his or her clean laundry? Fold it (if you're feeling especially generous) and place it on your family member's bed. Unless he or she is a contortionist, your loved one will have to put away those clothes before going to sleep that night.

Transform a shutter into a clothing rack. Next time you see an old wooden shutter at a flea market, grab it. In a few simple steps, says Norman MacLean, you can turn it into an excellent bedroom clothes rack.

First, screw a few conventional clothes hooks into the frame of the shutter, then hang the shutter on a wall with nails, screws, or wire and hooks. Hang your jackets, pajamas, hats, or bathroom towels on the hooks. You've hardly spent a dime, and you have a decorative clothes rack that will help keep clothes and even wet towels off the floor.

Hang a Peg-Board. Here's a quick way to get your clothes off the floor: Hang a few wooden Shaker Peg-Boards along a bedroom wall; then you (or your spouse) can whisk pajamas, jackets, hats—whatever—off the rug or chair and onto the pegs.

Drape your clothes on a doorknob. Create a quick hang-up for clothes by screwing several old doorknobs onto an old board (paint or stain the board if you like) and nailing or screwing the board onto your bedroom wall. This works well as a hanger for jackets, hats, or

towels—and it's so easy to use that maybe your spouse will be encouraged to hang up the stuff instead of dropping it on the floor—or hanging it on one of the functioning doorknobs.

Cleaning Up the Bedroom Closet

If your bedroom closet looks like a war zone, a natural disaster area, a time capsule—or a combination of all three—fear not, relief is on the way.

This rack won't help you catch more Zs, but it will get those wet bath towels off the bedroom floor and (worse) the bed. Hang a wall-mounted quilt rack on the back of the bedroom door, on the wall behind the door, or on the wall near your closet. Then, when your well-meaning spouse migrates from the shower to the bedroom to get dressed, he or she can hang up the damp towel right there instead of dropping it on the floor or flinging it across the bed. Here's the bonus: You can use the shelf at the top of the quilt rack (most of them have one) for grooming supplies, hair accessories, and the like, all organized in cute little buckets or ceramic dishes.

Another option is to place a freestanding quilt rack in a corner of your bedroom for wet bathroom towels, so you won't have to pick up those towels from the floor or the bed. When they're dry, just toss them in the hamper or return them to the bathroom where they belong.

Our experts are sworn deputies of the closet-control force, and their mission is to help you get rid of what you don't need, find what you *do* need, and store it within reach so you can grab it and go.

"Start by taking everything out of your bedroom closet and cleaning it," says Diane O'Halloran. "When you put clothes back into the closet, include only items that are in style and that can be worn with at least one other complementary item. If you don't wear an item of clothing every other week, you probably don't need it (unless it's a formal gown or seasonal clothing). So donate it to charity or a friend." Unfortunately, today's fabrics don't store well for long periods of time, so it isn't worth holding on to garments for months or years in the hope of handing them down to someone else.

Diane's principles work for jewelry, too. "Give away what you haven't worn in a year unless it's valuable to your estate, because you probably won't ever wear it."

CORRALLING YOUR CLOTHES

Once you've emptied your closet, be ruthless about what you keep and what you let go. Having a hard time? Follow the guidelines suggested by experts such as Diane O'Halloran and Addy Eshbach, an attorney who lives in a small condominium (about 650 square feet) in Boston, and you'll get your wardrobe—and closet—pared down to the best of the best.

Make sure each garment has a match. "Is your closet filled with stuff that you can't wear because it doesn't go with anything?" asks Diane. Then get rid of every piece of clothing that doesn't have at least one other current item to complement it. (Don't go shopping to find matching items—you'll just spend more money and stuff your closet tighter.) In the long run, you'll save space (your closet load will be lighter) and time (you won't be pawing through clothes in a quest for a matching outfit). And once you complete this exercise, you'll probably shop smarter too.

Many older homes don't have bedroom closets at all. Maybe yours has a closet, but it's too small to hold all your stuff. Just build your own closet, says Diane O'Halloran, an interior designer from East Kingston, New Hampshire. The best part is that you don't have to be a carpenter or a design expert to do it.

First, decide on the dimensions of your closet. Second, cut strips of 1-inch by 1-inch lumber to match the perimeter measurement and nail them to the ceiling. Next, measure the distance from the ceiling to the floor. This measurement, combined with the perimeter measurement, is how much fabric you'll need to create your closet "walls." (Alternatively, use attractive bed sheets or curtains for the "walls.") Cut and sew the fabric to make the "sides" of the closet. Finally, attach the fabric to the lumber strips with a staple gun to enclose the space that is now your closet. Create an entrance to your closet by leaving a space between two pieces of fabric at the front, or enter the closet at a corner through the opening where two pieces of fabric meet.

Create an instant closet with fabric.

Enlist the help of a friend. Can't decide which pieces of clothing to keep and which to toss? If you're having trouble parting with that peasant dress or leisure suit, ask a friend to help you. Choose someone who knows you well and whose taste you respect. Chances are, your friend will be honest and objective—and who knows, he or she might even take a few unwanted items off your hands.

Buy one, give one. Every time you buy an item of clothing, donate another item to charity. For instance, if you absolutely *must* have that new sweater or pair of shoes, fine. But head right to your closet and vote out an old pair of shoes or a sweater. This will maintain the equilibrium in your closet—and give someone else something "new" to wear.

Unload uncomfortable clothing. Get rid of any uncomfortable clothing—no matter how much you paid for it—because (admit it), it will sit at the back of your closet forever. So if the shoe pinches or the skirt binds, pass it along to

Make a "Grandparents' Box"

A TOUGH TASK for any parent is prying a child away from a toy that's no longer in use. Often, kids want to keep their stuff long after they stop being really interested in it. But they wail when their cherished game or toy is carried off—even if they need to make room for something new. Here's how Madelyn Gray, a grandmother in Amesbury, Massachusetts, dealt with some of her son's and daughter's favorite toys after they had outgrown them.

Madelyn designated a single box for toys that she and her husband would save in the attic for future grandchildren. Once that box was full, that would be it for saved toys. This kept her attic from being overrun with toys. Of course, her son and daughter forgot about the toy box until they each had their first child. But they were delighted when Mom brought out the box of toys—and their own children toddled around pulling a wooden dog on wheels, even coloring with much-loved but long-forgotten crayons.

the gift, just explain that you've lost (or gained) weight recently and can't wear it—so you decided to pass it along to someone who would appreciate it. You'll open up a little space in your closet without losing a friendship.

Organize your clothing by function . . . One way to avoid closet confusion is to organize objects according to function, says Diane O'Halloran. Hang all your blouses together, then all your skirts, then all your slacks. This way, you can put together an outfit quickly—just pick one item from each category and get dressed.

. . . Or by form. Another way to organize your closet is by color—reds, blues, greens, whites, blues, or blacks together. This way, you can pluck out a navy blouse from one side of the closet to go with your khaki skirt on the other. But we won't try to tell you which colors are stylish together—that's another book entirely!

Lose your closet pole. Want to add space to your bedroom closet? "Get rid of the closet pole," advises Diane. "It just takes up space, and you only need about one-third of a closet for long clothes anyway." Instead, install shelves—either shelves you build yourself or modular shelving that you can buy at any home improvement store.

Move out-of-season items to higher ground. If your closet has a high ceiling, take advantage of the air space to combat clutter,

a friend or a charity that can use it. You'll probably decrease the clutter in your closet by at least 10 percent.

Look gift horses in the mouth. Just because your best friend gave you that rhinestone-studded, pea-green sweater doesn't mean you have to wear it—or keep it, says Addy Eshbach. Donate it to charity. If your friend asks about

LIKE ALMOST EVERYONE else she knows, Linda Allen of Exeter, New Hampshire, has made some questionable clothing purchases—but once the money is spent, she hates to cut her losses and give the items away. Linda also tends to keep favorite garments long past their natural life span, all of which makes thinning out her bedroom closet a painful process. But recently, she found a solution to the problem: her 9-year-old daughter.

One day daughter Marjorie was sitting on the bed while Linda pulled skirts, slacks, and jackets out of the closet in an effort to figure out what to keep and what to let go. Soon Linda noticed a pattern: Periodically, Marjorie would burst out laughing at certain items. Pretty soon Linda was laughing too. She'd discovered a foolproof method for making the decision—as she held up each piece of clothing, if Marjorie collapsed in giggles, it went in the Salvation Army pile. If she could keep a straight face, it went back in the closet. Now they have a little get-together like this at least twice a year, and Linda's closet is much less cluttered. She also makes very few shopping mistakes any more. As she tries on an outfit in a store dressing room, she asks herself, "Would Marjorie laugh at this?"

suggests Addy Eshbach. Hats and out-of-season clothing are perfect candidates for a high closet shelf. If your closet doesn't have such a shelf, you can easily install one of the modular shelves available at any home discount store. If you store these items in cardboard boxes, be sure to label the boxes clearly.

Try some shoe solutions. A sure way to increase space in your closet is to organize your shoe collection—assuming you have more than one pair. Here are a couple of hints to get you stepping in the right direction.

• Shelve your shoes. Okay, so you aren't Imelda Marcos, but your shoes are stashed in boxes or lying in a jumble on your closet floor, and you have no idea how many pairs of clogs you actually own. Once you take inventory and toss the pairs you don't need, double your shoe space by placing lengths of plywood on cedar blocks on your closet floor to give you two levels of shoe storage. (You'll have to measure and cut the wood according to the dimensions of your closet.) Not only will you have room for more shoes (just in case you can't break the shoe-buying habit), but you'll also be able to see exactly what you have.

• Toss 'em in a basket. Have sneakers and other knock-around shoes lying around on the floor all over your bedroom? Toss them in a basket in your closet. That way, they'll be out of sight, but easy to find when you need them. And they won't get ruined by this type of storage as good shoes might.

DEJUMBLE YOUR JEWELRY

"Ever notice that when you go to a jewelry store, all the pieces are laid out neatly and actually inspire outfits? Well, jewelry isn't inspirational when it's hidden in those little boxes in your drawer," says Diane O'Halloran. Not to mention the fact that those little boxes add to the clutter in your dresser. Here, Diane and our other experts will show you how to organize those precious jewels once you get them home and out of the box.

Store jewelry in a flatware divider. "It's easy to organize your necklaces and bracelets," says Addy Eshbach. "Just buy the kind of plastic divider that's sold in kitchen departments for flatware." Insert the divider into a dresser drawer or even a nightstand or desk drawer. When you open the drawer each morning, you'll be able to find the jewelry piece you're looking for—without having to paw through a tangled mess.

Put ice cube trays to work. Another way to organize rings, earrings, and pins is to drop them into a plastic ice cube tray and slide the tray into your dresser or nightstand drawer. The compartments are the perfect size for small jewelry items, and are a great way to keep track of them. We admit that this idea may not win any design awards, but keep in mind that the tray will be out of sight and that it works.

Pop jewelry into a shoe pouch. Jewelry boxes can become the black holes of accessoryland. So try this, says Diane: Pick up one of those shoe organizers with clear plastic pouches at any discount housewares store and hang it on

confessions of . . . an Accumulator

MOST PEOPLE who visit Ann Winter's home in Exeter, New Hampshire, say it's lovely. Having spent several years in the real estate business, she has gleaned plenty of good ideas for everything from window treatments to hand-painted furniture. Ann has seen how other people deal with clutter. But she has her own confession: Since she and her husband, Bill, are parents to three grown children and grandparents to one granddaughter, their house has become a magnet for everyone's stuff. So when company is coming and Ann wants to straighten up the bedroom fast, she sweeps everything into plastic grocery bags and stuffs the bags in the bedroom closet. Hey, wait, you say—that doesn't really solve the problem. But there's more. Ann waits. After about a year, she says, she simply tosses the bags out. If she hasn't needed whatever was in those bags in a year, she doesn't need it now—and out it goes. She admits that her method "isn't pretty," but it works!

the back of your closet door. (Clear pouches allow you to see immediately where everything is.) Drop a bracelet or necklace into each pouch, and you're all set. Each piece of jewelry has its own pouch, and you can grab whatever you need as you're dressing. This system works best for chunky fashion jewelry as opposed to fine jewelry, which could become tangled or damaged.

Hang earrings from a ribbon. Have a pile of earrings with no place to live? Buy a length of pretty grosgrain ribbon at a fabric store (it will cost you only a few cents) and hang it against a closet wall or on the back of the closet door, suggests Diane. (Tap a nail into one end to secure it, or screw a small cup hook into the wall or door and punch a hole in one end of the ribbon so you can slip it over the hook.) Then sort through your earrings (this is a good time to take inventory of what you want to keep and what you can get rid of) and pierce each pair through the ribbon. This way, your earrings will stay organized and within plain sight of the clothes in your closet—so you can grab outfit and earrings at the same time when you're ready to get dressed each morning.

Hang around with your necklaces. Necklaces are notorious for getting tangled and snarled. And it's a sure bet that, once you have several necklaces locked in a struggle for space, you won't wear any of them. Here are two ways to hang them neatly so you can see them all and choose the one that will make you the belle of the ball.

• Hook 'em. Organize those tangled necklaces by hanging them in your closet. Buy some small cup hooks and screw them into the back of your closet door or to an inside closet wall and drape one or two necklaces over each hook. They'll be easy to see, and you'll probably wear them more often because you won't be wasting time rooting through individual boxes or a single drawer where they will probably languish in a tangle.

• Use a belt hanger. Organize your necklaces with a belt hanger—one of those plastic-covered hangers with multiple hooks intended for belts. Drape one or two necklaces over each hook and hang the whole thing in your closet. Your necklaces will be organized, and you'll be able to choose the one you want without a hassle, even when you're in a rush.

NEATENING NECKTIES, UNSCRAMBLING SCARVES

Neckties and scarves have adorned aristocratic necks for centuries, so you'd think that someone might have come up with a better way to keep them organized by now. Well, *we* have. Check out some clever hints from our experts before you crumple your silk ties at the back of your dresser drawer.

Hang 'em. Does your necktie drawer look like it's teeming with little silk snakes? Well, they won't bite, but they may drive you crazy. Get your finery out of the drawer and hang them in your closet on a fabric-covered clothes hanger. (If you don't have one, make one by wrapping a hanger with fabric from a cut-up T-shirt, pillowcase, or the like.) Drape each tie over the hanger, and you're in business. Not only will you cut down on clutter, you'll also reduce the amount of ironing you'll need to do each morning. Or pick up a necktie hanger designed to hold a few dozen ties in as little space as one shirt on a hanger.

Keep your scarves in view. Silk scarves can quickly turn into a slippery mess in a drawer. To prevent this from happening, "buy a small, clear plastic box at a discount store or in the kitchen section of the supermarket," recommends Addy Eshbach. "Then fold your scarves and place them in the box like a card file, so you can see each one." Addy keeps her scarf box on a shelf in her bedroom closet, but you can easily slide one into a dresser or nightstand drawer.

Drawers, Nooks, and Cubbyholes

You may think that every piece of your bedroom furniture is giving its all, but we'd bet that you can take it a step further by organizing what's inside those drawers and cubbyholes and on those shelves. Here are some hints from our own small-space dwellers and designers.

Raid the sewing department. Head to the fabric or craft shop and pick up a sewing thread organizer, suggests Diane O'Halloran. Why? "The organizers have lots of tiny boxes and are great for storing earrings, pins, and other little doodads. And since the boxes are clear, you can see what you need." Set the organizer inside your dresser or nightstand drawer.

Celebrate (shoe) boxing day. Organize socks and tights in open shoeboxes that you

keep right inside a dresser drawer, suggests Sue Morrill, a retailer and mother of two now-grown boys. The Morrills live in a small house in Amesbury, Massachusetts, making Sue the queen of clutter control while her boys were growing up. She even separated her husband's and sons' socks (and her own tights and hose) by color, assigning each color to a separate shoebox in the drawer.

Just for Small Bedrooms

Small bedrooms pose their own special challenges for clutter warriors. Sometimes these bedrooms aren't even separate rooms—they might be one corner of a studio or half a room shared by two children. Addy Eshbach knows exactly what we're talking about; her 650-square-foot condominium was advertised as a "studio plus," and her bedroom is really a small alcove. But she—and other small-space dwellers—have come up with some excellent ways to beat back the tide of bedroom clutter. And even if you are blessed with a spacious bedroom, you can try these tips to make your bedroom look even bigger.

Add antiques to your decor. Older furniture, whether it's officially antique or not, is often scaled well for smaller spaces, says Linda Stone. So if you live in an older home or a rented crawl space in New York, raid your grandparents' attic (with permission, of course) or prowl the flea markets and yard sales for smaller pieces for your bedroom. Using this smaller furniture will give you more space to move around the room, making it feel less cramped and cluttered.

Hang your goodies on the bedpost. Don't have room for a nightstand in your tiny bedroom? Pack a few necessities in a small tote bag, backpack, or colorful sack and hang it over a bedpost. Everything you need will be at your fingertips, and no one will be the wiser.

Get your linens out of the closet. Don't have a linen closet in your apartment? No problem, says Addy Eshbach. "Use the bottom drawer of your bedroom dresser for bed linens,"

CLUTTER CRUSADERS

Find a Treasure Chest

LINDA STONE AND HER HUSBAND, PAUL, an interior design team, live in a beautifully restored antique farmhouse in Hampton Falls, New Hampshire. But as lovely as their home is, the rooms are tiny—including the bedroom. So Linda makes the most of every inch of space by making sure her furniture works double time—or overtime. Her particular pride and joy is a small chest of drawers nestled against her side of the bed, which she uses as a nightstand. What's so special about this little chest? It has 14 small drawers, which allow her to compartmentalize a variety of treasures, from nighttime necessities to jewelry.

she advises. The bottom drawer is often deeper than the others, and can easily hold several sets of sheets or a couple of blankets. Not only will you save space by using your dresser this way, you'll also save time. When it's time to change the bed, your clean sheets are practically at your fingertips.

Try the dining room. You don't have enough space for clothes or linens in your tiny bedroom—well, the clutter rule book doesn't say you have to jam them all into your sleeping quarters. Instead, keep them organized in the dining room hutch the way Addy does. Her living room space is larger than her bedroom space, so she pressed an antique hutch into use—the glass top portion contains colorful quilts folded for decorative effect (and easy to find when she needs them) and the bottom half hides heavy winter clothes and ski sweaters. This way, she avoids having to put her winter things in separate storage, and she has the items she needs just steps away from her bedroom.

Move a medicine chest into the bedroom. Make use of wall space in your small bedroom to get clutter off the floor or away from your dresser top. Hang a pretty mirrored medicine cabinet over your dresser, where you can hide items such as tissues, eyeglasses, a hairbrush, jewelry, and the like.

Kids' Bedrooms

Kids' rooms are synonymous with clutter. Every parent, grandparent, and foster parent knows the pain of stepping on a plastic action figure with a bare foot. Every grown-up has uttered the command "Clean up your room!" thousands of times. If the tidal wave of stuff seems to be pouring out of your child's room and into the rest of the house, if you can't tell whether those lumps under the bedcovers are your kid or a herd of stuffed animals, and if you're afraid to look under the bed because something might be dead—or alive—under there, you need help. Of course, you need to decide which of these many prizes can hit the trash (or just head elsewhere). Then it's time to put the rest away. One tip to keep in mind is that kids are more apt to clean up clutter if they have storage that's easy and fun to use. Here are a few tried-and-true tricks.

Throw it all in the trash. "Wait," they protest. "That's my favorite stuffed giraffe!" No problem. Reassure your kids that they can keep their favorite toys *and* toss them in the trash. Diane O'Halloran tells you how.

1. Pick up a metal trash can at the hardware store and remove the handle from the lid.

2. Cut a circle of plywood 6 inches larger than the diameter of the trash can opening. Let the kids paint or decorate the plywood, then bolt the plywood circle to the trash can lid, where you removed the handle.

3. Fill the trash can with stuffed animals, toy trucks, building blocks, sports balls, or whatever fits the bill.

Put the plywood lid on top and the toys are out of sight—but easy for your little tykes to find. Here's the bonus: With the lid in place, you have a wooden tabletop that stays securely in place because it's attached to the lid of the

Create a storage space for toys—and an instant table—with a metal trash can and plywood lid.

trash can. Another option: Pick up a new metal or plastic trash can and let the kids paint it or decorate it any way they want. Stash it in their room and watch them fill it with toys.

Capture their shoes. Kids seem to leave shoes strewn everywhere—one under the bed,

another behind the fish tank. Trying to get them to arrange their shoes in a neat row along the closet floor is a losing proposition, regardless of what they're threatened with—loss of allowance, no dessert, no TV. Here's a simple solution. Put a large basket somewhere in the room—in a corner, in the closet, wherever works best. Then just ask your precious to toss his or her shoes in the basket at the end of the day. This way, shoes are all collected neatly in one place—and are easy to find each morning.

Give kids their own hampers. It's easy to find your kids—they're at the end of the trail of clothes that wends through the bedroom and down the hallway floor to the family laundry hamper. If you'd rather not follow this particular trail, put a hamper—an open basket, a canvas tote bag, or even an open cardboard box—right in their room. Stipulate that all clothes in need of washing go into the

FOUR WAYS TO GET KIDS TO PART WITH OLD STUFF

Trying to pry an old toy out of the hands of a child—even if the toy hasn't been used in a year—can make any adult feel like a monster. But kids' bedrooms would turn into the local dump if we didn't shovel out the toys they've outgrown. So here are a few tips for helping children practice their own version of clutter control by letting go of toys they no longer play with.

1. If a toy is broken and can't be fixed, use this excuse to throw it out. But don't toss the toy behind your child's back—let him or her do it.

2. When your child receives a new toy, suggest giving an old one away—to a friend, a family member, or to charity. Children love to give things to other people.

3. Set a date to pack up a box of toys for charity. While you are doing this, talk about how happy some other children will be to have the toys.

4. Get together with some friends for a toy-trading party. You may come home with as many toys as you started out with, but at least you won't have more!

"**B**ut everyone else has one!" Some of the best-selling pieces of children's furniture do nothing but crowd or clutter a child's room. Here are three to avoid.

1. AN EXTRA TWIN BED. "For when friends sleep over," the marketers say. But really, kids are very attuned to sleeping bags and most likely will have pajama parties on the floor. Meantime, the extra bed catches all the childhood debris—and takes up unnecessary floor space.

2. A STUDY DESK. Here's another clutter collector—the flat surface that seems to magnetically draw the day's papers, apple cores, CD covers, you name it. If you feel compelled to provide your child with a study surface, make it a sturdy, small plain table, not an overpriced desk with lots of nooks and crannies to absorb junk.

And ask yourself, "Does this kid need a space in his room to study, or does he do his best work on the family-room floor in front of the television?" Another low-clutter option is one of those lap desks that a child rests across her knees so she can write from the couch, bed, or armchair.

3. THE PREFAB BOOKCASE. If you can, build your own shelves to make more efficient use of space. Most of the prefabricated bookshelves marketed to kids have too-deep, too-high shelves and allow kids to stack items two deep—a big clutter no-no. At the same time, they don't have appropriate spaces for, say, sports equipment or a VCR. Instead, space shelves so your child can store paperbacks, and give shelves the right dimensions for your kid's stereo (or whatever is on your storage priority list).

hamper—or else! (If you need to enforce the rule, deduct a fine from their allowance for any clothes you find on the floor.) With all the clothes in one place, kids' bedrooms will be neater—and you'll have an easier time collecting clothes on laundry day.

Slip a sled under the bed. Kids are notorious for shoving all kinds of things under their beds—clothes, puzzle pieces, broccoli.... Here's a way to store things under the bed neatly. Head to the basement or garage for that shallow plastic sled that your tyke has outgrown but you haven't yet found another use for. Make

sure it's clean, then reassign it to your child's room and place things in it that he or she likes to play with, but that you want stored out of sight. Slide the sled under the bed and let your child practice pulling it out with the rope, then slipping it back under the bed. Now you have real storage under your kid's bed, and your child can use it all on his or her own.

Use pillowcase storage space. Old pillowcases make great storage bags for kids' stuff, says Diane O'Halloran. Sew a plastic or fabric loop onto the open end of a pillowcase, and you can hang it almost anywhere—on a closet hook, over a bedpost, on a doorknob. Children can stuff Beanie Babies, doll clothes, LEGO pieces, action figures, and so forth in a pillowcase, making room cleanup quick and fun. Here's the bonus—if the kids want to play with those toys in another room, they can just carry the pillowcases with them.

Take a tub. Empty plastic butter tubs—of all sizes—are perfect for collecting tiny objects

that your child simply can't part with, such as beads, stickers, miniature cars, doll accessories, hair clips, and so forth. The tubs are lightweight and easy for even young children to carry around the room as they pick up little bits and pieces of stuff. Weed out broken or mismatched objects from the tubs on a regular basis, say, once a month.

CONQUERING KINDER CLOSETS

Kids may fear that monsters will spring from the closet at midnight, but their parents (and grandparents) don't have to wait for nightfall for closet-related nightmares to materialize. Just what *is* that smell emanating from the right rear heap in your preteen's closet? Will a cascade of board games and notebooks crash on your head if you open the door? Are the hand-smocked dresses your Great Aunt Matilda made lost for good in your 6-year-old's mess? A kid's closet is treacherous, the clutter catcher to end all clutter catchers. How to tame the closet monsters? A fresh start, constant culling, and a bit of fun should do the trick. Try these tactics.

Make sure sesame can open. Even the best-intentioned, most responsible kids can't keep their stuff organized in a closet unless the door will open and shut easily. And we mean open and shut without the special nail file that springs the knob, without an adult to heave the door back on the runner, without clearing six boxes and the upright vacuum from the doorway before your child can put away her pajamas in the morning. So first things first: Clear a path to the closet door, and then do any necessary repairs to the door so it will glide open with ease. That means sanding or planing the bottom if it has never closed easily since you installed the wall-to-wall carpet, installing the runners for sliding doors, replacing any knobs that have fallen off the folding doors, and so forth. And of course, make sure the door's firmly attached to its hinges! You can't expect a kid to open a door if it might fall on her in the process.

Take it all out. Kids grow so fast, the only way you'll know whether they still need what's in their closet is to take it all out. That's also the only way to reorganize the closet storage devices, including shelves, rods, and bins, to suit kids' current needs. Set aside an afternoon and give yourselves a fresh start. Pull everything out, and then carefully choose what will go back in and what heads for the kiddy consignment store. One ironclad rule: Nothing goes back in without being opened and evaluated. Otherwise, how can you discover that the box labeled "trophies and stuff" really contains packing peanuts? Or that someone's made off with all the money and dice in the Monopoly game, rendering it useless? Review the Q.U.I.C.K. steps in chapters 2 through 6 if you need a refresher.

Lower the bar. Since kids are already allergic to hangers, at least make it easy for them to reach the rod in the closet to hang their clothes. Install a rod at around eye level—your kid's eye level, that is. And then follow up by removing the higher-hanging rod and replacing it with a shelf.

Go halvsies. In today's casual society, most kids, particularly the very young and boys, don't even need a hanging rod that runs the length of the closet. Consider one of those closet organizers with a half-length rod for hanging clothes instead. Or, in the case of one-Sunday-outfit-only kids, just put an extra-strong, 4- or 5-inch-long peg on the back or side wall of the closet. It should be able to handle four or five hanging items, and you can save the rest of the

OUT-OF-THE-BOX IDEAS

Roll Out the Clutter

GETTING CHILDREN'S toys organized is only half the battle, says Volena Askew, an Adult Home Economics teacher and supervisor in Knox County, Tennessee. You also have to organize so that the kids themselves can keep the toys in their place. Volena has one toy-organizing idea that worked when her three children were growing up, and still works with her preteen grandsons. "I bought those stacked plastic drawers with the rollers on the bottom, the type people use in their home offices," she says. "They're great for the small and midsize toys, but best of all, the kids can roll them around the room in the evening to pick up their toys, and then roll them right into the bedroom closet."

confessions of . . . an Accumulator

FRANCES HALL is in the catbird seat for clothing hand-me-downs: She has five female cousins just a year or two older than she is. That's a windfall for her frugal mother, Rose Kennedy of Knoxville, Tennessee, but it's also a major clutter challenge. "I'm a pack rat to the core," says Rose. "All these wonderful clothes kept coming in, and almost none of them ever went out again! Franny's closet would be overrun with stuff that hadn't fit anyone in years, and, worse yet, she could never find clean socks or mittens or her folk-dance skirt."

One day, inspired by a chat with a friend, Rose took charge. "My friend recommended separating outfits in your suitcase by placing them in plastic zipper bags," said Rose. So Rose tried it for 10-year-old Franny's everyday clothes, inserting a complete outfit, with underwear and socks, all in one bag and then leaving the bags in plain view on a single closet shelf. Franny would take an outfit out of its bag in the morning, put it back inside that night, and transport it to the laundry room.

"I emptied the bags into the wash, and then put the clothes right back in, organized by outfit, when they came out of the dryer," says Rose. And the see-through bags yielded a clutter-cutting bonus: "I knew immediately when a piece of clothing didn't fit or Franny wasn't going to wear it—it never made it into one of the 'outfit' bags," says Rose. "It was a no-brainer to decide which clothes to send on to my niece after that."

closet for more useful stacked boxes and open shelving.

Share the shelves. This is one of those rare instances when instead of kids' stuff overflowing into every room of the house, you can let some of the other household goods find a place in your child's closet. If you put your child's stuff higher than he can comfortably reach in the closet, you're courting disaster, because kids will climb. And, of course, he'll have the perfect excuse for never putting his stuffed animals back on the shelf: "I couldn't reach it!" Instead, put your child's items low in the closet (or elsewhere in the bedroom or rec room) and store seldom-used household items in the hard-to-reach spots. If you have (or can create) one deep shelf on the top of the closet, it's ideal for comforters and sleeping bags that won't fit elsewhere. The filling won't be tamped down during storage, and, should the inevitable avalanche occur, no one will be injured by flying down-fill.

Skip the stacks. Nancy Byrd of Indianapolis, Indiana, has an aversion to toppled heaps of clothes, and she also has two elementary school–age children. How to avoid the mess? "We don't stack folded clothes in drawers or on closet shelves," she says. "If you do, someone always wants something at the bottom of the stack and the whole pile goes down." Instead, Nancy purchased several small cardboard chests of drawers for each child (with wallpaper designs that match her decor). She placed the chests on the closet or bedroom floor. "Most people probably use them

FOUR FUN WAYS TO LABEL, MABEL

Sure, you know where everything in that spiffily organized closet should go, but do your kids? If you don't communicate in some way, you can't complain when the wet bathing suits end up hanging on the hooks designated for the dress-up necklaces, or the dirty socks end up on the floor, not in that bright red plastic milk crate you bought for laundry. Visual reminders on the storage receptacles are quicker than a map or an argument, and help everyone get used to the new system more quickly, parents included. Luckily, you're in the kids' rooms, so labels won't ruin the decor. And if you get the kids to help with the labels, you'll also get their "buy-in" on putting things back in the proper place. Here are four fun labeling solutions.

1. NEON POST-ITS. Just note what goes where and attach the Post-it. The neon colors are terrific because they're impossible to miss. And Post-its are perfect for the older child or the more formal house, because they're simple to remove once everyone's caught on to the new system.

2. LABEL GUNS. Remember the label guns that had their heyday in the 1960s? They're still around, and still lots of fun, particularly if your child is a new reader. Click out some labels, and, just for fun, add a couple to storage areas everyone is already familiar with: a "Mandy's Ear" label on her bedroom phone receiver, for example.

3. POLAROIDS. Take snapshots of the stuff that goes in each storage area, and tape or pin them to the appropriate place. There's plenty of room for humor here, too: Tape a picture of someone holding his nose and some stinky socks for the laundry basket, for example.

4. DRAWINGS. Let kids young or old illustrate either the objects to be stored in a bin, or the act of picking up that object. This is a place for humor, and it also reinforces the message for the very young child: This is what goes here.

for lingerie or socks," she says. At her house, the kids store one or two items of clothing per drawer. "The cardboard isn't fancy, but the drawers are light so the kids can pull them in and out easily," Nancy points out. "And you can always see precisely what's in each drawer without rummaging around or pulling things over."

Clear the floor. No matter how neat your closet, an object that ends up on the floor will end up behind or under another object. What good is that? The best policy is to replace that clutter-magnet floor space with containers, preferably those that roll or have drawers. An open box is okay, as long as it has wheels so you can pull it out and see what's crept into the corner. As for what to store in the containers on the floor, try shoes and boots, sports equipment such as skates and soccer balls, or even toy trucks and cars. Keep in mind that this is one of the spaces in a child's room she can reach. So if there are things you particularly want her to be in charge of cleaning up, or things you want within easy grasp—like her Barbies, art supplies, or inline skates—consider those as candidates for closet-floor containers.

Narrow your clutter. A clutter-cutting bylaw is never to store one object behind another. So while you may need some depth on your child's closet shelves for, say, a dollhouse or a kite, make most shelves deep enough only to house a single item—one toy bulldozer or piggy bank, for example. What if you already have deep shelves? Create the effect of more narrow shelves by placing a set of cubbyholes, like a cardboard sock organizer, across the back of the shelf, or lining it with open shoeboxes stacked to look like bricks.

Double your doors. Another creative kids' closet solution: Make more doors. That is, fill the closet, top to bottom, with narrow shelves, then place lightweight cabinet doors on the shelves. That way, you can put hooks and knobs outside the cabinet doors for hanging items—and still close the main closet door to hide the whole shebang.

Nix Clutter in the Nursery

It was probably Adam and Eve who first marveled at how many mounds of stuff it seemingly took to keep two tiny morsels like Cain and Abel alive. The clutter that babies can generate is stupefying. It's probably always been that way, but it's not all inevitable. No, there's nothing you can do about the dozens of diapers and outfits and bottles they go through each week. But if you keep your head, you can declutter the nursery decor—and maybe prevent some unneeded junk from ever reaching the baby's

room in the first place. Here's how to nurture your baby without nurturing clutter.

BEFORE THE BIG EVENT

The majority of clutter-control mishaps occur with new parents and new grandparents. That's because they're still chock-full of ideas of "how things should be"—everything from the baby needing a stroller, cradle, and bassinet to the dear thing getting the room "I always wanted and could never have." So most of your before-the-birth clutter-control work will involve questioning—the ads, the advice, even the *Goodnight Moon* gift sets. Here's how to prevent clutter before your baby arrives.

Get a list of "must-have" items from the pros. Instead of purchasing items based on the "helpful" list prepared by the toy store or a parenting magazine (often emphasizing the products sold by their advertisers), ask for a list of necessities at your obstetrician's or pediatrician's office. This will decrease the number of coats and fancy outfits you'll accumulate. (Bear in mind that those garments have to be stored somewhere!) And it will also move the extra baby appliances, such as jumping seats and baby tubs, off the "must-have" list and into the "nice to have if space allows" category.

Shower them with hints before the baby shower. So that you won't get three cushiony wall calendars (or three of *anything* that you don't feel you can give away), tell whoever throws your baby shower precisely what your

There's a lot of advertising talk about furniture that will grow with your child from infancy to college. Sure, such pieces will help you save money, but they're also important for clutter reduction in your child's room. When a child physically outgrows her kiddy-size furniture (or its Blues Clues motif), it becomes one more piece of clutter to deal with or ignore. One piece that need never move from your child's room is an armoire or wardrobe. Modern or antique, it's suitable storage for the nursery because you can use the closet portion to hang baby's clothes at *your* eye level and store diapers and such in the drawers. When your toddler becomes hell on wheels, the clothes will be too high for her to pull down, and when she's older, the armoire will become a suitable teen closet. It can even function as a computer table (if you add a shelf) or stereo cabinet.

baby needs and you want. If you're particularly close to the hostess, let it be known that you'd prefer for everyone to go in on one large necessity, like the crib. If you're not comfortable with that, at least voice your preference for practical stuff, like disposable diapers and plain T-shirts, over music boxes and dress-up outfits (there's never room in the closet for them, anyway). That way, when your mother-in-law inevitably gives you the music box and froufrou outfit, at least you won't have two of them cluttering up the nursery. Of course, if registering for baby showers is acceptable in your circle, you can make demands with impunity!

Think soothing and simple. A newborn baby needs comfort, not stimulation. The nursery doesn't need to scream "baby," nor does it need tons of kid stuff in it. Newborns will thrive with just one soft toy, a few high-contrast patterns to look at (like a checkerboard pasted on the wall near the crib), and lots of fresh air. Decide whether you want or need the mass quantities of stuffed animals, the kid-size chairs and tables, and the collection of children's classics right now. You can always get them later, once your child is old enough to enjoy them and you've seen how much nursery space he needs for the bare necessities.

Don't set a theme. Professional interior decorators unanimously pan "theme" nurseries. While their reasons are usually aesthetic, the principle is sound: Following a theme when you decorate the nursery will almost invariably lead you to put too much stuff in there. That's because so many theme accessories come as a package deal, from the little lamps and throws to the plastic Mickey Mouse bookshelves. Then it all collects dust and takes up space you might need for, say, the nursery monitor or a comfortable chair for breastfeeding. And look down the road a bit. If your daughter turns out not to be the Barbie type when she's 3, and her room is coated in Barbie tables, Dream Houses, and the like, that's one big, expensive decluttering and redecorating exercise in your future. Much better to select a few decorative items that you like yourself, and let the themes evolve as your child gets older.

Look baby gift sets in the mouth. It seems like every manufacturer is happy to group baby wares for you, from bath sets or hair sets to book and doll sets. Fact is, lots of times you'll only need, or use, part of what's in that set, leaving the rest to just clutter up the nursery. So experiment with products individually instead of buying the whole kit and caboodle. If you get a gift set, see what you use the first week or so, and then give the rest to a local women's shelter.

Streamlining a Sickroom

Sometimes a loved one needs special care, and you have to convert a bedroom (or other room) into a sickroom. If caregivers are coming and going, and if the patient is bedridden or housebound, it's pretty easy to see how the clutter can build up quickly. But keeping clutter at bay in a sickroom isn't so difficult if you try a few of these practical tips from our experts, Cindy Roach and Maureen Cronin, both of whom are registered nurses. Cindy is an elementary school nurse and an educator at a diabetes clinic in Portsmouth, New Hampshire, and Maureen is a community health nurse who specializes in home care. Both

FIVE EASY WAYS TO CUT NURSERY CLUTTER

When you're trying to control clutter in the little one's room, even the smallest steps can mean a lot. Try these five fast, surefire ways to cut clutter in the nursery.

1. QUIT THE TOY- AND BOOK-OF-THE-MONTH CLUB. Chances are, your child will have plenty of developmentally appropriate toys without a new one arriving in the mail every month. That's a lot of boxes and packing material to toss, too! As for the books, why buy them sight unseen when you can check out books from the library and then purchase copies of the ones you really like?

2. DON'T DUPLICATE DIAPER-BAG ITEMS. Instead, habitually bring the diaper bag into the nursery and get wipes and diapers out of it. After all, the baby can only be in one place at a time! There's no need for two complete sets of diaper-changing accessories.

3. BUY DIAPER-WIPE REFILLS. We *know* they make great compost holders and toy boxes. But even if you reuse diaper-wipe containers like a fiend, you eventually get too many. The refill packaging goes in the trash, so there's no clutter.

4. STORE BABY'S LAUNDRY IN THE WASHER. Instead of using a "holding place" for dirty baby clothes, load them directly into the washer, pretreating them on the spot. It's just a few extra steps, but it takes away the need for a messy laundry bin in the nursery, and keeps baby's room smelling fresher, too!

5. BUY BABY CLOTHES IN ONE OR TWO COLORS. Then, if only part of the outfit is messy, like the T-shirt, you don't have to change the whole thing. That saves on laundry, sure, but you also can buy fewer outfits—which means fewer clothes to store!

professionals emphasize that streamlining helps caregivers deliver assistance more efficiently and effectively—especially if a patient requires care from more than one person. You'll also see how a well-organized sickroom can increase a patient's independence, whether in moving around the room or simply being able to answer the telephone or get his or her own snack.

ORGANIZING THE ROOM

Both Cindy and Maureen agree that organizing a sickroom is an important part of patient care. The way furniture is arranged can affect a patient's independence, says Maureen. The nurses suggest removing unnecessary furniture that caregivers and your patient can trip over. Putting scatter rugs—which someone could slip on—on a wooden floor is a big no-no as well. Try to set up the furniture so the patient can walk from one place to the next with support if necessary. Carefully choosing furniture for its function and arranging it this way will help keep the room clutter-free.

Cut the (telephone) cord. Cut the clutter—and add safety—immediately by removing the traditional telephone and replacing it with a cordless model, says Maureen. Place the new phone within easy reach of your patient. You'll not only reduce clutter by omitting the cord, which can knock things over or get caught, you'll increase safety by giving the patient a portable lifeline for help.

Store bath items right in the basin. If your patient requires bed baths, where do you

A well-organized sickroom is safer for the patient. It's easier for him or her to navigate, and all his or her needs are conveniently located within easy reach. It's easier on the caregiver, too!

Good lighting in a sickroom can actually reduce clutter. It helps keep a patient oriented to time of day and objects in the room, which makes it easier to reach and put things away where they belong, explains community health nurse Maureen Cronin. Here are three simple ways to lighten up a sickroom.

1. Keep window coverings sheer or lightweight to allow natural light to enter the room.

2. Make sure that each area of the room has access to a lamp that is easy to turn on and off.

3. Plug in a night-light in case the patient needs to get up at night.

keep all the bath stuff? "Right in the bath basin," says Maureen. In a large basin, stack bathing items—soaps, powders, even dental care items—with two hand towels and two washcloths for each bathing session on top. Then stash the basin inside a nearby closet or nightstand, out of sight but ready for use.

Organize for the patient _and_ the caregiver. Organizing your patient's dresser will save you or any other caregiver plenty of time and aggravation. "Try to use the top two drawers of a dresser for items that a caregiver needs ready access to," suggests Maureen. Neatly place underwear, incontinence pads, hospital johnnies or comfortable sleepwear, and fresh bedding in those drawers. That way, bed and clothing changes will be quick and easy.

Try the layered look. Frequent linen changes are a fact of life when someone is ill. To save time and linen-storage space, layer the sheets right on the bed, advises Cindy Roach. For each layer, start with a fitted sheet, then a disposable pad, then a draw sheet (a body-size sheet). Disposable pads and draw sheets are available at most medical supply stores. In many cases, dampness will be absorbed by the two top layers, reducing the number of times you'll need to change a fitted sheet.

Go with side rails. If you need to convert a room into a sickroom and have the opportunity to select a new bed, choose one with side rails. Side rails not only enhance safety by preventing falls, but they also keep the bed looking neater. If your patient tosses and turns while sleeping, blankets and sheets are less likely to pull apart with a side rail securely in place. In the morning or after the patient's nap, you'll probably only have to do a few nips and tucks with the bedding instead of remaking the whole thing.

ORGANIZING MEDICATIONS AND OTHER ESSENTIALS

Maureen and Cindy stress the importance of putting necessary items within reach of your patient. "Try to anticipate the patient's needs," says Maureen. For instance, place a walker or cane near the bed or armchair if that's where the person spends most of his or her time. Here's more of their expert advice.

Drop pills in a med-slot box. The best way to organize pills and tablets is with a med-slot system, those plastic boxes made especially for the purpose. A med-slot box has separate compartments for each dose of medicine. This will help you and your patient avoid confusion over which medications are to be taken at what time of the day and reduce the likelihood of mistakenly double dosing or missing a dose. And it's a whole lot neater than trying to pick through multiple bottles of medication.

Stash necessities in a sack. "Make a little sack for holding medication, inhalers, and other necessities," says Cindy. Use a pillowcase or stitch together two square pieces of fabric with a loop on the open end so you can hang the sack on the back of a chair near the bed, on a wall hook next to the bed, or on the back of a

wheelchair or walker. The sack keeps all those important items stored in one place and within reach of both the patient and the caregiver, instead of being littered all over the room. The sack is also washable and portable—it can travel anywhere the patient goes.

Arrange essentials on a tray. Another way to keep essentials organized is to set them on a tray on a nightstand, table, dresser, or similar surface, says Cindy. That way, either the caregiver or the patient can readily identify dressings, an inhaler, tissues, a cordless phone, or anything else. At the end (or beginning) of each day, the tray can be restocked if necessary. And the tray can be moved around the room or to another room for convenience.

The Organized Traveler

Living with clutter is burdensome, but traveling with clutter is downright depressing. Out-of-control clutter will make you anxious and put a damper on the fun of a vacation. ("Where did I put those tickets?!") On a business trip, disorder can easily hamper your productivity. ("I thought I packed my calculator!") And when your things are a disorganized mess, you're much more likely to lose something.

It doesn't have to be that way. There are many steps you can take to organize yourself before you leave the house and stay organized while you're gone. The keys to clutter-free travel are packing light by eliminating unnecessary items,

---

KEEP A COOLER NEARBY

Maureen Cronin, a community health nurse who specializes in home care, visits a number of homebound patients each week. If a person is bedridden, it's tough for him or her to get to the fridge for a cold drink or snack. So Maureen suggests filling a cooler with cold beverages and snacks, and placing it within easy reach—on a table, nightstand, or chair. This will increase the person's independence, keep drinks and foods fresh, and organize them all in one place.

You've found what you think is the perfect carry-on bag. The salesman even assured you that it was the correct size. You're able to pack the bag neatly with everything you might need during the flight, plus an extra set of underwear and toiletries in case your other luggage gets lost. But when you get to the airport, the ticket agent tells you that your carry-on bag is too large and must be checked.

Here's how to avoid that frustration: When you shop for carry-on luggage, take along a measuring tape and measure the bag yourself. Federal Aviation Administration regulations state that carry-on luggage can be no larger than 45 linear inches. To calculate that figure, add the length plus the width plus the height (in inches) of the bag. The total needs to be less than or equal to 45 inches. So if the bag you're considering is 22 inches long, 14 inches deep, and 9 inches high, that's 22 + 14 + 9 = 45, so you're right on the money.

---

and keeping what you *do* take neat and organized. And it all starts in the bedroom, where most of us plan and pack for trips. Here's how to cut down on clutter when you're on the go.

Practice advance planning. We know you're excited about your trip. You've purchased the tickets, booked the hotel, and stopped the newspaper delivery. (You *did* stop the newspaper delivery, right?) Now you just want to toss everything into your bags and get the show on the road. But trust us, before you pack a single item, you need to draw up a complete list and check it twice. Here are two ways to make sure you leave with everything you need.

1. Contemplate your day. One terrific way to make sure that your packing list is complete is to mentally run through your day, from morning to night, making note of the activities you do (take shower, dry hair, brush teeth) and the items associated with each of those activities (shampoo, hair dryer, brush, toothpaste, toothbrush). Visualize your whole day this way, jotting down items as you go, and you're certain to remember the most important items.

2. Keep your list with you at all times. Trying to compile a packing list at the last minute is asking for trouble. Rushing is stressful, and the pressure is bound to cause you to forget something. Instead, start your list days—even weeks—in advance of your trip. Get yourself a small notepad and a pen, and carry them with you everywhere you go. That way, as you remember items you want to pack, it's a snap to just add them to the list.

Round up the usual suspects. Shampoo. Deodorant. Toothbrush and toothpaste. Some items are vital for almost any trip you take. If you forget them, it's no big deal, because you can easily and inexpensively buy what you need on the road. But then you end up with more clutter when you get home—a real no-no. Here's a better solution: Pack those items in a travel toiletry kit that you keep in your suitcase. Of course, this means you'll have to buy a spare toothbrush (if you don't already have one) and invest in travel-size versions of other items, but if you store them permanently in your luggage, you'll always have them packed and ready to go. Just make sure you check toiletries like shampoo and toothpaste before you leave to see if there's plenty, and replace or refill as needed.

Pack like a matchmaker. Have you ever arrived at a vacation destination, only to realize that you packed eight shirts and one pair of pants for a 3-day trip? Or maybe you found out that none of the blouses you brought go with any of the skirts.

Eliminate those gaffes and lighten your load by packing only pieces of clothing that you can wear with every other item you packed. That means every shirt you pack must match or coordinate with every pair of shorts, every skirt, every pair of pants, and vice versa. Sticking to basic colors—navy, tan, black, gray—may make it easier for you. If you want to add splashes of color, do it with space-saving accessories like scarves and jewelry.

Packing this way has many advantages. First, it allows you to carry less clothing, thereby decluttering your suitcase. Second, it makes choosing an outfit while you're traveling a breeze. Third, since you'll have to lay all your clothing out ahead of time to make sure everything coordinates, you're less likely to forget something. And fourth, if you do forget a blouse or pair of pants, it won't matter, because you'll still have something to take its place!

Nix the jeans. If the previous tip has you thinking "blue jeans," you might want to reconsider. Yes, jeans are comfy and they go with just about anything. But they're also heavy and

AIR OUT YOUR DIRTY LAUNDRY

At some point in your travels, you'll probably to have to deal with at least a little dirty laundry. And if you're carrying only one suitcase, those dirty duds will have to cohabit with your clean clothing. Icky? It doesn't have to be.

While you're packing, place one or two fabric-softener sheets inside a clean cotton pillowcase (cotton breathes better than cotton-poly blends and synthetics), and then pack the pillowcase in your suitcase. As you accumulate dirty laundry, fold it neatly (if you wad it up it'll take up more room) and place it in the pillowcase at the bottom of your suitcase. The fabric softener sheet keeps the whole suitcase smelling fresh, and the pillowcase keeps the soiled laundry away from your clean clothes. If you wash your clothes while you're traveling, don't forget to wash the pillowcase, too.

take up lots of space in your suitcase. Wrinkle-resistant khakis or chinos are a much better wardrobe choice.

Plan a wash day. It was the famed French writer and aviator Antoine de Saint-Exupéry who said, "He who would travel happily must travel light." One way to accomplish that is to do laundry while you're traveling. Even if you wash your clothes only once during a 2-week trip, you might be able to cut your wardrobe by half—if not more.

If you're staying with friends or family, call ahead and ask whether you can take advantage of their facilities. If you're staying at a hotel, find out whether the hotel offers a laundry service—most do. If all else fails, you're sure to find a Laundromat anywhere you go. And if you don't want to spend time doing your own wash, find out whether the Laundromat offers drop-off service.

Opt for layers, not bulk. When you travel to chilly climes, you may be tempted to take along several bulky sweaters or even a heavy coat. But those items take up a lot of room in your luggage and add unnecessary weight. A better way to keep warm without carrying heavy items is to dress in layers. For instance, a layer of silk or polypropylene long underwear worn beneath a microfleece shirt and a windbreaker can keep you just as warm as a thick sweater—with half the weight and bulk. Of course, sometimes you can't avoid carrying a warm coat. In that case, down outerwear is the best choice, because it compresses well, which keeps it from eating up as much space as a heavy wool coat.

Declutter your baggage—with Baggies. It can be tricky to keep all your belongings neat and organized when you're living out of a suitcase. One system used by many veteran travelers is packing items in resealable plastic food storage bags. Snack-size bags are perfect for holding cotton swabs, cosmetics, or a small sewing kit. You can use larger bags to store and organize T-shirts, scarves, hats, gloves, socks, slippers, and underwear. In addition, the bags keep bottles from leaking, and they can hold wet items such as bathing suits or washcloths until you can dry them. Since the bags are clear, you always know what's inside without having to rummage through a pile of loose items. And they're reusable.

Plan for incoming items. Part of the fun of traveling is collecting souvenirs. But if you don't

---

SHARE THE BURDEN, CUT THE CLUTTER!

Traveling with a friend? Reduce both your loads by eliminating duplicate items. A hair dryer and toiletries like shampoo are obvious choices to share, but you may also want to consider lending each other books and magazines and some clothing items like sweaters and jackets.

plan for them, you can end up with an armload of stuff and a suitcase that won't close. Fortunately, there is a simple solution. Take along an extra collapsible bag—one that, when empty, folds up and fits inside your suitcase. Anything made of rip-stop nylon would be ideal, because that material is ultralightweight. When you start to accumulate souvenirs, just whip out the bag and start filling it up.

Keep your jewels organized. When it comes to expensive jewelry and travel, the best policy is to leave it at home. Costume jewelry is another story. It can spruce up your look and make an outfit sparkle. The tricky part is keeping those baubles neat and organized. The good news is that we have several options!

1. Buy a jewelry carrier. These specially made pouches are designed to carry jewelry when you're traveling. Some are made from leather, others from fabric. Some roll, others zip. Shop around and pick the one that works best for you. Many companies sell them, including online and catalog retailers like Magellan's (www.magellans.com).

2. Make your own. If you don't have the time (or the inclination) to buy a jewelry carrier, you can make one for bracelets and necklaces in a pinch. You'll need the cardboard tube from a roll of toilet paper, some cotton balls, and good-quality masking tape (any other tape might leave residue on your jewelry). Stuff the tube with the cotton balls (to keep it from collapsing) and tape the ends to keep the cotton inside. Wrap your necklaces

and bracelets around the tube and use a little more tape to secure them.

3. Improvise an earring holder. Head to the fabric or crafts store and buy a square of felt that's at least 8 by 8 inches square. Attach your pierced earrings to the felt, going right through the fabric. It's best to keep all the earrings at one end of the square. After all your earrings are attached, roll the felt and secure it with some ribbon or even a couple of rubber bands. The felt keeps the earrings together and keeps them from getting scratched.

4. Pack it in a compact. Lipstick cases, the inexpensive kind with a snap closure and a small mirror inside, are handy for carrying rings and earrings. The cases are available at most department and discount stores.

Use your shoes. When you travel, especially for an extended period, there's lots of important information to keep track of: 800 numbers in case you lose your credit card, travelers check numbers, your passport number, phone numbers. It's vital to keep that information organized and, more important, safe. Here's a simply ingenious way to do just that.

First, write all the information neatly on a *small* piece of paper. Better yet, type the information in a word-processing program using a very small but clear font size; try Geneva or Helvetica at eight points. Print out the paper and trim it to the smallest size possible. Place it in a plastic sandwich bag (not the zip-top kind) and use just a little transparent tape to secure it. Next, remove the insole of one of your shoes—

Seven Travel Uses for Old Prescription Bottles

IF YOU or someone in your family takes any kind of prescription medicine on a regular basis, you may have lots of those empty plastic bottles hanging around. Remember that you can recycle the plastic containers. Or you can unload them by giving them back to the pharmacy. But don't get rid of them all! You can reuse some of them to organize your travel goodies. Remove the existing labels with warm water, then relabel the bottles with a permanent magic marker. Here are seven ways to put these handy containers to use on your next trip.

1. CARRY OVER-THE-COUNTER MEDICATIONS. Along with prescribed medicines, those little bottles are perfect for painkillers, antacids, antinausea pills, and other drugstore buys. (And remember, when you're traveling with prescription medicines, it's a good idea to carry a copy of the prescription in case there are any questions or you run out.)

2. CREATE A TRAVELING SEWING KIT. Wrap some neutral-colored thread around a small piece of cardboard. Place the cardboard, along with a needle or two and a couple of small safety pins, right in the bottle.

3. MAKE A MINI FIRST-AID KIT. A couple of adhesive bandages, a wrapped moist towelette, and some single-use packets of antibiotic ointment and alcohol preps will fit neatly into a bottle.

4. TAKE ALONG SOME NAIL-POLISH REMOVER. If you like to give yourself manicures while you're on vacation, but don't want to carry a big bottle of nail-polish remover, try this: Soak several cotton balls in nonacetone polish remover and stuff them into a prescription bottle that has a childproof lid. (Use the kind of lids that say "Push Down & Turn"—the snap-off lids aren't leakproof.) Just to be on the safe side, pop the bottle into a resealable plastic bag. Use the cotton balls to remove your polish, then throw them away.

5. PACK SOME BATTERIES. AA and AAA batteries fit easily into standard-size bottles.

6. STORE CHANGE OR TOKENS FOR TOLLS. Fill one bottle with quarters, another with dimes, and yet another with nickels. Keep them all in your glove box, and you'll always have exact change.

7. CARRY YOUR FAVORITE LOTIONS. Bottles with childproof lids can hold toiletries like shampoo, conditioner, lotions, and Vaseline without leaking. (You should still put those bottles inside a plastic bag in case they're accidentally crushed in your suitcase.)

most shoes, but especially sneakers, have removable insoles. Place the bag flat inside the shoe and reinsert the insole. You may have to make some adjustments with the paper or the bag, but when it's all said and done, your important information will be safe and sound! For the first day or so, you may be aware of the bag, but it should not be uncomfortable.

CHAPTER 10

Bathrooms and Laundry

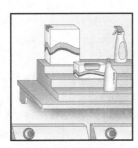

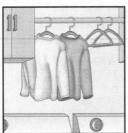

Envision yourself relaxing in a bubble bath after a hectic workday that was compounded by a bumper-to-bumper commute home. Now, picture yourself wrapped in a warm, freshly scented towel just plucked from a dryer. Soothing images, right?

Our bedrooms provide us with a soothing place to sleep, our kitchens take care of our taste buds, and our living rooms cater to our need to be entertained. But above all other rooms in the house, the bathroom is an oasis of comfort. So how is it that the most soothing—and smallest—spot in the whole house can fill up with so much stuff so quickly? Where *did* all these towels come from? Why are there 14 bottles of shampoo in the shower? And what are bottles of multivitamins circa 1986 doing on the top shelf of the medicine cabinet?!

CLUTTER CRUSADERS

Sailing to Success

FOR LA DORIS "SAM" HEINLY and her husband, Daryl, home sweet home is a 48-foot sailboat docked at the Balboa Peninsula in Newport Beach, California. That's 48 feet from bow to stern. During the week, Daryl is the chief executive officer for an electronics firm and Sam works as the Memories in the Making coordinator for the Orange County Chapter of the Alzheimer's Association. But weekday nights and weekends find the couple at the helm of their comfy and cozy boat, aptly named *Diversion*.

Sam and Daryl could easily live in a spacious home with multiple bathrooms, and they have during their 30-year marriage. But they purposely picked the boating life because it gives them the freedom and flexibility to set sail and feel the ocean breeze whenever they like. Sam and Daryl are both nearing 60, and their goal is to take a 3-year sailing excursion to Mexico, through the Panama Canal, the Caribbean, and beyond once they retire. For now, ship living is keeping them shipshape. Their bathroom (known as a "head" in sailor jargon) is basically a small closet the size of a phone booth equipped with a shower stall, a toilet, a sink basin, and a little shelving.

The Heinlys have learned a valuable clutter secret: Don't keep duplicates or triplicates of items. Those two-for-one bargains can produce more than you bargain for, stealing precious space. Sam and Daryl have made use of the vertical space in their shower stall by gluing on a three-in-one dispenser that contains shampoo, conditioner, and liquid body soap. "When we lived in a house with lots of space, we were forever keeping things that we didn't ever use. All they did was take up space in our cupboards and shelves," says Sam. "I think living on the boat has made us smarter about the use of space. We feel less encumbered."

When friends want to give the Heinlys gifts for special occasions, they diplomatically request selections that won't take up space they don't have. "We have our friends and family 'trained' when it comes to gift-giving," says Sam with a chuckle. "We ask them to give us only things that we can consume. Gift certificates to dinners or spas are especially appreciated."

Sound a little *too* familiar? When it comes to organizing bathrooms—and laundry areas—there's no need to dash your hopes down the drain. In fact, this chapter is loaded with clutter-cutting tips from top experts (and some ingenious everyday folks) to help you succeed.

Marshalling Your Forces

Before you empty a single drawer or pluck an item off the shelf, devote some time to surveying your bathroom and laundry areas. Like any good general, you need a battle plan before you blitz-clean these areas of your home.

Look at these rooms as if you were seeing them for the very first time. Look up, look down, look under, look all around. Sketch out the layout of the bathroom on a piece of paper. Indicate the location of existing shelves, cabinets, and other storage areas, suggests Karla Jones, a professional organizer from San Mateo, California, who helps homeowners and

corporations plow through the chaos created by clutter.

Get the kids involved. If you have preteen children, turn cleaning and organizing into a fun contest, suggests Maria Gracia, founder of Get Organized Now!, a professional organizing company in Milwaukee, Wisconsin.

"The younger the child, the more enticing games will be," says Maria. "Before dinner, try playing the Roundup Game. In it, your kids run around for 15 minutes putting things away. You can designate the bathroom one night. If they beat the clock—for example, finish neatening the whole room in under 15 minutes—reward them with a special batch of cookies or the chance to spend an extra 30 minutes before bedtime watching a favorite video or being read a favorite story."

Another game is called Erase the Evidence. "Your child spends 5 minutes cleaning up an area of the house so that no one is able to tell what was there before," says Maria. Your kids have erased the evidence!

Farm out the kids. If you have very young children, seriously consider taking on the bathroom when they're not underfoot. "Don't try to clean and organize and 'mother' at the same time," says Margaret Dasso, co-owner of The Clean Sweep, a housekeeping agency in Lafayette, California. "Arrange in advance to have your children stay with a sitter, a friend, or a relative. Or have your spouse take the kids to the park or some other outing so you can clean and organize in peace."

OUT-OF-THE-BOX IDEAS

Turn Clutter into Creativity

AS A FORMER KINDERGARTEN TEACHER and now a professional creativity expert, Courtney Watkins hates to see items go to waste. However, that doesn't mean she's a fan of clutter. In fact, Courtney, who lives in Los Angeles, California, thrives on helping families turn scraps and odds and ends into one-of-a-kind creations. She has been called "the Mary Poppins of the New Millennium" by Donny Osmond of the former *Donny and Marie* daytime talk show.

As you unearth spare strands of dental floss, odd buttons, old pantyhose, and other items in your bathroom cleaning binge, Courtney encourages you to use those materials to boost your child's creative powers. "I think I have the most fun cleaning and organizing when I look at my collection of things and say, 'What else can this be?'" says Courtney. "Playing the game of What Else, you push that muscle of creativity and ingenuity both in your child and in you."

Know your monetary limits. Major bathroom renovations and additions can be very pricey. So unless you scratch off a high-paying lottery ticket or gain some windfall of cash, chances are good that you'll need to work with the bathroom you have. Accept, even embrace, this reality. That way, you can focus fully on how to fine-tune the room and not be distracted by daydreaming about your fantasy bathroom: one as big as a bedroom, complete with a whirlpool, a self-cleaning separate shower stall, and endless counter space.

Banish Clutter from the Bathroom

Bathrooms are often the final frontier when it comes to household organizing. It's easy to shove things into drawers or toss them into the deep cabinet under the sink and forget about them. But before you know it, there's a mountain of tiny mouthwash bottles, a pile of half-used toothpaste tubes, and far too many outdated makeup items swallowing up space in your bathroom.

"Make an appointment with yourself and put it on the calendar," says Karla Jones. "Tell yourself that on Saturday morning you will tackle the downstairs bathroom. Pull everything out of the cabinets and drawers, because too often, items have lived in these places for far too long. I had one client who still had a can of starch

from the 1970s." Here are some ways to keep that from happening to you.

Make a clean sweep. Once your bathroom is devoid of all items, take this rare opportunity to give it a ceiling-to-floor scrubbing. That includes dusting the light bulbs! But start with your vacuum cleaner, not a sponge or mop. "If you first run the vacuum across dry surfaces, you will be able to remove hair and other dirt," says Margaret Dasso. "Then, follow up with your soapy sponge and floor mop." Be sure to aim your vacuum nozzle into the crevices and deep corners of your cabinet drawers to suck out trapped hair, makeup powder, and other debris.

Wax off residue. You can remove the soapy residue on shower tile and glass doors easily if you turn to a surprising cleaning ally: lemon oil furniture polish. "Don't laugh until you try it," says Margaret. "Wipe on the lemon oil with a clean soft rag and let it work awhile. Then polish the tile with a dry cloth." You'll also save time and elbow grease the next time the tile needs cleaning, because the furniture polish leaves a slight film that acts as a protective barrier against future soapy buildup.

Flush out stubborn stains. If your toilet bowl doesn't come clean with regular cleaning, Margaret has a solution that you can really sink your teeth into: Toss two or three denture-cleaning tablets into the bowl. Let them fizzle fully before you flush.

WHAT STAYS, WHAT GOES

Two words: Be merciless. Size up each item in your bathroom, make a stay-or-toss verdict, then move on to the next item. Remind yourself that clutter is often rooted in the failure to designate a home for each bathroom item. The mess piles up as those nomads roam from drawer to countertop with neither rhyme nor reason. So stand firm, be brave, and purge, purge, purge!

Have bags and boxes. Take a big plastic trash bag and a couple of big boxes with you to your bathroom battlefield and keep them within easy reach. Be sure that the bag is sturdy enough to handle the weight of all the items that you'll discard. Tops on the list: old tubes of toothpaste, the empty carton that used to be full of cotton swabs, the cologne your husband never, ever wears. When the job is done, tie it up and make one trip to your trash cans.

As for the boxes, use one to temporarily house absolute necessities and other items you use frequently. As you examine each item, keep this motto foremost in your thoughts: When in doubt, throw it out. This is the first step in the all-important sorting strategy. Into the second box go items that you want to keep but that don't belong in the bathroom.

Touch and toss. Be brave. Open the medicine cabinet and remove every single bottle, vial, and other shelf resident. It's critical that you remove everything *before* you decide what stays and what gets tossed. "You can't just open the cabinet and say, 'Okay, I want all this stuff,' and close the door," says Karla Jones. "You need to physically touch every item. It makes tossing so much easier."

Evict the expired. Remember that nasty cold or flu you had back in 1998? Probably not. But there's a reminder hogging space in your medicine cabinet—the half-used prescription that expired 2 years ago. Outdated medications are space gluttons, and they're potentially dangerous if you have children or pets. And to top it off, because medicines lose potency over time, they're no good to you anyway.

So give them the royal flush—pour the pills and liquids down the toilet, then toss the empty containers into the trash or recycling bin. While you're at it, check the expiration dates on all of your other bathroom products, such as toothpaste, antibiotic cream, sunscreen (yes, it expires), peroxide, and mouthwash.

Face the facial facts. In general, most cosmetics, including facial creams, lipsticks, blush, base, eye liners, and the like have a shelf life of only about 6 months. There's a good reason: Old cosmetic products deteriorate with age, and can actually cause rashes or other problems for sensitive skin. Do what Marcia C. Smith, a newspaper sportswriter from southern California, does. "When I buy new cosmetics, I mark the purchase date on them with a permanent marker that won't smudge," says Marcia. "And I've gotten into the habit of immediately

CLUTTER CRUSADERS
A Tidy Kid Takes Off

WHEN PRESSED FOR AN ANSWER, Maria Gracia will 'fess up. "I admit it. Growing up in Jersey City, New Jersey, yes, I was definitely a tidy kid," she says. "I shared a bedroom with my older sister, who was a bit of a slob, and I was forever tidying up our room. My mom is what I affectionately call an 'organizing maniac,' so I guess it's always been in my blood to be a neat and organized person."

Her innate need to be neat is now reaping dividends. After working for marketing and management companies, Maria left the corporate confines a few years ago to pursue her true passion: helping people get their lives and their homes organized. She founded her own company, Get Organized Now!, wrote a book to help other people get organized, *Finally Organized, Finally Free*, and runs a clutter-cutting Web site, www.getorganizednow.com.

"I don't like to see people held back from their goals or dreams because of clutter," says Maria. "There's so much people are capable of, and it would be a shame for something simple like clutter to be their obstacle."

Throughout her life, Maria has always lived in one-bathroom homes. She currently shares a comfy two-bedroom, one-bathroom condo in Milwaukee, Wisconsin, with her husband, Joe. She looks at a lifetime of one-bathroom living as a challenge, not a limitation. "I've had so much fun figuring out ways to maximize our one and only bathroom that I'm not sure what I would do if I had *two* bathrooms," she laughs.

CLUTTER CRUSADERS

No Longer in Dryer Straits

WEB SITE DESIGNER PAUL HAYES of Santa Ana, California, lives in a 28- by 70-foot doublewide mobile home. It's been his place of residence for more than 15 years. It is *truly* small-space living. During this past decade, Paul began losing his hair. So he started to crop his hair short—about a half-inch in length. "I vowed that if I ever lost my hair, I would never try to hide my baldness by combing strands of hair over my head," says Paul, who's 45. "To me, that looks ugly and ridiculous."

Surprisingly, the loss of his locks freed up a little space in his one and only bathroom. "One day, I suddenly realized that I didn't need my big hair dryer. It was gathering dust and taking up a lot of space in one of my bathroom vanity drawers, so I gave it the heave-ho," says Paul. "I'd recommend that other guys who are losing their hair consider doing the same thing."

tossing the old lipstick to make room for the new one."

Share your shampoo stash. Most of us are particular about the types of lotions, bath oils, and shampoos we use. So what do you do with all the bathroom toiletries you received from well-meaning friends that you never intend to use? You're too guilt-ridden to throw them away. "I say give them to a battered women's shelter," says Karla Jones. "Often, women there don't have extra money to spend on cosmetics, fancy soaps, or other nice things. So give those women a little bit of well-deserved pampering."

There are several ways to find a local shelter. Check the blue government pages of your phone book under Social Service and Welfare Organizations, Health and Welfare Agencies, or a related category. Also, shelters are sometimes listed in the classified section of local newspapers.

Take a time out on towels. La Doris "Sam" Heinly is stingy when it comes to towels. She needs to be. She and her husband, Daryl, live on a 48-foot sailboat in Newport Beach, California. The couple keeps a set of "his and her" towels hoisted on a hook in the ship's head (bathroom) and stashes four more tightly rolled towels on an enclosed shelf. "I've discovered that you really can have too many towels," says Sam. "Now, we have a number that is practical for the two of us." Take a look at your own towel collection: Do you have dozens more than you need? Maybe it's time to pass a few along to the kids or Goodwill.

Color by design. The Enos family of Loxahatchee, Florida, never feuds when it comes to deciding which towels and toothbrushes belong to whom. That's because Shelly Enos, a first-grade teacher, came up with an elementary plan that works. "I color-code my family's towels and toothbrushes," says Shelly. "My husband Tony's color for these items is blue; my daughter Amanda's color is pink; my son Corey's color is purple; and my color is yellow." That means family members don't have to grab a fresh towel each time they need one, then leave it lying around. Everybody knows exactly which towel is his or hers.

ORGANIZING WHAT'S LEFT

Congratulations! You've weeded out excess and useless items. Now it's time to put your bathroom back together—but in better-than-ever shape. Discover the extra storage spaces you never knew existed! Now's the time to buy the added shelves, containers, or other storage allies that you'll need to complete the reorganization successfully.

Practice counter intelligence. Horizontal space, especially smooth countertops, seems to beg to be loaded up with clutter. But resist, says Maria Gracia. "Walk into many bathrooms and you may not even be able to see the countertop because of all the candles, hair dryers, towels, tissue boxes—you name it—littered on top of it. It's enough to stress you out. I suggest that you reserve the counters for the few items you use a lot throughout the day, such as toothpaste, toothbrushes, and brushes. Store your cosmetics, your shaving cream, your razor, and the like in the bathroom cabinet, out of sight. Freeing up this space will make your bathroom more appealing."

Add a mate for your countertop. If you're looking to add to your countertop space, think vertical, not horizontal, says Sharon Hanby-

Robie, a professional organizer and interior designer from Lancaster, Pennsylvania. She suggests placing a pier cabinet on your countertop. Pier cabinets are small, standing less than 3 feet high, but pack lots of storage. "With the pier cabinet, your countertop is still usable, but

confessions of . . . a Collector

THINK YOU'RE GETTING something for nothing when you take home all those complimentary shampoos, conditioners, hand lotions, shower caps, and sewing kits provided during your hotel stays? If you travel a lot—as Debra Moore, of Allen, Texas, does as an internal auditor for JC Penney—you quickly pay the price for these hotel freebies: You'll amass a mountain of the mini-size items in your home before you can say "Holiday Inn."

"At first, I thought it was great, taking home all these toiletries," says Debra. "But after traveling sometimes three or four times a month, I came to the conclusion that I would *never* use them all." Debra now practices restraint. She keeps a set of toiletries in her overnight bag for visits to friends or family. In her guest bathroom at her home, she keeps two shampoos, two conditioners, two lotions, and one shower cap in a decorative wicker basket on the counter. They're for houseguests who may have forgotten to bring their hair care products with them. "I stick to these amounts, then every 6 months or so, I replace them with a new set," says Debra. "Otherwise, I leave these 'freebies' where they belong—back in the hotel room."

way up high. Mount a shelf near the ceiling, and use the above-the-forehead space for extra supplies such as toilet paper and tissue boxes, the type of things that you need to get to but don't necessarily want to look at every day.

Make the right curtain call. You can make your bathroom look bigger than it is by using a monochromatic (single) color scheme when you decorate. Choose neutral, light colors for your walls, countertops, and sink basin. Complete the larger-than-life look by selecting a clear or light-colored shower curtain. Dark curtains tend to shrink the look of your bathroom.

Remember your toilet. Not that you could forget. But one of the most underused spaces in many bathrooms is the area above the toilet. Professional organizer Linda Koopersmith, author of *The Beverly Hills Organizer's House Book*, recommends mounting a stacked cabinet above the toilet. There, you can store some of the items that you now keep under the sink—extra toiletries, toilet-paper rolls, tissue boxes, and a few hand towels.

Store trash bags where you use them. While you're in this cleaning mood, use the opportunity to save yourself some time in the future. Store plastic garbage bags in the bottom of the bathroom wastebasket, right under the bag that's in use. You'll free up storage space under your bathroom vanity and always have a fresh bag at hand when it's time to toss the old bag.

you've gained a great deal of storage space right within easy reach," says Sharon.

Reach for new heights. There is often an untapped treasure of available space on high—

Lasso that hair dryer. Hair dryers—and their crafty accomplices, curling irons—are clunky and take up lots of space inside a bathroom drawer or undersink cabinet. So set them free! Mount a hook on your bathroom wall and hang your small appliances from it. A word of caution: Location is vital. Situate the hook well away from your sink or tub so that you don't accidentally drop the curler or hair dryer into water while you're using it.

Give jewelry the hook. Barbara Lee, a family therapist in San Marcos, California, has far too many orphaned earrings. "Before I went to bed at night, I'd take off my watch, ring, and earrings in the bathroom and place them down on the counter right next to the sink," she says. "Sometimes I'd be so tired that when I washed my face and hands before going to bed, I accidentally knocked an earring down the sink. Not only that, but my watch and ring were usually swimming in a puddle of water on the counter."

To solve the problem, Barbara mounted an inexpensive but decorative hook on the wall— and away from the sink. At night, she slips her watch and ring onto the hook. She drops her earrings into a satin sachet, pulls its drawstring, and loops that on the hook, too, for safekeeping. It's turned out to be a jewel of an idea!

Take a recess. Sharon Hanby-Robie has toured the bathrooms of many homes, historic and contemporary. "Being both an interior designer and a real-estate agent gives me a unique perspective," she says. "I see the home as a place

CLUTTER CRUSADERS
The Retirees

AFTER RAISING A FAMILY OF THREE, Shirley and Howard LaBounty looked forward to retirement and downsizing their lives, including their living space. They gladly sold their sprawling 3,000-square-foot home with four bedrooms and three bathrooms in West Palm Beach and bought a two-bedroom, one-bathroom mobile home in a quiet retirement development in Zephyrhills, Florida.

Howard, a retired handyman and trucker, put his mechanical skills to use optimizing the limited space in their single bathroom. He used two-by-fours to build a wooden cabinet above the toilet. The couple keeps items too tall or bulky for the medicine cabinet, including hair spray and perfume bottles, there. They save space in the bathtub by sharing one bottle of shampoo and one bottle of conditioner that get stored on a hanging shelf on the showerhead.

for living, but I also see it as if I'm a prospective buyer. I especially look for areas of clutter or chaos."

Sharon's space-saving tip for people stuck with small bathrooms and no place to expand: "Whenever possible, recess into the walls," says Sharon, author of *My Name Isn't Martha, But I Can Renovate My Home*. "It's amazing how much you can accomplish with just 4 to 6 inches of recessed space. Use the space for towel bars, mirrors, even shelves."

CLUTTER CRUSADERS

This Idea Is a Home Run

PROFESSIONAL SPORTSWRITER MARCIA C. SMITH travels all over the country reporting on various sporting events. She was at Camden Yards in Baltimore, Maryland, the day Orioles third baseman Cal Ripken Jr. took himself out of the lineup to end his league-record consecutive game-playing streak at 2,632 games. And she covered the action for her newspaper, *The Orange County Register*, when the Los Angeles Lakers captured their second consecutive NBA title in 2001.

When Marcia returns from these trips, her suitcase always sports some new mementos, including plastic drinking cups that commemorate the special event. Rather than stash these cups in a closet—or worse, on a top shelf in her office to collect dust—Smith puts them to practical use. She has given the bathroom inside her Southern California apartment a sports theme.

In the Ripken cup, she stores her brushes and combs. In the Lakers cup, she stores her nail polish and nail polish removers. She sets these cups and others on the shelf under her bathroom sink. "Everything I need is compartmentalized in several sports cups," explains Marcia. "I just open the cabinet door and reach down for the cup I need. It frees up a lot of counter space."

If you're a skilled do-it-yourselfer, you can create the recesses yourself with a few supplies, including a stud finder and a saw, says homebuilder Richard Beaver of Knoxville, Tennessee.

Just ask for advice at your local home store. If such a project intimidates you or if there's wiring in the wall, call a handyman or carpenter to do the work for you. Look for numbers for these professionals on the bulletin board at the home store or in the Yellow Pages under Building Contractors.

Plop doodads in plastic. What can you do with all those little odds and ends that you simply can't part with? Left inside drawers, bobby pins, nail files, cotton swabs, and other little items can easily get lost in the shuffle. Store these items in small, clear, stackable plastic containers—you'll find them at most discount stores. Stash them inside the drawers or on shelves for easy access.

DOUBLE YOUR SINK STORAGE

Are you taking full advantage of that deep space in the vanity under your sink? Many folks don't. Here are a few ways to make it work harder in your quest to cut the clutter.

Add a shelf. Shelly Enos added space under her sink by adding a permanent shelf. "My husband, Tony, is handy with tools, so I convinced him to build a shelf in the cabinet under our bathroom sink. It doubled my space down there. I use the top shelf to store my feminine products and stockings, and the bottom shelf to store my lotions, creams, and bubble baths." If you're not so handy, visit a kitchen store and purchase a small plastic-coated wire shelf on legs. This clever product allows you to store items on—and under—the shelf.

Hang a caddy. Many kitchen stores sell caddies that mount on the inside of kitchen cabinet doors. These caddies, designed to hold dishwashing liquid, scouring powder, and the like, work as well in the bathroom. Mount one on the inside of the door to your vanity and use it to hold toiletries or cleaning supplies.

Take your stuff for a spin. Make better use of that deep space under your bathroom sink with a low-cost lazy Susan. Place your toiletries and other bathroom essentials on these mobile trays, which are widely available in discount and home stores. When you need something, simply spin the tray until the desired item pops into view. This trick keeps items from disappearing from sight—and mind.

Draw boundaries. Most under-the-sink cabinets are deep and tall, but rarely is the space used to its fullest. To make the most of the space—*and* save time—try this: Place all cleaning products on the left side of the cabinet, and all your extra soap and shampoo bottles on the right side. Keeping the two types of products segregated will save you from having to rummage through everything under there each time you need one.

MORE CLEVER CLUTTER FIGHTERS

Of course, there's more to your bathroom than the vanity and toilet areas. It's time to tackle the rest of the room with our experts' ingenious suggestions:

Rack 'em up. Who says that a paper-towel rack belongs *only* in the kitchen? Certainly not Maria Gracia. She suggests installing a paper-towel holder in your bathroom right above the towel rack. When you need to clean the counters or toilet lid, just reach for a spray cleaner and a paper towel. Then toss your used towel in the trash.

"Paper towels eliminate the need to keep old sponges under your bathroom sink taking up space," says Maria. "These sponges can cause mildew, harbor germs, and create clutter. The paper towels are a much cleaner alternative. And you can match the color of your paper towels to your bathroom towels."

Get toys out of the tub. If you have a young child, your bathtub is probably full of toys. Get them out of the tub and up on the wall. Hang a hook on the wall above or near the tub, hang a plastic basket or fabric mesh bag on the hook, and store all your child's must-have bath toys there. "You'll discover that in addition to the fact that you'll reclaim the family bathtub, your child's toys will stay cleaner and dry much faster because air can circulate around them," says Maria.

Hoist the shelf in your shower. Keep yourself from fumbling over the bottles of shampoo, conditioner, shaving cream, and other shower essentials by hanging a tiered,

The Family Therapist

FOR MORE THAN 2 DECADES, family therapist Barbara Lee of San Marcos, California, has helped couples mend their relationships and individuals cope with some of life's most stressful situations. She also has some good advice about how to create extra space to store towels in a bathroom.

"Too often, we don't realize the wonderful space we have behind a door," says Barbara. "It's a perfect place to hold extra towels." Barbara fastened three hooks in a semicircle pattern about two-thirds of the way up on the back of her door. Each of these hooks holds a full-length bath towel, freeing up space in her linen closet for bed sheets, pillowcases, and extra blankets.

plastic-coated, lightweight shelf over the neck of your showerhead. For the few dollars you'll invest, you'll reap priceless benefits. This shower caddy can amply hold all those items—plus your razor and washcloth—in a neat vertical space. You'll find the shower caddies in most home improvement stores.

Stick with the two-for-one approach. One way to keep clutter from taking over your bathroom (and laundry area) once you've dug out is to discipline yourself the next time you shop. Sure, you're tempted by all the neat gadgets, but if you do make one purchase, then make it a rule that you'll eliminate *two* old items when you get home.

Place new items in back. You've worked so hard organizing your medicines, shampoos, and other tonics. Here's how to keep them neat and tidy. Store similar products in the same place, then when you buy a refill, place it *behind* the half-used one so that you empty the original before you open the newer item. This way, you will know exactly when you need to buy more.

Be ready for the beach. If you love relaxing at the beach or by the pool in the summer, here's a way to keep your beach gear organized and within easy reach. Anne McAlpin, owner of Pack It Up in Jacksonville, Oregon, recommends hanging a tote bag on a hook on your bathroom door. "I just love tote bags. I hang them all over my house—they're truly underrated organizers," says Anne. "Just place your bathing suit (clean and dry, of course!), a fresh towel, sandals, and sunblock in the tote bag. When you're ready to head for the beach, you don't have to waste time hunting and gathering all your beach items."

Wire your bathroom for space. Hang inexpensive three-tiered wire baskets from a hook in your bathroom. The baskets are a space-saving way to hold your—or your child's—washcloths and soaps. The best baskets for the bathroom are plastic coated; plain metal baskets might rust.

Bring the kitchen into the bathroom. If you're redecorating the kitchen, don't toss out that plastic flatware organizer. Give it a second life by turning it into a clutter-cutting tool—in your bathroom. It's perfect for organizing small, long items such as makeup brushes, eyeliner, tweezers, and nail clippers. Relegate each one to its own special slot so there is no intermingling of the cosmetic clan.

Suction it up. Looking for a nook to hook your razor on so it's always in reach when you need it? Joely Johnson, a publications editor from Alburtis, Pennsylvania, uses a clear suction cup on her shower-stall wall.

"I don't have a big bathroom, and there's no real shelf space to speak of in my shower stall," says Joely, who lives in a two-bedroom, one-bathroom house. "It was a real pain to be constantly bending over to reach for my razor in the shower. A few times, I stepped on it—ouch! Then I got smart. I placed a suction cup with a little hook on it right under my showerhead. My razor hangs from the hook, making it easy to grab when I need it." You'll find suction hooks at most home supply, discount, or hardware stores.

Lightening Up the Laundry

Having access to your very own washer and dryer really is one of life's perks. If you get the urge to wash clothes at midnight, you don't have to worry about waking the neighbors or fumbling for quarters to pay for the load. Still, many of us fail to completely utilize this very

You've bid bye-bye to the unmatched socks, the expired prescription bottles, and the year-old cosmetics. You've also discovered new sources of space up, down, and all around. Now comes the final challenge: How do you keep this masterpiece of neatness from returning to mayhem?

Heed the 30-second rule. Linda Koopersmith helps people minimize their messes in less than a minute. Best known as "The Beverly Hills Organizer," Linda employs what she refers to as her 30-second rule.

"It's something I came up with many years ago," says Linda. "I use this as a guilt trip with people." In a nutshell, the rule reminds you just how little time it actually takes—usually 30 seconds or less—to put back an item you're finished with. How could you *not* return an item to its rightful place? "Keep this up," says Linda, "and in no time, it becomes a habit." And a real time saver, sparing you from wasted minutes—even hours—spent trying to scare up your hairbrush or blow dryer.

important part of our home. Here's a laundry list of ways to cut the laundry room clutter, all the while saving you time, space, and money.

Remember your laundry room's true identity. If you're having trouble reaching your washing machine, it may be because you've fallen into the habit of using your laundry area as a catch-all for other items— like your set of golf clubs, a toolbox, or a stash of flower vases.

Try to limit the occupants of your laundry area to items that are related to cleaning clothes. Otherwise, you'll only end up caught in confusion (and clutter), wondering exactly where you misplaced your laundry basket. "Laundry areas should be reserved for washing and drying clothes—period," says Karla Jones. "You need to put things in places where they make sense; otherwise, you become confused and spend needless time searching for things in all the wrong places."

Try the tiered tactic. One way to maximize the space around your appliances is to use tiered storage devices. Use three-tiered hanging baskets, as we suggested for your bathroom, to house lightweight laundry items such as fabric-softener sheets. Consider expandable shelves built like little stairs to store heavier items such as the laundry soap and bleach, suggests Linda Koopersmith.

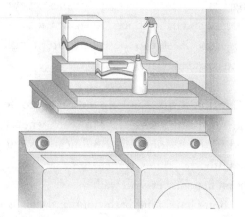

Stepped shelves make it easy to reach all your laundry supplies. No more digging!

BED SHEET CLOTHESBAG

If you can't part with an old bed sheet, turn it from yet another piece of useless clutter into a laundry sack. Use it to store your laundry until washday arrives. That's what sewing and craft expert Pamela Hastings of Wall, New Jersey, uses instead of a bulky clothes hamper.

"The laundry sack is collapsible, so it doesn't take up as much room as a hamper," says Pamela. "You can use it to hold your dirty laundry or dirty bedding. Then you can empty the whole bag into the washing machine and clean it in one nice, tidy bundle. My sister is a seamstress, and even she was amazed when she saw what I created!"

Here's how to make your own: Use a double-, queen-, or king-size flat bed sheet for ample room to store your dirty laundry. Buy about 80 inches of nylon cord from a camping store (or hunt around your house for some extra cord). Then:

1. Fold the sheet in half widthwise. Sew the short side closed, then sew up the long side to about 2 inches within the edge.

2. Fold down the edges of the top of the sack to form a 1- to 1¼-inch seam. Thread the cord through the seam to make the sack's drawstring. Tie a knot at each end of the cord big enough to keep it from slipping back out of the seam.

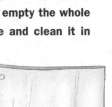

Sew up the sides.

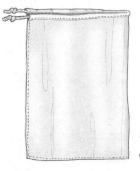

Insert the drawstring.

Let shirts hang out. Keep the iron in its storage place by using a collapsible rolling clothing rack to hang shirts and other pieces of clothing that can't be dried in the dryer. "A rolling clothing rack air-dries clothing wonderfully, and it's also great to use when you take clothes fresh from the dryer that you don't have time to fold and put away," says Maria Gracia. "The rack prevents wrinkles from forming, and when you don't need it, it tucks neatly away."

Add hanging space. Does this sound familiar? You're pulling clothing out of the dryer. As you do, you place each item on a hanger. The trouble is that after a while you run out of places to hang the stuff up. So you resort to hooking the hangers on cabinet shelves, doorknobs, maybe even the hamster's cage. Hold it. Here's an inconspicuous way to expand your hanging space. Hang a closet rod between storage cabinets above your washer and dryer so that it fits snugly. Or locate the rod between a storage cabinet and wall. The rod creates a dandy new space to hang up clothes as they're pulled from the dryer.

Add space to hang your clothes by installing a closet rod in the laundry room.

Lose your ironing board—sort of. If your laundry room is really cramped, you can get rid of your conventional ironing board and replace it with an over-the-door ironing board. These ironing boards work like Murphy beds: They hang on the door, and when you need to iron, you pull the board down. When you're through, you just flip the board back up flat against the door.

These ironing boards are sold by many stores that specialize in home organizing products. To find an online or mail-order store, search the Internet using the keywords Over, Door, Ironing, Board. One such vendor is www.containerstore.com. A similar idea that's just as good: wall-mount ironing-board holders. They save closet space, and many models have a slot for the iron, which frees up shelf space, too.

MAKE NEAT WORK OF A LAUNDRY AREA

Keeping laundry supplies orderly and handy at the same time can be a challenge, especially if space is at a premium (and isn't it always?). Depending on your laundry area layout, one of these two approaches will work to keep laundry products neat and nearby.

1. To make use of vertical space in your laundry area, pick up an inexpensive, four- or five-tiered metal workshop shelf unit (available at home improvement stores). Situate the shelf right next to the washing machine, and soap, bleach, and fabric softener bottles will be easy to reach. Go one step further and use old hand towels or dish towels that have passed their prime to line the metal shelves; they'll soak up detergent drips effortlessly, and you can just throw them in the next batch of wash to get them clean again.

2. If you lack up-and-down space but have horizontal room to spare, install a single long, narrow shelf above your wash station. The shelf should run the length of your machines to maximize storage, and be just wide enough for your largest detergent bottle—but not so wide that it prevents your washer lid from opening all the way. Again, you can put old towels to good use here as absorbent, easy-to-keep-clean shelf liners.

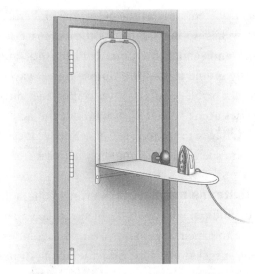

A fold-down ironing board is a great space saver.

each family member a different color of hanger.) The shelf is where each family member's folded laundry goes, and that's where he or she picks it up!

Use wall hooks. Save valuable floor space in your laundry area by hanging your mop, broom, and dustpan on wall hooks. This also prevents you from knocking over the whole collection of mops and brooms stacked in a corner every time you try to extract one. Keeping those tools airborne will also extend their life spans, because they won't be collecting dirt from the floor.

Try a triple threat. Maria Gracia considers her three-bag laundry sorter an absolute godsend. "As clothes need to be washed, we immediately put them into their proper bag: darks, whites, or delicates," says Maria Gracia, who shares her many space-saving tips on her Web site, www.getorganizednow.com. "When my husband or I are ready to do a load of wash, we don't waste time sorting clothes because it's already done."

Name your spot. Here's a way to save time delivering laundry to its proper family member and prevent clean laundry from cluttering up the laundry room. Install a long shelf in the laundry room to hold the newly folded laundry. Designate individual space on this shelf for each family member and post their names on the edge of the shelf. (For hanging items, assign

Stash the sheets. If your linen closet is in or near your laundry room and is crammed full, take a tip from retirees Shirley and Howard LaBounty. They don't even have a linen closet. But they have managed to squeeze out space when they need it inside their two-bedroom mobile home in Zephyrhills, Florida. "We need only four sets of bedding," says Shirley, a mother of three and grandmother of four. "I keep an extra set of sheets under my bed and another set under the bed in our guest room. It works for us."

Make sorting a game. Turn laundry duty into a fun game with your children. Show them how to sort light clothing from dark clothing so you don't have to wade through their clothing at laundry time. Store two clothes hampers in the bathroom and praise your children for tossing the lights into the light hamper and darks into the dark hamper. Who knows—they may even use the opportunity to practice their jump shots with a balled-up T-shirt.

Save time sorting. As a mother of two active children and wife to an equally active husband, Shelly Enos needs to wash two loads of laundry each day. She saves time by assigning each family member a specific kind of clothing to keep track of.

Here's how it works. Dark clothes that need to be washed go into a hamper in her husband's bedroom closet; fine washables go into her closet; dark clothes such as blue jeans are stashed in a basket in her son's bedroom; and light-colored clothes, including T-shirts, are housed in her daughter's closet. "Corey is especially messy, so I hooked a toy basketball net over his closet door so that he can 'shoot and score' the clothes," says Shelly.

As Shelly makes her nightly rounds, she plucks a basket from one of the rooms and puts it into the washer. In the morning, she gets up early enough to place the load into the dryer. After sipping some coffee, reading the newspaper, and enjoying a little quiet time for herself, she wakes up her family. As they prepare for work and school, the dryer load finishes, and Shelly is able to fold the clothes right away to prevent wrinkles. All this saves clutter since dirty clothes aren't scattered throughout the house, but it saves time, too, because Shelly doesn't have to spend time sorting dirty laundry.

Unite their undies. If you run a household with children who are close in age, then you've come to expect arguments over whose underwear or socks are whose. Stop the sibling rivalry and contain the clutter of dirty laundry by giving each family member his or her own mesh lingerie bag. Instruct them to place their socks and underwear inside their bags. To stop any confusion, select bags in different colors or designs, one for each member of the household. Come laundry day, each family member needs only to give the drawstring on the bag a tug to close it up. Toss the bags into the washer, then the dryer. When the clothes are dry and ready to take out of the dryer, sorting the items will be a breeze.

CHAPTER

Entryways and Mudrooms

The main entryway—be it a back room, a mudroom, or a back door—is the workhorse of the average family home. And whatever you call it, it can be trouble. Sure, some people are able to maintain a lovely public foyer—you know, the kind with a chandelier and a single large vase of the freshest, brightest flowers to welcome guests. But rest assured that even those people have a "real" entry somewhere, where the kids plop everything from rock collections to inline skates; where the adults dump their briefcases and purses; where shoes, shoes, and more shoes are put on and taken off, then tossed at random.

Entryway and mudroom clutter can easily get out of hand, even with the best intentions. And for those who live where the winter climate is cold and snowy, the clutter problem grows exponentially with the dropping of the temperatures and the adding of soggy hats, mittens, and scarves and dripping winter boots. But you're not without recourse. In this chapter we've gathered the very best tips and advice to help you dig out. Our experts include interior design author Glenna Morton, who explains how "no-fly zones" can help you keep clutter moving out of the entryway. All-around organizing pro Maria Gracia offers her tips about clearing out the entryway and mudroom and storing odds and ends such as umbrellas. There's loads more, too, including several ingenious ideas from the original clutter cutters, the Shakers.

Getting Started

Whatever sort of entry or mudroom your home has, it needs to be well-designed and well-thought out to prevent clutter from leaking into the main part of your house. Even if you have only a little space just inside the door, careful planning and strategic placement of a few essential elements will make your entry space efficient, functional, and maybe even nice to look at!

Think of the mudroom or entry as a containment area. Much like an antibiotic or calamine lotion, its purpose is to keep infectious

WHEN CLUTTER COMES HOME TO ROOST

Does the main entry to your home look like a flea market after a cyclone? You're not alone. But before you try to sort through it all, let's see how bad things really are: In the following list, make note of how many of the items apply to you.

- [ ] When you open the door to your home, you must wade through a sea of shoes to reach the entry table to dump today's mail, which you flop on top of a pile that has been there since you moved in.

- [ ] Although there are lovely benches in your entry to sit on while removing footwear, you can't use them because the bench is hidden somewhere under a damp, yet colorful, mound of jackets and backpacks.

- [ ] To pull off your own dripping boot, you usually balance on one foot, then set it firmly on top

of Spot's rawhide chew bone. More than once you've managed to step off the bone, only to have your foot land in Spot's water dish.

- [ ] The last time the UPS guy stepped into your entryway, he asked when you folks are planning to move. You're not moving.

- [ ] At the bottom of a mountain of clothes on your coatrack, you once found an article of clothing you thought your child had lost. By the time you found it, that child had a child of his own.

- [ ] Your home has no "entryway." All of the above happens in your kitchen.

If you nodded your head in recognition as you read these items, you need help. But the first step of getting help is knowing that you need help—and you've come to the right place.

clutter from spreading into your house. Here are some ways to vaccinate your home against entryway and mudroom clutter.

Start from scratch. We've said it once and we'll say it again: Whatever the size of your entry area, to begin decluttering it, you must first empty the entire area. "You'll be better able to get your thoughts together," says Maria Gracia, creator of GetOrganizedNow.com and author of *Finally Organized, Finally Free.*

Pick a warm, dry day and toss the contents of your entryway out onto the back step if you have to. Toss it into boxes and bags, or into the adjacent kitchen. Whatever works. But empty the area to its bare boards! You won't get rid of clutter, you won't be able to accurately assess an item's potential worth, and you won't be able to see the possibilities for reordering things unless you can truly see and feel the effect of their absence. In the decluttering process, absence does *not* in fact make the heart grow fonder. Instead, it makes you say, "Hey, look at all this space!" and you'll never want to slide back into your cluttered ways again. This is a good thing. If you need a little help getting started, review chapter 3, which is devoted solely to getting rid of what you don't need.

Give everything a home. To achieve a less cluttered entry area or mudroom, rule number one is to create a place for every entryway interloper and make sure all household members know what and where those places are. Call a family meeting if you have to! Interior design author Glenna Morton, a guide with the Web site About.com (http://interiordec.about.com), recommends that once you've designated a place for everything, you must enforce the idea that these are "no-fly zones."

A no-fly zone? Once an area is designated as such, no other clothing, supplies, or equipment are allowed to "fly" there. The top drawer of a chest might be the mitten zone, which means that socks are verboten. Likewise, a hall closet might be the kids' jacket zone and the tennis racket zone, but not the hockey equipment zone. Glenna even recommends putting up signs until all the family members get the idea.

THE LAUNCHPAD THEORY

A good way to think about your mudroom or entryway is as a launchpad. That's a spot from which items leave to be returned to their proper places.

In her online newsletter, *Get Organized Now!,* Maria Gracia recommends that every room have a designated launchpad. A decorative basket at the bedroom door, for example, is the place to dump the magazine that's on its way to the recycling bin.

This launchpad mind-set might help you reduce clutter in your mudroom or entryway by helping you to keep items moving out of the area, or at least on their way to moving out. That will give you the physical and mental energy to efficiently deal with the items that *do* belong there—coats, hats, bags, and the like.

Publicize the rules. If the clutter at your main entry or mudroom is largely created by children, make it clear where backpacks, books, and papers should go when they come in the door. This may sound obvious, but you'd be surprised how often the rules aren't clearly stated. Nobody is born knowing where to put their stuff, so repeat the message early and often.

Even a childless household will experience entryway clutter-control problems. It's easy for harried adults to fall into the habit of putting things down on the first available spot inside the door, then never quite getting those items to their proper places. This can be a primary source of marital sniping, particularly when one spouse works outside the home and one spouse is home during a large part of the day. On closer examination, it hits you that your working spouse isn't really a lazy slob. It's just that she doesn't know where exactly to put the stuff she brings home because it doesn't have a designated storage spot.

To combat the problem, housemates need to agree on where those commonly dropped items will live. It may be that one spouse assumes that such a place already exists, but it's productive to reiterate.

Tidying Tiny Entryways

Not everyone has a kitchen-size mudroom off the back entrance space or even room for a couch in the foyer. If your entryway or foyer is tiny, you'll need to have a realistic idea of its storage potential, says Betty Belnoski, proprietor of Organize 123 in Fogelsville, Pennsylvania. "The entrance to your home should make people feel pleased, calm, and in control," she says. "The foyer should be an open area that's aesthetically pleasing." If you have other storage options elsewhere in the house, store or display only a few items in your foyer, Betty says. You might also consider installing a mirror somewhere in the entryway, to open the area and make it seem less cluttered.

And if your whole home is tiny and you're fighting for every inch of storage space? Use the foyer and the front hall closet to their best advantage, Betty says. Here are some ways to maximize storage space and minimize clutter in small entryways.

Forget the throw rug. A tiny piece of floor demands a tiny rug, right? Well, in the foyer that's not such a good idea. Any rug in a high-traffic, cramped area just gathers dirt, bunches and slides, and keeps you from opening either the front door or the front closet easily. So consider moving the throw rug elsewhere. If you're a diehard decorator and can't stand the look of bare floors, consider stenciling patterns or painting a rug pattern directly on the floor. Just make sure to seal your paint job with several layers of a protective coat, such as polyurethane.

Look for lots of drawers. If space allows only one piece of furniture in the foyer, make it one with several drawers, Betty says. "That way you can store lots of smaller things, including scarves and car keys." You also won't have to

Okay, Collectors. We know you're loath to give up your knickknacks, your curios, your gewgaws, your tchotchkes, your objets d'art, your dust collectors. But here's a way to get them out of boxes and on display in a clutter-free way.

Hang shelves around the perimeter of your mudroom or entry close to the ceiling. How close depends on the size of the objects you plan to display. Arrange your antique milk pitchers or your stuffed pink flamingos on the shelves. Then, when friends stop by, you can point to your neatly arranged treasures, but they won't be in anyone's way.

Add display space with a high shelf.

worry about upsetting a stack of objects to get to one on the bottom—only one or two objects will fit in a small drawer.

Declare recess. With as little as 4 inches between the drywall and frame, you can create recessed spaces in the walls of your foyer and fit the spaces with shelves or cabinets. "They're great for books, knickknacks, and family photos," says homebuilder Richard Beaver of Knoxville, Tennessee. Creating recesses yourself requires enough handyman know-how to be able to cut Sheetrock and find studs, Richard says. You can find directions at almost any home store. If you don't feel confident of your skills, hire a handyman or carpenter to do the job for you.

Keep in mind that these recessed shelves or cabinets *do not* have to be at eye or hip level,

Betty Belnoski says. "Consider the whole wall, floor to ceiling. You can gain a lot more space if you go higher with the shelves, and lower, at floor level."

Fold the closet door. One major source of clutter in a cramped foyer is the front closet door. It always seems to be open, revealing closet clutter and interjecting itself into the already tight space. To make the space tidier, consider converting your closet door to one that folds into accordion pleats. Even when it's not properly closed, it won't be in the way.

Park it on the porch. If your tiny foyer continues to be barraged with all the stuff that comes in the house, consider installing a metal icebox (the kind fishermen use) or vintage milk box on the front porch. Widely available at thrift stores and discount department stores, these metal boxes are the perfect place to stash anything from roller blades to mittens. To make sure everyone in the family understands the new plan, use masking-tape labels that describe the intended contents of the icebox. To better your chances of success, also make a sign for the closet door or the foyer floor, describing items that can no longer "park" there. If you're feeling really creative, issue parking tickets with fines when unwanted items do land there.

Tools You'll Use

In many homes, the entryway is a dumping ground from which nothing moves unless the EPA declares the area a toxic waste dump. Broken items gather there awaiting repair; tools stand ready to be returned to toolboxes and garages; glass and newspaper due for recycling sit in a corner; overdue library books linger awaiting return; and the dog's leash sits on the floor ready for the next lap around the block.

It's human nature to let items make a temporary stop in your entryway; it's nothing to be ashamed of. But even during a short stay, good planning can contain that stuff and keep it from looking quite so, well, dumpy. The key here is containment, coupled with rules of your own devising about how long items can stay there, how often they must be cleared out, and who, exactly, is responsible for the clearing.

Here are some tools you can rely on to keep the clutter at bay.

THE JOY OF BENCHES

Interior designers say that the one essential element every mudroom or entry needs is a place for people to sit when they're removing shoes and boots. But since space is at a premium in most entryways, that bench should do double (or even triple) duty. Choose one with built-in storage or even just an open space below for stashing shoes, boots, and other miscellany. Need more ideas? Here are some tips to help you choose—or build—the perfect bench.

Try a plastic model. Some well-known companies that sell plastic storage bins and food containers—Rubbermaid is one—also sell lightweight plastic storage benches. Those benches are a relatively low-cost, low-maintenance, but attractive option for providing seating and storage in your mudroom.

Finish an unfinished bench. Many unfinished furniture stores and woodworking outlets sell several styles of storage benches. Look for "blanket boxes" designed for use in bedrooms or sturdy children's toy boxes, and use one for seating and storage in your mudroom or entry.

Personalize storage benches. One theater designer we know used his stage design skills to break the entryway clutter clog created by his two young daughters. He built each child a personalized sitting and storage bench.

The bench has pegs for hanging coats and backpacks; storage in the seat for stowing mittens, hats, and scarves; and space underneath to tuck shoes and boots. Dad applied his artistic skills to personalize the benches for each child. He claims his children take ownership of their benches and are proud to have their items properly hung and displayed there—and sibling rivalry keeps their personal items from migrating to the wrong bench!

Bring outdoor furniture indoors. Lawn and garden stores often sell a variety of outdoor storage benches designed for storing hoses and other gardening tools. These benches may work as well in your mudroom as they do in your shed; all you need to do is paint or decorate the bench to match your decor. Here are several ideas for turning outdoor benches into indoor seating and storage—we'd bet you can come up with even more.

• Hit the deck (kits). Check out deck design kits, which are available at most home improvement stores. The kits often include some kind of outdoor bench seating with underseat storage. Many of these plans can be easily adapted to fit your indoor entryway space and are relatively easy to construct.

• Dip into your own collection. If you have an extra picnic table bench in the yard or shed, bring it inside and use it in the entryway or mudroom. Paint it to match your decor, then stow baskets or plastic bins underneath for storing shoes, hats, or mittens. You may even be able to add an open drying shelf (see "Turn your bench into a dryer," below) between the legs to create a mitten drying area.

The next two ideas work for garden benches or benches designed to be used indoors.

• Turn your bench into a dryer. If you already have a bench that isn't working quite as hard as you'd like, add some open cross shelves under the seat. Then, when winter rolls around, you can place the bench over the heating vent in your mudroom or entry and use the shelves as a drying rack for damp hats and mittens.

• Consider a bench with a drawer. One clever bench style, based on a Shaker design, features a pull-out drawer in its base. This bench does triple duty, providing seating, open storage right under the seat, and closed storage in the drawer. Such a bench would be ideal in a mudroom: Bags and books can be stowed in the middle open area, and shoes or boots can go in the closed area.

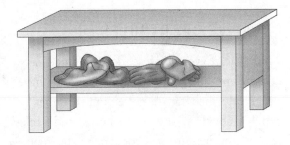

By adding a shelf under your hall bench, you can create a discreet drying rack for wet socks and mittens.

Opt for Bucket Seats

NEED EXTRA KID-SIZE SEATING? How about extra kid-size storage? With just a 5-gallon bucket and some other inexpensive materials, you can make both. It's a storage bucket seat. Inside go your child's hats, mittens, small toys, or other personal items. The cushion on top gives kids a place to park their backsides while they take off their shoes and boots.

You'll need a 5-gallon bucket, round or square—the kind that paint, spackle, or bulk laundry detergent often comes in. Bakeries and food co-ops sometimes give them away, but you can buy them at home improvement centers or hardware stores. A plain bucket with no writing is ideal, though you can remove any existing labels or try covering them with your own designs using a sturdy high-gloss or semigloss paint to match your color scheme.

First, sew a cushion or purchase one that fits the shape and size of the bucket lid. You may find cushions on sale at summer's end in the outdoor furniture departments at discount stores. Attach the cushion to the lid with Velcro, then let your child decorate his or her bucket with markers or stickers to give it a personal touch.

Store this bucket seat under shelves, a table, or Peg-Board in your entry or mudroom to keep it out of the way when not in use. The handle makes it portable, and that means this storage seat will work in other child-cluttered areas of the house, as well.

A 5-gallon bucket makes a great kid's seat and storage bin.

CREATIVE CUBBYHOLES

Think back to your high school or college days. Did the entrance to the library or cafeteria have cubbyhole shelving—a collection of cubes in which students stashed their books and backpacks? This institutional concept has been embraced by contemporary experts in home interior design and can be an excellent tool for making your mudroom or entry efficiently, yet beautifully, uncluttered. Cubbyholes are ideally suited to storing hats, mittens, children's toys, pet supplies, gym bags, sports equipment, and other mudroom clutter culprits. You can buy ready-made cubbyholes from home stores such as IKEA, or you can make your own. Here are some cubbyhole hints to get you started.

Style your cubbyholes. In top-of-the-line cubbyhole design, each family member

With minimal carpentry skills and basic tools, you can build a mudroom storage and sitting bench. The instructions below are for a 16-inch-high, 4-foot-long storage bench, which you can construct from one 4- by 8-foot piece of ½-inch plywood, with no leftover wood.

What you'll need:

One 4-foot by 8-foot sheet ½-inch plywood, cut as directed below

Paint or stain to match your decor

One good-quality paintbrush

One box 1½-inch drywall screws

Power screwdriver

Upholstery foam, batting, and fabric, enough of *each* to cover an area at least 16 inches wide and 4 feet long. Choose a thick, durable, easy-to-clean fabric. Foam and batting are available in fabric stores and sewing centers.

Staple gun and staples

Spray-on fabric protector (optional)

Three baskets of any design, each no larger than 16 inches square

1. Cut the plywood into six 16- by 48-inch strips.
2. Cut five of the six strips into three 16- by 16-inch squares, 15 squares in all. Do not cut the sixth 16-inch by 48-inch plywood strip. That's the seat for your bench.
3. Sand the plywood to give it a smooth finish if desired. (Some plywood comes with a prefinished side that won't need sanding.) Paint or stain the plywood pieces to match your entry or mudroom decor.
4. Use the drywall screws and screwdriver to construct three cubes from the 15 plywood squares. Each cube will have one open side.

Step 4: Bench cube

5. Make sure that the paint or stain on the bench seat is dry, and then sand any sharp or pointed edges. Place a layer of foam, and then a layer of batting on the bench seat.
6. Center the fabric over the bench seat and pull it almost taut on every side. Attach the fabric to the underside of the board with the staple gun. If desired, treat the fabric with fabric protector.
7. Place the three boxes side by side, with the open ends facing forward. Attach the bench seat to the boxes with drywall screws. Make sure the screws are evenly spaced and that the seat is attached to each box in at least two places.

Place this bench in your mudroom or entry and place one basket in each cubbyhole.

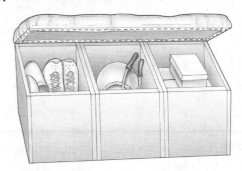

You can also turn the open end of the boxes upward, use your cushioned seat to cover the openings, and add hinges.

CLUTTER CRUSADERS

The Original Clutter Cutters

THE TRULY CLUTTERED in our contemporary culture could learn a thing or two from the Shakers, an American religious sect born in 1747 but now nearly extinct. The Shakers constructed beautiful, simple furniture and decorative pieces that have inspired styles to the present day *and* hold ingenious answers to modern clutter control problems.

For their designs, the Shakers drew inspiration from two beliefs: To do a thing well was an act of prayer, and every item should be designed based on its ultimate function. Look through any book of Shaker furniture or walk through a Shaker museum, and you'll probably find a functional piece that would work beautifully in your own entry or mudroom. Penney Martellaro of Dovetail Designs, a Missouri crafter of Shaker furniture, isn't surprised. She knows that Shaker pieces are perfect for mudrooms or entryways. "It's a style that fits with contemporary, country, antique—anything," says Penney, whose furniture is exclusively featured at a store called Simply Elegant in Golden, Colorado. Her choice for a mudroom? A pine cupboard. "There's a lot of space inside where you can store things."

The Shakers loved benches, too, and their hutches and chests always featured cleverly designed and well-placed drawers. One design especially well-suited for a mudroom is a bench that holds boots and shoes in their own compartments. Beneath those compartments is a hidden tray where dirt and mud can fall. The tray can then be pulled out to empty it.

gets his or her own cube. The cubbyhole is fitted with a perfectly sized decorative basket to contain personal belongings while keeping them out of sight. If you like a unified look, choose identical baskets for each cube. If you prefer something more creative, use a hodgepodge of baskets and other containers. Since family members will need to be able to identify and remember which basket belongs to whom, there might be additional merit in choosing a bunch of different baskets.

Turn shelves into cubbyholes. There's no law that says cubbyholes must be perfectly square. Think of a bookcase as a set of rectangular cubbyholes. Place the bookcase near your entry or mudroom door and designate each shelf a cubbyhole. Label the shelves with the names of family members and require that personal belongings be placed only in the properly labeled cubby.

Use baskets and bins. If you don't have (or don't want to use) a bookcase as a set of cubbyholes, hang shelves on the wall with decorative brackets, then place baskets on the shelves. Designate the baskets either by type of item (shoes, toys, pet supplies) or by a household member's name. In lieu of baskets, you could use plastic storage boxes, milk crates, sturdy laundry baskets, or even sturdy cardboard filing boxes in the same way—as long as whatever you choose has handles for convenient retrieval.

Add Fencing, Add Storage

PICKET FENCES aren't just for front lawns anymore. They can migrate to your mudroom and help you get clutter off the floor.

Attach a premade section of white picket fence to a wall in your mudroom. Install it as you would wainscoting, up to about 36 inches. Next, pick up a collection of inexpensive, colorful plastic buckets, the kind toddlers use at the beach. Hang the buckets from the pickets by the handles, or use craft wire, depending upon the weight of the items you wish to stash in them.

Fencing makes a clever storage display.

GET HOOKED UP

Unless your entry or mudroom has a big walk-in closet, you'd probably benefit from hanging good-quality, sturdy hooks on the wall for coats and other items. If you have children, place some of the hooks low enough, about 36 inches high, so that the little ones can reach them. If there's enough room, hang two sets of hooks on separate walls, one for adults and one for children; if not, hang the hooks in two rows, but make sure that a couple of the child-height hooks are lower than the others to accommodate long adult coats.

Even with a well-designed coat-hanging area, vigilance is required. Don't let one hook become overburdened with two or three out-of-season or outgrown coats, for example. Anything not worn daily should be stored elsewhere in your home. And there are items that should not be hung on pegs or hooks. According to Glenna Morton, your best coats should be hung conventionally. "But if your coat closet is brimming," she says, "try categorizing your outerwear into formal and casual, then stow more formal items, such as your good wool coats, nice raincoats, and the like, on hangers," she says.

So without further ado, here are more ways to make the very best use of hooks and pegs in your home.

Hang it all—on pegs. The Shakers may not have invented the idea of hanging items on

Ski Your Way to More Storage

HERE'S A VARIATION on the old hook-on-the-wall theme that'll add a little interest to your mudroom. Check your attic or a flea market or antiques dealer for an old wooden ski. Mount coat hooks on the ski at 6- to 10-inch intervals (if you place the hooks too close together, the wood might split), then mount the ski on the wall. This idea might not work so well in a formal foyer, but the ski will look terrific in a rustic mudroom.

pegs, but they are nonetheless renowned for their ingenious use of pegs all around their simple and elegant dwellings and meeting-houses. (See "Clutter Crusaders," page 204.) The Shakers hung everything from drying flowers and herbs to dining room chairs to household tools such as brooms and mops on the pegs. Of course, you don't need to be a Shaker to take advantage of pegs. Here are three arrangements to try.

• Combine your pegs with a shelf. Here's a Peg-Board design that you can adapt for a mud-room or entry. Buy a ready-made setup or just put the pieces together yourself. First, hang a long shelf on the wall, then hang a row of pegs on the wall underneath the shelf. This arrangement provides a surprising amount of storage space: Hang coats, jackets, and bags on the hooks; on the shelf store decorative items or small baskets into which hats and mittens can be tossed.

• Go for the cupboard option. Another shelf-and-peg design features pegs hung on the wall under a long, narrow cupboard. The cupboard adds even more storage space than the shelf does and can hide and contain small items that might look like clutter on top of the shelf. The top of the cupboard can be used as a display shelf or storage for more decorative items.

• Add space for umbrellas. Yet another variation on the Shaker shelf-and-peg idea combines pegs for hats and coats with slots for holding umbrellas, sports equipment such as baseball bats, or utility items such as brooms and mops. This is a good option if your entry or mudroom must also serve as a utility closet.

• Enlist old clothespins. Attach sturdy clothespins (the old-fashioned wooden, spring-

A Shaker-style peg shelf can replace a hall closet or coat rack.

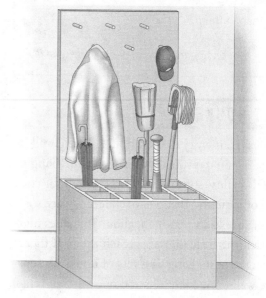

Why settle for an umbrella stand when you can create a multipurpose storage setup like this?

A Marriage of Form and Function

AN INGENIOUS ARTIST we know mounted a ceramic soap dish to the wall in his entryway. But it's no run-of-the-mill soap dish. This one is shaped like a hand, its palm turned upward and the fingers slightly spread. When our friend walks in the door, he tosses his keys into the palm and hangs his sunglasses from one of the fingers. If the hand idea is a little too out-there for your decor, keep in mind that there are all sorts of wall-mounted decorative soap dishes, metal and ceramic, that won't look at all out of place in your entry or mudroom.

loaded kind) to the wall with finishing nails at a child's height. Use these new clips to clip hats, mittens, or other small items and keep them out of the way.

• Plant a hall tree. A hall tree—a mirror surrounded by heavy-duty pegs designed to hold hats and coats—is an excellent clutter-cutting choice for a formal entryway.

• Bag it. You may be able to get more storage help from the pegs or hooks in your mudroom by hanging a bag from each in which you store small items. For instance, hang a pretty beach bag from one hook and fill it with lightweight beach toys and picnic items, or hang a gym bag to hold workout clothes and supplies, like free weights, sweat bands, and a jump rope.

• Rack up storage space. If wall space is limited in your entry area but you have ample floor space, an old-fashioned, freestanding coat rack might be the best option for corralling heavy coats and jackets. We say *might*, because the coat rack can put you on a slippery slope. In fact, some experts recommend against them for many folks. "Coat trees can seem like a good idea, but they can become top-heavy with piles of coats, which only adds to a cluttered look," says Glenna Morton. But we hate to dismiss racks altogether because there are ways around the problem. One is to reserve the rack for guest coats only.

Stand in the middle of your mudroom and slowly turn around. Is every inch of wall space being efficiently used? How about those corners?

Corners are one of the most underused elements in the mudroom—or any room for that matter. But that doesn't have to be the case. These days you'll find corner shelving and corner cupboards in all shapes, sizes, designs, and materials: Get a teeny-tiny one to display a single knickknack or houseplant or a small bowl for keys. Or choose a large corner cupboard, where you can stash books, tools, even boots. Choose a floor-to-ceiling model or a waist-high design. Select wood or glass or plastic. The storage possibilities are nearly endless!

MISCELLANEOUS TIPS AND TOOLS

Here's a collection of mudroom and entry tips that don't quite fit in any one category—but are too good to leave out!

Design your own. You don't need to spend big bucks to customize your mudroom or entry storage system. Look into tools for designing your own closet, available at most hardware and home improvement stores or from an online outlet. (Search on the keywords Closet, Storage, System.) Though usually designed for enclosed spaces, the pieces can be adapted easily to fit your space and give it a custom look, especially if you think of your mudroom or entry as one big closet.

Arm yourself with an armoire. To add shelves *and* hide the contents you store on them, take the advice of Glenna Morton and get yourself an armoire.

"Closed storage areas are essential for keeping an entryway clutter-free," Glenna says. "An armoire can hold a ton of stuff. And it doesn't have to be fancy; just fit the inside with lots of shelves and perhaps a few hooks."

In small spaces, use the door. If the door to your mudroom is just hanging there and not helping you fight clutter, put it to work. Hang a shoe bag on the door and label the pockets with each family member's name. Use the pockets to store pesky small items such as mittens, workout water bottles, library cards, ice

OUT-OF-THE-BOX IDEAS

Use Strong Medicine for Storage

WHEN IT COMES to cutting clutter in the mudroom, you need to consider all storage systems. One clever mom we heard about mounted a medicine cabinet in her mudroom. Don't worry—it's decorative, so it doesn't look out of place. Family members check their look in the mirror on their way out the door and store small items such as sunglasses inside. You can take the idea one step further by placing screw hooks in the cabinet bottom and hanging your keys from them.

scrapers, and change purses with milk or toll money inside.

Hide stuff with a homemade hammock. Here's a simple, clutter-cutting craft project. It's a small fabric storage hammock that hangs on the door. You can get all of the supplies at a hardware store. You'll need a dowel that's a little less wide than your door, two dish or hand towels, two over-the-door hooks, and some light-gauge picture wire.

Sew the two long sides of the dish towels together to make a tube. Turn the tube inside out (to hide the seams) and slip it onto the dowel. Place the hooks on the door as far apart as the dowel is long. Cut two pieces of picture wire and attach both ends of the dowel to the hooks. This homemade hammock is terrific for storing lightweight seasonal items such as hats, mittens, and beach towels.

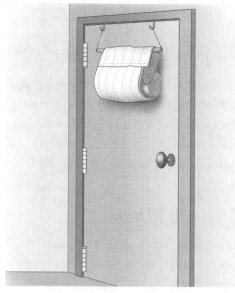

Dish towels make great hanging storage space.

Add a table for contents. If you have the space, a small table can be a terrific addition to your entry or mudroom. Place a decorative basket or bowl on top to catch small items—keys, loose change, stamps, and the like. You can even designate the table as the temporary landing strip for incoming mail. (See "The Launchpad Theory," page 197.) As always, though, you must be vigilant to make sure the mail gets sorted in a timely manner, then moved to the home office or other bill-paying or paperwork area.

Here are some other ways to choose an entry or mudroom table and to make it work harder for you. (For helpful advice about controlling mail and other paper clutter, see chapter 16.)

• Stash stuff out of sight. Any table is terrific for storing items out of the way, but one with a shelf beneath is even better.

• Sofa, so good. A sofa table, because it's long and narrow, can fit in even a small or narrow entry or mudroom and provides storage on top and beneath. Some have a shelf where you can add decorative storage baskets or bins and/or a small drawer perfect for things like car keys, stamps, or take-out menus.

• Add a tablecloth. You can organize your less-attractive items out of sight (and turn a not-too-pretty table into a lovely one) by adding a tablecloth to your mudroom or entry table.

• It's a shelf! It's a table! If you don't have (or don't want) a table in your entry or mudroom, attach a narrow shelf at table height with brackets along the perimeter of the entry or mudroom. The shelf serves the same purpose as an entryway table, but adds a distinctive design element and provides the same opportunity for

PAINT YOUR WAY TO A BIGGER MUDROOM

Sometimes it's the little things that can make the most difference. Are your mudroom walls a dark or dingy color? Is the wallpaper busy? Either can make any room feel more cramped and cluttered. Paint the area a pale, neutral color, and you'll increase the sense of space. And the fresh paint job will look so great it may inspire you to keep the rest of the room neat and orderly.

stowing stuff underneath and out of the way. To save space, consider installing a shelf you can fold up against the wall and hook into place when it's not in use—similar to a wall-mount ironing board.

Take a tip from the kitchen. If the stuff you have to store would overwhelm a simple table and you have the space, consider installing kitchen cabinets and a countertop in your mudroom. You'll give yourself a durable work surface and tons of storage. You can even stash overflow kitchen tools there!

Can the cabinets, keep the counter. If cabinets seem like too much, consider installing just a countertop supported by sturdy shelf brackets or fireplace mantel supports on one wall or around the room's perimeter. Store items on top and underneath.

Storage is looking up. If you're lucky enough to have a house with post and beam construction, look up. See those beams? Why not hang baskets with handles from them to hold small items that you'd like to keep out of sight?

Keep wet umbrellas contained. If you're tired of family members trailing wet umbrellas from the front door through the living room and to the hall closet, take a tip from Maria Gracia. She recommends placing a container for the umbrellas in the entryway or mudroom. "It could be a small wastepaper basket, or even a small pail," she says. But the container should have a weight in the bottom so it doesn't tip—even a brick would do.

Stowing Specific Stuff

Implementing the tools and tips we've suggested is an excellent first step toward gaining control of entryway clutter. Next, pay attention to those pesky little items that can easily multiply and thwart your valiant efforts at clutter control.

MITTENS AND GLOVES

It's quite possible that the only way to truly control wayward mittens and gloves in your entry, especially if there are children in the house, is

---

THE OPULENT MUDROOM

If your goal is a truly elaborate mudroom, interior designers recommend that you install a janitor's sink for taking care of tasks such as washing the dog, rinsing pet dishes, and cleaning gardening tools. A janitor's sink is lower than a kitchen or bath sink and can even be installed at floor level if shampooing the family pet is its primary purpose. The sink can also come in handy during large gatherings at your home, filling in as a huge ice bucket or a place to stack accumulated dirty dishes. Some contemporary upscale mudroom designs include two sinks—a janitor's sink and a regular sink designed for gardening and laundry uses.

CLUTTER CRUSADERS

Don't Forget the Shoe Rack!

Maria Gracia is a professional organizer. She knows a thing or two about organizing, and her mudroom would never be without a shoe rack. "You can put it on top of an absorbent mat right by the door," she says. That'll make clear where everybody's shoes should go when they enter the house—and you'll never hear "Where are my blue shoes?" again.

For storing shoes, anyway, Maria doesn't care for plastic shoe bags, the kind that hang over a door. "They tend to become messy with street dirt," she says. "My favorite is the bookshelf type, the kind with two tilted shelves. You can stack them and, if there's room, each family member can have his own."

to move closer to the equator. Barring that, the suggestions below may help.

Bring hangers out of the closet. When winter rolls around, try this temporary clutter-cutting solution to double, triple, even quadruple your storage space: Hang a skirt hanger, the kind with several rows of clips, from a hook on the wall and hang hats, mittens, and gloves from the clips.

Get loopy. Sew a loop onto your child's mittens that is just big enough to fit around the buttons on her winter coat. Use the loop to attach the mittens to the coat while it hangs in your entry. Not only does this idea keep mittens from cluttering the room, it helps your child keep track of where they are!

Plant a tree. Another old-fashioned item that combats mitten and glove clutter in entryways is a mitten tree, a freestanding rack with a series of angled pegs that each hold one mitten. These are fun for kids to use and excellent for allowing maximum drying of soggy mittens.

An old-fashioned mitten tree keeps gloves and mittens dry and together.

PET SUPPLIES

It's not for nothing that a bunch of cats is known as a *clutter* of cats. But felines aren't the only clutter culprits. Like kids, cats and dogs seem to spontaneously generate it. With their toys, food dishes, flea sprays, collars, and chew bones, you can probably find pet stuff underfoot everywhere, perhaps especially in the mudroom or entry area to your home. Here's how to manage.

Make space for bins. If your mudroom is home to sacks of dog food or bags of cat-box litter, do yourself a favor and invest in a plastic pet food storage bin. The bins, which come in 50- and 100-pound sizes, are lockable and stackable, and they keep rodents out. You'll find these bins at larger pet supply stores—Blitz is one popular brand name. To find an online dealer, search the Internet using the keywords Stackable, Pet, Food, and Storage.

Get them off the floor. Sometimes just getting those bags of dog or cat food or cat-box litter off the floor in your mudroom is all it takes to clear some clutter. Many stores sell plastic wall-mounted bins that store and dispense dry food or litter. One model, the Stack-N-Store, made by Blitz, can hold 40 pounds of chow.

Roll out the barrel. If you have the floor space, invest in a dual-function dog or cat feeder. Several models are available; the largest looks like a medium-size plastic trash can. It serves as a storage bin for Fido or Fluffy's food, but it also doles out the correct portion of food for him every day. You'll find the feeders on many pet-related Web sites and in larger pet supply stores.

Bring in the garbage (can). If all else fails, a clean, lidded garbage can makes a fine container for storing pet food in your entry. If your pet is fed at specific times of day, store her empty dishes inside the same container, on top of the food. The dishes will be just where you need them for the next feeding time.

Stairways

Stairways are the source of many clutter problems—and solutions. Here's how to minimize the former and maximize the latter.

Add a shelf. The walls along a stairway that leads to a basement are among the most over-

OUT-OF-THE-BOX IDEAS

From Bakery, to Mudroom

KEEPING TRACK OF PET SUPPLIES—leashes, toys, food, carriers, and the like—can turn into a clutter nightmare. But there is a solution that may work for you: a baker's rack. It's an open shelf unit, usually made of metal or wood. They're designed for kitchens, but are useful in the mudroom, too. Stow bins of pet food on the lowest shelf, hang leashes from one of the supports, and organize grooming supplies and toys on the other shelves.

A baker's rack creates storage space that's as decorative as it is useful.

looked storage spaces out there. Consider whether you could hang a shelf from the ceiling or wall just inside the stairway door and within arm's reach of one of the stairs. A shallow shelf there is an ideal place to store a few cellar or utility-type items you keep in quantity elsewhere—a few basic cleaning supplies, lightbulbs, extension cords, and maybe a second set of small hand tools such as a hammer and screwdriver. The idea here is to have things handy, saving yourself a trip or two down into the cellar or out to the garage to look for these items when you need them most.

If you don't have room for shelves, consider lining each side of the cellar stairwell walls with hooks, then hang long-handled items such as a broom, wet mop, or dust mop there. Again, the idea is to have these tools handy where you need them most but off the floor and out of the way. If your cellar door is just off the kitchen, those stairwell walls could be an ideal place for your kitchen-cleaning tools (or for a second set of them if your kitchen is farther away). If you're tight on space in the kitchen and the cellar's nearby, consider hanging skillets from the walls along the cellar stairway.

Create a closet under the stairs. Why not use all that space below your cellar stairs to store seasonal items or things you use only occasionally? Make a closet under an open stairway by hanging shelves with brackets directly on the wall or buy a premade shelf unit that fits the space. Enclose the shelf area with a simple door, perhaps just a piece of plywood cut

confessions of . . .
a Not-So-Dumbwaiter

"IF I STILL HAD all the money I've paid in overdue library fines, I'd be a rich man," says Tom Cavalieri of New York City. "In fact, I'm pretty sure that my fines are supporting New York's public library system. It's not that I don't live near my local branch—quite the contrary. I pass it three or four times a week. The problem is that once I've read a book, tiny elves emerge from the woodwork and bury it under a stack of paper, under the bed, or in a stack of other books.

"When I finally got sick and tired of losing track of my library books and paying the late fees for them, I decided that all our books should live in the front hall. That way, I'd always see them on my way out. On one of the walls in my entryway is a door that leads nowhere—it used to be a dumbwaiter, but that's long gone. Now there's just an empty space behind the door. I removed the door, built a small bookcase, and fit it into the space. It's only a couple of shelves, but it's made all the difference. Not only do I keep my library books there, but I also toss my keys, sunglasses, and wallet there when I come in the door."

to fit and hinged. A set of old bookcases in graduated sizes can also be put to work, storing items under the stairs and out of sight. For easiest access, turn the bookcases into roll-out carts by attaching wheels to the bottoms, then set the shelves perpendicular to the wall just underneath the stairs.

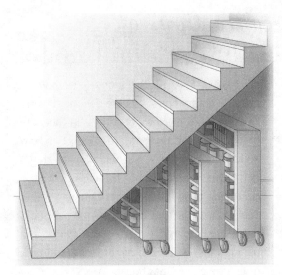

Put that unused under-stair space to work with rolling bookcases.

Seize a stair basket. The stairs in the more public areas of your home—those that lead to your upstairs bedrooms or second-floor living areas—can easily accumulate clutter, but there are some design tricks you can take advantage of to disguise clutter and add more space.

The Shakers, who were unlikely to accumulate much clutter (see "Clutter Crusaders," page 204), invented the ingenious stair basket, an important tool for any two-level home today. A Shaker stair basket fits on one of the stair treads and looks like a beautiful decorative basket. In reality, it awaits all those pesky items that are trying to make it up or down the stairs and back to their rightful place—a pair of dirty socks, a magazine for recycling, small toys, somebody's school notebook.

Toss these items into the stair basket, then make a household rule that nobody goes up the stairs without taking (and emptying) the basket. That may be harsh, but household guidelines are required here.

However, if you have only one basket and keep it at the top or bottom of the stairs, you risk having it in the wrong place at the wrong time. Perhaps your home will need two stair baskets to solve this dilemma. Of course, any basket with handles that is small enough to fit nicely on your stairs without falling off will suffice in lieu of the Shaker basket. So no one trips, make sure that the baskets are clearly visible to people climbing or descending the stairs, and that they don't take up so much space that it's hard to walk safely on the steps.

A Shaker stair basket will help you get your stuff where it belongs.

CHAPTER

Home Office

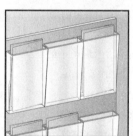

The business of running even a one-person household can become overwhelming if you don't prepare for the paperwork that leaks in through the mail slot and waltzes through the front door each day. Setting up a small home office, even if it's just one corner of the kitchen where you pay bills, can help you shovel out before the papers become piles.

As more and more people telecommute or start small home businesses, controlling clutter can become a lost cause when files and piles mount. And by the time the bank ledgers have merged with the bills and marketing data and the kids' report cards, productivity has ground to a halt. That can make you feel like a failure, says professional organizer Lynne Silvers of Finally (!) Organized in West Roxbury, Massachusetts.

"People are ashamed of the fact that they aren't more organized in their home offices. It's not a character flaw—it's a skill that you can learn."

Nancy Black of Organization Plus in Beverly, Massachusetts, has been helping people organize their work spaces for 18 years. She says that the first thing to remember is that a perfectly neat work area is not the goal. "Most of the time, clean desks exist only in magazine photos," she says. "The goal is to be able to find information as soon as you need it and to put things away before they distract you."

Setting Up a Clutter-Free Home Office

The first step toward organizing those scattered bills and stray files peeking out from under the sofa is to figure out why your work has spread into every room of the house. "If you're constantly bringing work into the kitchen, it's probably because your office isn't set up right," says professional organizer Barbara Clement of OrganizationWorks in Wellesley, Massachusetts. It may be too dark. It may have no phone, or you may have a cheap filing cabinet that doesn't work properly. Or maybe you're paying the bills in front of the TV each month because you don't have a work space at all. Choose the right space with the right furniture and organizational supplies, Barbara says, and you're halfway there. Here are some ways to do just that.

CHOOSING THE PERFECT SPOT

Just because you don't have a spare bedroom waiting to be converted into a sparkling new office doesn't mean you're out of luck. Far from it. You can still devote a spot in your house to paperwork or running a business. All it takes is a little creativity. Here's how.

Be a closet organizer. If you're lucky enough to have a spare closet at home, you may have a spare office. You'll probably need to clean it out, install a shelf at what would be desk height, and boost the overhead lighting. But there's probably room to add a filing cabinet or an overhead shelf to stack books or reference materials. And there's a bonus: At the end of your work sessions you can close the door, hiding the whole shebang, and no one will be the wiser.

Adopt an alcove. Anne Braudy runs her own home business. She's a professional organizer and owner of Before & After in Brookline, Massachusetts, but she hasn't dedicated a room in her house to the business. Instead, she works in a kitchen alcove. "I share counter space with the toaster oven," she confesses. Anne wanted to work near her kids, and that meant setting up shop in the heart of the home. She keeps the computer there and uses an electronic personal organizer for her to-do list, which keeps paper at a minimum. Because she has no room for a filing cabinet, she uses cardboard filing boxes that she can tuck away in a closet at the end of the business day. "They hold my current files, so I can see them all the time and they don't pile up on my tiny desk space," she says.

Cart your files around. If there really is no other space except the dining room table on which to do your work, that's okay, too. Simply invest in a rolling file cart, available at any office supply store and many home stores. Choose one with space for hanging files and a drawer at the very bottom where you can store office supplies and a checkbook. Simply roll it out of its hiding place (a closet or laundry room), then roll it back at the end of your workday. This won't be the setup for a burgeoning Fortune 500 company, but it will keep an ordinary household running smoothly.

confessions of . . . a Tosser

LAST YEAR, WRITER DEXTER VAN ZILE moved into a new house in Brighton, Massachusetts. The only trouble was that his new office space was about half the size of his old space. "It really pushed my Tossing buttons," he says. He doesn't usually have trouble with this except that several of his editors stipulate in his contract that he has to hang on to his notes, research, and rough drafts for certain stories for up to 12 months after they have been published. "They never look at it, but they want me to keep it," Dexter says. His solution was simple. He bought three or four file box containers. At the end of each project he dumps the related files into the boxes, marks the date when they can be thrown out, and stores them in a nearby closet. When that date rolls around, the boxes go out the door.

ADDING FURNITURE

Every month seductive catalogs arrive in the mail, their glossy pages full of streamlined computer desks, spiffy barrister bookcases, and matching desk accessories. Of course, you know better than to spend thousands of dollars on a new mahogany desk. But the question remains: What does the home office truly need to stay organized?

Lose a door, gain a desk. Dexter Van Zile of Brighton, Massachusetts, knew that he couldn't afford a new desk when he began his writing business 3 years ago. He also knew that he'd need as much file-drawer space as possible. Dexter's solution was to purchase a couple of filing cabinets and a single hollow-core door from a home improvement center. He set the two cabinets a few feet from each other and put the door on top, making a serviceable desk for a fraction of what a new one would cost. "The only trouble was that one file cabinet was about 4 inches taller than the other," Dexter says. His answer was to stack phone books on the smaller of the two to even them out. "It works fine for my purposes, and it didn't cost much," he says.

Don't cheap out on your chair. If you're going to spend more than $100 on any piece of office furniture, which should it be? The chair, of course, says Barbara Clement. "It's the only item in your office that really matters. A good

chair can be adjusted for height and angle to keep you ergonomically correct," she says. "That way, you won't tire quickly and you won't have to worry about your feet and back."

Filing cabinets? Buy the best. It's tempting to pick up one of those cute half-size filing cabinets from a discount store. After all, the price is right and so is the size. But that flimsy cabinet might not hold up to even a few months' use. Paper is surprisingly heavy, and you'll probably find that the drawers of cheap cabinets won't open when they're full. Or worse, the cabinet will fall apart completely and you'll have to replace it. So buy good-quality, sturdy metal cabinets, and they'll last for years. If you can't afford a brand new filing cabinet, check your area for stores that sell new and used office equipment. Even thrift stores sometimes carry them. If all else fails, it's okay to use the sturdy cardboard filing boxes available at moving and storage companies and at most office supply stores. Even cardboard will hold up better than flimsy discount metal.

Think laterally. You've decided to spend the extra money on sturdy filing cabinets, but now you have another choice to make. Traditional or lateral files? Nancy Black uses only lateral files in her office. They're the kind whose drawers store files side to side rather than front to back. "I like them better because you don't lose space at the back," she says. "They also look better than traditional cabinets because they're shaped like a bookcase and don't stick out so far from the wall."

Perhaps the best reason to go lateral is that these files offer more vertical space on top. You can use this space as an additional shelf for frequently used books, keeping them close at hand and up off the floor.

ORGANIZING YOUR DESKTOP

When you first set up your desk it seemed huge. Then you added your computer, the phone, the Post-its, the organizer for your mail supplies, the stapler, the Rolodex, the tape dispenser, the pencil cup, and the paper clip holder. Oh, and your World's Greatest Mom mug. Now there's hardly any space left, and even when your desk is clear it's too small. How did this happen? Relax. There's no need to buy a bigger desk— just read our tips for freeing up a little desktop real estate.

Extend your work space. Old end tables can come in handy when you're trying to free

---

HELP! I CAN'T FIND MY DESK!

Spend a lazy afternoon sipping tea instead of organizing your office? Not you, not with three deadlines looming, a doctor's appointment to get to, and a phone bill that went AWOL 2 weeks ago. You need to dig out—fast. Here's how. Grab four manila folders. These will be what professional organizers call action files. Label them as follows.

1. To Do. Here's where you put the catalog orders you need to check on, the invitation to which you need to respond, the budget you're preparing that's due today, and that phone bill (when it surfaces). All that stuff will now be in one place, easy to find when you need it. But don't let this file become a place to hide tasks that need to be done. As each item goes into the folder, write down the task on your to-do list. Add the deadline, too, so that you know when it has to be done.

2. To File. Here's where you put tax-related receipts, memo drafts, and old correspondence that's sitting on your desk collecting dust. This is stuff you haven't filed because you can't get motivated to put it away. So as you place items in this file, get out your calendar and make an appointment with yourself to file them so they will never bother you again.

3. Pending. This is the file for everything you've acted on but are still waiting to hear about. This is where you put a copy of the budget after you've sent it but before the client has approved it. Or the confirmation number of your airline tickets after you've purchased them but before they arrive.

4. To Read. This is where you put all those articles and newsletters and personal correspondence that you don't have time for right now. They'll come in handy while you're waiting in line at the DMV or the doctor's office, though. This file will collect your reading material and be ready for you when downtime strikes.

---

up desk space. Tuck one at the end of your desk and use it for your fax machine, printer, or any other toy that you don't want cluttering up your desktop. You could go one better and use a filing cabinet to extend your desktop and increase your storage space.

Borrow a card table. If your work area is one of those little computer desks or a small writing desk that originally came with a bedroom set, then your work space really is too small. No matter what your business or home office needs, a computer user needs space on either side of the keyboard to lay out papers and do some writing. And small writing desks won't accommodate files and piles both. Solve the problem by borrowing a card table from the basement and setting it up next to your current working desk in an L shape. Expand the space slowly and see how your energy for work increases, too, when you can see it.

Change your angle. A small writing desk or old typing table can free up work space if you use it as a stand for your computer monitor and keyboard. Many people put those items on their desktops, where they just waste prime writing space; then they have to scoot to one end to do anything other than type. "Wrap the work space around you in a kind of L shape, with the computer to one side," Lynne Silvers says. Then, when you don't need to type, you can turn your chair slightly and spread out those files or make a phone call.

Make the most efficient use of your office space with an L-shaped arrangement.

Shelve small items. Lynne also advocates moving staplers, tape dispensers, Wite-Out, and other small items off the desktop. You use them only once a week (if that), so don't give them pride of place on your desktop. Try this instead. "Hang a narrow shelf above or next to your desk," Lynne says. "It should not be wide enough to hold books, or you'll be tempted to stack some there." Ideally, it should be the width of an ordinary knickknack shelf, no more than 5 to 5¼ inches. That's the perfect size for holding a stapler, a tape dispenser, a pencil cup, even pictures of loved ones. They'll always be in easy reach, but they won't take up space you need to do your work.

Banish non-work items. Photographs of your beloved cat Fufu do belong in your office. The question is whether they belong on your desk. Framed photos, signed baseballs, and lucky charms take up valuable space, and the truth is that they'll look just as nice decorating

Into the Kitchen

THAT TOP DRAWER in your desk has become a collector of junk, when it could help you get things off the top of your desk, says Nancy Black. Her advice is to head into the kitchen (or to the local home center or kitchen supply store) and get yourself a couple of drawer dividers. The ones used for organizing silverware are ideal for holding the little items destined to collect dust on your desktop or hide forever in drawers: binder clips, paper clips, pencils, rubber bands, thumbtacks, and the like.

Box yourself in. Keeping desk drawers neat is a challenge for many of us. It's easy to just sweep anything and everything off the desktop into the drawers, where it becomes a tangle of unusable stuff. There is a better way. Craft stores sell small boxes made of pressed cardboard. They come in all shapes and sizes and are terrific for organizing desk drawers. Remove the lids, paint the boxes any color you want (or leave them bare), and use them to hold pushpins, scrap paper, or anything else that collects in your drawers. "The idea is not to have a perfectly neat drawer," Nancy Black says, "but to be able to see what's there when you need it." It'll also keep you from accidentally pricking your finger on a loose pushpin while digging for a paper clip.

the bookshelf across the room. Reserve your desk space for work and it will always look and feel less cluttered.

Add height to increase work space. Can't expand the horizontal surface on your desk? Think about expanding vertically—with a hutch. Some are as simple as a single shelf, others include cabinets and multiple shelves. Others have doors so that you can close them up and make the whole office space look neat. Most are available in home improvement centers and office supply catalogs or stores. Any kind of hutch will help you get items such as computer monitors, mailing supplies, and file folders off your real work space, while still keeping them in easy reach.

Digging Out Your Office

You know that the first step toward getting organized is throwing away most of what's cluttering up your desk and file drawers. The question is, where to begin? Fifi Ball and Sally Brickell, co-owners of Squared Away in Newton, Massachusetts, have thrown away more paper than they care to remember. Their advice is simple: Just start. It doesn't matter where. "You can begin in one corner or with the scariest pile or just spin around and plop your finger down," Fifi says. After you've picked a pile, the important thing is to focus on working systematically. Your second focus should be on throwing things away. Need help getting started? That's why we're here!

Take baby steps. The thing to remember about throwing things away, says Sally, is that it's a skill. "You'll get better at it over time," she says. Her advice is to do a little each day, rather than trying to organize the entire office all at once. "The first few times you try to do it, you'll hang on to more than you throw away, but in time you'll be ruthless."

Turn piles into files. Sally says that as you throw papers away, you should be sorting the remaining ones into preliminary files. First, separate the personal or home files from the business files. "They should go on opposite sides of the room, because ideally, they'll go in different filing drawers or different rooms." Second, sort the business piles into three different piles based on how often you'll need them. These files don't have to be fancy— they're broad categories that you'll sort more specifically later. (For more on managing pesky paper piles, check out chapter 16.)

1. Hot files. This pile is for bills, pending invoices, or new projects, things you look at every week or possibly every day. When you're through sorting, they'll end up close at hand, such as in the bottom right-hand drawer of your desk.

2. Reference files. These files contain information, such as the current year's tax information, your résumé, or recently completed

projects. These are things you might look at once or twice in the coming year. They'll end up in a filing cabinet across the room, where they'll be close at hand but not in your way.

3. Archive files. These are files that you may not need again but can't part with, such as old love letters, drawings that kids bring home from day care, or research for the novel you're going to write someday. They're going to find their way into a storage container destined for the basement or attic. Label each container carefully, so you can retrieve anything you should need years from now.

Include an expiration date. Once you dig yourself out of disorganization, you're probably vowing never to let things get this bad again.

A TAXING QUESTION

Need a good reason to separate your home business files from your personal files? How about the IRS? These days many people who run a business from their home take the home office deduction, which allows them to deduct a percentage of their mortgage and utility expenses as business expenses. But you can claim this deduction only if the space in question is used strictly for business. (Planning kitchen renovations, signing report cards, and paying personal bills don't fall under that category.) If you do run a business out of your home, check with your tax adviser to get more specific advice about setting up your office.

Anne Braudy advises acting on that promise by putting a note on your calendar for 6 months from now. By then you will have accumulated more clutter, and several of your current files will have become outdated. "Regularly making time for organization will help you stay focused," Anne says.

Simple Filing Systems That Work

Barbara Clement will never forget the filing nightmare that awaited her in one client's house. "She had duplicated all of her files at least eight times," Barbara says. The harried woman spent all her time making copies of every piece of paper she thought she'd need again. And she had a filing system for each one. One was alphabetical, one was numerical, one was by category. "I've forgotten what the rest were about," Barbara says. With a little help, the woman was able to let go of her duplicates and use a single system that she could feel confident about.

"People are afraid to file because they don't trust their own systems," Barbara says. "That's why they stack papers on the desk, chair, and floor. They're afraid that if they file it where they can't see it, they'll never be able to find it again." That's not true, of course. Creating a system that will work for you is easy and will free up your life for new projects and opportunities. Here's how.

"One recent December, as I was recopying phone numbers and addresses and birthdays into my latest date book, my husband said, 'You know, if you had a Palm Pilot, you wouldn't have to recopy that stuff every year.' I loved my date book, but the prospect of avoiding writer's cramp every year was intriguing," says Lori Baird, a freelance writer and editor who lives in New York City.

"A few weeks later, my husband bought me an electronic organizer for my birthday, and I haven't looked back. It holds my address book, my to-do list, and my memo pad. It also has stripped-down versions of Word, Excel, and Quicken so I can edit a document or a budget in a pinch or enter an ATM withdrawal.

"Everything is cross-referenced, so, for instance, if I entered my friend Michelle's name in the Find function, I'd get a list that included her birthday, her address and phone number, and the date of her baby shower.

"The best part is that my organizer is practically fail-safe. It came with something called a 'hot-sync cradle' that allows me to easily and quickly back up everything on my computer. So even if I forget to change the batteries, my information is safe and sound."

THE NO-FILE FILING METHOD

Lynne Silvers was straightening and systematizing offices for years before she came to a startling conclusion. "Filing doesn't work for everybody," she admits. "That was a hard concept to accept." Natural organizers (and surely they must exist somewhere) love to file things and feel great about retrieving them. Other people practically need a tranquilizer to put papers into file drawers.

"It's important not to force yourself into any one type of organizing," Lynne says. If you love to pile, then find out why you love it. If it's just because you don't have enough filing space, that's easy to fix. And if you have some deep-seated psychological aversion to files, fear not, because there are ways around them. Here are a few.

Use a notebook. "One woman I know told me she couldn't bear to put things into drawers," Lynne says. "She said that not being able to see what was in there made her afraid that she'd forget about it and never find anything again."

Lynne came up with a better approach. She put the woman's important papers into three-ring binders and used dividers instead of folders to separate categories. The binders sat on a bookshelf near the woman's desk, their labels announcing their contents, so the woman never had to worry about losing or forgetting about anything. And she lived happily ever after.

Think vertical. People who love piles quickly run out of horizontal space on their desks. That's when they resort to piling on the floor, where the papers get stepped on or kicked around and always look messy.

"Going vertical will give you more space for your piles," says Lynne. She advises getting those hard plastic wall units that you often see in doctor's offices. The units are usually mounted on a door or wall and hold several patient files at one time, or they hang inside the waiting area, holding pamphlets for patients to take. In the home office they can hang on a door or on a wall adjacent to the desk and serve a similar purpose, holding files or stacks of papers that pertain to different ongoing projects.

Doctors control office clutter with these plastic file holders. You can, too.

Hang it all. For those who have more than a few files—or piles—to organize, Lynne recommends getting a hanging file-folder frame, available for just a few dollars at any office supply store. Set it up on any end table or on the floor near your desk, where it will hold dozens of files. This is a good compromise for nonfilers, she says, because the labels and files are still visible, but aren't cluttering up the room.

Try a file to go. Some people pile papers around because they're constantly taking off to sales calls or meetings and need to see the files they're going to stuff into a briefcase on the way out the door. An alternate solution is a plastic minibriefcase, a hard plastic folder with dividers inside. Pilers on the go can keep their files inside and still be able to see the labels easily.

Simple Filing Systems That Work | 225

FINDING WHAT YOU FILED

One of the hassles of retrieving papers from your filing system is trying to remember not only which drawer they might be in, but also what the file name might be, says Lynne Silvers. "You're left wondering how you were thinking when you filed a paper 5 or 10 years ago." Did you file a warranty under Appliances, Household Stuff, or Warranties? "That's scary," she says. The good news is that there are ways to make the process less frightening and more logical. Here's how to get started.

Choose broad categories. There's no law that says you have to file alphabetically. Go ahead: Throw away those lettered dividers, because there's a better way. In fact, you can make your files work the way those piles used to. Honest. Simply divide your life into three to six broad (or super) categories. Nancy Black divided her office files into three categories: Administration files, Client files, and Promotional files. Yours might include the following.

• Bills
• Home improvement
• Insurance
• Medical
• School

Color-code them. After choosing her broad categories, Nancy assigned each its own color and bought colorful hanging files to go with them. "People who are creative or right-brained

tend to like color-coded files," Nancy says. Her Administration files are green, Client files are red, and Promotional files are purple. Now, when she opens her drawer looking for a client file, she knows to go right to the red section. "It's important to remember to stick to broad categories," she says. "Don't go crazy with lots of colors, or they won't mean anything after a while."

Designate subcategories. Once you've decided on four to six broad areas, you're ready to start adding subcategories to them. Some will be obvious: Within Bills you'll probably have files for Gas, Electricity, Cable, Telephone, and Credit Cards. But a category called Medical might be trickier. It might include a file for medical and dental files and one for insurance. Will it include a file for your health club membership? Your nutritionist? Only you can decide, but it's worth thinking about right now. "Don't think in terms of encyclopedic logic," says Lynne. "Think in terms of where you're going to look for it tomorrow, next month, next year." If it takes you even 20 seconds to figure out your system when you're looking for something, your system isn't working.

Add more subcategories. If you're like most folks, you'll probably need another layer of categories. For example, in the file called Medical or Doctors you'll probably have a folder for each member of the family, or one for each doctor that you see. In the Telephone category, you might have separate files for

KEEP UP-TO-DATE

Many people make travel files for themselves where they store restaurant reviews and stories about interesting destinations they'd like to visit. The trouble with these files is that they age rapidly. If magazines or newspaper travel sections provide fodder for your travel and food files, remember to cull them regularly. A 5-year-old restaurant review is certainly no good. The place may have closed or changed chefs a few times. Keep the file up-to-date and it won't take over your filing cabinet.

your cell phones and landline phones "because when you pull each file, you'll be flipping through four or five pieces of paper looking for something, rather than 50," Nancy says. The idea, after all, is to shorten your steps.

Leave some empties. As you set up your categories and subcategories, make sure to leave some spare files in each. Files expand—that's what they do best—and hunting around for another green file when you open a new bank account is going to result in a pile on your desk rather than a filing system that works.

MAINTAINING YOUR FILING SYSTEM

Nobody likes paging through file tabs wondering where that one file went. It's equally frustrating to have used a file successfully only to be clueless about where it came from. How will you ever return it to the system so you can find it again? Our experts share their hints.

Neatness counts. Not being able to read your own handwriting accounts for more than a few lost files. If you take the time to invest in a small label maker, your files will always look professional and always be easy to read.

Keep an index. "If you find that you're having trouble remembering exactly what files you have, keep a list of all the folders in a drawer and tape it to the front," says Lynne Silvers. That sheet will be your index for what's inside. Be aware, though, that you'll probably have to update it as the files change.

Make crib notes. The frustrating thing about having files out on your desk is trying to figure out where they came from. This morning you grabbed the file that contains your dental records to make an appointment. Now do you put it back under Doctors? Dental? Or is there a folder with your name on it that contains all your medical records? Save yourself the frustration by writing a crib note on the outside of the folder that tells you which hanging folder to slip it back into.

TO-DO KNOW-HOW

Sure, you have a to-do list. In fact, you have 8 or 10 of them floating around the house. The trouble is, they never seem to end up on one master list. You need a better system! Here are some ideas to get you started.

Make your to-do list work for you. Anne Braudy is a big fan of detailed to-do lists. If, at the end of the day, you're making a list of people you need to call, go ahead and pencil in their numbers next to their names. If you're going to be pulling together informa-

---

ADVICE FOR . . . TOSSERS

You've always prided yourself on your home office. It's where dated reminders and ancient receipts are never allowed to linger. After all, once you're done with a piece of paper or information, it gets filed in the trash. Right?

Not so fast. There are some crucial categories of paper (aside from your tax forms) that you should hang on to even if you'll never need to look at them again. It sounds crazy, but it's true.

1. Investment information. Go ahead and throw away those monthly statements from the brokerage firm, but keep the confirmation notices of your investment purchases. You'll need to keep those at least until you sell those shares or that investment (think capital gains tax) and probably for several years afterward, if it has tax implications. Check with your accoun-

tant about any forms you're not sure about.

2. Information about assets you've purchased and copies of receipts for tax deductions. You'll need to file these until 7 years after you sell the asset or 7 years after the tax year in question. Your accountant can give you more specific advice for your purposes.

3. Medical information. Perhaps you had an illness or an operation a few years back. It seems as though it's all in the past, but you'll still want to keep records of your treatment. In fact, you should request copies of your entire medical file from your doctor. It will be handy if you ever change physicians or suffer a relapse. What's more, the information will be crucial to your children, who may face similar circumstances.

One of the first mistakes people make when it comes to filing is using the premade labels that come with most packaged files. For example, most of us have filed car insurance information in a file labeled Automobile. "But when was the last time you actually referred to your car as your automobile?" asks professional organizer Barbara Clement of OrganizationWorks in Wellesley, Massachusetts. The next time you look for a copy of your car insurance policy, you'll linger over the files in the C section looking for Car Insurance, having forgotten that you filed it under A for Automobile 3 months earlier. All of this wasted time and effort keeps you from wanting to bother filing at all. The solution? When you set out to label your files, start with blank labels and use the same language you use when you talk to your friends.

tion for a presentation, list the places where you've filed information. This will reduce the number of items you'll need to do in the morning and give you a boost of momentum—and you're less likely to get distracted if everything is in front of you. "It's like the way chefs pull their ingredients together before they start to cook. It's called *mise en place*," Anne says.

Use one calendar for all. Although you should probably keep your personal files separate from your work files, the one exception to this rule is the planning calendar. After all, your life has only one time line; it won't do to schedule an important meeting one afternoon only to find out later that this is the day the kids have a half-day at school. Your master calendar should include all of your planned activities, including the dates when bills are due. This will keep details from falling through the cracks.

Make a date with yourself. Once you have a to-do list, it's important to make it work in concert with your calendar, says professional organizer Judie Yellin of Newton, Massachusetts. "Plot important tasks in your appointment book the way you would a dentist appointment," she says. "Then add 20 percent to your time estimate, because things always take longer than you think." This will give you an estimate of what you can realistically accomplish in 1 day, and it will help reduce the feeling of failure you're likely to get when you can't cross everything off the list. This scheduling practice will help you estimate project lengths in the future and help you to use your time more wisely.

Give yourself a gimme. The thing about to-do lists and calendars is that they're constant reminders of things that have to be done. Anne Braudy tells her clients to schedule in some fun things, too. "Making an appointment to go to the gym or get a baby gift for a friend isn't a

Professional organizer Nancy Black deals with lots of executives who have never really used to-do lists because they insist that they can keep everything in their heads, even though they're running to meetings 10 minutes late and can't find their airline tickets. Here's the advice she gives them.

1. Brainstorm all the things you need to do; number them if you want. Don't try to make a perfect, beautiful list; it'll keep you from getting anything done.

2. Break down each task into small, definable goals. Items such as "plan a wedding," or "design an ad campaign" are overwhelming. Short-term goals will lead to short-term successes when you cross them off your list.

3. Separate items that you need to do today from what you need to do soon. Most lists have too many things on them. They're unrealistic.

4. If there are a lot of items left on the list at the end of the day, don't recopy the list. Just cross off the things you've done and highlight the things you need to do tomorrow.

5. If important tasks keep floating from day to day, get out your calendar and make an appointment with yourself to do them at a specific time. An artificial deadline can really get you going.

6. When a task lingers for weeks, you may have to get brave and admit that you're never going to do it. Delegate it or just take a deep breath and cross it off the list. Allowing pesky tasks to nag at you will just make you avoid your list.

---

crime," she says. "People think that everything in their day has to be do-or-die, but that's not why you work at home. The important thing is to be as deliberate as possible about how you spend your time."

Decluttering Your Computer

Invisible clutter may be harbored inside your home office. Byte by byte, with each tap of your keyboard or click of your mouse, you could be unwittingly clogging up your computer's hard drive.

"Just because you can't see clutter doesn't mean it doesn't exist in your computer," cautions Richard Nielsen, owner and operator of 24HR Computer Housecalls in Oceanside, California. "Too often, people get into the black hole concept when it comes to their home computers. They think the space is limitless. Unfortunately, it is not. Before you know it, your machine is sluggishly slow or worse, it crashes."

In the world of computers, Richard is a lifesaver—the guy who comes to your aid by retrieving lost documents and getting your computer humming happily again. "I feel like a detective searching for clues and solving a case each time I make a house call," he says. "I love wowing people and watching them 'ooh' and 'aah' as I make their computers work as efficiently and as quickly as possible."

Richard and our other computer experts help

point out some surprising sources of computer clutter, and share their best ways to make your hard drive cruise.

BASIC ORGANIZATION

It's not just new computer users who benefit from remembering the basics. These tips will keep you in good (uncluttered) stead—no matter how expert you are.

To each his own—folder, that is. If your kids like to use your computer to research school projects and store downloaded video games, you'll want to find a way to keep their files out of yours. One way to do that is to give each member of the family his or her own folder on the hard drive. A special folder will help them organize their files. It will also keep them from having to go through *your* files while they're looking for their own.

Name your files creatively. You're trying to find a consumer complaint letter that you wrote a few months ago and sent to Smith Enterprises, but you've already opened a half-

---

PHOTO OPTIONS

We *know* you love those photo screen savers of little Audrey, your black Lab, or the new boat. But do you have any idea how much space those photos take up? Stored photos can be a major source of computer clutter, taking up space and slowing your machine to a crawl. "A single photo can easily use up 20,971,520 bytes of memory," says Carol DaSilva, a computer expert from Emmaus, Pennsylvania. "That's more space than it would take to store Shakespeare's complete plays!"

Of course, you could save your photos for your office wall. But now there's another option: You can store them on a CD. Thanks to the miracles of technology—and a handy device called a CD burner—you can store hundreds of photos on a single recordable CD, which can hold 700 megabytes of data. These CDs come in two versions, CD-R, which you can "burn" or record once, and CD-RW, which can be used over and over. When you want to look at photos, just pop a disk into your CD-ROM drive and enjoy to your heart's content. They won't be taking up a single byte on your hard drive!

If you're buying a new system, you can get a CD burner as part of a standard package. But they're also available as separate components (called an external CD-RW drive or a portable CD-RW drive) for a couple of hundred dollars—and even less, of course, if you buy one used. These portable units are no bigger than a portable CD player, so they won't clutter your computer desk space.

The best part is that it's easy to copy files, photos, music, and so on onto the disks—and they hold so much, you won't need to make space to store stacks of floppies. More clutter conquered!

---

dozen computer files on several different disks with names like "Smith" or "SmithE" or "S-Ent" and none of them is the right one. You've found games, budgets, geneaology files, but no letter. Next time, shorten your trail by following three simple steps to create a file name that describes what's in the file.

1. Code them. Come up with a list of short abbreviations that designate the document type and use those abbreviations in file names. For example, SmithLET.doc, CableLET.doc, and TomLET.doc would all be letters. RogerINV.doc and AttINV.doc are invoices.

2. Date them. If you'd rather keep track of files by date created than by type, add a simple date abbreviation to your file name to keep track of when you created it. (The computer will keep a record only of the last time you saved it.) Smth91901.doc was created on September 19, 2001.

3. Mark the hard copy. Once you've printed an important letter and sent it, you might want to print a hard copy for your files. If you do, take a moment to write the computer file name in the top left corner of the first page. Then, when you see the document, you'll know where to find its electronic counterpart.

HIDDEN SPACE GOBBLERS

Are you the keeper of too many cookies? Are you aware of temporary files? Do you re-member to clean out your recycle bin? Left un-touched, these three areas can quietly overload your hard drive.

Toss those temporary files. Don't let the name "temporary" fool you, says Paul Hayes, a Webmaster who maintains more than 20 business Web sites from his Santa Ana, California, office. Each time you visit a Web site, temporary files are stored on your hard drive. Many of these files are "cookies," which are small chunks of information Web sites dump on you that track how often you visit a site, plus save your logon name and passwords. "Cookies and other 'temporary' files don't just vaporize into the air by themselves," says Paul. "And these files aren't storing just text, but also graphics and possibly, sound files, which can eat up a lot of space." His advice: Each week—say every Monday—get rid of those files.

To do that, Windows users should go to the Windows folder on the hard drive and open up Temporary Internet Files. Hit the Control button and the letter *a* to highlight the files, and then hit Delete. Mac users can get rid of those files by throwing away the Cache folder for the browser they're using. That folder will be in the Preferences folder within the System folder.

Reclaim your recycle bin. Mac users have it made: When they drag a file or folder into the trash and then empty the trash, those items are gone. A common mistake among Windows users is to delete files and think that they are—

CLUTTER CRUSADERS

Have Laptop, Will Travel

Sportswriter Marcia C. Smith must be mobile at all times. She relies on her laptop computer—not a desktop model—to write and file her stories for the *Orange County Register* in Santa Ana, California. One night, she may be covering the Los Angeles Lakers basketball game, and the next, flying to Seattle to do a feature story on an Olympic-bound athlete.

For her, space is a precious commodity. She must often pack a quick overnight bag and a second carry-on that includes her laptop, a few paper files, and floppy disks.

"As a reporter, I'm writing stories nearly every day, so I've learned the importance of titling documents in such a way that I know immediately what they mean—and am able to retrieve them quickly," says Marcia, of Seal Beach, California. "Fortunately, programs these days allow you to give very specific titles to your documents. Rather than title something 'Iverson,' I can identify the file as, say, 'Iverson060601,' which tells me the subject and the date I filed the story. By labeling accurately and specifically right from the start, you can save a lot of time in the long run."

Chuck old versions. In your excitement to install a new version of *Jeopardy!* on your hard drive, or your haste to update your antivirus software, don't forget to completely uninstall the older versions, says Cheryl Wilhite, who troubleshoots and repairs personal computers in Plano, Texas. "Ask yourself, do you really need two versions of a word processing, chat, or landscape design program?" Cheryl says.

Windows users can completely uninstall programs by going to Add/Remove Programs in the control panel after the new program has been installed. Don't just delete the directory. Otherwise, you could clog up your hard drive's memory. Mac users have at their disposal uninstall programs that will delete all the files associated with a software program. Those programs are usually available from the software company's Web site.

Count on compression. You may own a computer blessed with a 160-gigabyte hard drive, but if you store lots of big files—photographs and movies—even that will fill up fast. But there is software that compresses files and makes them smaller—sometimes less than half their original size. WinZip for PCs and StuffIt for Macs and PCs are two of the most popular programs.

poof!—gone forever. Wrong. These files stay in the bin until you retrieve them or empty the recycle bin. It's easy to empty the bin: Simply right-click on the recycle bin icon on your desktop and choose Empty Recycle Bin. Bye-bye, unwanted files—forever!

AUXILIARY SPACE SOURCES

To maximize the speed and efficiency of your hard drive, it's best to keep files and programs that consume a lot of space to a minimum. How? Store your memory gobblers (music files, digital photos, graphics, and the like) on separate disks.

And remember, you always need to back up *all* your computer files onto disks as well.

Why back up files? The information on your personal computer is often more valuable than the machine itself. Backups are cheap insurance to protect your system's applications and the data you've worked hard to create. Practice two backup habits: full backups and increment backups. Full backups make a protective disk copy for every file in your system. Increment backups save only those files that have changed since your last backup. This is a good way to protect any new or changed files in a time-saving fashion. Retrospect is one of the best-known and frequently recommended backup programs, and it's available in both Mac and PC versions.

"I've learned the hard way—by having my hard drive crash and losing everything—to back up and store files on floppy disks, Zip disks, and CDs," says Larry Lachman, Psy.D., a psychologist from Carmel, California, who specializes in family therapy and animal behavior. "Now, I keep my hard drive pretty tidy."

How often should you back up your files? That depends on how much you store—and *what* you store, says Richard Nielsen. If all you do is surf the Web, play occasional games, or balance your checkbook on the computer, consider incremental backups every month and full backups four times a year. But, if you write a lot of vital data files, such as word processing documents or money data files, back them up to disks *each time* the data changes. Backup and storage sources come in three primary forms: floppy diskettes, Zip disks, and CDs.

Use floppies for the small stuff. Three-and-a-half-inch hard plastic floppies are one of the oldest ways to store files from your hard disk. Floppy diskettes are small, easy to tote, and inexpensive. A multipack of 10 sells for under $5. The downside is that these diskettes provide limited capacity—only 1.44 megabytes of space. You can quickly fill a tray of diskettes that will take up valuable shelf space in your home office. Also keep in mind that these disks are probably going the way of the 5¼-inch floppies in favor of Zip disks and CDs.

REV UP YOUR RAM

You've cleaned out every temporary file, every piece of junk mail, memos from 1993, and games you beat long ago, but your computer still crashes and runs slowly. What's the problem?

It could be your RAM, or random access memory. Think of RAM as your computer's brainpower—if there's not enough of it, your computer will be sluggish and unable to handle more than just a few tasks at once. Especially if your computer is an older model, it may have come with too little RAM to run the files you need.

The good news is that you can usually add more RAM to your machine. The chips are available from your machine's manufacturer and most computer stores.

Store larger files on Zip disks. For backing up and storing big files, like a book manuscript, consider Zip disks. A little bigger and thicker than the 3.5-inch disks, Zips are magnetic disks that cost about $10 each but can store up to 250 megabytes—or, nearly 200 times more information than a floppy. Zips are perfect storage stashers if you want to store large photo files. The downside: Zip disks require their own drives. But most newer computers already have them installed, and if you're using an older computer, you can buy an external Zip drive.

Learn the ABCs of CDs. The newest generation of auxiliary space savers are CDs. These coaster-size disks can store up to 700 megabytes. You could store the same amount of information on one CD that would fit on 450 floppy disks!

CDs come in two varieties—CD-R and CD-RW. The *R* in CD-R stands for "recordable." These are one-time-use disks, meaning that once you fill the disk to capacity, you can't erase the disk and reuse it. You can copy the information back onto your hard drive and use it from your computer. These disks are inexpensive, about 40 cents apiece, and are best for storing data that you don't need to access frequently.

The *RW* in CD-RW stands for "rewritable," which means that you can erase information from the disks and reuse them. CD-RWs are a bit pricier than CD-Rs, at nearly 2 bucks a pop. But they're still a bargain compared to Zip disks, and with their ultrathin jewel cases, CDs take up a whole lot less room.

confessions of . . .
a Former Paper File Collector

RACHEL GOLDMAN, a technical writer in Plano, Texas, can navigate shortcuts on her hard drive and maneuver software applications with ease, but she admits to one flaw in the so-called paperless world of computers: She is a printout junkie.

"I grew up as a big pen-and-paper person," says Rachel, a self-taught computer whiz who often helps friends with their ailing home computers. "When writing a story, I like to print it out and hold it in my hand while I read it. The problem was that I was filling my drawers with lots of paper printouts."

Rachel is weaning herself off her printout tendencies by regularly backing up her computer files and storing them on specifically labeled CDs. "One CD can hold up to 700 megabytes," she reminds us. "That little disc takes up considerably less space in my house than mountains of paper printouts."

Hey Mabel, label! Disorganization can create a classic case of what's-in-this-diskette syndrome. Always label your disks and CDs in great detail, including the topics stored, the file names, and the date the disk was created, urges Cheryl Wilhite. Store them in a logical order in disk containers or shelves that are out of direct sunlight to protect them.

Learn how to save Web sites. In researching Web sites, you often find great information you want to save. Do what Larry Lachman does. "When you go to a Web site, you have the option to save the information as a text file or other options that include all the graphics," says Dr. Lachman. "Save it as a text file, because it takes up less room on your hard drive. Doing this also keeps my speed on the Internet from slowing down."

Organize your e-mail. Think of your e-mail as a mailbox. If you're not careful, it could be stuffed with junk mail. Rachel Goldman, a technical writer from Plano, Texas, recommends archiving old e-mail messages you wish to save as text files, and then burning them onto a CD for storage. The rest? Delete them right after you read them.

Dealing with Everyday Office Clutter

No matter how organized you get at any one time, things are going to creep up. They always do, and it's no fault of yours. Junk mail is going to arrive uninvited, ATM slips will accumulate, and somebody is going to borrow your scissors without remembering to put them back. That's just life. Here are some strategies to help you cope before your next big dig.

ORGANIZING OFFICE SUPPLIES

Nothing's worse than searching high and low for a few pieces of computer paper when you're on deadline or making a special trip to the store to get a ruler only to come home and discover that you already have one. Get control of your supply cabinet with these strategies.

Shelve your office supplies. Office supply stores love to sell stacking paper trays. Most professional organizers say that those trays don't save desk space, but according to Nancy Black, they're great for adding emergency shelf space to your supply closet. There they can hold Wite-Out, Post-it pads, index cards, and any other short items you need to store.

"They're also ideal for computer paper," Nancy says. Set up the stacking trays next to your printer. One tray can hold letterhead, another can hold plain white paper, and a third can hold colored papers, or simply the extra ream you haven't opened yet.

Take a tip from the kitchen. If you have only one spot to contain all your office supplies, that space can get tight in a hurry. One way to add shelving is to take a hint from your kitchen cabinets. Home improvement centers often sell racks that form makeshift shelving in kitchen cabinets to help store dishes better. They'll also

work in your supply cabinet to give extra shelf space for paper and other supplies. "The plastic-covered wire racks work best because they're easy to clean," says Nancy.

Wire racks designed to add space to kitchen cabinets are also ideal for office supplies.

Label it. Barbara Clement often hears from people that their Scotch tape has wings. The scissors get up and walk out of their home offices. If your family knows that you have office supplies, they'll be tempted to use them far more often than they'll actually put them back. She suggests using a strategy that crafty mailroom workers use in corporations. "Label your stuff," she says. Use a label from a manila folder that says "Mom's Office" and secure it with Scotch tape. It will serve as a not-so-subtle reminder to borrowers that whatever leaves your office must return.

And get some spares. Your scissors and tape may be walking off because there aren't

Organizer Nancy Black meets many Collectors who, although drowning in paper, still can't bear to part with a single business card. Her advice is to invest in business card filing sheets, which are available in any office supply store. The sheets fit into a three-ring binder. Once the binder is set up, Nancy helps her clients organize that pile of business cards into loose piles. "Of course, it would be easier to set up an electronic database with everyone's name, address, and phone number, but if you love cards, you love cards," she says.

The trick is to organize the cards the way you'll need the information. Let's say you're a marketing specialist. You go to a trade show where you collect business cards from writers, printers, paper suppliers, and graphic artists. Alphabetizing the cards by the person's last name makes no sense. (After all, you don't know these people.) Instead, organize them by what they do, artists on one page and printers on the other, and so on.

Same thing with household business cards. Sure, it's nice that your plumber's name is Louie Piper, but that won't help you find his phone number when your faucet is leaking. Put his business card under Household Maintenance or some other category that will be easy to find.

any others in the rest of the house. Give in this one time and get a spare—or two—and label them for locations in the house (such as kitchen and den). Now, when someone tiptoes into your office to borrow the tape "just this once," you can send them off to another source.

Stem the tide of business cards. Everywhere you go these days, someone is handing out a business card. You get them from bankers, department store salespeople, and the plumber who's fixing your toilet. Go to a networking function and you'll come home with a dozen of them. Go to a convention and you'll come home with hundreds. You can't escape them, and throwing them away seems so wrong. What else can you do? Well, the first step in combating business card clutter is to figure out why

exactly you wanted the card in the first place, then moving that info to your master address file or e-mail file and getting rid of the card. Now it can never bother you again.

Rid yourself of the rotary card file. Barbara Clement wants you to know that there's no law that says you have to have a rotary card file (also known as a Rolodex). "I hate them," she confesses. "They're so ugly, and it's not like you can put them in your briefcase and take them with you." Barbara puts phone numbers and contact information in the pertinent project folders. Medical files have doctor's numbers. Client folders include their names, numbers, and addresses. "It keeps all relevant information together," she says. And it gets rid of that ugly Rolodex.

SORTING EVERYDAY FINANCIAL INFORMATION

Credit card receipts and ATM slips seem so important—and they are, for a short time at least. The question is how long to hang on to them and when to let them go. (For advice on sorting all sorts of other paper piles, turn to chapter 16.)

Stick it to your receipts. Receipts for your purchases are important for three reasons. First, they serve as proof of purchase if ever you need to return something. Second, they help you reconcile your credit card statement at the end of the month. Finally, they're backup for the tax deductions you'll want to make at the end of the year. Many people keep receipts long after they're useful. For example, once you've worn that blouse and sent it to the cleaners, you won't be able to return it, so why keep the receipt?

To keep your current receipts from floating around the office until you're ready to toss them, get one of those metal spindles from an office supply store. Impale your receipts as you get them, then when your statement comes, just remove the stack and check them against your bill. File the ones that have tax implications and toss the rest.

Check, then pitch. Nancy Black often has to remind people that ATM slips serve only as a check against the bank's monthly records. Electronic mistakes do happen, and the receipt is proof that you deposited money when you said you did, and withdrew money, too. As soon as you've reconciled that month's balance, however, they're just dead paper and can be safely tossed.

ADVICE FOR . . . COLLECTORS

Professional organizer Lynne Silvers loves to help people find extra space in their houses, but she occasionally finds it difficult to convince people that it's okay to throw stuff away. "Usually, when you tell someone that there's no need to hang on to electrical bills from 5 years ago or even last month, they joyfully run to the trash can," she says. Most of them, anyway.

Lynne once had a client who was an accountant. He was so fastidious about his personal finances that he'd kept all of his monthly bank statements for the past 40 years. He refused to throw them away, even though he was moving to a much smaller house and could ill afford the space they consumed. "He told me that he had to keep them in case the bank made an error," she says. "I finally convinced him by telling him that if the bank made an error on his account, he'd have to find it during the current month. There's no way it was ever going to reimburse him 35 years later."

With that, Lynne helped the accountant haul the boxes to the trash. "I told him that if he needed old statements, he could buy them from the bank. He'd pay a small fee, but nothing compared to the space he'd be saving."

Unmingling Business and Home

For most people, the major trouble with a home office is that every piece of paper in the household tends to float there as if by magic. It's difficult sifting through a stack of papers looking for the catering plan for a client only to find a piece of artwork by one of your kids or the garden plan for this coming spring or even a stray grocery list.

Others have the opposite problem. The books and paperwork that are supposed to live in their home office seep out onto every flat surface in the rest of the house. Neither plan is ideal for organization or sanity. Here are some ways to keep things separate.

Take a tip from kindergartners. To keep her business work separate from her personal work, Anne Braudy uses a system that's worked in kindergarten classrooms for decades.

"In preschool classrooms, every activity has an action area," she says. There's one area for coloring, and near that area are shelves for putting away coloring books. Right next to the area where kids play with blocks are bins where kids can get the blocks and (more important) put them away afterward. You can do the same in your home, says Anne, by keeping your home files *completely* separate from your business files. You may even want to keep them in another room, storing a small portable file holder in the kitchen where you like to pay bills and plan the garden.

Dedicate a drawer. Folks who can't spare separate rooms for business and personal records aren't out of luck, says Lynne Silvers. "If you have one desk area and that's all you can spare, dedicate one drawer or file box under that desk for your household stuff." That will keep the piles on your desk from getting mixed up.

Turn, turn, turn. You can further separate work and personal files by setting up a small desk or card table adjacent to your work space. Then you can simply turn your chair 90 degrees to focus on home tasks when they come up. "That's a good way to mentally change channels when you need to go from home tasks to work tasks," Lynne says.

CHAPTER 13

Workshop

Having a workshop may be a natural extension of home ownership. A house requires a lot of work, and unless you can afford to tackle virtually every home repair with your checkbook, sooner or later you'll need to buy a hammer, a set of screwdrivers, and a few paintbrushes and rollers. Before you know it—bam!—you're buying a toolbox and it's too late to stop.

Then there are the gearheads among us, those men and women who simply *must* have the next big thing, be it a tool or a piece of hardware. The problem with having every specialty tool under the sun is keeping it all under control. Collectors and Concealers might say, "There's no mess that can't be solved with more Peg-Board." But before you buy more of those 4-by-8 sheets of holey heaven, read the tips in this chapter and then make a plan to cut the clutter in your workshop.

Getting Started

You can manage your clutter-cutting efforts better merely by reflecting on why you have a workshop and how you use it, says Bill Keller, a longtime do-it-yourselfer from Lemont, Illinois, who produces videos for the home improvement industry. "Knowing your handyman *modus operandi* will help you plan your workshop space to avoid clutter," Bill says. He finds that most folks fall into one of the following three categories.

1. The reluctant do-it-yourselfer. This handyman accepts home improvement tasks as

necessary evils. His workshop—home to the remains of a dozen home improvement projects—is more a tool graveyard than a work area. (These folks will want to review chapters 1 through 5.) Half-empty paint cans and old brushes and rollers that haven't been cared for properly litter the area.

A good strategy for this handyman style is to buy only the materials he needs for the current project when he shops, Bill says. "If you need a couple dozen nails, under no circumstances should you purchase the 5-pound box, even if it seems like a better deal. It's no deal if you'll never finish the box. All you'll be left with is a bunch of clutter taking up space."

2. The weekend warrior. This handyman enjoys the challenge of each project she tackles. She has a healthy outlook, too: No matter how the project turns out, she looks back with pride and says, "I did it myself."

The weekend warrior constantly tries new projects and isn't afraid to amass a collection of tools and materials. Her best clutter-cutting strategies: careful shopping and regular purging to avoid workshop duplicates—and performing detailed feasibility studies before pitching headlong into new projects.

3. The avid craftsman. The avid craftsman looks forward to building and fixing things. His workshop is probably larger than those of the other handyman styles, and that's as it should be, because he's constantly completing necessary jobs and hobby projects. Because the avid craftsman's workshop gets more use than the others, it runs the highest risk of becoming disorganized. It's not realistic to expect an avid craftsman to give away lots of tools and materials, but he can streamline the mess and create space with strong organizational skills and clever storage ideas.

KEEPERS, TOSSERS, AND WHICH ARE WHICH

Once you've determined what kinds of fix-it jobs you do and thus how much workshop you need, it's time to start decluttering space. But start several rooms away, in an easy chair, with a cool drink by your side. Seriously—begin with a logic check. "All clutter control involves finding a logical space for everything, somewhere you can return it to after you're done with it," says personal organizer Carol Keller of Portland,

Oregon. This is particularly important in the workshop, which contains a lot of objects you use so rarely that they don't have a home.

Take a few minutes to jot down what you—not Norm Abrams, not the adorably handy couple on *Hometime*—logically expect to find in your workshop. Say, "If I were looking for ____, I would head to the workshop." Anything that can reasonably fill in that blank goes in the workshop; stuff that doesn't goes elsewhere.

Ask your family members to fill in their own blanks, then compile all your answers in a list, and check the list against what's actually in your shop. If you couldn't imagine looking for the Clue game or the Sterno cans from last month's fishing trip in your workshop, don't let them take up space there.

"Of course, this isn't meant to be a rigid exercise," Carol says. There will be items not appearing on your list that you do want to keep in

---

BATTLE CLUTTER, NOT YOUR SPOUSE

The average man thinks he never has enough tools, says professional organizer Janet Hall. Even though Janet got paid to cut other people's clutter for 5 years, "I could never stop my husband from buying more tools. He always wants the newest and the best. I'm amazed by the variety of hammers you can buy, for example. How could you ever use them all? But my husband's theory is, 'Great, I'll take one of each.'"

If you're the tool-skeptic half of a similar couple, says Janet, the workshop is one area where you'll need to tread lightly. "Sometimes relationships are more important than a few extra items you don't need." You may be able to help your mate organize the tools to identify duplicates or evaluate which ones don't work anymore, but you probably aren't equipped (at least in your mate's view) to judge what stays and what goes. Still, you aren't powerless, Janet says. "Your budget constraints are another discussion entirely, and together you and your spouse can establish a limited space where the tools can be."

the workshop, but listing your expectations will help you to more readily spot items that don't belong. Remember, this is *your* bible. If you and your family expect the popcorn popper to be in the top right cabinet above your worktable, or the dog's toys in a bucket at your feet, let it be. Once you know what should stay, you're on your way. Now all you have to do is figure out what goes. Here are some surefire ways to do just that.

Be realistic. Instead of considering what a handyman "should" have in his workshop, sit down and make a list of what you'll actually use and what you'll never touch in a year of Sundays. You may even want to rethink the whole idea of having a workshop. Perhaps you'd be better off with a few toolboxes for the house and car, a couple of (well-organized and labeled) boxes of stuff in the attic, and a local handyman's number on the speed dial, says Bill Keller. "If you're not into fixing things, you're wasting that workshop space. Consider reorganizing so you can use the space for something you love, like a library or a home gym."

If it ain't broke, keep it. Toss any item that doesn't work or that is of no use to anybody. "There are few other places in our homes where we would harbor broken items, and there's no reason to keep them around in the workshop, either," says personal organizer Janet Hall, president of OverHall Consulting in Port Republic, Maryland. "In fact, if old power tools have frayed cords or don't work correctly, it's dangerous to keep them." Old paint. Rusted nails. Split, frayed boards. Broken fans. Rusted chains. The list goes on and on. This is a good time to have a Tosser with a strong back around. But even if you're on your own, make those trips to the dump and the garbage can until you have nothing left but usable items.

DEAL WITH THE DUPLICATES

When all your workshop paraphernalia is out in front of you, it's easy to see duplicate items. (One family we know had nine identical, brand new, unopened sponges for glazing walls.) This is the time to keep the latest and greatest, and get rid of the rest. Here are a few ways to deal with and prevent duplicates.

Get it out in the open. Don't fudge on the Quantify step of the Q.U.I.C.K. process in your workshop (see chapter 2 for a review). You need to look over everything you have and pair like items—especially if you lend tools, share a workshop, or are using an inherited space or tools. "I did this grudgingly, because it took almost a day to haul the stuff out of my garage workshop, but it was well worth the trouble," says Wade Slate, a lawn care professional and avid do-it-yourselfer in Knoxville, Tennessee. "We found seven pairs of those industrial-strength scissors. After restocking every art box in the house, I still had two left for me," Wade says. "I realized I had two identical drills that had never come out of their boxes. My mother had accidentally given me the same gift 2 years in a row. My brother sure was glad to get the extra. More important, I noticed I was missing a Skilsaw and one of my stepladders. I'd lent them to a neighbor, and if I hadn't pulled everything out of my workshop, I might not have remembered to ask for them back."

Refuse second helpings. Lots of us, particularly Accumulators, feel that having duplicate items is a good thing. Think about it. If one drill fails, you'll have another at the ready. But the reality is that power tools and building

---

OUT WITH THE NEW, IN WITH THE OLD

"My grandfather, Red Scott, was a construction worker most of his working life," says Rose Kennedy of Knoxville, Tennessee. "He helped build some of the most important buildings in Washington, D.C., including the Washington Monument and the Pentagon. When he died, I somehow got his level. All through college and during my single years, I displayed it someplace in the house. I used it to hang posters in the dorm and do other such jobs. Today it's on my mantel, and I wouldn't exchange it for 100 new models. When I need a level for a project, I take it off the mantel and replace it when I'm done. I don't need a new one because the old one works. That's a good clutter message as far as I'm concerned. It's fine to keep around sentimental items, and if they can pull their own weight, as most old hand tools can, there's no reason to buy new models."

materials are like batteries or vegetable seeds. They tend to wear out or expire whether you use them or not, so it's silly to keep an extra. Ditto for extras of craft and project items. If you haven't used even one package of minihinges to make wooden jewelry boxes, what are the chances you'll ever need seven?

Isolate iffy items. If you can't identify an immediate project for an extra tool or material, get rid of it. That's the word from Janet Hall. And if you think you'll need something for a not-so-immediate project? "Don't kid yourself," Janet says. "Start a box or a bucket where you can hold the tools and materials you think you might need later, but store things there for 6 months at the most. If you haven't found a way to use those objects after that long, get rid of them."

Consider selling. If your tools are in decent shape, you may be able to motivate yourself to pare your collection by selling a few. "High-quality hand tools definitely hold their value," says Ollie Belcher, an antiques dealer in Corbin, Kentucky. For power tools in good repair, she recommends consignment stores. "There are small stores in almost every community," she says, "but they do have requirements about what they'll accept." You'll find local consignment shops listed in the Yellow Pages under "Consignment Service."

If you're willing to part with vintage tools, particularly picturesque ones such as cross-cut saws, try flea market dealers, Ollie says. "People frequent flea markets specifically to buy tools, so many flea-market booth owners will know what you have and what it's worth," she says. "Their overhead isn't as high as the typical antiques or collectibles dealers, so they're more willing to work with you if you don't have a lot to sell." Don't count on making loads of profit selling old tools through a flea market. You'll probably make only a little pocket money. You may even be able to talk a friendly booth operator into coming to your workshop and helping you find some things to part with, Ollie says.

Show off vintage tools—just not in the workshop. You might want to hang on to tools with sentimental value, such as the old ripsaw you used to make your first tree house (even though you now have three electric table saws). Why not free up room in your workshop by displaying a few of the most interesting or attractive tools inside the house? Awls, hammers, tongs, and handsaws add a rustic look to a room when hung from nails on a brick fireplace. You can even dangle plumb bobs from the top of a bright window as an ornament. "Restaurants often decorate with vintage tools and implements," says Janet Hall. "I've seen people decorate the exteriors of their work sheds or the walls outside their workshops with tools, or display items on a curio shelf around the ceiling." Make sure the items are out of reach of little ones, and be sure to hang them securely.

Share your workshop wealth. People know that they can donate food, clothing, children's items, and the like to the needy. But there's just as much demand for home maintenance and workshop items—the traditional "guy" stuff, says Janet, who is writing a state-by-state guide to organizations that recycle and reuse household clutter. Her recommendation: nonprofit organizations.

"They usually need tools and building supplies just to keep up with the repairs on their own offices or buildings," she says. "Those that serve needy families may also distribute supplies that help people keep up their homes, and because most of the stuff they get is used, it wears out or breaks down quickly, so they need frequent replacements." To find out about nonprofits in your area, call the local United Way or council of churches, or look in the Yellow Pages under "Charities" or "Social Service and Welfare Organizations." Here are specific or-

TWELVE INSTANCES WHEN TWO TOOLS ARE BETTER THAN ONE

Sometimes you should keep or even purchase duplicates of items you use in the home and in your workshop. Even though you'll end up with more stuff, you'll have less clutter because you won't have to put a project on hold to find a key tool or search high and low (and make a mess) to find, say, the masking tape when you want to paint. But—and this is a very important but—you must establish a way to keep the workshop version organized and in the workshop. Consider painting the handles of the workshop items bright yellow, where possible, and tagging other items with strips of bright yellow electrical tape. Here are 12 tools that you may want to duplicate.

Broom	Handheld vacuum
Cordless screwdriver	Heavy-duty scissors
Duct tape	Household bleach
Flashlight	Masking tape
Garbage bags	Staple gun
Glue gun	Steel wool

ganizations that might welcome your workshop castoffs.

1. Habitat for Humanity. According to its national office, the group is opening local thrift stores that concentrate on building materials and tools, large and small, in good condition.

2. The high school vocational class. Depending on how sophisticated the students are, they might welcome anything from power tools to drafting paper.

3. Local or high school theater groups. Consider pulling together a couple of toolboxes full of stuff appropriate for constructing sets. The groups can probably use house-painting supplies, too.

4. The Boy or Girl Scouts. Who knows what they might need for projects that will help them earn badges or enter box-car derbies? If you have lots of extra hammers, nails, or scrap wood, you could even suggest a project to a local troop, and then volunteer to help them with it.

Break up the inheritance. People tend to treat a tool inheritance reverently. Rarely do you hear about, "the great saw Uncle Ned left me." No. It's usually, "I have Uncle Ned's tools and I'll leave them to my daughter, the architect." But as much as the tools' previous owner deserves reverence, there is absolutely no need to keep the collection together in defiance of all reason or space restraints. You can, and should, cherry pick, keeping the best of the collection and giving away or selling the rest. In fact, there may be someone in the world right now who envies your inheritance, someone who would dearly love to have even one worn ratchet set. Sometimes just realizing that you can split the set (the sky will not fall) will help you clear dozens of duplicates from your workshop. It will definitely help you get more enjoyment from the treasures you choose to keep.

Easy Organizing Tactics

Particularly if you're a Collector or Accumulator, you may resist getting rid of anything. That means you need to concentrate on organizing what you have, says Bill Keller. As a home-repair book author and producer of several home-improvement industry trade videos, he's seen dozens of effectively organized workshops up close, and learned lots of effective strategies, including these.

WORKBENCH WISDOM

To choose a suitable workbench and make the most of it, you don't need to know as much

> ### A WORD OF WARNING
>
> **N**ever store dangerous chemicals such as turpentine, paint stripper, or solvents on shelves or in cabinets above eye level. Accidental tipping or spillage could cause burns, blindness, or worse. Always store chemicals on the floor or on a shelf close to the floor, in a cabinet or room that is *always* locked and inaccessible to young children and pets.

about different fancy models as you need to know about yourself. Whether you plan to buy or build, consider your clutter habits as you consider workbench features

Skip permanent features. If you take on only a few big projects each year that require a steady, sturdy surface, top two sawhorses with an old wooden door and forget a permanent workbench. The door can go up in the rafters when it's not in use, the sawhorses stack—and you'll have more floor space.

Get one that's big enough. If you do lots of woodworking, purchase a workbench whose surface is large enough for your large-scale projects. Don't buy (or build) a too-small workbench that will just take up space and attract clutter. Instead, use the time-honored sawhorse-and-wooden-door makeshift workbench until you have more space.

Put it on wheels. If you feel that a permanent workbench is worth the space it takes up, consider a model with wheels. That way, you can easily wheel it out of doors for 1-day projects, which should reduce cleanup and clutter in the workshop. Of course, the wheels should lock when you're working.

Choose a few bells and whistles. If you're an avid craftsman and can't do without a permanent workbench, consider whether you can save space with a model that has holes, loops, and shelves for tools. But exercise that option only if you plan to store tools that have no other home on the workbench. Otherwise, you'll just end up with lots of duplicates, one in the cabinet, one in the workbench.

Improvise. If you find it nearly impossible to resist placing (and leaving) items on any available clean, flat surface, opt for a folding table as a portable workbench. Put it away when you've finished a project and it will never collect clutter.

Build your own. Ready-made workbenches available from hardware or home improvement stores are typically either 30 or 36 inches tall. But those sizes might not make the best use of your space, says garage organizing expert Bill West of Fort Collins, Colorado. So rather than buying one of those, build or buy a workbench that's longer and, to use the space that you have more efficiently, one that's taller. Bill's workbench is 42 inches tall. "When I'm doing work, I don't have to stoop, which puts a strain on the back," says Bill. Also, because the bench is so

CLUTTER CRUSADERS
Outline Your Plan

Ed Jensen of Hastings, Nebraska, has traced the outline of each tool right where it goes on the Peg-Board he hung over his workbench. That keeps his work area free of clutter because he always knows where each tool belongs—and when it's missing.

tall, he can use the space below it to store trash barrels and a wet/dry vac. Here are some more ways to make your workbench work.

THE PERKS (AND PERILS) OF PEG-BOARD

In many workshop circles, a man is measured by the size of his Peg-Board. But, Bill Keller says, "It's not how big the Peg-Board is, it's how you use it." Here are some of Bill's expert tips for using your Peg-Board to its fullest.

Don't overdo it. One sheet of 4-by-8 Peg-Board hung above the workbench will do the trick for most people, Bill says. You'll need about an inch of space between the wall and the Peg-Board for the hooks. To do that, attach pieces of 1- by 2-inch furring strip to the wall as spacers and attach the Peg-Board to those spacers.

Go deep. If your shop has unfinished walls, consider hanging Peg-Board instead of drywall or paneling on one wall. That will allow you to use every square inch of your wall space for hanging tools. "Using Peg-Board is a great, convenient, flexible way to find permanent or temporary homes for all kinds of stuff," Bill says. "However, in the wrong hands, Peg-Board can just consume valuable storage space." His advice: "Don't go wide—go deep." Rather than hang just one tool per hook, buy hooks that are 6 inches to 1 foot long and hang several tools on each one. "I have all my tools grouped on long hooks, one for paintbrushes, one for scrapers,

GET WITH THE GROOVE

If Peg-Board is a little "old school" for your tastes, give your shop an upgrade with slat board. Slat board is a solid composite board with inconspicuous horizontal slats that accept special hangers. Originally used in retail stores, it's now available for home use. The slat board has a finished front and can hold lots of weight. It's more expensive than Peg-Board and may not be as versatile, but it has a very polished look. StoreWALL is one company that manufactures slat-board storage systems for residential use. Slat board in general and storeWALL in particular are available through closet companies, office furnishing companies, architects, and building contractors.

one for saws, and so on." And if your tools don't have convenient holes for hanging, Bills suggests, "Start drilling."

SHELVING SAVVY

Shelves can be the salvation or the downfall of the workshop. Some versions provide essential storage that helps you keep your shop clean and organized. Others hide everything you need, harbor useless stuff, collect dust and grime, and sag or break. Problem is, you can't tell which is which merely by looking at the unit—or the price tag—in the store. Even the most luxurious unit may not work in your workshop. Instead, solve the good shelf/bad shelf question by following this advice from personal organizers and Bill Keller, who has organized many a workshop.

Don't start shelves on the floor. In almost any room of the house, floor-to-ceiling shelves give a unified, uncluttered look. But they're not practical in the workshop. For one thing, if your workshop's in a damp basement or garage, you don't want anything, not even a shelf, touching the floor where it could get wet. For another, it's inconvenient to have to crouch down and lift heavy items from floor level. And anything that's difficult to access runs the risk of being duplicated or expiring before you use it. You can have massive shelving units, but you should install them starting at knee height, not on the floor.

Stock them single file. If you're going to use shelves in your workshop, choose narrow units, says Carol Keller. "Otherwise it's way too tempting to stuff items in the back where they get hidden by other items. In that case, you'll probably forget they're there. As for shelves that are tall enough to stack several items, keep in mind that sooner or later you'll need the thing on the bottom. If you have two of one item, you can place one behind the other, but that's the only time, says Carol. "Put the open, oldest one in front and the other right behind it."

STORING SPECIFIC TOOLS AND HARDWARE

When it comes down to stashing workshop stuff, it's time to start thinking creatively. Here are some suggestions to get you started.

Opt for office furniture. Office furniture isn't just for the workplace; consider it for the workshop, too. There are many inexpensive, self-contained office units available that you could adapt. Freestanding cabinets that open and feature a pull-down desktop can work as a project table, for example. They're designed to provide loads of storage and close up neatly. File cabinets are also a useful addition to any

---

THE TRUTH ABOUT BABY FOOD JARS

Baby food jars may be the first thing that pops into your mind when it comes to cutting clutter in the workshop. Someone will always pipe up with, "You know, you can use baby food jars to store nuts and bolts." Yes, you can. In fact, it probably wasn't long after the baby food jar was invented that someone started drawing up plans for a rack to hold jars of washers and cotter pins.

Here's great news: This chapter is loaded with storage ideas that are *even better* than baby food jars. Don't get us wrong. We love baby food jars. If you're blessed with a little bundle of joy, save as many empties as you can use. But don't hoard food jars like toilet paper during a hurricane, because there are plenty of places you can always find more should you need them.

workshop. They're relatively inexpensive to buy new, and just as easy to find used. For the new ones, look under "Office Furniture" in the Yellow Pages; for the used ones, look up "Thrift Stores" or "Consignment Stores" in the Yellow Pages or check out garage sales.

File cabinets are perfect for storing owner's manuals, project plans, receipts for tools and hardware, and home store circulars. Use hanging files to organize your sandpaper by grit. Even without files, file cabinets have large, deep drawers that are perfect for storing everything from power tools to plumbing supplies, too.

Milk crates for storage. If you're not sure whether or not heavy shelving would work for you, experiment first with plastic milk crates.

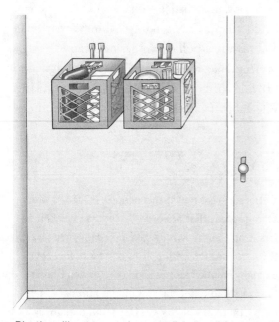

Plastic milk crates make great "shelves" for tools and accessories.

CLUTTER CRUSADERS
Let the Good Tools Roll

Rose Kennedy's father, a mechanical engineer, has always put rollers on heavy furniture so it can be moved around easily. "Then I saw a similar concept on a garden show. They used a rolling pallet to transport big, heavy pots to different areas of the house," says Rose, a veteran writer for the HGTV cable channel's Web site. Nowadays, Rose uses the rolling concept in her workshop. "Nothing goes directly on the floor," she says. "Instead, we store the heavy stuff, like paint cans, on wooden pallets that my husband attached rollers to. They're the same kind of wheels you might put under a bed frame," Rose says.

Rose and her husband also store gallons of paint and heavy materials, such as bags of concrete, in a child's wagon they keep under the bottom shelf of a wall-mounted bookcase. "That really helps with the clutter, because you don't have to shuffle heavy stuff around on the shelves. You just wheel the wagon out to see what you have," she says.

Attach several to the wall with shoulder hooks or your favorite hanging device. The crates are strong enough to hold power tools and paint cans, but not so deep or high that you risk cluttering up the place by stacking or hiding one tool behind another.

Make a case for cases. Power tools come with accessories; and in the workshop, accessories mean clutter. No matter how many power tools you own, the best way to keep them organized is to keep each one in its own case, Bill Keller says. If the model you want doesn't come with a case, buy one when you purchase the tool. A case doesn't need to be specially made for your specific brand or model of tool, but it should have a lid, a lock, and enough room for all your accessories: blades, bits, chargers, and the like. Soft cases are becoming popular, but hard cases—metal or plastic—are durable and stack nicely.

Bags aren't bad. Not all power tools come with cases, and sometimes you can't buy one that fits. Don't worry, though. We're not going to suggest that you store your Sawzall in the bedroom. Home improvement enthusiast T. J. Wilson has a better idea. He covers his tools with clear plastic bags. "Always use clear plastic so you can see what's under it," T. J. says. He uses thumbtacks to attach the bags to the wall behind the shelves that he stores the tools on. That way the bags don't get misplaced and he knows exactly where to return the tools when he's finished with them.

Attract clutter better. Hardware and home improvement stores sell magnetic strip tool holders, similar to the ones you may use in your kitchen to store knives. You mount the strip on your wall, then hang your tools from the strip. They're a terrific way to get clutter off your workbench. But if you choose to buy the strips, be sure to get the large, strong ones.

They'll hold your tools much better than the smaller models.

Make a screwdriver holder. Rather than dig through your toolbox or cabinets every time you need a screwdriver, store them in plain sight, neatly and out of the way. Here's how. In a strip of wood, drill holes of varying sizes at 1½-inch intervals. Use wood screws to fasten the strip of wood horizontally to the wall studs over your workbench. Simply drop the screwdrivers, handle up, into the holes. The screwdrivers with the thinnest heads go in the narrower holes and the bigger screwdrivers go in the wider holes. You can use this same method to store all sorts of tools, from wrenches to awls.

Bag the rags. You have to have rags in the garage or shed—they come in handy for so many jobs. But storing rags neatly can be a problem. If you have an old laundry basket, you have a place to tidily store those old rags: Just stuff them inside. You could also store the rags inside a laundry bag hung from the wall. Draw the top tight, then cut a small hole in the bag's bottom so that you can get out rags as you need them. Don't store rags that have been soaked in gasoline, paint, or other flammable substances. That's a fire hazard. However, before throwing those rags in the trash, check with your local public works department to find out the proper way to dispose of them. They could be considered hazardous waste by some communities.

Reach for baby wipes. Baby wipe containers are a welcome addition to most any workshop. Not only are they relatively large, lightweight, and stackable, but they also hold a 5-pound box of nails or screws perfectly. They're durable, to boot. Of course, you'll have to get used to pastel colors—pink, blue, and unisex green. The only real problem is that because the containers aren't clear, you can't see what's inside. You could label each container with a permanent marker, but here's a better idea. If you're storing nails, screws, or some type of connectors inside, use a hot-glue gun to attach a sample of the contents to the front of the container for easy identification. It's a terrific storage solution that cuts searching time to a minimum.

LINERS ARE FINER

If you use the kind of tool chest that has drawers, be sure to use drawer liners. The liners are made of thin foam or rubber and prevent tools from sliding around when you open and close the drawers. At a home improvement or hardware store, you can buy liners specially made to fit your brand of chest or buy it in rolls that you cut to size. You'll be surprised by how much they help you keep the drawers neat. If a lot of debris accumulates in the bottom of the drawer or if a few tacks or staples get loose in there, it's a simple matter to uproot the liner and shake it out, and that's much easier than dusting the drawer with a cloth.

Try this prescription for storage. Empty prescription bottles make terrific containers for small pieces of hardware such as screws, nails, tacks, and washers. To remove the labels, just wash the bottles in warm water. To relabel them, write directly on the plastic with a permanent felt-tip marker. If the bottles are going to be stored in a drawer (or anywhere else where they might get knocked over and roll around), use bottles with childproof lids, which are less likely to open accidentally and spill.

Take advantage of shoe-bag storage. Plastic shoe bags, the kind with plastic pouches, can come in handy for workshop storage. You can use a plastic shoe bag to store everything from tools to hardware to rags to instruction manuals. And if you choose a bag with clear plastic pouches, you'll be able to see what's inside.

Keep track of blister packs. If you're not purchasing small pieces of hardware in bulk, then you're probably buying them in those little blister-pack packages. If your usual habit is to tear the package apart to get to the hardware inside, you need to slow down a bit. That's because once the package is ruined, you'll need to find another container for the pieces of hardware you don't use or they'll get scattered, cluttering up your workshop even more.

Next time, open the packs carefully and, once you've used what you need, seal them up again with a piece of masking tape. That way you can rehang the packages on a nail or hook in your workshop just the way they were hung in the hardware store. Crush the plastic down a little to fit more packs on one nail if you need to. If you group your blister-pack hardware in some kind of logical order (screws on one nail, washers on the next), you'll be able to find what you need at a glance.

Declutter dowels and lumber scraps. Scrap lumber like molding and dowels has a way of making your workshop look messy, especially when it's strewn here and there. Here's an inexpensive but practical way to keep those pieces organized.

Get yourself a 2-foot-square cardboard box with sides that are about 2 feet tall. Fill the box with 2-foot lengths of PVC pipe set on end—choose a variety of diameters to accommodate different-size pieces of lumber. Wedge as many pieces of piping into the box as you can to keep them from tipping over. Now just place your extra pieces of molding, dowels, and even short two-by-fours into the tubes to organize and store them out of the way.

Mobilize your tools. Having a workshop is all well and good, but if you're fixing a leaky faucet in the kitchen, then you need to take your tools with you to the place they're needed. If you don't have or don't want to use a conventional toolbox, toss your tools into an empty 5-gallon spackle or paint bucket with a handle. It's spacious enough to carry several tools.

If you want to get really organized, you can buy organizing systems made especially for spackle buckets. These organizers, available at home improvement centers and big hardware stores, usually feature loads of pockets and holsters and other fancy gizmos. BucketBoss (www.bucketboss.com) is one manufacturer.

UNEXPECTED STORAGE

One of the joys of cutting clutter is finding storage space you didn't even know you had. That holds true for the workshop, too.

Finagle the floor joists. If your workshop is in an unfinished basement, you may have storage space you never dreamed of. Look around the room, then look up. If you see floor joists with nothing between them, you're missing out on one of the workshop's best-kept secrets. You can tuck long materials or tools, such as poles, pipes, and molding, between the floor joists. All you need to do is fasten a couple of pieces of wood to

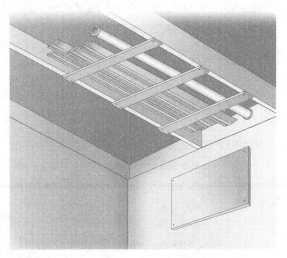

Storing lumber, pipes, and so on between floor joists gets them off the floor and out of harm's way.

the bottom of the joists to keep your tools aloft. Furnace ducts running along the joists create little cubbyholes that are perfect for storing wallpaper rolls and short scraps of wood. For more tips on making the most of your basement space, see pages 303 to 310.

Pipe in storage. If there are pipes running through your workshop on the ceiling, take advantage of them to hang light items, from paint rollers to bar clamps.

Set your sights on the ceiling. The largest area of uninterrupted space in any workshop is the ceiling. Even if you have a finished ceiling, suspend two parallel sections of board like a trapeze from the ceiling and use it to hold long sections of pipe or lumber. "You can purchase these contraptions ready-made from a home store," says Janet Hall. "Or you could make your own from lightweight pieces of plywood, suspended by a chain, or maybe even an aluminum garage door. Basically, it looks like an upside-down table."

Preventing Workshop Clutter

Even with all the see-through plastic tackle boxes and rolling pallets in the world, your workshop will still attract clutter—unless you're content to stop buying tools, or repairing small items that break down at the house, or dedicating several weekends in a row to one big, glorious woodworking project. Still, there are lots of ways to keep new clutter to a minimum without depriving yourself or defeating your do-it-yourself goals. Here are just a few.

Operate at less than full capacity. Janet Hall recommends making space in your workshop for what you have, and then creating some more space for irresistible items that might come into your life later. "Especially when there are all those wonderful tools and workshop materials out there, there will be other things you'll want," she says. Clutter can easily gain the upper hand if your space is completely full, Janet says. One more wrench or glue gun and suddenly your workshop feels overstuffed again. She recommends keeping 10 to 20 percent of a workshop's space open for future items.

Make time before you spend money. Workshop shelves and floors all around the world are littered with debris from unfinished projects. In fact, if you're a typical American, your workshop is also harboring materials from projects that never got off the ground. How to break the habit of optimistically, dreamily buying all the stuff for a project you don't have time to do? Try this. Before you write a check (or even visit a home store or do-it-yourself Web site), act like a contractor and prepare an estimate. Figure out how many hours you'll need, add 50 percent to that estimate, and then grab your calendar. On what days can you work that many hours into your schedule? Make sure to check the household calendar and your spouse's daybook while you're at it. If you can't commit the time in pen, there's no point in buying the materials, because

---

TURN DOWN THE TAJ MAHAL OF TOOL CHESTS

It's often difficult for a handyman or -woman to walk down the tool aisle without stopping to stare in wonder at the towering spectacle that is a mechanic's tool chest. Like a sports car, it sits there in brilliant candy apple red. You can practically see your reflection in the paint job. The wide, shallow drawers are perfect for storing hundreds of mechanic's tools, but these lavish tool chests are not practical for most home workshops—they're just too darn big, says Bill Keller.

As a producer of videos for the home improvement industry, Bill has seen dozens of high-end workshops, and few of those include the Corvette-quality tool chest. "Sure, they're a great ego boost," Bill says, "but unless you do a lot of automotive work, leave them to the mechanics." Instead, choose a portable toolbox with two to four drawers. "You can take them where you need to do the work, and they're a lot less expensive, but they still have drawers for keeping your tools neat."

they'll only take up space. And if you can see the available hours only in the distant future, wait until then to buy the materials.

Rent, don't own. Particularly if you're not all that fond of tools, consider renting what you need for major projects. "Most good rental shops offer a wide assortment of basic power tools such as drills and saws, as well as specialty tools such as ceramic tile cutters," says Bill Keller. If you are having trouble justifying the cost, jot down a space comparison instead of the cost comparison mentioned in the previous tip. For example, instead of telling yourself, "If I bought a table saw instead of renting and used it three times, it would pay for itself," consider, "A table saw would take up as much space as my workbench, and I'd have to put the rolling tool chest somewhere else, but I'd only use the table saw twice a year at the most."

Select standard sizes. When you plan a project, try to go with commonly available, home store-type materials and hardware: two-by-fours instead of custom-planed boards, standard finish nails instead of the antique Monticello-style tacks you saw at a salvage store 600 miles away. That way you'll be able to return or exchange your materials easily, which will keep them from lying around the workshop indefinitely. And since you'll be able to purchase what you need for repairs and replacements nearby, you won't be tempted to overbuy "just in case."

confessions of . . . a Tosser

"I'M A CONFIRMED TOSSER," says Lori Baird of New York City. "But I'm married to an Accumulator. My husband Tom is almost 40, but he still has T-shirts he wore in high school. But the T-shirts aren't as big a problem as the tools and hardware once were.

"We live in a small apartment with zero storage. Tom occasionally does art installations and is an avid do-it-yourselfer, so we have lots of tools and hardware around. Unfortunately neither one of us is particularly neat, so some stuff ends up in places it shouldn't. One day, I 'accidentally' threw out a bag of expensive hardware. Okay, I threw it away on purpose, but only because the stuff inside looked like a collection of mismatched, junky metal pieces.

"As luck would have it, Tom only realized that his security hangers had gone AWOL when he was on his way out the door to a job for which he needed them. That was bad. It was worse when I told him what happened to the hardware. We realized that we needed a solution that would fit both our styles. We bought a cheap set of plastic drawers on rollers that fits under Tom's desk. When I'm tossing in a frenzy and find washers and picture hooks and such, I toss them into the rolling drawers. When the drawers get full, we've decided that he'll cull that hardware and get rid of what he doesn't need. Now I can toss to my heart's content—I just have to toss it in the plastic drawers. And Tom can accumulate, but only until the drawers are full."

FIVE WAYS TO SCRAP WOOD SCRAPS

Whatever the reason, some people like to hold on to wood scraps—half-sheets of plywood, one railroad tie, or a single foot-long strip of molding that didn't make it onto the wall. If you examine these scraps with logic, not sentiment, you'll lose a substantial amount of clutter, says professional organizer Janet Hall. "Take a realistic look at whether you'll be able to use the wood before it goes bad. If you can't, it's much better to give it away now, while someone else can still use it, rather than let it rot or warp in your damp or drafty shed." Here are five ways to reduce scrap wood in your workshop.

1. Discourage yourself from keeping wood scraps in a detached workshop that's not well sealed by reminding yourself that it could attract termites or even mice and snakes, who might consider piles of wood a nice place to live.

2. Always check the return policy when you buy wood for a project, and return boards you don't use for a refund.

3. Donate scraps that you can't return to a Habitat for Humanity thrift store, which specializes in building supplies.

4. So you can't rationalize that a board hasn't been in your shop all that long, hot glue a penny from the current year to the end of a board when you purchase it, unless you use it at once. You could also write the date on the face of the board, but the hot-glued penny won't mar the board surface in any way. Once a year, clear anything with last year's penny on it.

5. If you're an avid woodworker, once a year take a day to build bluebird or bat houses from leftover untreated boards. If you can't use them, local elementary schools, nursing homes, or bird-watching groups will probably welcome your creations. Any board still standing at the end of the day goes to the thrift store.

Take two trips. Leftovers are a major workshop bugaboo. The project is done, and you have an extra packet of bolts. Turns out you had enough stain left in the old jar and never needed to open the new one, and so on. Don't let those unnecessary extras sneak into the drawers and cabinets of your workshop, Bill Keller says. "At the outset of a project, plan two trips to the store," he says. "Buy what you need on the first trip, and return what you don't need on the second." And just as you make a "buy" list for the first trip, make a "return" list for the second.

Send the expert on buying expeditions. Seems logical: If the household handyman is going to slave away on big projects, the least his spouse can do is pick up the supplies. But this is actually a habit that encourages workshop clutter. It's far too easy for someone who's not intimate with building terms to buy something that's close . . . but not quite right. And that not-quite-right item may never make it back to the store. "It's the fine shade of difference that will kill you," says Wade Slate. "My wife bought superglue when I needed ceramic glue. Another time, she picked up the entire kit to make a lamp, instead of the cord, which was all I needed. Spray adhesive instead of the brush-on kind, playground sand instead of builder's sand, that kind of thing. We live 20 miles from the home store, so of course no one wants to make the drive to return any of the items."

Another downside of inexact purchases, says Wade, is that the wrong material might stall the project, and then it sits around the workshop until the next weekend. "If the person doing the project can't make the trip himself, he should at least get on the phone with the hardware store to make sure they have pre-

cisely what he needs. Then someone else can pick up the packages."

Save receipts. Even when the expert does the buying, there will be returns. And on this planet, returns generally require receipts, so don't let them get away from you. Wade isn't formal with receipts, just effective. He slaps them directly onto the project workbench with masking tape, and there they stay until the project is complete. "That way, when I clean up, it's natural to check out the receipts and see what needs to go back," he says.

Small-Space Workshops

For the past 20 years, artist and art installer Tom Cavalieri has worked in some of New York City's snazziest and largest apartments. To do his job effectively, Tom needs to have lots of tools and hardware on hand. The problem is that Tom's own apartment is a lot less sizable than those of his clients. To complicate matters, Tom is an avowed Accumulator (see "Confessions of a Tosser" on page 258).

But this is a success story! After years of dancing on the edge of clutter chaos, Tom—who is also an avid do-it-yourselfer—has effectively organized his tools and hardware in very little space. He's living proof that your workshop doesn't have to be the size of a warehouse to be efficient: All it takes is a spare closet or cupboard—or some space in a closet that is already

A Handy Apron for the Minimalist Handyman

LET'S SAY you don't even own enough tools to organize. Maybe your collection consists of a couple of screwdrivers, a measuring tape, a small hammer, and a utility knife. If that's the case, you probably don't even need a toolbox. Instead, get yourself an apron. That's right. A good, full-length apron with a couple of big pockets can serve as your kit. You don't need to invest in an expensive carpenter's model, either. An old kitchen apron will work just fine, as long as it has pockets. Hang your new tool kit in a closet, then when you need to make a simple repair—say, touch up some paint—put the apron on and you're ready to go. And the apron not only stores your tools, but it protects your clothes, too.

"This was a natural solution for me," says Tom Cavalieri. "My wife, Lori, and I like to backpack, and I'm always amazed at how, with a little planning and thoughtful packing, I can carry so much stuff in so little space." The best part of using a daypack is that all of your tools will be in one place, so you can take them where you need them. And when you're not using your tools, the pack can live in the bottom of any closet.

You don't need to buy a top-of-the-line camper's daypack. A book bag or even a heavy canvas rucksack from the Army-Navy store will work just fine, but keep in mind that better-quality bags will have more ergonomic designs. Make sure that any bag you use has at least three compartments, with one deep enough to hold your largest tool. Finally, check to make sure that the shoulder straps are snugly attached to the bag.

Here's a partial list of the tools that Tom is able to fit in his 2,000-cubic-inch-capacity tool kit.

in partial use (one of Tom's solutions). Take it from us. If Tom was able to create a clutter-free miniworkshop, so can you. Here's how.

Backpack your tools. What to do if you're really pressed for space and can't set aside an entire closet for your tools? You could buy one of those tackle box–style toolboxes. But they can get very heavy, and unless you buy a big one, larger tools such as a cordless drill with its charger won't fit inside. The answer? Store your tools in an ordinary daypack.

In the main compartment

- Carpenter's apron with a tape measure and pencil in the pocket
- Cordless drill with its charger
- Electric drill with an extension cord
- Empty prescription bottle filled with spackle (for patching dings in walls)
- Hammer
- Resealable plastic bags that hold screws, nails, and other assorted hardware

In the medium-size compartment
- Awl
- Extra pencils
- Locking pliers
- Medium-size Phillips-head screwdriver
- Medium-size slot-head screwdriver
- Needle-nose pliers
- Scissors
- Slip-jaw pliers
- Small bottle of white household glue
- Small notebook
- Small spirit level
- Utility knife with extra blades

In the small compartment
- Drill bits
- Nail set
- Screwdriver bits for drills
- Swiss Army-type multiblade knife

A pack holding these tools weighs about 20 pounds, but it's possible to carry even more. When Tom's pack is full of tools, it weighs about 40 pounds. "But when I'm on the subway or walking down the street and see someone lugging a heavy toolbox or a suitcase by its handle, I'm grateful that my load is on my back or shoulder strap," Tom says. "It's much easier to carry."

Encourage hang-ups. In addition to using a rolling plastic cart, Tom stores many of his tools on the back of the door of the closet that serves as his miniworkshop. The space is too

small for Peg-Board, so Tom uses a much simpler device, the common nail, to hang his tools. Here are five tools that you can hang and organize with just a few nails.

- **Hammer.** Drive two nails at a downward angle into the door or wall of your tool closet. Place the nails side by side and just as far apart as the width of your hammer's handle. Make sure the nail heads protrude far enough to hold the hammer under its "shoulders."

- **Spirit level.** A 2-foot spirit level is a handy tool, but only if you can find it when you need it. Just like a hammer, the level can be hung on a couple of nails on the wall or door. Hold the level against the wall you want to hang it on and use a pencil to mark the spots where a couple of nails will hold it best. Now it has a permanent home.

- **Scissors.** Drive two nails into the wall or door and hang the scissors by their handles, blades pointing down.
- **Small saws.** Hang coping saws and hacksaws by their handles or by the space between the blade and the frame. To protect the saw blade (and your hands), cut a length of garden hose the same length as the blade. Split the hose open, then slip it onto the blade.
- **Rasps and files.** These tools often have small holes in their handles that make it easy to hang them from nails.

Keep your sandpaper together. On the back wall of the closet that serves as his workshop, Tom has hung a clipboard. He clips all of his sandpaper sheets, sorted by grit, to the board.

CHAPTER 14

Garage and Shed

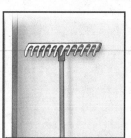

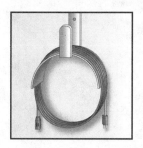

For many people, the garage is a clutter graveyard, a seemingly handy place to chuck that broken toaster oven, last year's throw rugs, and dozens of half-empty cans of paint. Add a snow blower, some lawn furniture, and a few power tools, and it's no wonder that so many of us can't even fit our cars in there anymore.

The good news is that there is probably lots more space in your garage than you realize—maybe even enough to make room for your car. Our experts will help you find and make the most of that space, whether you want to use it for storage, as a workshop, or as a parking spot.

They'll share some of the uses they get from their garages. For example, we'll introduce you to a real-estate broker and garage-organizing expert who uses his garage as a home gym. He also manages to host cigar-smoking night in there. You'll also meet professional organizers Pat Moore, who started her business 10 years ago when she discovered that the man she married was a pack rat, and Cherri Smith, whose friends and clients call her the Dirty Girl, because, as she says, if you're going to organize a garage or shed, you're going to get dirty.

Of course, your first step is to clean it out. Before you panic, know that our experts will be right beside you, showing you the fastest techniques for getting rid of junk. They'll offer easy ways to decide what's worth keeping (the flowerpots that you'll use next spring), what you need to get rid of (the crib that your 17-year-old son once slept in), and how you can get rid of it.

Then they'll help you come up with a plan to organize what's left. You'll learn what to hang on the walls, how to find extra storage space in the ceiling, and how to construct and organize shelf space so you'll never waste another minute looking for those finishing nails. You'll also learn how to use items you probably already have on hand, such as coffee cans or scrap wood, to help you store your stuff in a clutter-free fashion. With help from our experts, you'll get the maximum use of the space that you have in your garage and shed, and you'll never trip over another dead toaster oven.

Clearing Out

You've decided how you're going to use your garage or shed. Maybe you've settled on using it for storage, or perhaps you want to move your exercise equipment into it. Whatever your intentions, the first thing you need to do is get rid of the things in it that you don't need. "There are three steps to organizing a garage or shed," says Lynne Silvers, a professional organizer in West Roxbury, Massachusetts. "Decide what you need to keep, sort what's left, and then store it. A mistake many people make is to store first. They skip the step about deciding whether they even need to store it." Unfortunately, making that decision is often easier said than done, because sometimes it's difficult to part with items, and other times it's tough finding someone to take them.

WHAT TO KEEP, WHAT TO TOSS

Garage organizing expert Bill West of Fort Collins, Colorado, follows a simple rule when deciding what items in his garage or shed to keep and what to toss. "When in doubt," says Bill, "throw it out." Other professional organizers and everyday experts have their own guidelines. Here are some of them.

Play the memory game. "Ask yourself, When was the last time I used this?" says professional organizer Nancy Black of Beverly, Massachusetts. "If you have a 10-year-old bike and it's not good enough to ride and not old enough to be an antique, get rid of it and free up some space." Honestly, if you haven't used something in the past year, what are the chances that you'll ever use it again? Remember that

your life, your interests, and your abilities are always changing, and the things you choose to store should change with them.

Don't get emotionally attached. Parting with an item that was once important to you, such as an old bicycle or your Little League baseball bat, can feel like betraying an old friend, says home improvement enthusiast T. J. Wilson of Monticello, Illinois. Don't let that stop you from doing what you need to do to get your garage or shed organized. "Objects are not our friends," T. J. points out. "They don't have emotions."

Go ahead: Be a fool for love. There is one exception to the above rule, says Lynne Silvers. Once you've asked yourself whether you've used an object or if you really need it, you can ask yourself one other important question: Do I love it? "You probably don't need your 25-year-old Little League glove, but you probably love it, so it's okay to keep it," she says. At that point, you need to make a commitment to find a place for it. Make an appointment with yourself to check these items you love in a year to see if your ardor has cooled.

Use it now or lose it. Keep only the things that you're really going to use, says Lynne. If, for instance, you have lots of wood scraps and a dream of doing a building project with that wood, but you know you're not going to do it in the next 6 months, throw the wood away. "Be realistic," says Lynne. "You can get more wood.

WHEN DONALD AND NANCY SEATON moved into their new house in Hastings, Nebraska, they decided to renovate several rooms. A few months into the project, they found that they had lots of leftover materials and equipment that seemed important to keep. They had leftover paint, extra tiles from the bathroom and kitchen, scraps of drywall that would be good for patching holes, and lots of scrap window casing and baseboard. "It piled up in the garage for a while, and then I decided to organize it," says Don, an avid Collector. He went shopping for a shelving unit and found one he liked, but it cost more than $100.

Don almost bought the shelves, until he realized that if he totaled up the cost of replacing all the things he planned to store on it, it would be far less than the cost of the shelves. "Organized junk is still junk," reasoned Don. So he scrapped the shelving purchase and the leftover materials, and has lived happily without both ever since.

never use again. Or you might have a computer that cost $2,000 6 years ago but is now totally out of date." These are items that, despite the money you once paid for them, you need to get rid of—they will no longer serve any purpose for you.

GETTING DOWN TO BUSINESS

Preparation is the key to doing a good job of clearing out your shed or garage, says Cherri Smith of East Troy, Wisconsin. Here's her advice about making the job run smoothly.

Listen to the weatherman. When you clean out your garage or shed, choose a day when there's no rain in the forecast, because it will be much easier to organize everything if you can move it onto the lawn or the driveway as you work. It's also important to move everything out of your garage or shed before you start, because it can give you the sense that you're starting with a clean slate, and that can be a great psychological boost.

Recruit friends. Bribe them with pizza and cold drinks if you have to. It's no fun cleaning out the garage alone. Plus, if you have help, you can have someone driving stuff to the dump or to the Goodwill shop while you clean. That will save time, and the sooner you get rid of the items you don't need, the better. You won't be tempted to talk yourself out of throwing away that exercise bike you haven't used in 5 years.

If something is not that expensive, can be easily replaced, and you can't identify the specific reason for keeping it, get rid of it."

Forget the price tag. Throwing out something that was expensive to buy can be a big psychological hurdle to get over, says T. J. Wilson. "For example, you might have a chair that's too good to throw away, but that you'll

Give yourself enough time. Don't underestimate the size of the job. It's going to take twice as long as you expect. "If you're planning to do it in 1 day, give yourself a second day," Cherri says. "If it took you 20 years to make the mess, you're not going to undo it all in one afternoon."

Have your tools ready. Don't waste time in the middle of the job trying to find a broom or a dustpan. Have your garbage bags, shovels, barrels, and recycling bins at your side when you begin. It might even be a good idea to set up a card table so that you can sort small items as you remove them from the garage. If you plan to get rid of anything that day, and you need a truck to do it, have the vehicle parked at the curb and ready to go.

Keep refreshments at the ready. Clearing out the garage and the shed is going to be sweaty work. So do yourself a favor and have a cooler full of ice-cold drinks and snacks nearby. That way you won't have to spend valuable decluttering time running back and forth to the refrigerator.

Call the dump. Before you start piling up the trash, make sure you know what your town dump will and won't accept. And make sure you know what its business hours are. You don't want to be stuck with a pile of trash sitting in your driveway or in the bed of your truck for too long. Also, if you have curbside trash pickup, call the town public works department and find out what the trash trucks will and won't take and in what form they'll take it. For instance, does scrap wood have to be tied up into bundles, and how big can the bundles be?

Build it first. If you plan to add cabinets or shelves to the walls of your garage or shed, buy them and assemble them *before* you begin cleaning. That way, once you're finished cleaning, you'll have a place to store the items you moved out of the garage before you began clearing out.

WORDS TO THE WISE

Garages collect a lot of junk because they're catch-alls. Every member of your family probably has his or her designs on the space. One family member might want to park the car in there. Another may want to use the space to work on home improvement projects. Another might want to store gardening equipment and tools there. Take time to discuss your family members' expectations and the best uses for space before you completely reorganize or invest in shelving or a workbench.

Be aware, though, that trying to settle on a single use for your garage or shed can create family conflict. If you decide that the garage is off limits to gardening tools, be prepared to suggest an alternative location for them. Making an agreement that everyone is comfortable with will keep uninvited clutter from creeping back in.

Take notes. When you start to clean your garage or shed, make sure you have a notepad handy. As you come across pieces and equipment for other projects you want to work on, such as the molding for the fireplace, write them down so that you can come back to them later. Also, this is a good time to make a list of the items that you want to give to charity.

Start with the big stuff. As you're cleaning, take care of the big things first so that you can see you're making progress. "This is not the time to start sorting nuts and bolts and placing them into individual jars," says Cherri Smith. "Get them into a big, sturdy box and add the sorting to your to-do list."

Know where it's going. As you pull stuff out of your garage, designate separate areas for trash, recycling, charity, consignment, and so on. Don't just create a big pile that you'll have to go back and sort through again. That's a waste of time.

IT'S GOTTA GO—BUT WHERE?

Your local dump or trash collector probably won't take paint, insecticides, car batteries, oils, or other environmentally hazardous materials. Many communities set aside hazardous waste days every couple of months on which residents can bring their materials to the dump. Check with your town hall or sanitation department (usually listed in the blue government pages in the telephone book) to find out when the next hazardous waste day is. If you have lots of old paint, plan your garage or shed cleanup around that day. Here are some other hints about getting rid of that stuff in your garage or your shed that you don't want or don't need.

Use paint to get rid of it. Cans of latex paint can be a problem to get rid of, even on hazardous waste days. There is a solution, however. Pour or paint it onto a flattened cardboard box or a piece of plywood and let it dry. As long as the paint is dry, most trash collectors will take the cardboard or the wood with the rest of the trash. Mix larger amounts of latex paint with cat litter, sawdust, or sand in a cardboard box lined with plastic. Let the mixture dry and put it out with your regular trash. Some dumps will accept cans of latex paint if you first fill the can with sand or dirt to sop up the paint.

Throw a painting party. Some types of left-over paint can be consolidated and put to use: Latex paint has a shelf life of about 10 years, and as long as it hasn't been frozen and mixes without lumps when stirred, you could still use it to paint the doghouse or shed.

Don't ditch the computer. You've finally realized that the old Macintosh computer you bought in 1989 (and replaced in 1992) is nothing more than a giant doorstop. Before you toss it in the trash, though, be aware that some states consider it hazardous waste and will refuse to pick it up. What's worse, you may get fined for trying to throw it away.

If your town dump refuses to take it, don't despair. You have a couple of options, even if you have several of those digital dinosaurs to get rid of. Many charities are happy to take even out-of-date computers, and you may be able to deduct the book value of the machine on your

---

ARE YOU GETTING THE MOST FROM YOUR GARAGE?

Most people think that the garage is just a storage area. Garage organizing expert Bill West of Fort Collins, Colorado, couldn't disagree more. "The garage is the most underutilized, underappreciated room in the home," Bill says. That's not the case in his home. Bill's garage is not only a parking space and a workshop, but it's also a home gym, a party room, and a smoking lounge. How does he do it? First, he keeps it free of clutter. Second, he uses the space in shifts. Here's how.

1. IT'S A GYM! It's an exercise room! Bill keeps his treadmill in one corner of his garage. So that he doesn't have to stare at a wall as he runs, he set up a TV/VCR unit on a wall swivel shelf. The VCR comes in handy in the workshop as well, because many home improvement products include how-to videos.

2. TURN IT INTO A PARTY ROOM. When Bill throws a big party at his house, he moves the car and any other big equipment into the driveway. He also secures any potentially dangerous items so that the garage can serve as an overflow room for guests. Bill recently hosted a seventh-grade graduation party for his son, and most of the action took place in the garage. "It's a great place to throw a party with kids. They can make as big a mess as they want, and all you have to do is hose the floor down when it's over."

3. LIGHT IT UP. Bill enjoys inviting some of his friends over for occasional cigar-smoking nights, and he doesn't have to worry about fumigating the house the next day. All the puffing takes place in the garage, and his 42-inch-high work-bench serves as the bar. "We don't call it cigar night," says Bill. "We call it cigarage night." Of course, before anyone lights up, Bill makes sure that there are no flammable products in the garage, such as oil cans or gasoline cans for the lawn mower.

Rather than throw away or give away items that you come across while cleaning your garage or shed, you might be tempted to try selling them at a garage sale. If so, keep in mind that you're not going to be able to hold a garage sale and clean your garage at the same time. You'll be too busy haggling over the price of that 15-year-old Big Wheel to get any work done. However, you still might be able to make some money while you're making your garage or shed a more manageable storage facility. If you have a couch or a bike or another big item that you want to get rid of, set it out on the lawn with a for-sale tag on it and a firm, nonnegotiable price.

tax return. There are also some recycling centers opening up that can extract usable or recyclable materials from these machines. At least they'll take them off your hands. Call the repair center that services your model of computer. It can direct you to the nearest computer recycling service.

Think before you donate. Professional organizers know that when we feel guilty about throwing things away, we often settle on another solution. We decide to give them away. How generous of us. Unfortunately, our trash does not automatically become a friend or relative's treasure, especially if it's been sitting in storage for 5 years. "If you come across a toy, don't assume that it needs to go to cousin Suzie because she's planning to have a baby," says Cherri Smith. "If she hasn't had a baby, don't give it to her. You're just giving your problem to someone else. Besides, she'll probably get lots of toys at her baby shower anyway."

Don't use Goodwill as a trash dumping ground. If you do need to give something away, first make sure that it's not broken, stained, or damaged. Then, give it to charity, where it will go to someone who truly is in need.

Don't donate old baby furniture. Giving old but usable items to charity is always a good idea. Remember, though, that certain toys and baby furniture might not be accepted. Items such as high chairs, baby seats, or even old baby baths go out of date much more quickly than other items. As child safety laws improve, many child-related products are recalled or revealed to have hidden dangers. You certainly don't want to give away items that could be a danger to others, and charities certainly don't want to accept them. In some cases, these items belong in the dump, where they can't hurt anyone. There's no liability on the part of the donor of such items, but you can check the safety status of an item by visiting the Consumer Product Safety Commission's Web site (cpsc.gov, or go to your favorite search engine and use the keywords Consumer, Product, Safety, and Commission), which lists all recalled items.

SWEEP IT AND SCRUB IT

Organizational experts will tell you that clutter attracts dirt and that a dirty room invites clutter. Part of organizing your garage means cleaning it, too. In addition to sweeping it, you'll want to rinse it with soap and water to remove all the dust and grease that can soil whatever it is you want to store. Use dishwashing liquid (the concentrated kind) to scrub oil off the concrete. After you've cleaned the floor thoroughly, you'll want it to stay that way. Here are some ways to make sure that it does.

Visit the sweep hereafter. T. J. Wilson believes that if your garage or shed is clean and neat to begin with, you'll be more likely to keep it that way. "If the place looks clean, you're going to have more respect for it and return items to their proper places, stacking them neatly," says T. J. He makes sure his shed stays clean by keeping a broom and dustpan in it, and whenever he cuts his lawn or shovels snow, he takes a few minutes to sweep the floor after putting the equipment away.

Give it a fresh coat. After you've cleaned your floor, consider painting it or applying a sealer to it. "Keep it neat, no concrete," is the motto of Bill West. The coating on his garage floor protects it from motor oil and other corrosive fluids. And since the surface has remained so smooth, it's easy to sweep or mop the floor. Buy a top-quality product, says Bill, especially if you park your car in the garage. Otherwise heat from the tires will cause the coating to begin chipping and peeling in as little as 6 months. Bill's coating of choice is a Kelly-Moore product called Envira-Poxy.

Fix the cracks. When garage floors take a lot of abuse, they can get cracked. Those cracks are magnets for dirt and debris, and grow larger

---

EVOLUTION OF THE GARAGE

If you live in an older home, one more than 50 or 60 years old, you probably have a detached garage. That means you have to walk outside your house to get to the garage, making it a less convenient storage spot. But the detached garage wasn't just a passing architectural fancy. In fact, it was more a matter of safety than of fashion.

When autos were first mass-produced in the '20s and '30s, homeowners were afraid that they would explode, so builders constructed the garages a safe distance from the homes. In the '20s, building codes were first enacted that required a fire wall to be built between a house and an attached garage, but it wasn't until the '50s and '60s that people started to become comfortable enough with cars to accept attached garages. Of course, by then, Collectors and Concealers were also discovering how easy it was to fill the garage with everything but the car.

without repair. You can fill hairline cracks as wide as an eighth of an inch with concrete crack filler or an all-purpose urethane caulk. To repair larger cracks, you'll need a mortar compound. Be sure to remove any debris from the crack before you repair it. You may also want to scrub away any stains that cover the crack, or the adhesive won't work. Once the crack has been fixed, go ahead and paint or seal the floor.

Getting Reorganized

As a real-estate broker with 25 years' experience, Bill West has seen more than his share of messy garages. "People approach their garages with a landfill mentality," says Bill. "They just shove or toss things into the garage, never to see them again." The key to a clutter-free garage or shed is to have a system that makes it easy to get what you want and to put it back where it belongs. Here are some tips on how to do that.

CREATE A PLAN

Before you start storing items in your garage or shed, get yourself some graph paper and make a diagram of the floor plan, then map out what's going to go where. Professional organizer Pat Moore of McKenney, Virginia, likes to divide and store items in categories: sports, camping, pets, gardening, painting, tools and hardware, and the like. Some of those categories may need to be divided further into subgroups. Sports, for

example, can be divided into golf, water sports, winter sports. Do the dividing, cautions Pat, before you purchase hooks, nails, or shelving. That way you'll have a better idea of what you need. While making your plan, here are a few other things you'll want to take into account.

Clear a path. When you're coming up with a floor plan for your shed, remember that you'll need to be able to roll your lawn mower or snow blower in and out. So be sure to create a corridor.

Leave room on the floor. Keep the floor space in your garage or shed as clear as possible for the items that you can't hang on the walls or from the ceiling, such as your garden cart or wheelbarrow.

If it's out of season, get it out of sight. There's no need to have your skis handy during the summer, and you don't want your pool

CONSIDER YOUR CAR

Perhaps you'd *really* like to turn your garage into an elaborate workshop and home gym, but alas, that may not be practical. Before you banish your car to the driveway, remember that it's probably your family's largest investment after your house. Keeping your car in the garage and out of the elements can add years to its life and help maintain its resale value.

equipment stowed out of the way during the summer. In the spring and summer, you can store your skis and ski poles in the rafters of your garage or shed and your shovels and hoes along the walls. Then, in the fall and winter, when you don't need to get to your gardening tools, switch their place with the skis. Here's a caveat for downhill or backcountry skiers: If you do store your skis in the garage, make sure that the roof doesn't leak. The edges on metal-edged skis are made of steel and will rust if they're not stored in a dry place.

Keep tools accessible. It's a smart idea to store items such as hand tools at eye level using shelving, cabinets, or hooks, because you don't want to have to stoop down to find what you need. You can see larger items at a quick glance, so it's okay to store them on or near the floor.

Don't fight the tide. When you look around your cluttered garage in its preorganized state, take note of the sorts of clutter that gather near each door. If certain tools, such as the rake and hoe, always end up near the garage door, take your own hint when designing the new floor plan. Make sure the items you use most often are stored right next to the door of your shed or garage. Why? Because that's where they're going to end up, anyway. By the same token, you'll want to store those big bags of extra paper towels, toilet paper, or garbage bags somewhere near the door leading into the house.

Ensure many happy returns. Keep in mind that the easier it is to return an item to its storage spot, the more likely it is that it will end up there. Don't make a plan that calls for storing your lawn mower in an out-of-the-way place during the summer.

KNOW WHAT GOES WHERE

You have lots of stuff to store in your shed or garage, but keep in mind that some items are better suited to one or the other.

A shed, for instance, is a better place than a garage to store fuel because of the potential for fire and noxious fumes. (Make sure that the shed is vented so that the fuel fumes can escape.) Paint, on the other hand, should go in the garage because it's not good for it to freeze.

If you do store paint in the garage, you may want to install a thermometer. Most products have storage temperatures listed on their labels,

and the thermometer will let you keep tabs on the room temperature. And that can help you decide where to store it.

In addition to safety concerns, consider location. If you're going to use something frequently in the yard, such as a rake or lawn mower, it makes sense to store it in the shed rather than the garage so that you don't have to haul it so far. However, items that need to be loaded onto your car every time you use them, such as skis, are better off stored in the garage with the car.

Keep two sets of tools. T. J. Wilson stores two sets of tools in his garage, one for woodworking and one for fixing his car. His organizational plan keeps those tools separate because they do different jobs and make different kinds of messes. "Saws tend to get dusty, and car equipment tends to get greasy," says T. J. "And when wood and dust mix, it makes a big mess." That's why he keeps his woodworking tools in one corner and his automotive tools in another.

Making the Most of Your Space

A good storage plan calls for getting the most use out of all available space—including the floor—with the help of shelving, the walls, and the rafters. "Think laterally," says Bill West. "Look at the walls, posts, even the ceilings. Lateral thinking maximizes vertical storage." Our professional organizers and everyday experts have plenty of ideas that will help you maximize the storage space.

MAXIMIZE YOUR SHELF SPACE

Whether you already have shelving in place, plan to buy some, or are thinking of building your own, here are some tips that will help you get as much of your stuff as possible up off the floor.

Plan ahead. If you're going to build or buy shelving units for your garage or shed, have an idea of what's going to go on the shelves before you build them. There must be lots of room between shelves that will accommodate large or tall items. But if you plan to store small items on

---

BUILD YOUR OWN SHELVES—EASILY

If your garage or shed has exposed wall studs (as opposed to wallboard or plaster), you can easily add shelving between the studs. These narrow shelves will be a great place to store small but potentially dangerous items such as automobile supplies or gardening supplies. To build the shelves, all you need are a length of 2-by-4 pine (the length depends on how many shelves you want to build), a hammer, some 3-inch nails, a saw, and a yardstick or a tape measure. Here's how to do it.

1. Measure the width of the space between two studs. It will probably be 14 to 15 inches.
2. Cut off a piece of the two-by-four to fit the space between the studs. That will be your shelf.
3. Wedge the newly cut shelf between the studs. If you don't own a level, use the yardstick or the tape measure to make sure it is at the same height on both sides.
4. Use the hammer to drive two nails through the stud and into each end of the shelf.

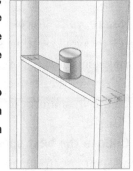

Wall stud shelving

---

the shelves, then you can place them close together. "If you build shelves too far apart, you're wasting space," says Lynne Silvers. "You don't want to waste any vertical space. And you don't want to stack items on shelves if you don't have to, because that makes it harder to get to them."

Think plastic. If you're going to purchase a shelving system from a home improvement center, Nancy Black has one word for you: plastic. "Plastic shelving units usually don't require tools to assemble, so they're easier to put together. They don't dent or rust, and they usually cost less than the metal ones," says Nancy.

Box up your clutter. One way to get the most use out of your preexisting shelf space while keeping things organized is to put like items such as paintbrushes or pet supplies together in boxes that, if necessary, can be stacked on the shelves. Several small boxes are better than large ones because they're easier to move around and it's easier to find what you're looking for. Just remember to clearly label each box.

Reuse your boxes. If you have to stack boxes to avoid wasting shelf space, consider storing items in shoe boxes or oatmeal canisters. They're sturdy, easy to open and close, and because they're uniform sizes, stack neatly.

Choose the best spot on the shelf. Place items you use frequently near the front of shelves, says Pat Moore. For example, keep paintbrushes near the front and tall cans of paint near the back (and for safety purposes, keep them on a high shelf). "You're far more likely to need those brushes before you ever use those old cans of paint," says Pat.

Put extra dish tubs to use. Spare dishwashing basins are great for keeping your shelf space organized. Place a bunch of small items in one, put a label on it, and slide it onto a shelf.

Bottom's up. While you're piling things on top of the shelves, don't forget about the space underneath. You can use clear glass jars, especially baby food jars, to store different-size hardware. Unscrew the lids and use screws to attach them to the underside of the shelves. Then fill the jars with nails, nuts, or bolts and screw them to their lids. Since the jars are glass, you can see what's inside them and won't have to label them.

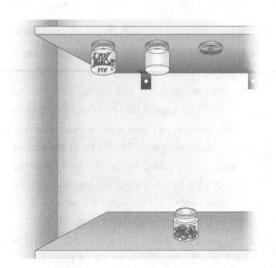

Attaching baby food jars under shelves keeps nails and other small supplies organized and in plain sight.

Stack 'em high. When you're planning to buy or build shelves, remember that it's okay if garage or shed shelves are higher than, say, a bookshelf. You can use those shelves near the ceiling, the ones you need a stepstool to reach, to store seasonal items such as flowerpots or Christmas decorations, stuff you need to get to just once a year.

Rotate your stock. Once you've stacked those Christmas ornaments or lawn toys on the top shelf, be sure to rotate them to a lower shelf when they come into season. For example, you can store winter sports equipment on a high shelf in the summer, but move it down in the fall. Do the same with gardening equipment and any other seasonal tools that you don't need for half the year.

Label your shelves. When you have lots of shelves, it can be a good idea to label them with numbers or letters—shelf number 1, number 2, or A, B, C, and so on. Make a master list of the things stored on each shelf and post it somewhere in the garage or shed. Having the list nearby will shorten your steps when you're looking for specific items.

CALLING ALL WALLS

Any wall space that's not holding up a shelf could be holding some type of tool or equipment. "Hang every item that you can on the wall, even some that you wouldn't think of hanging," says Pat Moore. For instance, she

CLUTTER CRUSADERS

Downsize Your Paint Cans

CHRIS BEAN OF WINCHESTER, MASSACHU-SETTS, doesn't waste space in his garage by keeping large paint cans with small amounts of paint in them. Instead, he pours the leftover paint into smaller containers, such as baby food jars. (He has an infant son and therefore an endless supply of baby food jars.) That way the paint is handy for touch-ups but doesn't take up a lot of space. For larger amounts of paint, he uses old detergent containers (he does a lot of laundry) or even plastic water bottles. The detergent containers have a wide mouth, so it's easy to fill them from a paint can. "Make sure you dab some paint on the outside of the detergent container so that you know what color is inside," says Chris. "You'll probably need a funnel to fill water bottles, but like the detergent containers, they're airtight and easy to pour from. And like the baby food jars, you can see what's inside them."

hangs folding lawn chairs. "They can take up a lot of floor space," Pat says, "but when you hang them on the wall, they're out of the way but are still visible." Here are some other items you can hang from the walls of your garage or shed, and some ingenious ways to hang them.

Drop it in the bucket. A bucket makes a great container for small tools. Just hang the bucket from a hook on the wall and drop in the tools. But be sure to stick a label on the bucket so you'll know what's inside.

Can it. If you want more permanent small-tool holders, nail coffee cans to the wall and place hand tools inside.

Zip it. Store small items such as nuts or bolts in small, resealable plastic bags. Then you can either hang the bags from a bulletin board with thumb tacks or store them together in one box—a tackle box, say, that you can place on a shelf.

Use a shoe bag. Shoe bags, the kinds that hang on the back of a closet door, can hold as many as a dozen pairs of shoes—or 24 different types of smaller items, from golf tees to wing nuts, that would otherwise end up lost in a junk drawer. You can buy these canvas shoe bags at any household goods store, and instead of hanging them in the closet, hang them on the wall of your garage or shed. Be sure to buy one with see-through compartments so that you'll have no trouble finding what you're looking for.

Rack your rakes. If you'd rather hang your rakes and shovels from the walls, there are simple ways to do that. Here are two.

1. Handle up. Hammer nails or screw hooks into the walls at about eye level, then drill holes into your tool handles and hang the tools directly from the holes onto the hooks or nails. If

CLUTTER CRUSADERS

Stand 'Em on End

CHRIS BEAN OF WINCHESTER, MASSACHU-SETTS, grew tired of tripping over his shovels and rakes every time he stepped into his shed. So he nailed some strapping (1-inch-by-2-inch strips of wood) horizontally to the shed's exposed wall studs at about waist height. Now, with the pole end down, he can drop his shovels and rakes behind the strapping and between the studs.

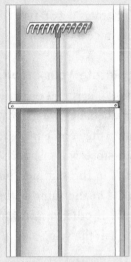

Wall-stud storage

you're having trouble drilling holes that are large enough to fit over the nail heads, simply thread a piece of twine through the handle hole and make a loop that will hang on the hook.

2. Handle down. You can also hang tools the other way around, handle down. Drive two nails into the wall. Make sure the space between them is just larger than the width of the handle, and hang the rake or broom end on these nails. The only trouble with hanging tools this way is that you have to swing them upside down to store them, which can be dangerous, and may

Reuse Those Rollers

THE PROBLEM WITH STORING ELECTRICAL TAPE or duct tape in the shed or garage is that if the roll falls on the floor or your workbench, its side picks up all kinds of dust and dirt, and then the tape won't adhere well. Professional organizer Pat Moore has a way to avoid that problem, particularly if you've recently had your bathroom redone. "Fasten a toilet paper holder to the inside of a cabinet door or right to your wall. Instead of holding toilet paper, it can hold big rolls of tape."

Use a simple hose hanger to organize your extension cords.

damage other things in the garage. If you don't mind spending a little more money, buy brackets or hooks that attach to walls and are specifically designed to hold rakes and brooms. They are available at hardware stores and home improvement centers.

Hold on to that hose hanger. Garden hose hangers have become somewhat obsolete now that you can buy those big roll-up units for your hose. But don't throw away your old hose hanger. Instead, hang it on the wall of your garage or shed and use it to hold heavy-duty extension cords. If you use nails or hooks to hang a cord, you run the risk of puncturing the cord's protective rubber coating. That's not a problem if you use a hose hanger.

Strap them in. Anyone who owns a set of bungee cords knows how useful they can be. Here's one more chore they can handle. Store skis and other narrow items between two exposed studs with a bungee cord stretched across to hold them in place. Attach the ends of the bungee cord to hooks or nails that have been fastened to the wall studs.

UP IN THE RAFTERS

You've filled all your shelves with boxes and bins and covered every inch of wall space in your garage or shed with brooms, shovels, and rakes, but you're still looking for somewhere to store that extra lumber you'll be using next month to build some additional shelves. Look up. There's plenty of room in the rafters of most sheds and garages, as long as they were built with a gabled roof. You can lay long, flat items directly on the ceiling joist or you can store smaller items in the rafters by first laying a piece of ¾-inch plywood across the joists. The plywood won't cost you more than $10 at a home improvement center, and it will allow you to create a kind of attic for storing seasonal items up and out of the way until you need them. Here are some other ways to use the space above.

Use the space between the rafters. Fasten strips of wood or lengths of heavy rope across the bottoms of the ceiling joists and store items such as skis, ski poles, hockey sticks, or tomato plant posts on top of them.

Organizing Specific Stuff

How many times have you gone to fix something around the house and spent more time searching for the right tools than working on the project? Or how often has the start of a game been delayed while you tried to dig through a pile of sports equipment looking for the ball? Help has arrived. Our experts have some solutions that will create a place for everything—from screwdrivers to soccer balls—and make everything easy to find.

AUTO MOTIVES

If you'll be storing your car in the garage and plan to add shelving or cabinets, you'll want to measure how much space you have for these items while your car is *in* the garage. Make sure you have ample space to open all four car doors as well as the trunk and hood. Also make sure that you have space to walk in front of and behind the car. The next time someone carries big bags of groceries into the house, he or she will be grateful that you checked these details. Here are some other car-related factors to keep in mind.

Store smart, avoid scratches. You probably worry that those scratches on your car came from the guy who parked too close to you at the supermarket. In reality, most scratches occur closer to home. Reduce this problem by carefully storing bulky items such as folding lawn chairs or bikes. Make sure they're close to the door or leave a clear path to the door, and you'll save your paint job while you keep your garage neat.

Park perfectly. One way to increase space in the garage is to position your car properly. Pulling in too far wastes space near the wall that you might otherwise use.

Here's how to position your car perfectly each time: Pull the car in once, making sure you have the right amount of storage space near the wall. With some string, a nail, and tape, suspend a Ping-Pong ball or tennis ball from the ceiling so that it just touches the windshield. Now, whenever you pull into the garage, you'll know to stop just as the ball touches the glass.

Solve other parking problems. You know where the car goes, but do your children know where to put their bikes, wagons, and other big toys? With a little bit of fluorescent electrical tape, you can solve these problems by marking out a space for each on the floor.

SPORTS EQUIPMENT.

You're tired of having to kick basketballs and soccer balls out of the way every time you want to take the car out of the garage or pull the lawn mower out of the shed. Sporting equipment is

---

MAKE A CHAIN GANG

A chef gets the most use of his or her kitchen space by hanging pots and pans from a ceiling rack. You can do the same in your garage or shed by making a kind of ceiling rack for your gardening hand tools. Here's an easy way to make one.

1. Hang a length of heavy-duty chain from the rafter with an S hook so that the bottom link is within easy reach.

2. Hang additional S hooks from several of the lower links, also within easy reach.

3. Insert eye screws into the top of your tool handles and simply hang your tools on this improvised hanger.

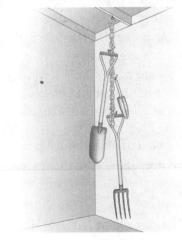

Create a ceiling rack for trowels and other hand tools.

From the Kitchen to the Garage

KITCHEN CABINETS ARE GREAT for organizing and storing items in the garage or shed, but if you've ever remodeled your kitchen, you know that cabinets can be very expensive. Of course, if you do renovate your kitchen, your old cabinets, regardless of how awful they looked above your sink and below your countertops, might be just fine for your shed or garage. And best of all, they're free.

If you're not redoing your kitchen, maybe a friend is redesigning his or hers. Or, check with a cabinetmaker or a home improvement center. It might have some cabinets that were returned because they were the wrong size, or wrong color, or maybe they had some scratches in them. Whatever the case, if they have reject cabinets taking up space in their storeroom, they're probably willing to let you take them off their hands for a very reasonable price. "The cabinets in our garage were custom made for someone else's kitchen, but they were the wrong size," says T. J. Wilson of Monticello, Illinois. "We got them for a song."

into the yard when they go out to play and then back into the garage or shed when they come in at night. The bin will give them an easy way to pick up and store their toys, which will make it less likely that you'll have to do it.

What goes up doesn't have to come down. Footballs, baseballs, and basketballs don't sit still when you place them on a shelf, but there are ways to keep them off the floor.

One way is to hang a mesh shopping bag or laundry bag from a hook or nail on the wall. The bag will expand to hold the balls, and because it's mesh, you can see what's in the bag. Or, if you're building a shelf, fasten the front of the shelf a little higher than the back. That will keep the balls from rolling off the front of the shelf. For extra security, fasten a lip along the front and side edges of the shelf so that balls can't roll off.

Bag your bats. Your old golf bag might be too worn to carry on the course, but you can

usually either round or bulky, which means it's seldom easy to store. However, there are some solutions.

Roll out the toy chest. If your kids have lots of sporting equipment such as soccer balls, Frisbees, and Wiffle ball sets, you might want to give them a rolling bin that they can move

Hold Them in a Hamper

CHRIS BEAN, of Winchester, Massachusetts, found a good use for an extra laundry hamper. He put it in his shed and uses it for storing balls and bats and other bulky sports equipment. "You can also use a clean garbage can," says Chris. "But be sure to label the outside clearly so that no one tosses garbage in there, too."

still get some use out of it. Fasten it to a wall in your garage or shed and use it to hold long, tall items such as baseball bats or fishing poles.

Get it off the floor and onto hooks. Scooters, hula hoops, jump ropes, and even bicycle helmets can roll around your garage floor, under the car, and underfoot, driving you crazy and possibly causing a dangerous fall. Get them out of the way by hanging them on large, plastic-coated utility hooks from the hardware store. Attach the hooks to the interior wall of your garage (find a stud for better security) at a level the kids can easily reach. The hooks are cheap, they won't scratch your stuff, and they'll help keep your garage junk-free.

Join the bucket brigade. For smaller balls—baseballs, softballs, old tennis balls, footballs—use a bucket. An old bucket with a handle can be stored anywhere in the garage within easy reach of both kids and adults. The bucket handle makes it easy to carry the whole collection around, so you can stash it in the car for trips to the beach or park. With all the balls in one place, you won't have to search for that certain one that rolled behind the paint cans or under the lawn mower.

Tote the toys. Gillian Davies, an environmental scientist in Acton, Massachusetts, has two little boys and a passion for outdoor sports. Gillian's also passionate about keeping clutter under control. So she sorts the boys' things—beach toys, balls, and the like—into plastic beach bags or canvas totes. She hangs the bags on old brass coat hooks that are screwed into the garage wall. "It's great, because their gear doesn't get scattered all over the garage, and I just grab the bag with the right stuff whenever we head to the beach or the park," Gillian says.

Be a great dresser. Have an old chest of drawers languishing in the basement? You know, the one that's in such bad shape (or style) that you know you'll never use it again, but you can't bear to part with it? Haul it out to the garage or shed and fill the drawers with baseball gloves, elbow and knee pads, goalie's masks, whatever. Your gear will stay clean, dry, and organized—and your bureau will have a new life. You can even let the kids paint or decorate it with sports logos or stickers. But remember, it's important to choose a dresser that you don't want to refurbish at a later date, because ex-

OUT-OF-THE-BOX IDEAS

Put Your Hammock to Work

HERE'S A great way to use the hammock that someone gave you as a housewarming gift: Hang it from hooks screwed into the exposed ceiling joists of your garage. Then toss some of your lighter-weight, seasonal sports gear in it during the off-season—like basketballs, soccer balls, and pool toys in the winter, and hockey gear, plastic sleds, and snow saucers in the summer.

treme changes in temperature, as well as any dampness in the air, are likely to warp the wood over time.

Pick up the laundry. Plastic laundry baskets are great catch-alls for sports gear that tends to spread itself all over the garage. If you have several baskets—and lots of stuff—designate each basket for a particular category: one for balls, one for kneepads and elbow pads, one for helmets. Or assign a basket to each household member. Any way you slice it, your old laundry baskets can cut the sports clutter in your garage or shed.

Make it a clean sweep. Canoe and kayak paddles can take up a lot of space if they're just lying around the garage or shed. So take a tip from your spouse's uncluttered cleaning closet: Hang metal broom clips along the wall of the garage and stick your paddles in the clips. (The clips are available at most hardware stores.)

This way, your paddles are out of the way but easy to locate. However, if you have detachable kayak paddles, take them apart and hang each section separately, blade up, to prevent oxidation from damaging them at the joints, says Joel Thomas, owner of New England Small Craft in Rowley, Massachusetts.

Try this lifesaving advice. Who wants to trip over damp, musty boating life jackets (or personal flotation devices) that are lying around the garage floor? No one. Here are two ways to get them off the floor.

1. Toss 'em in a bag. Let your life jackets dry out before putting them away, then store them in the garage or shed in a space where they get plenty of air. If you use clothes hangers (hung on plastic-coated hardware hooks attached to the wall) or a mesh bag (hung from the wall or ceiling), your jackets will be off the floor, not to mention fresh and ready to wear next time.

STASH THE SKI POLES

No matter how well you think you've propped them up, ski poles have a way of sliding to the floor in a tangle like a set of pick-up sticks. But when that happens, you don't feel like playing a game. You can ward off the ski-pole mess in your garage by building a very simple stand. First, cut a 2-foot-long piece of 1- by 6-inch pine board (available at any lumberyard or discount home supply shop) and two 4-inch-high squares (for legs). Attach the legs to the bottom of the board with screws or nails. Turn the stand over, and it will look like a small footstool or bench. Next, drill holes in your stand with a ⅜-inch bit (you can go larger or smaller if your poles are extra thick or super skinny), counting one hole for each pole. If you drill the holes in two rows, about 4 inches apart, you'll have enough room for six pairs of poles with average-size baskets. If you're feeling especially crafty, you can sand the edges of your pole stand and add a coat of paint or polyurethane. Otherwise, tote it out to the garage or shed as is and plunk your poles, baskets up, into their new home.

2. Hang a rod. You can also hang life jackets on hangers from an old closet pole or wooden curtain rod suspended from a ceiling joist. Measure the rod and screw two eyehooks into a joist, lined up with each end of the rod. Attach a length of rope between each screw and the end of the rod, at the height you want. Then hang your life jackets, wetsuits, or any other outdoor sports clothing items on the rod just as if it were in your closet.

Park your bikes. Bicycles can take up a huge amount of space in your garage. And when one topples over and hits your car, you're ready to ditch them forever. Here's how to save the family cycles—along with the finish on your car—and still have room to walk around in your garage.

1. Get them off the floor. John Gromek, owner of Exeter Cycles in Exeter, New Hampshire, suggests that for each bicycle you screw a pair of heavy-duty, plastic-coated utility hooks (available at any bike shop or hardware store) into the exposed ceiling joists in your garage. Hang the bike on the hooks upside down by the wheels or just by the back wheel.

2. Improvise hooks. Do you have several heavy-duty metal hanging-plant brackets lying around the garage? John suggests that you clean up the clutter—and hang up your bike—by screwing a pair of eyebolts to the exposed ceiling joists in your garage. Then hang your bike upside down with the wheels on the lower hook of the brackets and put the upper hook through the eyebolt.

3. Buy ready-made storage. Spend a couple of bucks ($13 to $30) for a fold-down bicycle rack that attaches to your garage wall. Closet Masters (www.closet-masters.com) is one online dealer that carries several varieties.

4. It's curtains for those bikes. Here's another great way to get your bikes up in the air: Grab a pair of old wooden curtain brackets and attach them to the edge of a 2-by-4 board at a width that lines up with your bicycle wheels. Hang the board against the garage wall, attached to studs if possible for security. Then hoist your bike onto your new rack, hanging it upside down by the wheels. You can also attach the brackets to a ceiling joist and hang your bike there.

LAWN AND GARDEN TOOLS

The thing to keep in mind about the tools and equipment you use for your garden and lawn is that they'll get a lot of use in the spring, summer, and early fall, but you'll barely touch them in winter. So store them out of the way when it gets cold, maybe in the rafters of your garage or shed, and make sure they're very handy the rest of the year. The other thing about lawn and garden tools is that they can quickly clutter a shed or garage if they're not put away properly. Here are a few ways to keep them handy and keep them from cluttering your storage areas.

Roll out the barrel. A plastic trash barrel is a great place to store your rakes and shovels.

And if the barrel has wheels, you can wheel your equipment right out of the shed or garage into the yard.

Get a handle on them. Some tools get used together: gardening gloves, a trowel, fertilizer, and knee pads, for instance. You might find it useful to store those kinds of items together in a basket with handles. Then you can grab the basket on your way to the garden without having to hunt around for the tools on all their different pegs, hooks, and shelves. The same idea can work with car-cleaning products. All those sponges, chamois cloths, and cleaners can go into a single bucket that's easy to pick up when you decide to wash the car. For a 5-gallon bucket, you can also add a wraparound cloth apron with pockets so that you have separate compartments for additional tools. The aprons can be found at home improvement centers and cost less than $2.

Create a mower maintenance kit. You've eked out a spot for the lawn mower in your garage or shed, but don't forget about the supplies you need to keep the mower up and running. Gather all those items together and keep them in a clear plastic storage bin, preferably one with a handle so that you can take your kit out to the field for

SHED KNOW-HOW

Wondering if a shed is a good idea for you? Well, it depends. Whether or not it's worthwhile to put a shed in your yard or against the side of your garage usually depends on the size of your property. If you have lots of acreage and do your own landscape work, you probably have a large lawn mower, a snow blower, a wheelbarrow, and other such equipment that would quickly suck up the space in your garage. And sheds are convenient because they allow you to store lawn and garden equipment and supplies out in the yard, closer to where you're going to use them. If you decide that you simply can't live without a shed, heed these two expert tips to keep it from becoming a clutter dumping ground.

MIND YOUR HEAD (SPACE). If you do buy or build a shed, make sure that it's tall enough to stand inside. If you have to stoop, you'll be less inclined to spend much time in there putting things back in their proper places, and all your supplies and equipment will quickly become very disorganized.

DON'T DO WINDOWS. Many fancy new sheds come with windows and even window boxes, so that they look like tiny cottages rather than tool closets. If your heart is set on a shed that matches your house, then go ahead and buy one of those. Be aware, though, that the windows are just expensive add-ons that take up valuable wall space. A salesperson will tell you that windows add light so that you can find things. Actually, you're going to have the door open when you're in the shed, and that will give you plenty of light to see by. Of course, be sure to buy a shed with a door wide enough for you to get your equipment in and out easily.

quick repairs. Here's what to put inside.
- Can of oil
- Fuel funnel
- Miscellaneous spare parts
- Replacement air and oil filters
- Sharpening stone or file to get nicks out of the blade
- Spark plugs
- Wrench

Sort Your Seeds

WOULDN'T IT be nice to organize those little seed packets that always seem to scatter to the four winds in the garage? Look no farther than the accessories of your favorite trading-card collector. That's right. The protective sheets designed to hold baseball and cartoon trading cards have multiple slots that are the perfect size for seed packets. Store the sheets in a three-ring binder. You can stash planting directions, articles and newspaper clippings, and catalogs in the front pockets. That way, even if you keep seeds on hand mostly for day-dreaming, they'll be where you want, when you want them—and it's easy to see whether they're out of date, too. If you use a vinyl binder, it's weatherproof, so you can take it out to the garden. And since you can store the seeds with the packet openings facing up, there will be no more incidents of accidentally picking up a seed packet by the wrong end and spilling 72 radish seeds across the floor to attract mice.

Keep your garden tools upright. If your storage plan for garden tools consists of leaning them against the wall inside your garage and hoping they stay right side up, then lend an ear. With one simple and subtle addition to your system, your garden fork, shovel, and spade will stay in place while you're not using them—and remain sharp all season long, to boot. Here's the secret: Lay a length of 12-inch-wide common pine board on the floor underneath the tools. That's all there is to it! The wood protects the metal edges from getting dinged up on the concrete floor and acts as a moisture barrier to keep your tools rust-free. And standing on the softer surface, they'll be less likely to fall over!

Go postal—in a good way. Even if the extent of your garden is the few hanging boxes and planters on your deck or patio, you still need to keep your tools organized neatly. Here's a terrific way to keep your supplies handy and protected, but otherwise unobtrusive: Store them in a vinyl mailbox, available at home improvement stores and hardware stores. Rubbermaid makes several models.

These mailboxes are made to withstand the elements. A medium-size box will have a large covered opening, and it's the perfect size for a few hand tools, gardening gloves—even a small box of fertilizer. Several styles are available. You can mount some models on a post, and hang others on a wall or the railing of your deck.

Tote a six-pack of tools. Sure, you could buy a fancy garden-tool caddy to carry your

TRY POT NETS

Terra-cotta pots are real space wasters. You can't stack them, because they expand and contract with the temperature and could chip or fracture when you try to pry them apart. And that means you have to give each one its own spot on a shelf, right?

Don't give in so easily. Those net bags that onions and lemons are sold in can keep terra-cotta pots from sticking together, even if they're dirty or it's hot. You'll need one net bag for each pot. Place the pot in the bag, then nest it inside another pot. Tuck the topmost net bag inside the pot, so you can grasp it when you need to pull the stack apart. Another nifty benefit: If the mesh is narrow enough, you can use it as a liner to keep soil and drainage material from washing out of the drainage hole when you pot the plants. The netting also makes it easier to pull root-bound plants from the pots.

hand tools around the yard, but then you have to find a place to store the caddy! Here's a better idea: The next time you head out to do a little weeding or digging, place your hand tools, your gloves, or even a few bulbs in the compartments of an empty cardboard six-pack holder. Of course you're being clever, but you're being frugal, too. When you've finished for the day, you can just put the six-pack holder back in the recycling bin. And depending on your soda or beer-drinking habits, you may have a steady supply of these cartons!

DRIVE CLUTTER OUT OF YOUR CAR

Judging by the clutter we leave behind, we Americans don't just drive in our cars—we eat, play, work, and sleep in them, too. So, while you're out in the garage pondering organization, why not take on the family vehicles?

Have a can waiting at the end of the road. Lots of travel Web sites and travel clubs recommend handy car garbage containers, and they can be nice. But instead of focusing energy on getting garbage into a bag, concentrate on taking it completely out of the car. Make it convenient by keeping a garbage can or wastebasket within steps of wherever you park the car, ideally next to the door into the house. Then make it a habit to put all of that day's trash into the can the second you close the car door. If you're diligent about it, you won't need a 3-gallon bag taking up space in your vehicle.

See your way clear to a title. Sure, you want to be logical, but keeping your car's registration and title in an accessible place could also mean precious time spent shuffling through coupons, graduation announcements, and CD covers while the officer of the law glares at you skeptically. A nice choice for in-car storage of these documents is a see-through plastic pencil case, the kind kids clip into three-ring binders. The case will be easy to identify because you'll see the contents inside it, it opens and shuts easily, and it's small enough to fit easily inside the glove box or lie flat in the pocket of your side door.

Sponge up ashtray clutter. It seems like all the tiny things, from earrings to safety pins to Chiclets, and—of course—your loose change, find their way into the ashtray, where they become a grimy mess. Curtail this clutter magnet by cutting a new, flat household sponge to fit the bottom of the ashtray. It will keep the small objects from rolling into each other, and make it easier to pick out, say, your train ticket from among the other debris. Plus, the added height makes it harder to overload the ashtray with a tangle of tiny objects. And when things *do* get grimy in there, just lift out the sponge, trinkets and all, then sort, wash, dry, and replace.

Change how you handle change. Never thought too much money could be a problem, did you? But too many coins in your car can get grubby and start spilling all over the place, and they take up space in the ashtray where you'd rather put your parking garage access card or something else that really belongs in the car. One way to stem the tide of coins is to start carrying a penny roller in your vehicle. Every time you get pennies, put them right in the roller—it will hold up to 50 cents. Then, when you pay at drive-throughs or gas stations, make exact change with the pennies—this will cut down on silver coins, too. Best of all, if you fill the penny rolls, you can usually unload them at the gas station.

FOUR WAYS TO KEEP FOOD TRASH OUT OF THE CAR

Wrappers, crumpled napkins, drink cups. . . . Somehow, when food enters the car, the trash seems to make it no farther than the floor (or, if you're lucky, the ashtray). Here's how to break the cycle:

1. Pay at the pump. When no one goes inside the gas station, no one brings out jelly doughnuts, slushes, or gum.

2. Stop driving through. When you can, particularly on long trips, opt to sit down at fast-food restaurants instead of taking your order on the road. You lose only a few minutes (usually the inside line is much shorter), and the trash stays at the restaurant.

3. Drive junk food out of the car. Make a new rule: The only food allowed in the car is fresh fruit, bagels, and bottled water. Cut out the sodas, crackers, candy bars, and fast food, and you cut out most of the messy packaging—and the spills and crumbs. And another thing: Those snacks are healthier, too!

4. In the winter, ask for drive-through drinks with no ice. It's almost inevitable that a cup of ice left over from a soda or iced tea will end up melted in the trash bag or, worse, tipped over on the floor. Save the slop and the mildew by drinking soda straight, at least in the cold months, when the beverage will stay cool by itself until you've finished drinking it.

Pack up your supplies in your old diaper bag. Lots of companies sell special storage bags that you can sling over the headrest of the passenger seat. Many of them are pretty neat, too. But before you commit to this organizing tool, experiment with an old diaper bag. It costs nothing (if you have one on hand), and it's easy to dispose of it if it doesn't work out. Use it to stow the items you want to have inside the car: your maps, CDs, tissues, moist towelettes, and so on.

Organize your tunes. They're a lot less bulky than eight-track tapes, but CDs can contribute their own clutter to your car. Here are two terrific ways to get them organized.

1. Use a visor CD organizer. These handy contraptions are inexpensive, about $10, and usually hold a dozen CDs. Some even feature extra pockets for change, gum, pens, and business cards. The organizers are available at car accessory shops and online—The Container Store (www.containerstore.com) is one site where you can find them.

A note of caution: Before you purchase one of these handy devices, make sure that your visor is in good working order—many are used so seldom that they fall when you fold them down, or won't fold down at all. And never, ever clip something to the driver's-side visor. Even the most careful among us occasionally forget to clip the case securely or load the contents properly, and you don't want falling objects endangering lives.

2. Choose the music before you leave home. CDs clutter your car even if you have a nice, padded, waterproof CD organizer. That's be- cause the case is not really the issue. What makes the mess are the CDs you can't put away while you're driving, unless you have a full-time passenger to neatly change the music, replace the CD, and refile the jacket. So, instead of concentrating on containers, why not change the music while you're at home? Most of the time, you'll rarely play more than one or two CDs per trip. So load one, leave its case at

Paperwork: Out of Sight and Over My Head

LIKE SO many of us, independent lawn-care professional Wade Slate needs to hang on to receipts for his taxes. "The problem is, I get about eight receipts every day that I *don't* need to save, for coffee, milk, dry cleaning . . . ," says Wade, who has about 40 regular clients in Knoxville, Tennessee. So that he doesn't have to repeatedly weed through stacks of slips, or worse, lose a tax deduction, Wade stows the business-related receipts out of sight—on the ceiling! "My truck ceiling is metal, and I've collected several of those flat magnets that businesses give away," he says. "I stick the important receipts to the ceiling with a magnet. When I run out of magnets (I have about six), it's time to take the receipts down and put them with my records." With this strategy, Wade knows any bits of paper on the floor or in the ashtray can be quickly tossed into the garbage. The important stuff is over his head!

home, and carry another. Skip the bulky storage container and the dozens of empty cases that sneak into the side pockets, under the seats, and into your grocery bags and other inappropriate places.

Need more variety per trip than a couple of CDs can offer? Consider purchasing a CD player with a six- or eight-CD cartridge, and make your selections before you leave for work (or a road trip). This approach yields clutter benefits at home, too: If you draw CDs from a central location, you'll never have to search high and low, in your vehicle and your spouse's, at work and in the den, to find your favorites.

Organize the trunk. Is your car trunk just a big bucket of clutter? It doesn't have to be that way. Aside from the items that you really *must* store there (See "10 Car Essentials—According

to AAA"), wouldn't it be nice to be able to stow the groceries there for the ride home? Or maybe actually know where the Frisbee is when you want to play on the beach? Here are a few inexpensive items you can use to get things organized down under.

1. A large cooler. With or without the lid, you can use a plastic cooler to stow your beach toys or any other smallish items. And when your groceries include frozen items, you can temporarily displace the toys and store the frozen goods inside for the ride home.

2. Milk crates. Line the bottom of your trunk with as many milk crates as it will hold. When you go to the grocery store, the bags will fit in the crates, which will keep them from tipping over. When you're not toting groceries, you can use the crates to organize your emergency car kit and other items.

10 CAR ESSENTIALS—ACCORDING TO AAA

A critical part of decluttering your car is realizing what isn't clutter, too. One essential that should live in every vehicle is the car emergency kit. Here are the 10 must-have items for your kit, courtesy of the American Automobile Association.

1. Blanket
2. Cloth or roll of paper towels
3. First-aid kit with pocket knife. This should include adhesive bandages, first-aid tape and gauze.
4. Flashlights with fresh batteries
5. Ice scraper
6. Jumper cables

7. Small bag of abrasive material, such as sand or salt, for ice on the road.
8. Small shovel
9. Tire gauge
10. Warning device in case of accident or breakdown: flares or reflective triangle

If you live in an area that has particularly harsh winter weather, add some high-energy food, water, tire chains, and hats and gloves in autumn, so a winter storm doesn't catch you by surprise. (We like to carry the super-light-reflective "space blankets," too.) In year-round warm climates, of course, you can dispense with the sand, salt, and ice scraper.

3. Old ammunition boxes. These waterproof boxes are terrific for carrying your car tool kit. (They're great for first-aid kits, too.) You can also get removable dividers designed specially to turn old ammo boxes into tool kits. Both are available at Army-Navy stores.

ORGANIZING THE TRASH

There's really no way of getting around it: Your recycling bins are going to clutter your garage or shed. You might be able to get them off the floor and place the bins on a shelf, and you can certainly stack newspapers on a shelf. If the grocery store that you shop at uses paper bags with handles, you can hang a bag from a hook or nail on the wall and fill it with newspapers. Be careful, though. If you overload the bag, it's going to tear.

Be square. If you're going to store your trash barrels in your shed or garage, your best bet is to buy square barrels rather than round ones. Square barrels will fit flush against the walls and take up less space.

Pick your spot. If you store your barrels and recycling bins near the garage door instead of near an interior door, you'll have a shorter distance to move them on trash day, but a longer distance when carrying trash from the house to the barrels.

One might be enough. If you're filling up just one barrel a week, guess what? You don't need that second barrel, and there's no need to take up valuable storage space with it.

Keep a lid on it. It's okay to store your barrels outside, as long as you keep them out of sight and keep the lids fastened so the barrels don't become midnight snacking spots for all of the neighborhood varmints. But there are a couple of problems with storing recycling bins outside. Since most don't come with lids, the contents get wet when it rains, and that can cause quite a mess. You can buy an outdoor alcove, which will take care of the rain problem, but unless you thoroughly rinse all of your recyclable plastics and cans, they're going to attract animals, who will also create quite a mess.

CHAPTER

Attic and Basement

The problem with attics and basements can be summed up with one old chestnut: Out of sight, out of mind. Cramming endless items above or below your everyday living space may *seem* like an easy way out of the clutter trap, but it's actually one of the biggest pitfalls for a homeowner.

You probably use very little of what's in your attic or basement on a regular basis, or even on a not-so-regular one. In fact, according to Don Aslett, author of *Clutter Free! Finally and Forever*, 85 percent of the stuff we store in our attics is junk. If you think that's bad (and it is), basements are even worse—containing up to 95 percent junk. Talk about wasted space!

This chapter will help you distinguish the clutterers from the keepers, and offer expert advice about how to store the keepers safely in the unique environments found in attics and basements. You'll also learn how to "weather" catastrophes caused by climatic criminals: basement dampness and attic heat.

Most important, this chapter offers oodles of ways to use every bit of space efficiently, allowing you to make the most of these ultimately very useful areas. In some cases, you can actually give your basement and attic a practical face-lift and turn these former forgotten household junkyards into jewels of new space with special themes. Ready? Then read on!

Getting Started

Once you've made your way up to the attic or down to the basement, the real work begins. And unfortunately (or fortunately, if you're the bad-news-first type of person), the toughest part comes at the beginning: sorting through your collection of forgotten stuff. This painstaking process involves making piece-by-piece decisions, says James Sledd, a personal organizer in Bryn Mawr, Pennsylvania. "As you consider each item, remember that less is more," he says.

Professional organizer Sharon Hanby-Robie of Lancaster, Pennsylvania, recommends clearing the floor space, then conducting a three-step evaluation of each item. Ask yourself the following questions.

1. Will I use it again?
2. Is it worth storing?
3. Should I throw it out or give it away?

Answer those questions and you're well on your way. Here are more essential tips to help you make the right decisions about each item as you start sorting through your attic or basement.

THE THREE FACES OF CLUTTER

As you decide what to store where, consider the three categories into which stored items most often fall and the characteristics of each, says Cheryl Ross, member of the Minnesota chapter of the National Association of Professional Organizers and founder of Amazing Space, Inc., in River Falls, Wisconsin.

- **ACTIVE STORAGE.** The kind you like to (or need to) have access to every day of the year. Everyday pots and pans, your work wardrobe, and frequently used reference books are some examples of items often kept in active storage.

- **SEASONAL STORAGE.** You need these items at certain times of the year but not during others. They include off-season clothing, holiday decorations, and sports gear such as bikes and golf clubs. The basement makes a good choice for things in this category.

- **DEAD STORAGE.** This is the worst clutter-causing category; it encompasses those things you know you want to keep, but hardly ever use or even look at. This group includes sentimental memorabilia such as old photos, wedding dresses, and family heirlooms. Dead storage almost always winds up in the attic, but can sometimes be found in the basement as well.

When we lose a loved one, every photo, every article of clothing, every personal possession belonging to that person can become a painful reminder of her absence. After an elderly relative passes on, the responsibility of handling her home and (potentially numerous) belongings often falls to the children or grandchildren.

"Give yourself the gift of time," says Sharon Sobel, founder of Let's Organize in Haddonfield, New Jersey. "Before you can declutter, you need to give yourself enough time to mourn. It's unfair not to do that." How much time depends on you. If you're lucky enough not to be rushed in your responsibility to tend to your loved one's property, then wait until you feel up to the emotional task. Pay attention to how your emotions are faring and you'll know when the time is right.

If, on the other hand, real estate needs to be sold or your time is curtailed for other reasons, there are ways to move the process along without it being too harsh on you. A good solution is to ask one or more family members to help you—there's no need for you to go it alone. Besides, having another relative involved could turn a sad time into an opportunity to reminisce about happier days. If all else fails and you absolutely *must* empty Granny's attic before you feel ready to do so, take a path that's becoming more common these days. Have a moving company transfer everything to a rented storage facility. When you've had ample time to grieve, sorting through your relative's belongings may even be easier in less sentimental surroundings.

FIRST STEP? CLEAR THE STAIRS

First things first. If you can't even get to your attic or basement because the stairway up or down is covered in clutter, you have a problem. Not only does stairway clutter look bad, but it can be dangerous, too, says Betty Belnoski, who runs Organize 123, an organizational training program in Fogelsville, Pennsylvania. "It's a real hazard—I don't advise storing *anything* on the stairs," she says. On your path to decluttering, do yourself a favor and make your steps safer with these tips.

Think vertical and you'll stretch your available space. Take a look at the walls to the left and right of your staircase. Chances are, there's plenty of unused wall space that can be pressed into service. If the width of your stairway allows, install shelving or closed cabinetry, Betty says. Stairway too narrow? Hang a series of large hooks, or use a ready-made hook system to hang specific items such as brooms and mops. You can find these easy-to-install devices in well-stocked hardware stores.

Take the right step. If you're blessed with big, blocky wooden steps leading down to your basement, convert the lowest step into a handy storage bin. Simply hinge the top of that

ANNE MCALPIN of Jacksonville, Oregon, lacks the willpower to bypass antiques stores, especially if she spots an old trunk or hat box in the window. She also has a weakness for tote bags and can't begin to tell you how big her collection is. "My grandparents had old trunks and hat boxes and to me, they conjure up the mystery and romance of a time gone by," says Anne. "In those days, travel was romantic. Today, it is exhausting and certainly not as elegant."

But her suitcase, trunk, and tote bag hobby doesn't waste space. Anne stores tax records in trunks, off-season clothes in suitcases, and items for the beach in her tote bags for quick access. Instead of listing her contact information on the suitcase tags, she lists the contents of the suitcase. "It's a great way to save space and not waste time looking for things," says Anne, who honed her love of travel and packing into a successful business she calls Pack It Up in Jacksonville, Oregon. "I keep my mittens, hats, and scarves in one suitcase, my 'fat' clothes in another in case I gain weight, and my bathing suits and sun hats in a third. All I have to do is look at the tag and I know exactly what's inside."

stairways common to many attics, consider this easy way to make your steps safer. Attach rubber or grit-covered tread appliqués to the top of each step, suggests Sharon Hanby-Robie. You'll find these materials in the bath or deck department of any hardware store. The next time you're climbing up or down with a sight-blocking armful of boxes, your feet will appreciate the safe purchase and sturdy footing. While you're at it, test the traction for your basement stairway as well.

Search high *and* low beams. Unless you're part owl and can see in the dark, you know how frustrating it can be to try to climb into a pitch-black attic or walk down into a basement when the lightbulb has burned out or, worse, the power goes off in your house. Here's a (literally) bright idea: Mount tap lights, also known as touch lights, to the wall just inside your attic entryway and at the top of the stairway leading down to your basement. Tap lights are small, round lights that are available at home improvement centers or hardware stores and can be mounted almost anywhere. You just tap the dome to turn them on and off.

Casting Off the Unwanted

Now that you've categorized your clutter, all that remains is to deal with it. It helps to think in a businesslike way, delegating when you can and remaining unemotional, especially when it comes to the items you've finally decided to do

bottom step so that it can be raised or lowered. Store little odds and ends inside, such as an extra extension cord or a spare flashlight.

Make stair surfaces safer. Whether you have an actual staircase or one of those folding without. These tips will help you handle the piles you've probably found in your attic or basement. For even more ideas for getting rid of the clutter you find, review Chapter 3, the Unload step of the Q.U.I.C.K. process.

Make a memorable gift. Heirlooms and antiques often find their way to the attic or basement. The items may seem too delicate for your rough-and-tumble household, or they may simply not match the decor of your living space (like that antique butter churn or vintage Native American battle headdress).

You don't have to junk these special items. A better alternative is to make unique gifts of your unused heirlooms. Mark Dolar of Los Angeles remembers a special Christmas present from his dad. "My father came across my old Cub Scout graduation plaque when he was cleaning out the attic," says Mark. "He went to the trouble of wrapping it and putting it under the tree, and both he and my mother beamed when I opened it up."

And remember that family members aren't the only ones who could benefit from your beloved items; friends, too, might appreciate being gifted with a special item from your past.

Go ahead, use the good china. You may be conditioned to think that Grandmother's china or other breakables will be out of danger if they stay in the attic. But where's the sense in that? Why not bring that china or silver tea service out of storage and use it once in a while, or at least display some of it in a hutch or on a wire plate holder that you hang on the wall? It's especially important to reconsider valuable, delicate items if you no longer have young children or rambunctious pets. Lots of times, people forget to switch to adult mode and remember

---

RELIVE THE MEMORIES

When parents bring out the dusty old photo albums, most children can't help but start yawning. Page after page they endure. Why not share a story from the past with your children once a month by letting them see, feel, and smell real memories stashed in your attic?

Creativity expert Courtney Watkins of Los Angeles says there are "thousands of stories in everyone's attic. All you have to do is open a trunk or unzip a garment bag. The next time you need to make a trip up to the attic, have your child accompany you. Let your daughter try on the dress you wore when her father proposed to you as you share what qualities attracted you to him. Or, have your son slip on the old catcher's mitt that you wore when you played high school varsity baseball, and go that extra inning to recall one of your favorite games against your rival school.

"Share your family history with your children through stories," says Courtney. "It's a nice way to bridge the generation gap."

---

that they are now old enough and careful enough to use—and deserve—the "good stuff."

Outfit your local drama department. Come across an old prom dress, bridesmaid dress, or wedding gown in your attic attack? If you don't plan to wear it again (and really, how many formal gowns get to "go out" more than once?), such glamorous garments might make creative costumes and be greatly appreciated by your local high school drama department, observes Cheryl Ross, member of the Minnesota chapter of the National Association of Professional Organizers and founder of Amazing Space, Inc., in River Falls, Wisconsin. "And this way, at least you'll know that someone is getting good use out of these things," she says. A bonus: The next time you decide to take in a local play, you may get to see some of your old finery up on stage. Talk about recycling in action!

Truck it to the curb. If all else fails, take the last-ditch approach: Leave your leftovers at the curb with a sign reading FREE TO A GOOD HOME. You can bet your clutter will be somebody else's treasure before dark!

Up in the Attic

If your attic isn't already packed with clutter, it may be only because the space is less than ideal. Unfinished attics often lack a true floor surface, making them unfit for storing anything heavier than a box of last year's gift wrap. If you live in

YOUR OLD SUITCASES WILL SUIT SOMEONE ELSE

While going through your attic and basement, you may come across old luggage. Don't toss it right away, because it will probably be appreciated by shelters for battered women. Women seeking shelter could gladly use suitcases instead of toting their possessions in plastic or paper bags. And toss a teddy bear or toy inside the suitcase to give a child a bonus.

an area with hot summers (or year-round heat), your attic temperature may also be too extreme to store heat-sensitive items. Making a few simple changes can help you use your overhead space to its full advantage.

Tackle clutter during a cool spell. Attics are notorious for their brain-searing heat in the summer—and much of the rest of the time, too. Even with an attic fan, the lack of cross-ventilation can make decluttering there an exercise in claustrophobia. Do yourself a favor and save your attic cleaning for the autumn or even early winter when the space will be a lot less sultry.

Be a fan of big fans. One of the best ways to ease the extreme heat in your attic is by installing an attic fan, says homebuilder Richard Beaver of Knoxville, Tennessee. Otherwise, attic air can reach 150°F in the summer. With a fan, the temperature really shouldn't exceed about 95°F. Your stored items will fare better in

Just for the Feng Shui of It

IF DECLUTTERING YOUR ATTIC OR BASE-MENT seems to you like a waste of time, consider this: Experts in the ancient Asian art of feng shui (an elevated approach to interior design to choreograph the movement of energy—*chi* in Chinese—through space) believe that attic and basement clutter has profound meaning.

In her book *Clear Your Clutter with Feng Shui*, feng shui expert Karen Kingston explores the symbolism that these spaces have for us—and the significance of the stuff we keep there. According to Karen, "A cluttered basement symbolizes issues from the past not dealt with, often very weighty issues."

She notes that people tend to put their bulkiest junk in their basements. Think of that the next time you have to squeeze past Great-Aunt Ethel's dusty old armoire, and you may start to think about letting go of some of the heaviness from the past that's filling up today's space.

Attic clutter, too, has more of an inner effect on you than you might think. "Things stored in your attic can restrict your higher aspirations and possibilities," she says. According to Karen, excess junk is literally "hanging over your head," threatening to crash down at any moment. Cleaning out the attic may just lighten up your mental outlook. It's certainly worth a try!

a cooled attic and your home will, too. That's because an attic fan will also keep the living areas of your home much cooler, reducing air conditioning costs in the bargain.

Put plywood to use. Uncovered attic joists practically invite an errant foot to poke an impromptu (and unwanted) skylight through the ceiling below. Protect your home's ceiling, make your attic safer, and provide solid storage space all at the same time by laying sheets of 1-inch (or thicker) plywood or particleboard flooring over attic joists. Secure the flooring with nails driven right into the joists; if you're covering a large area, be sure to stagger the seams (the places where sheets meet) to get the most stable surface.

Keep the area clear of combustibles. Now is the time to pay attention to those KEEP AWAY FROM HEAT OR FLAME label warnings. Never store combustible items in the attic; those include paint, paint thinner, gasoline, kerosene, camping fuel, and any other flammable liquid. Check labels and stow this stuff someplace cooler, or, if you won't be needing these substances any longer, call your local sanitation company or department to find out how to dispose of them properly.

Let there be light—and lots of it. When you hear the word *attic*, what image comes to mind? If you picture a dark, cobwebby space with lots of shadowy corners stretching far into a deep unknown, you aren't alone. Many attics

CLUTTER CRUSADERS

Store Sentimental Stuff with Care

SINCE 1976, BERNIE KELLMAN has seen 398 rock concerts, give or take a few. That's a lot of ticket stubs—especially since Bernie is an avid collector of all things rock-oriented. He also has posters, photos, commemorative T-shirts, programs, and vinyl record albums. This museum, as he calls it, has been displayed in only two of the five homes Bernie has lived in over the past 10 years, most recently in Nazareth, Pennsylvania. "This stuff takes up a lot of space," he admits.

Since his treasured items spend most of their time relegated to storage, careful consideration is called for to prevent damage. "When storing my collection for the long term, I always separate the paper items," Bernie says. He knows that ticket stubs and other paper memorabilia shouldn't be stored in damp basements, where they can quickly be destroyed by mildew. Instead, he keeps these items in photo albums with self-stick pages, then stores the albums in the attic. Vinyl record albums will quickly warp and become worthless (not to mention hard to listen to) if they spend even one summer in an oven-hot attic. Dampness won't do any harm to vinyl, so Bernie feels good about keeping his LPs in the basement—stored on end and carefully boxed up, of course.

"Simple shop lights with fluorescent bulbs make a good choice in the attic," says Betty Belnoski. You'll find these bargain-priced lighting fixtures at any hardware store, and they're easy to install. Fluorescent bulbs give off a bright white light, but the fixtures have a low profile, meaning that they'll do the job without taking up much headroom in an already cramped attic. If your attic is particularly large, you may want to use two or more fixtures, spaced evenly throughout the area, to get the best results.

rely on a single bare bulb to illuminate an area that's as vast as your whole first floor. Making full use of your attic space will be easier when you let plenty of light in.

SEVEN ITEMS YOU SHOULD NEVER STORE IN YOUR ATTIC

If you reach to new heights (say, your attic) for storage, you may feel new lows. That's because some items simply can't take the heat up there. Here's a handy list of what *not* to tuck up there.

1. Candles and anything else made of wax
2. Cosmetics, including Halloween costume makeup
3. Flammable items or substances (fireworks, gasoline, kerosene, lighter fluid, lighters, paint, paint thinner, propane camp-stove cartridges, and the like)
4. Food items of any kind, including those in cans and jars
5. Photographs and photo albums
6. Vinyl record albums
7. Wool clothing

PACK THE ATTIC PROPERLY

Are you guilty of the "toss and turn" approach to attic storage—you know, where you toss something in there, then turn and run? You aren't alone, but that doesn't mean there isn't a better way. With a little forethought, storing items in your attic and retrieving them when you need something need not be an anxiety-provoking experience. These tips will change your attic-packing attitude for the better.

Cover up. Some large items—the old baby carriage, the Christmas tree, your golf bag—may not fit inside dustproof boxes. In those cases, you'll have to improvise to keep things relatively clean while in attic storage. "Cover them with plastic sheeting, preferably the clear kind, so you can see what's underneath," says Betty Belnoski. Disposable painter's drop cloths work well for this purpose, but in a pinch (or to pinch pennies) you can also recycle a camping tarpaulin or even an old vinyl tablecloth. Drape the plastic over the item, then tuck the ends underneath for the best protection.

Keep inventory. Want to get your hands on your grandpa's baseball card collection or your grandma's wedding dress? You can do it in a matter of seconds, thanks to an ingenious

---

MAKE AN ATTIC INDEX

When you travel to a new city, what's one of the first things you do? Pick up a map. This approach to keeping track of your surroundings can be put to good use when you want to keep track of what you've stored in your attic. But instead of a map, make an attic index that indicates both contents and location. An index will allow you to find precisely what you want when you go into your attic, and it will come in handy when your kids are searching for the soccer ball or Christmas wrap. To create an index, make a simple line drawing of your attic's shape on a blank sheet of paper or graph paper. Indicate on the drawing the location of each category of item; you may want to give each area of the attic a number or letter for reference. On the back of the map (or on a separate piece of paper) make a list, by category and area, of each individual box and its contents.

Keep your index in a clear plastic sleeve or even a resealable plastic bag attached to the attic door. Update the list and the map whenever you add or remove a box. Here are some sample categories. You can mix and match, or come up with new ones to suit your family's particular storage needs.

1. Baby gear
2. Camping equipment (but remember—store propane-stove or lantern canisters someplace other than the attic)
3. Furniture
4. Holiday decorations/gift wrap
5. Memorabilia
6. Off-season clothing
7. Sports gear

tracking system created by Linda Koopersmith, best known as The Beverly Hills Organizer.

"I believe you can keep your whole life as long as you know where it is and can get your hands on it quickly," says Linda, author of *The Beverly Hills Organizer's House Book*. Linda recommends maintaining a master inventory sheet in your computer that details the contents of each box in your attic. For example, Box 1 may contain your grandpa's baseball cards and Box 4 may store your grandma's wedding dress. When you add—or, even better, take away—items in your attic, you can easily update your list with a few keystrokes.

"It's not unusual for someone to have 25 or more boxes in her attic," Linda says. "Keeping the computerized inventory makes finding things a snap. So, the next time you want to show your daughter just how hard your homework assignments were when you were in the fourth grade, you scan your list and know that it's in Box 25." (See "Make an Attic Index," page 301, for yet another ingenious method of keeping track of what's stashed in your attic.)

Use labels that last. A box without a label is a mystery. A box without a label at the bottom of a tall stack of other boxes without labels is a migraine. Save yourself the grief of crashing cartons and wasted box-shuffling effort by developing a lifelong labeling habit. As soon as you pack each box, immediately mark it on a clearly visible spot with lettering large enough to see from across the room. If you aren't sure just how you'll be storing your boxes, you may

CLUTTER CRUSADERS
A Picture-Perfect Attic

ENTER THE CLASSROOM OF FIRST-GRADE TEACHER SHELLY ENOS and you'll be amazed by how neat and organized it is—despite being occupied by 28 high-energy, eager-to-learn students. When she announces that it's time for her students to return to their chairs after testing their writing or math skills at specially designated workstations, she knows the books and flash cards will be returned to their appropriate spots.

"What's my secret? Well, I've learned that children are very visual learners," says Shelly, who lives in Loxahatchee, Florida, and is now in her ninth year of teaching. "So, I take Polaroid photos of each workstation and post them next to the stations so that my students can 'see' where things belong. This way, there's no guesswork or confusion."

Shelly carries over this picture-perfect strategy at home. She keeps a couple of photos that depict all the boxes and items stashed there near the entrance to the attic. This way, when her two children and her husband need to take something out of the attic, they know *exactly* where to return the item in its own parking spot in the attic. Of course, you could use this tip in the basement, too!

want to label more than one side of each carton.

If you use cardboard boxes, a thick, black, permanent marker pen may be all you need. For any other type of box, you can use large, white self-stick labels, or just pieces of note-paper attached to your boxes with heavy-duty strapping tape (the kind with visible fibers running through it).

"Don't use plain old cellophane tape to attach your labels," says Betty Belnoski. "They'll stay on for 6 months, but in a hot attic those labels will eventually fall off and land on the floor—making them pretty useless for identifying what's in the boxes."

Down in the Basement

There's no need to be down in the dumps about clutter in the basement. As the following tips demonstrate, lots of creative, space-saving, clutter-cutting storage techniques are

at your beck and call. Let's head down there and see!

BASEMENT BOXING 101

No, we're not going to recommend that you set up a speed bag or boxing ring in your basement (although, when you've finished decluttering, you'll probably have room for them). What we're talking about here are boxes, which are the natural choice for storing the items you decide to keep in the basement. They're inexpensive, easy to carry, and generally easy to store. But it's worth considering the details to do the job just right.

Boycott cardboard. Cardboard boxes are prone to harboring bugs or mildew in the base-

---

RENOVATION CONSIDERATIONS

One of the best ways to cut clutter permanently in your home is to add extra "finished" space for storage and living in your basement and attic. But you can't approach such renovations haphazardly—there are rules and regulations to cover in the process, and fines to pay if you're found in violation. "You don't want to cut corners, because there are really good reasons for building codes, including safety considerations and structural soundness," says Richard Beaver, owner of Beaver Builders in Knoxville, Tennessee. Before embarking on renovations, Richard encourages you to take your drawings and any questions to your area codes official.

"They'll help you comply and give sound advice, and you don't have to give them an address if you're nervous they'll look you up for an inspection," he says.

Here are just a few elements that might need to adhere to code.

- A window you can climb out of
- Ceiling height—usually at least 7½ feet
- Easy up-and-down access in case of fires
- Stair tread width and stair height
- Sufficient ventilation
- Wall thickness (also a fire regulation)

ment. Avoid those fates for your valuables by packing them instead in clear plastic boxes with lids. You can see what's inside and you'll have the added comfort of knowing that the plastic containers will protect your important items from dampness and humidity.

Try color coding. Brighten up your basement and make finding specific items easier by storing them in colored plastic boxes. Look for plastic storage bins in holiday colors—how about red for Christmas decorations and orange for Halloween costumes? A green bin could house gardening supplies, or maybe financial documents. Use your imagination.

Designate an odds-and-ends box. Even the most organized declutterer can wind up with a few bits and pieces that defy categorization. If you find yourself scratching your head and wondering what box to put the last small items in, stop fretting. It's perfectly okay to relegate otherwise oddball items to one general storage box.

Get your boxes off the floor. After Anne McAlpin of Jacksonville, Oregon, lost her high school diploma to a minor basement flood, she took steps to ensure that her possessions will never succumb again to an unexpected splash. She placed cinder blocks around the perimeter of her basement to give her stored items an extra leg up in case of a watery invasion. Anne puts her boxes right on the cinder blocks, but if you have more than just a few boxes, consider laying plywood on top of the blocks to make larger platforms.

Substitute shelves for stacks. Stacking boxes, especially cardboard ones, prevents air from flowing around them. Less airflow means a greater likelihood of mildew accumulation. And besides, if you have a stack that's four boxes high, Murphy's Law practically guarantees that the one carton you're looking for will be the one at the very bottom. Here's how to say goodbye to those stack attacks!

"Two words will save you: utility shelves," says Maria Gracia, owner of Get Organized Now! in Milwaukee, Wisconsin. "Shelves help you get everything off the basement floors, and you can categorize items into very distinct groups on the shelves." Shelves also allow for air circulation and spare your back, so that you can see and get to items more easily.

Location is everything. After the boxes are packed and labeled, take a few minutes to plan where they're going to go. To make your newly decluttered basement truly user-friendly, accessibility is key. Think about which boxes you'll be using most frequently compared to the ones you won't need for a longer time. Baby clothes, for example, could be stored on a higher shelf, while Christmas decorations or gardening equipment should be easier to find, preferably at eye level.

THE WORLD OF SHELVES

They're shelves—how complicated could they be? It's true that you don't have to be a rocket scientist to understand them, but there are some basics to keep in mind.

Maria Gracia shares a small two-bedroom condo in Milwaukee, Wisconsin, with her husband, Joe. Space is at a premium, but fortunately, Maria makes her living as a professional organizer. "We don't have an attic, but we do have a large storage area in our basement," says Maria. "This condo has been a test of my small-space organizing abilities. But it has really paid off. I'm even amazed at how much we've fit into this small space, and it's not cluttered at all."

What's her space-squeezing secret? Maria has given the four-shelf utility unit in her basement double duty. Instead of four shelves, she has divided it into eight specific areas by visualizing an imaginary Mason-Dixon Line down the middle of each shelf. This way, she has space for two specific areas per shelf. Here's how she breaks down the space, from bottom to top.

- **FIRST SHELF.** Laundry supplies (detergent, dryer sheets, and bleach) on one side, car wash supplies on the other
- **SECOND SHELF.** Household repair items (including tools and touch-up paint) share this space with picnic and barbecue supplies (such as the cooler and picnic basket)
- **THIRD SHELF.** Shipping supplies (including folded boxes and tape) share this tier with travel items (including luggage—a set of five matching pieces that store inside one another)
- **FOURTH SHELF.** Fishing gear—"I'm happy to declare that the other half of this shelf is empty!" says Maria.

Size up your shelves. When placing items on different shelves, rely on the waist test created by Sharon Hanby-Robie. "I tell my clients to put their most frequently used items on shelves at waist height," she explains. "Put items you use least often on high shelves, and the things that you use semioften on shelves below waist level."

Prevent a climbing catastrophe. When shopping for shelves, don't forget to pick up a sturdy step stool to go along with them. Keep the stool in the basement, right next to the shelves (and in plain sight), so that anyone reaching for boxes stored overhead won't be tempted to go climbing.

Go the ready-made route. If your basement walls are made of cement or stone, installing shelves can be tricky, requiring special tools and lots of care. You can get the shelf space you want without drilling a single hole, says James Sledd. "I like shelf units from IKEA," says Sledd. "They're sturdy and inexpensive, and I can adjust the shelf heights with very little work."

You can also find premade shelf units at superstores such as Home Depot, Kmart, or Wal-Mart. These handy (and often very economically priced) units are usually available in finished or unfinished wood, metal, or even waterproof, rustproof plastic.

AVOIDING THE BIG BASEMENT PILEUP

After you've taken the time and trouble to de-clutter your basement, wouldn't you like to keep it that way? The experts tell us that it's easiest to keep clutter at bay when every item has a home. Find a place for everything in your basement and prevent future pileups by following these space-savvy storage tips.

Say no. Prevent future clutter buildup by saying "no" more often, says Margaret Dasso, co-owner of The Clean Sweep, a professional housekeeping agency in Lafayette, California.

Say no to:
- Bargains. Ask yourself, "Would I want this item if it were full price?" If not, then you probably won't use it despite the money you "saved."
- Duplicates. How many hammers, watches, and other items do you really need?
- Impulse purchases. Ask yourself whether the item is a "need" or a spur-of-the-moment "want" item.

Don't lose an inch. Avoid a common mistake of many would-be declutterers, says Betty Belnoski: Use *all* of the storage in any given area. "Use the walls, use the ceilings—really maximize the space," Betty says. When you think you've run out of room, stand back and take a good look around. Have you done something with the triangular space beneath the stairs? The wall space above the cellar door?

To help you make the most of the nooks and crannies every basement offers, Betty recommends checking out the catalogs of companies that sell organizational aids. There are space-specific gadgets and devices that can help you find a use for every area, no matter how narrow or wide, how low or high. "The Lillian Vernon catalog is a good one to start with," she says.

Let things hang around. Getting items off the floor and out of the way of potential leaks is easy when you use hooks. Hooks can be especially useful for awkward or bulky things such as bicycles, motorcycle helmets, large backpacks, golf bags, and the like. For the most

OUT-OF-THE-BOX IDEAS

Subdivide Your Basement

PAMELA HASTINGS, a sewing and craft expert in Wall, New Jersey, was looking for more living and working space in her four-bedroom colonial home, and she found it.

Pamela measured her basement, and then used Sheetrock to divide the area into four distinct rooms: a playroom for her three children, an office for herself, a sewing room, and a storage area with shelves. "I positioned the playroom on the opposite end of the basement from my office, and with the Sheetrock walls, I'm able to muffle their sounds," Pamela says.

If you're not crazy about the prospect of working with Sheetrock, consider using bookcases or dressers to create minirooms and expand storage in your basement.

strength, be sure to sink your hooks into wooden studs or use masonry hardware and tools (including safety goggles) to secure hooks into stone or cement walls.

DEALING WITH THE DAMP

Perhaps the biggest challenge associated with stashing items in your basement is finding ways to dampproof the storage systems there. Dampness is often the status quo in basements, and unless you can afford to leave the space completely empty, the moisture in the air will have to be dealt with one way or another. These tips can help dry things out.

Pack them in plastic. Honestly, books, off-season or vintage clothing, and photographs are better off stored someplace drier than a damp basement. But if you're short on space (and if you've already weeded these collections down to the bare minimum—no storing useless items, please) there *are* ways to protect your "precious perishables."

Rigid plastic storage bins with snap-on lids are good (the kind manufactured by Rubbermaid are one example). The clear ones are even better, says Tara Aronson, mother of three in Pacific Palisades, California, author of *Simplify Your Household* and clutter columnist for the *San Francisco Chronicle*. "You'll be able to see the contents easily and won't have to rummage through more than one box to find what you need when you need it," she says. If your basement is really damp, add a moisture-absorbing product to the bin. One such product, made by Damp Rid, is the Damp Trap. The trap goes inside the bin, where it absorbs excess moisture. Damp Traps and other moisture-control products are available at most hardware and home improvement stores.

Make a yearly check. Even when you do take precautions, it's a good idea to schedule a yearly peek into the boxes, says Cheryl Ross. "You should just make sure that things aren't becoming mildewed," Cheryl says. If you do happen to notice any damage, you'll be able to move the items out of the basement before they are ruined completely.

SIX ITEMS TO KEEP OUT OF THE BASEMENT

Just as some items in your home can't stand the heat of the attic, other's can't abide the moisture in your basement. Here are six that you'll need to store elsewhere.

1. Any valuable items (such as expensive furniture) that could be damaged by mildew or flooding

2. Birdseed, grass seed, pet food, and other potential rodent fodder

3. Carpeting and area rugs

4. Gift wrapping supplies

5. Living plants

6. Suede jackets, pants, shoes, or boots

Use a dehumidifier. For mild to moderate basement dampness, try using a dehumidifier. Choose a unit that turns on and off automatically—on when the air gets too damp, off again when the machine has pulled enough moisture out of the air to reduce the humidity. Use a dehumidifier daily in the summertime; depending on the dampness, you may be able to put it away come winter. And you'll be surprised what a difference these devices can make—and just how much water they can remove from your basement environment in next to no time. (Don't toss the water that your dehumidifier absorbs—your plants will love it.)

Pick a pump for serious water problems. If you sometimes have standing water in your basement from heavy rains or a high water table, a dehumidifier won't do it. You'd be wise to install a sump pump, says Jack Summerlot, owner of Summerlot Home Improvements in Coopersburg, Pennsylvania. Otherwise, one day "you may have a swimming pool in your basement," Jack cautions. Unless your stored items can swim, you'll want to avoid this scenario, so call a contractor or other home improvement expert for advice on installing a pump safely and properly.

Fix up the floor. Most basements have floors of poured concrete. While these surfaces are inexpensive and generally low maintenance, they can leave much to be desired. For example, concrete floors have a tendency to generate dust. Not

BASEMENT BORDEAUX, ANYONE?

You can take tasteful advantage of the naturally cool, consistently dark environment of your basement by storing (or starting) a wine collection there, says professional organizer Cheryl Ross. If you pay attention to three fairly simple wine storage requirements, your bottles will age well and provide enjoyment for future celebrations or wine-tasting parties.

1. Sequester your collection to the darkest corner of your basement so that even when the lights are on, the glare doesn't shine directly onto the bottles. And of course, you'll want to keep the lights off most of the time. (Note: It's a good idea to keep a working flashlight handy here to scope out labels when searching for a particular bottle.)

2. Lay the bottles on their sides; this will keep the corks wet and prevent them from coming apart and floating around in your glass. You can buy a specially made wooden or metal wine rack for this, or even use a sturdy cardboard liquor box containing cubbies for individual bottles (turn the box on its side and store it off the floor on a shelf).

3. Keep your collection away from vibration. Vibration can cause air bubbles to form in the wine, and that degrades its quality. So store your wine away from the washing machine or dryer, and preferably not under a busy staircase. Also, try not to move the bottles unnecessarily; once you've selected a storage spot, keep relocation to a minimum.

only is this dust likely to get tracked throughout the rest of the house, but it can feel pretty nasty and gritty under bare feet, making impromptu, shoe-free decluttering visits very unlikely. Clear the space and give it a good sweeping, then put down a layer or two of concrete-sealing paint. The next time you set (bare) foot in your basement, you'll notice the difference.

Keep supplies under lock and key. Many people use the basement as an off-season gardening shed, storing shovels, potting soil, and even fertilizer and pest controls there. If this sounds familiar, consider putting any potentially poisonous substances in a locked box to prevent them from falling into tiny hands or furry paws.

Depending on the size of your basement,

DEFINITELY NOT CLUTTER: EMERGENCY SUPPLIES TO KEEP ON HAND

One of the advantages to getting rid of all that unnecessary stuff in your basement is uncovering the room to store the really important stuff—crucial, potentially life-saving items that you may or may not already have tucked away down there. In the midst of all the other junk, indispensable items such as a fire extinguisher are often missing from cluttered-up basements, says Lisa Wendt, member of the National Association of Professional Organizers and founder of Sort-It-Out in Eagan, Minnesota. "I am shocked by how many of my clients have no fire extinguisher or even smoke detector, for that matter," says Lisa. "Not having a fire extinguisher readily available is a big deal."

According to Lisa, besides housing a functional fire extinguisher, your basement should be the first place you and your family members can turn to in an emergency, such as a hurricane, tornado, blizzard, or other natural disaster (except floods, of course). And—again, with the exception of floods—the basement is the ideal place to store emergency supplies. If the time comes, you can either retrieve the supplies from their desig-

nated storage space, or hustle the whole family to the basement as a safe location, feeling confident that you have all you need right there. Store those emergency supplies in a waterproof container such as a plastic storage bin with a snap-on lid. Here's a sample inventory.

- [ ] A 3-day supply of food and water for each family member (1 quart of bottled water per person per day and a selection of dried foods and canned foods; don't forget a hand-operated can opener and basic kitchen utensils)
- [ ] Candles and waterproof matches or a reliable lighter
- [ ] Extra blankets or sleeping bags
- [ ] First-aid kit and manual
- [ ] Flashlight
- [ ] Fresh batteries for both radio and flashlight
- [ ] Plastic garbage bags
- [ ] Portable radio
- [ ] Soap, toothpaste, toilet paper

---

you could save space by employing a simple footlocker with a lockable latch. If you have room to spare, you might want to invest in one of those new plastic shed-size containers that are large enough to hold all of your gardening supplies and can be locked with your own padlock. Other hazardous materials, such as pool chemicals or paint products, could also be kept here.

Considering the Possibilities

One of the best ways to reclaim unused space in your home is to renovate your basement or attic. Fixing up those spaces is less expensive than building additions—and it's usually a lot less disruptive, too. Before you start or as you plan, consider the following tips.

Paint it white. The attic and basement are the two places in your house where otherwise boring white paint is the right choice for the walls and ceiling. White helps illuminate the space and makes it appear larger than it actually is.

Extend the climate control. To make the space truly livable, you'll have to extend heating and/or air conditioning into the basement or attic. This step can turn a formerly unusable space into a comfortable area safe for storing just about anything.

Make sure it's pestproof. When renovating, you'll also want to deal with any existing pest problems and make sure the new construction will be pestproof. Again, protecting your finished room from insects and rodents will make the new area much more useful for storage.

Moving It Out: Hiring a Storage Facility

At some point, you may decide that the best solution to your attic and basement storage problems is to stow your stuff in an outside facility. There are a variety of reasons for going this route. Maybe you've got a vast collection of treasures you simply can't part with, but you're tired of stumbling over them. Or perhaps you've inherited a houseful of furniture and need time to figure out what to do with it all. Off-premises storage also comes in handy if you're without premises yourself—say if your new house isn't ready yet, or the renovation is taking twice as long as expected. Whether your needs are long term or short term, a storage facility can be a godsend when there's too much stuff and too little space.

The catch, of course, is that off-site storage costs money. Generally, you'll sign an "occupancy agreement" or contract and pay a monthly rental fee. The fee is determined by the size of the space you need measured in cubic footage. That's why it's important to consider carefully just what items you want to store and how you want to store them. There are different types of facilities available, and their quality may vary widely. Because your possessions mean a lot to you (otherwise, why pay to store them?), it's worth doing your homework so you can choose the storage option that's right for you.

Take an honest look at your loot. In some ways, the prospect of paying to store your belongings is a good thing. It forces you to take a good, hard look at what you're hanging on to and ask whether it's really worth it. As you consider which items to put into storage, remember that the more space you need to rent, the higher your monthly bill will be. This will help you weed out items you don't absolutely need, and prioritize the ones you're keeping for their sentimental value. People who find it hard to let go of treasures often find it a lot easier when the alternative is to pay for their upkeep!

Do the math. If you're thinking about off-site storage but are balking at paying a fee, consider the cost of real estate: yours versus theirs. Have you ever thought about putting an addition onto your house, or even moving to a bigger place, just to make more room for all your stuff? You'd have to pay an awful lot of rent to equal the cost of adding even a single room, much less moving up. And besides the initial cost of expansion, an addition or a bigger house will raise your property taxes. Renting off-site is probably cheaper. In fact, if you live in an expensive community, you might be better off sending some of your things to a storage facility in a lower-cost area. The big advantage of having your stuff around you is that you can see, use, and enjoy it. But one solution that gives you the best of both worlds is to rotate your treasures between your home and the storage facility.

It may be a write-off. Another financial factor to consider is whether you can declare part of your storage fee as a tax deduction. Depending on your profession, the items you're storing may be considered useful to your work—for example, if you're a writer of historical fiction and want to store a large reference library that helps you keep your facts straight about Victorian England and ancient Rome. Talk to a tax adviser to see whether your storage fee would be considered a legitimate business expense.

Size up the cost. When you're starting to shop around for a storage facility, you'll want to get a preliminary estimate of your monthly costs. To do this, make a list of the items you plan to store. You don't have to measure everything, but if you're storing boxes, note their quantity and dimensions. For just about everything else, simply note the item and quantity: "Four dining room chairs, one large sofa, two bicycles," for instance. Most storage companies have guidelines for calculating space requirements and will be able to give you a rough estimate of your monthly fee. Once you write up your list, you can present it to several different storage companies and compare prices. Keep in mind, though, that a rough estimate is just that. Especially if you haven't yet gone through the process of sorting through and packing up your belongings, you may end up needing a lot more—or, with any luck, a lot less!—space than you're expecting.

Check 'em out. Sending your possessions away to live under another roof can be an emotional experience. Which is why you should never, ever choose a facility based on cost alone. Equally important, if not more so, is the reputation of the company to which you'll be entrusting your belongings. Unfortunately, in the moving and storage business, scams and "misunderstandings" are all too common. Before you sign with a company, do a background check: Call your local Better Business Bureau (or do an online search at www.bbb.org) to make sure the company's rating is satisfactory and no complaints have been lodged against it. In addition, if you're considering a warehouse facility, contact your local Department of Consumer Affairs to make sure that it is properly licensed.

Be sure it's secure. Some storage facilities come with a wide range of security features, including 24-hour guards, alarms, video surveillance, and motion detectors. And some offer very little security. It stands to reason that a guarded building where visitors are required to sign in offers more protection for your belongings than an unguarded drive-up garage-type unit. Before you commit to any storage facility, always do a personal inspection. Would you be

THE SIX STORAGE-FACILITY FACTORS

What you need to find out about a storage facility can be summed up in six items. Keep this list with you as you shop around, and you can't go wrong.

1. **REPUTATION.** Call the Better Business Bureau and get recommendations from friends and coworkers. When it comes to reputation, "good" is the only acceptable option!

2. **CONDITION:** It should be clean, dry, mold- and mildew-free (you can tell by the smell), fire resistant, and climate controlled.

3. **SECURITY.** More is better, especially if you're storing valuable items.

4. **SERVICES.** These can range from absolutely none to absolutely everything. Choose based on your needs, and don't pay for what you don't need.

5. **ACCESS.** Do you plan to retrieve items frequently and come and go often? Hours and terms of access vary among storage companies, so think about what's appropriate for you.

And of course . . .

6. **COST.** It's not the only thing, but it definitely matters!

comfortable going there alone, after dark, if you had to? You should feel confident that your things will be safe there and that you'll be safe when you visit the place.

Cover your assets. Will the items you store be insured against fire, flood, and other damage? Most self-storage companies claim no responsibility for your items. Even when local regulations require them to carry insurance, it's a minimal amount that may fall far short of what your possessions are worth. Find out to what extent (if any) you're covered by the storage facility, then check to see whether your current homeowner's or renter's policy covers items stored off-site. If neither is adequate, consider taking out additional insurance. Your storage facility probably offers coverage from an outside insurer—compare the cost of adding off-site coverage to your homeowner's policy to

THE TWO TYPES OF STORAGE

When it comes to professional storage companies, you have two basic choices: self-storage (also known as mini-storage) and warehouse storage. Here are their fundamental differences.

SELF-STORAGE

☐ You rent a separate, individual unit within the facility. These are available in a variety of dimensions, from closet size up to an area that will hold an entire house's worth of items.

☐ You provide your own lock and key; no one else has access.

☐ The monthly fee is determined by the size of the unit you rent.

☐ You're on your own: Moving your belongings in and out and retrieving items is your responsibility. (Some companies offer pickup and delivery services for an additional charge. But often you're paying just for the truck and driver, who won't help you load and unload. Inquire and plan ahead.)

WAREHOUSE STORAGE

☐ Your items are stored in a large open area, either on shelves, in wooden containers, or in cubicle-style units.

☐ You don't have direct access—if you want to "visit" your belongings, you must be escorted by a staff member.

☐ Your fee is determined by the cubic footage required to store your stuff.

☐ Facilities use inventory stickers or bar-coded labels to identify your items.

☐ Warehouse storage is usually offered through moving/storage companies that provide a full range of fee-based services, including packing and materials, inventory, pickup, and delivery.

☐ Storage fees may be significantly cheaper, especially on smaller amounts.

the cost of additional insurance available through the storage company.

Remember that you are *not* your stuff. When it comes to deciding what kind of storage is right for them, many people make the mistake of projecting their own preferences onto their possessions. "People would rather be in a room than in a warehouse," says Richard Barrale, owner and president of All-Star Moving and Storage in Brooklyn, New York. "Because they feel more comfortable in an averaged-size room, they think it's better for their things." For this reason, he says, many opt to put their possessions in a smaller self-storage unit. But that's not necessarily better or safer, and might not be the best choice for their situation. The important issues are whether the facility is clean and secure and whether the management has a good reputation. Beyond that, it's a question of what meets your needs best in terms of cost, access, and services.

Visit the facility. If you decide warehouse storage is right for you (see "The Two Types of Storage" on page 313), you'll never have to deliver or retrieve anything yourself, and you'll sign the contract and complete all necessary paperwork during a meeting at your home. In other words, you never have to see the warehouse where your belongings will be stored. But it's still a good idea to visit the place before making your final decision. Warehouses don't have to be beautiful, but they should be clean, and the air inside should feel dry, not damp. Ask about what security features are in place. Take note of how items are stored. They should be stacked neatly on shelves or in wooden containers and be clearly labeled. Taking a look at the facility before you send your stuff there is bound to improve your comfort level.

Keep a list. You're dying to share your old Nancy Drew books with your daughter, so you head off to your self-storage unit to dig up

---

A WELL-KEPT STORAGE SECRET

There's a little-known storage option that might be just right for you: document storage. This is a type of warehouse storage catering primarily to businesses, which use it to archive inactive files and records. But individuals can also use document storage to house their collections of books, magazines, comic books, phonograph records, CDs, audio-tapes, and videotapes—in other words, things you can catalog and store in boxes. Document storage has several advantages, the main one being that costs tend to be 30 percent to 50 percent lower than self-storage. Check your Yellow Pages to see if there's a document-storage facility in your area. It might save you some money.

your treasured collection. And there you see them: 17 large cardboard boxes, all labeled "Books." Wouldn't it be nice if you knew which one held *The Secret of the Old Clock*? It takes a little extra work during packing time, but just as you label boxes that will go into your attic (see "Keep inventory" on page 301), it's a smart idea to number and inventory the boxes you're sending away. Keeping a detailed list has two benefits: First, when you need something specific from your storage unit, finding it won't be such a mystery; and second, if your records are neat and complete, you'll be able to send someone else to fetch something if necessary.

Decide how much work you want to do. One of the key differences between self-storage and warehouse storage is service. With self-storage, the accent is on "self." You do it all: You pack, you transport, you retrieve. At the other end, the soup-to-nuts services offered by warehouse storage companies make this an ideal choice for some. They can deliver boxes and packing materials to your home (and will even pack and inventory your stuff if you like), transport it to the warehouse, and retrieve items for you on request. Imagine simply calling up and saying "Bring me box number 156, please." You pay for each of these services, but it saves you time and trouble, and that's worth something, too.

CHAPTER

Those Pesky Paper Piles

Papers are like snowflakes. They collect in piles and settle anywhere there's room. You'd think that with the 21st century's reliance on electronic communication, the last thing we'd need to worry about is a deluge of paper. Yet it makes its way to our homes from utility companies and credit card issuers; from school and church and the racquet club; and soon we're buried under pamphlets and notices and bills and magazines and junk mail.

How can you stop this mashed-pulp menace? Stop piling and start purging—we'll show you how!

Clutter That Comes In with the Mail

Whoever said that the advent of the personal computer would be the end of the paper trail had better be hiding on a remote island somewhere far, far away. The amount of junk mail, memos, catalogs, magazines, newspapers, and other paper that comes into the average American house each week is staggering. And if it sits around too long, it takes on a life of its own, cluttering countertops, tabletops, chair seats—you name it. Here's how to deal with the endless stream of paper that creeps into your home through the mail slot.

TOO MUCH MAIL

Someone once said that adolescence is the last time in your life that you're happy to hear that the phone is for you. Well, it's probably the last time you were happy to see your name on a mailing label, too, what with all the, um, junk that floods our mailboxes every day. The good news is that there are ways to reduce the number of labels you see your name on each day.

Sort your mail standing up. Newspaper publisher Don Seaton of Hastings, Nebraska, gets more than 10 pieces of sales mail every day.

Thanks to a few household remodeling projects he and his wife completed a few years ago, he's found himself on every home-related mailing list there is. Rather than let that stuff pile up every day, he uses a trick he learned long ago when he worked in the newsroom. Reporters—who get more sales mail than almost anyone—routinely open their mail while standing over the trash can or recycling bin. "Almost everything that doesn't have a first-class stamp on it is a sales pitch," Don says. Reporters know that, and so should everyone else. Toss the sales stuff before it gets a chance to clutter up your office or kitchen table.

Don uses the same tactic when he gets a roll of film developed. He looks at the roll while standing over the trash can and tosses out-of-focus, poorly framed, and underdeveloped photos. No need to keep them around if they aren't any good. (For more on dealing with photographs and the clutter they can create, see pages 326 to 328.)

Take your name off the list. Sometimes you get on a mailing list by mistake. You start getting pet supply catalogs when you're allergic or baby supply catalogs when you have no kids. Sometimes you get on a mailing list because one company with which you deal sells your name to another, unrelated company. Here are two ways to end the deluge.

1. Contact the company. Next time you receive a catalog from a company with whom you have no interest in dealing, tear off the address sheet and send it back to the company with a note that says "Take me off your list." Within a couple of months, the company should comply. If you prefer, call the company's toll-free number, which should be listed on the catalog, and request that your name be removed from its list. Make sure to request that the company take you off the lists that it sells, too, or the avalanche will continue.

2. Contact the Direct Marketing Association (DMA). The DMA is a trade association of businesses that market to consumers. Consumers can contact the DMA and request—by completing a single form—that their name be removed from a whole host of mailing lists. You can fill out the form online at

---

WHAT ABOUT THE MAIL I WANT?

"**H**oney! Where's the phone bill?" "I know that invitation is around here somewhere." "I just bought stamps last week!" Are these familiar refrains around your house? You're not alone. Dealing with the deluge of junk mail is bad enough, but then there's the mail you actually want (or have) to look at. Don't give up. Here are two ways to cope.

1. PROVIDE A PERMANENT PIT STOP. Keep mail clutter under control by designating one permanent place where the "real" mail (not sales mail) always goes, regardless of who brings it in. That can be a basket on the floor by the front door or some type of desktop bin on a coun-

tertop. Make each family member responsible for sorting through the mail and retrieving what's his or hers, then alert everyone that anything left in the bin by, say, Sunday afternoon, goes out the door for recycling, with no exceptions!

2. SORT YOUR SUPPLIES. Don't waste time searching for envelopes, stamps, and address labels when you have bills to pay or invitations to mail. Keep all postal-related items in one kit, along with some pens, blank note cards, and stationery. If you have a home office, that's the perfect place for your mini post office. If not, a kitchen drawer will do.

---

www.the-dma.org/cgi/offmailinglistdave (with a $5 fee) or send your request by mail (for free) to Direct Marketing Association; 1120 Avenue of the Americas; New York, NY 10036-6700.

CATALOGS

Catalogs are like junk mail, only prettier. They're chock-full of gorgeous photos that show suspiciously clean kitchens, spanking new gadgets you don't need, and perhaps even a couple of items you *do* need. That's why you keep them around, right? Well, most people hold on to them until they're tripping over the pile. Sound familiar? Just read the tips below for some ways to dig out.

Alphabetize them. Here's how professional organizer Sally Brickell of Squared Away in Newton, Massachusetts, tackles the catalog issue. "It sounds crazy, I know, but I alphabetize my catalogs," she says. They stand upright in a cardboard box in hanging folders. She adds letter dividers so she can find each catalog by company name. Sally doesn't do this because she's a power shopper, but because she wants to keep only the most recent catalog. "When a new catalog comes in the mail, I can easily find the old one and replace it with the new one."

Use an alias. Sure, they said they wouldn't pass your name along, but how can you make sure? Take up an alias or two, says Bob Kennedy, a retired engineer who lives in Toano, Virginia.

confessions of . . .
a Concealer

JULIE WINTERS of Greenville, New York, thought she was being organized and efficient by opening her mail each afternoon when she got home from work, never letting it pile up. And she thought she was being particularly clever by writing the due date and amount due on the outside of her bill envelopes. "But then I would put them in a drawer, to keep them out of sight, and well, sometimes they ended up being out of mind, too," Julie confesses. "I knew I had to do something to keep my bills better organized, but also visible so I wouldn't forget about them."

Then she had an idea. Why not use a desktop file organizer in her kitchen? She went to her local office-supply store and found a compact version that was perfect for one corner of her kitchen countertop. "I divvy up the bills in 10-day increments," Julie explains. "I put bills due the first 10 days of the month in the first slot, bills due the next 10 days in the next slot, and so on." Now her bills are out in the open so they won't be overlooked, and they're neatly organized.

In the 1970s, he wanted and used several mail-order tool and gadget catalogs. But to trace which company was passing his name to other companies, he often used a recognizable alias when ordering catalogs: a favorite was Leroy. If that name appeared on unsolicited junk mail, he knew immediately which company was at fault. In these days of computer-generated mailing lists, you'll have to use one alias per mail-order company catalog that you sign up to receive—and you'll need to fill out the "do not sell my name" paperwork before you can get miffed.

MAGAZINES

That you'll have leisure time for reading is one of the most dangerous fantasies out there. You know you've fallen victim when you have dozens of magazines sitting around the office or living room collecting dust. You want to read those trade journals and the newsmagazines and your favorite cooking magazines, but just don't have the time. And now you don't have any room in your den, either. What to do? Read on.

Weed out the weeklies. When you're looking to eliminate magazine subscriptions, eye the weeklies first. Not only can you cut out 52 periodicals per year (versus 12 or 10), but the reality is that weekly publications are the toughest to keep up with. They're also the ones least likely to find a second life at the library or senior citizens center because they go out of date so darn fast, so you'll be less likely to send them on their way once you're done.

Give yourself a deadline. Paring down a long list of magazine subscriptions won't be easy. One approach, says Judie Yellin of Managing Partner in Newton, Massachusetts, is to set a deadline of 1 to 3 months for reading certain magazines. Once they've become that dated, it's time to throw them out and cancel the subscription, because you're clearly wasting your money. You can still buy the occasional issue off the newsstand; it'll be much cheaper than paying for the whole year.

Rip and read. Judie also recommends tearing out the articles you really want to read when you don't have time to read the whole thing. "Let's face it, a magazine is two-thirds ads anyway," she says. Put the torn-out pages into a To Read file (see chapter 12 for more about clutter-free filing systems). The articles will be there when you're ready to read them, but the bulky magazine itself will be long gone.

Skip the trial. Rose Kennedy of Knoxville, Tennessee, is a veteran magazine writer and communications consultant. But she would never dream of accepting a so-called trial offer for one or more free issues of a magazine, particularly those that are prominent on the Internet. "The problem is, they require a credit card and action on your part—you have to cancel the subscription when the free period is up. I just don't trust myself to keep track of that." If Rose wants to try out a magazine, she skims an issue at a bookstore or borrows it from a friend.

Pay by check. Many credit card companies offer trial issues of magazines, then "allow" you to bill the subscription on the card. Thereafter, the subscription is automatically charged to the card. That's too easy—you hardly notice that you're re-upping for another year's worth of magazines. Instead, pay for all magazine subscriptions with a check. When the money runs out, the company will have to actively request a renewal—and you'll have to actively consider whether you want to continue to receive the magazine.

MAXIMIZE MAGAZINE LIFE

It doesn't have to be the *Sports Illustrated* swimsuit issue for a magazine to have a second life at a second location. For example, a friend of ours never leaves for the pool in the summer without an armful of women's magazines to pass out (and for other people to dispose of). The beauty of such an arrangement is that other folks get to enjoy your magazines, and you get to enjoy the space that's left behind when you give them away. Here are a few possibilities. Of course, you'll want to check with each of these places to make sure they want your castoffs!

- [ ] A local college library
- [ ] Child care centers, for use in crafts
- [ ] Dentists' and doctors' waiting rooms
- [ ] Hospital waiting rooms
- [ ] Senior centers, for reading or use in physical therapy activities
- [ ] The lunch area of your office
- [ ] Your local public library (sometimes libraries can sell old copies of magazines for small fund-raising events)

Get it at the library. You'd be amazed at how many magazine subscriptions your local library maintains, says Joanne Kennedy, a retired reference librarian in Toano, Virginia. Sure, you have to plunk yourself down in a chair on the spot to read them, but that may provide a more welcome break than trying to enjoy your favorite sports publication at home with your many undone chores competing for attention.

Don't see what you want on the shelves? "Often libraries solicit requests for materials," Joanne says, "or they can request what you want via an interlibrary loan." And if you're truly in no hurry for the latest scoop on Madonna or 40 ways to fix chicken, many libraries also circulate donated magazines. If your area is home to lots of branch libraries, scour the offerings frequently, and you'll soon detect where people donate the magazines you want.

Pass along your subscription. You may already be stuck with the financial investment of a subscription you've grown tired of, but you don't have to be stuck with the clutter. "Lots of people don't know that you can transfer the remainder of a subscription to another address or even another name at another location," says Rose Kennedy. "Our family once received almost 2 years of a *National Geographic* subscription from my husband's Aunt Aileen, who couldn't keep up with it. It was a treasured gift for us." If no one you know would want your subscription, consider funneling it to a local school library or community center. Just call to give them a heads-up first.

Newspapers

You've heard the expression "As useful as yesterday's news"? A day-old newspaper *should* be old news in your home. Get it out of there. We don't care if your spouse hasn't consulted his horoscope yet or your child wants to check the baseball scores. Get it out of there. This is an area in which the "Use it or lose it" rule applies. If you're just not that ruthless, at least set boundaries. Create a newspaper area, and if you ever see an unread newspaper outside of it, out it goes. Here are some other ways to keep newspapers from overtaking your living and lounging areas.

Cancel all or part of your subscription. This advice does not, of course, apply to the person who luxuriates in a morning cup of coffee and the soft rustle of the newspaper. But if you're a "glance at the headlines when I get home" kind of guy or read only the weekly home and garden section, consider canceling newspaper delivery to your home. Then you can see whether you're motivated enough to go out and buy a paper each day. If you are, deposit the day-old newspaper in the recycling bin on your way. Also consider canceling only daily delivery, or only Sunday delivery, depending on which you don't really use fully and appreciate.

Pass it along. If you really do use and read your paper every day, and carefully keep and refold it, consider passing it on to someone else to read . . . just not someone else in your house-

"When I was a kid in the '60s and '70s, Pittsburgh, Pennsylvania, was a two-newspaper town," says book editor Lori Baird, who now lives in New York City. "On Sundays, my parents wanted to read both papers, the *Pittsburgh Post-Gazette* and the *Pittsburgh Press*. As it turned out, so did our next-door neighbor. For several years, both households bought both newspapers. But after a while, everybody realized that, since nobody can read two newspapers at once, it made more sense for my parents to buy the *Post-Gazette* (which came out Saturday night) and for our neighbors to buy the *Press* (which came Sunday morning). Everybody swapped Sunday afternoon.

"Although this newspaper-swapping routine did save both households some money, more important to my mom was that it saved having two newspapers strewn all over the house. And when my mom was happy, everybody was happy."

hold. Do you pass a fast-food breakfast restaurant or a diner on your way to work? Drop your used newspaper there each day. Sorry if we cut the press out of some business, but it seems almost certain that soon some folks will come to rely on your paper being there and stop purchasing their own . . . which saves them money and you clutter. The receptionist at work might also appreciate a slightly used daily, as might a night-shift worker going off duty as you come in to work. If you don't encounter anyone outside the home who might need your paper, find out whether your building or neighborhood has a crossword puzzle fan, especially someone who's shut in or can't get out of the house to pick up a daily easily.

Seek news online. You don't need the paper to get the latest news or sports or entertainment information. It's all over cable and the Internet. So consider making your transition complete, and get all your news from an online news source, without printing out a single article.

Holiday-Related Paper

We love holidays. They're the times when we gather with friends and family. We enjoy wonderful food and fun times. Sometimes we exchange gifts. What's not to like? Well, there's the clutter. But don't fret—we've found some terrific ways to make the holidays nearly clutter-free and perfect.

GREETING CARDS

That greeting card is sweet when you first tear into the envelope, but at some point you're going to have to get rid of it. Okay, you can keep the ones from your 18th birthday or the first Valentine's Day you spent with your mate, but the others can take on a life (and several boxes and drawers) of their own. Start whittling away the unwieldy pile by taking out all the cards that don't have a handwritten message (or that have a meaningless, lifeless tone). Put them in with the recycling, or donate them to a preschool for craft projects. Here are a few other ways to say goodbye to greeting-card clutter.

Send a cyber card. You may not realize that e-mail greeting cards are free to sender and recipient. Although they're not necessarily perfect for folks who stand on ceremony, they are a genuine, heartfelt greeting—heartfelt, read once, then, blissfully, gone for good. If you'd like to encourage others to use these paper-free birthday and holiday gestures, get the ball rolling by adopting the habit yourself.

Cut down cards if you can't throw them out. You can turn old greeting cards into perfectly nice gift tags just by cutting them into small squares or rectangles.

Give 'em a home. If you send a lot of greeting cards throughout the year, create a special area just for storing ones you buy ahead of time, along with your addresses, stamps, envelopes, and the like. During the Christmas season, keep a special basket just for the cards you receive. Keep them until the following year, then when card-writing time rolls around again, send cards only to those who sent you one. This seems crass, but you'll save time, money, and effort by paring down your Christmas list. We

know of one very loving couple who has never sent a Christmas card, and no one seems to like them less.

GIFT WRAP AND RELATED CLUTTER

It may be better to give than to receive, but even giving gifts can create great heaps of mess at your home. And most of us don't designate space for outgoing gifts or have a whole closet to spare for wrapping and trappings (with the possible exception of Concealers, who probably have a swell $50 container designed particularly for bows). To cut down on gift clutter, try to avoid holding on to gifts longer than you have to, and minimize the stuff you keep around to wrap gifts. Here are a few solid strategies.

Send a gift certificate. Celia Hall lives in Anchorage, Alaska, where the mail is slow and the overnight shipping prices exorbitant. But she says that even if she lived next door to her nieces (who are several time zones away), she'd still give them gift certificates to their favorite hometown boutique to mark special days.

A gift certificate eliminates the need for exchanges, storage, or a trip to the post office, any of which can turn a potential gift into yet another undelivered pile of stuff in your living room or basement. You also won't need to stock wrapping, tape and boxes, or packing peanuts. Celia does take several steps to guarantee that her gift certificates are still personal. She buys them directly from the store, over the phone and at her leisure, then asks the manager or owner to call the recipient on her birthday to announce a gift "from Cissy, Dan, and the dogs." She eschews mail-order certificates, because she'd rather the girls shop where they can get immediate gratification and can visit several times before deciding on purchases.

Deemphasize holidays. Now that we're all grown-ups, can we forget a birthday here and there? Probably not, says Rose Kennedy, who regularly exchanges gifts with adults including her husband, a goddaughter, two parents, and five in-laws. "But I've learned to do one thing that really helps me with clutter at the house and also helps me give people better presents. Instead of waiting for the holiday to roll around, I give a present when I see something at a good price that the other person would like. I don't hang on to it. Then I send a card or give them a hug on the 'real day.'" Last year Rose sent her in-laws and her parents flannel sheets a few months before Christmas, for example, knowing they could enjoy them more starting in October than January (and not wanting to have them mailed to her home in the interim).

Leave it to the experts. One way to completely eliminate gift wrapping clutter is to have all your gifts wrapped by the pros. Large department stores usually have year-round gift-wrap departments. The service isn't always inexpensive, but if you really want to cut the clutter, it's the way to go.

CLUTTER CRUSADERS
Give Up Gifts

"YEAR AFTER YEAR, MY HUSBAND and I struggled to find the right Christmas gifts for my sister- and brother-in-law," says Lori Baird, a book editor who lives in New York City. "The four of us are pretty straightforward, so we talked about the situation. It turned out that we all dreaded the holidays and searching for gifts for each other. So we hit upon a solution. Rather than exchanging gifts each year, we decided to go out to dinner and enjoy a nice meal together. It's worked out beautifully, especially since we all live in New York City and have access to hundreds of top-notch restaurants. Not only does the idea eliminate paper and gift-box clutter, but it also eliminates mental clutter, which may be the biggest perk."

Keep it corralled. If you can't eliminate all traces of gift-related clutter from your home, you can at least keep it organized. Here are four ways.

1. Wrap it up. Store long tubes of gift wrap by unwrapping it from the tube and rerolling it to fit inside the tube. Cut a small piece of wrap and tape it to the tube for identification.

2. Keep boxes to a minimum. Hold on to only one or two used boxes for gifts. Store small boxes inside the big ones.

3. Avoid event-specific wrapping paper. You know: the kind that says Happy Graduation! or

New Baby! Instead, buy long, wide rolls of plain paper that can accommodate almost any present you might need to give.

4. Make your own. A graphic designer we know uses brown craft paper, rattan, stamps, and stencils to create beautiful handmade gift wrap and spectacular ribbons and geegaws for every gift he gives.

Prevail over Photos

Many folks list "put photos into albums" as a priority activity they'll take up when they retire. The only other time it's likely to actually happen is if a skiing accident sends you to bed for 6 months. In the meantime, you're stuck with bag and stack upon box and pile of photos—and mostly photos of red-eyed people and Aunt Myrtle's old boyfriend, at that. Just because that's how everyone (with the possible exception of Felix Unger) handles photos doesn't mean you're doomed to live with photographic clutter. Instead, adopt these tactics.

No need to get too fancy. Caroline Kirschner has built a substantial business as a scrapbooking consultant for Creative Memories, but the Jackson, Tennessee, resident has a contrary message for those who need to store photos: Forget the fancy scissors and the stickers. "It's far more important to complete a basic photo album," she says. If you wait until you have time to do the fancy book, you could end up with mass quantities of unidentified photos cluttering up the place. "Instead, get the photos into a book with acid-free pages, one that people will look forward to flipping through. And, most importantly, write down

---

HOW TO TREAT PHOTOS YOU WANT TO KEEP

When you carefully preserve the photos you like and want (and only those photos you like and want), you don't have to keep lots of extras around, and that reduces clutter. Follow these guidelines with "keepers," and you can toss the rest with confidence.

☐ **WRITE THE RIGHT WAY.** Never write directly on any part of a photograph. Use an acid-free adhesive label on the back or write on the album page.

☐ **STAY FREE OF ACID.** Mount photos only in albums with acid-free paper. Any other kind of paper or adhesive mechanism breaks down over time and can damage photographs.

☐ **WATCH THE THERMOMETER.** High temperatures can fade or ruin photos, as can humidity higher than 60 percent.

☐ **SAFETY FIRST WITH STORAGE CONTAINERS.** Some storage options damage photos over the long haul. Those include cardboard boxes, brown envelopes (especially with glue and a metal clasp), and rubber bands.

---

who is in the photos and what they're doing, what we call 'journaling' in the scrapbook business." Photo albums are easier to store than shoe boxes of photos, and selecting photos for a book helps you see which prints you can toss or mail along to Grandma, too.

Toss the bad shots. People seem to think that because they paid for the film and the developing, they are obligated to keep really lousy photographs. Well, they're not.

In fact, "if you don't know 'em, throw 'em," ought to be your motto. Sure, make a quick call to Aunt Suzie to be certain that no one can identify those folks gallivanting around the Christmas tree in matching plaid. But once you've established that you don't know who's in those photos, give them a toss.

The same goes for people in photos that you know all too well. If it's unlikely that *People* magazine will be calling for a record of so-and-so's early life, you don't need to keep photos of them.

Positively get rid of most negatives. The chance that you'll actually use a negative to make a copy of a photo is very slim. Keep only those negatives of prized photographs or truly meaningful events—and always toss negatives if you can't tell what's on them. Even without a negative, there are ways to duplicate photographs if it really becomes necessary. Store the negatives you do keep in their own envelopes and write a brief description of the contents on the outside. For permanent storage, use polyethylene transparent holders or a steel filing cabinet.

Don't dismiss a digital approach. Digitized photos can be stored on a personal computer, on disk, or on the Internet. As such, they take up a whole lot less room than traditional prints and are easier to sort, store, and share with friends. If you're at all computer phobic, don't panic. Just dip your toe into the digital water: Next time you develop pictures, get

NO PHOTOGRAPHS, PLEASE

Shutterbugs, beware. Unless your basement is truly temperature controlled, you'll need to store your snapshot collection elsewhere, says Lisa Wendt, a professional organizer in Eagan, Minnesota. "Technically, photos should be kept between 73°F and 77°F. That's a pretty precise range, and hard to maintain in the average basement," she warns. Your best bet: Place photos in albums and keep them in the living area of your house, where they can be enjoyed by everyone on a regular basis.

If you absolutely have nowhere else to keep your photos, Lisa says that you can offer your images at least a measure of protection by storing them in what are called "photo-safe boxes." These specially made boxes are available at camera shops and are intended to keep photos dry, dust-free, and at a relatively stable temperature.

them back on a compact disc (CD) that you can use in your computer's CD-ROM drive—the service is now widely available. From there, you can print the images yourself, manipulate them, incorporate them into documents, send them to friends, and organize them in albums. Photo CDs occupy a whole lot less space than traditional photo albums, and you don't have to worry about damaging the prints with tape or glue. You can also take the CD back to the photo store and have reprints made when you really need good-quality paper copies—a lot easier than searching for that missing negative strip when you want reprints.

What about your old photos? You can store those digitally also, but that requires a piece of equipment known as a scanner. A scanner, which looks like a small photocopier, converts ordinary photos into digital images, which you can then store on your computer and use in the same way as described above. With the right software, you can even change scanned photos and improve the contrast, clean up smudges, erase tears, and do other touch-ups (such as giving everybody silly hats). You can even colorize black and white photos! Using a scanner to re-create your collection of ancestral photography is a great way to share rare prints with other family members, or prepare a scrapbook for an upcoming family reunion.

If you find yourself really getting into digital photography, you'll probably want to skip the middleman (the developing process), dump your old-fashioned film camera, and purchase a digital one.

There is one caveat to the digital approach. Experts speculate that, over decades, CDs *may* degrade at a faster rate than prints. So rather than toss valuable photos after you digitize them, you may want to hold on to them.

Kid-Related Paper

A baby's primary function is to generate dirty diapers. Later, as he gets a little older, his job description changes to producing paper: artwork, permission slips, tests and quizzes, notices for soccer practice, and the like. What to do with it all? Here are some ideas.

MANAGING MEMOS, PERMISSION SLIPS, AND MORE

While you're yearning for the days of the one-room school house, use these tips to deal with the everyday reality of school paper.

Make a school-only bulletin board. Hang a bulletin board in the kitchen just for school-related paperwork. Use it to organize the following papers.
• Permission slips
• Report cards that need to be signed
• Schedules
• Special announcements
• Tests and quizzes
• Vacation day calendars
• Weekly school lunch menu

If you're a committed Tosser and don't want to clutter up your computer with tons of digital images, you can always let someone else store them. Many Internet sites allow you to upload your digital photos and create online photo albums. The online directory Yahoo (www.yahoo.com) provides such a service and also lists dozens of other Web sites that let you upload images, order prints of them, and share your photos with friends. Adobe ActiveShare (www.activeshare.com) and the Digital Fridge (www.thedigitalfridge.com) are just a couple of these services. Note that it can take a bit of time to upload your pictures to these sites, especially if you have a slow Internet connection.

Keep in mind that Web sites come and go, so if you can't find a suitable site right away, go to your favorite search engine and search on the keywords Digital, Photos, Store, and Upload.

Use a bin system. If you have children, your kitchen is the daily repository of school papers, memos from teachers, and sports activity schedules. Boy, what a logjam of paper! One of the easiest ways to get it all under control is to assign an area in the kitchen for each child's paperwork. It can be a box or basket on the floor, or a plastic or wire bin on the counter. The idea here is for each child to put each day's take-home papers (but not homework) in the bin so Mom and Dad can take a look at them. If there's a permission slip or sign-up for volunteer night, those papers should be on top. Your job is to go through your kids' bins every night, sign what you must, mark important events on your calendar, then replace the back-to-school papers in the bin for your child to retrieve in the morning. The rest can be recycled.

Once your family gets used to the new routine—kids put the papers in the appropriate bins each day, and parents dutifully check the bins each night—there will be no more frantic morning cries of "Where's my field trip permission form?" or "Did you sign my report card yet? Where is it?"

ARTWORK

Every week little Johnny comes home from preschool with a new set of finger paintings. They're beautiful. You ooh and aah just as you should and up they go on the office walls and the refrigerator. But tomorrow, there'll just be another set of drawings. And school papers and spelling bee honors. You barely have room for your own work. What do you do? Here are some simply ingenious ideas.

Let the kids decide what stays and what goes. So says Barbara Clement of OrganizationWorks in Wellesley, Massachusetts. It's okay not to keep everything. "It's not as though the kids are going to want to keep every grade-school project." You can even teach them the value of throwing things away that they don't need by talking to them about it. "Review the artwork they've brought home and ask them which ones they want to keep and which ones they don't." You'll be surprised at their astute choices. You may love everything they do, but they don't.

Open a gallery. Display your child's latest creations on the walls that line your stairways. Periodically change your displays there,

---

PARE DOWN FINGER PAINTINGS

Kid art tugs at our heartstrings, and even the most callous Tosser has trouble giving the boot to little Johnny's kindergarten paintings. There's good news: You can get the sentimental value without the clutter. Here's how.

☐ **HAVE A KODAK MOMENT.** Take a photograph of any piece you really like, keep the photos in a designated scrapbook, then throw away the original. You could also take a photograph of the child holding one or more pieces of artwork, so you can remember his age and interests at the same time.

☐ **PUT IT IN THE MAIL.** Let your kids use small pieces as stationery when they write letters to grandparents or other relatives.

☐ **GIVE THE GIFT OF ART.** Another way to get kid art clutter out of your house is to send it to someone else! Frame their masterpieces, then send them as gifts to grandparents.

---

keeping only the best samples until the wall is full. Then if you want to add one print, remove another one and toss or store it.

Archive old artwork. Kids create lots of drawings and artwork over the course of their lives. If you can't bear to part with a single masterpiece, you might try archiving them in a creative way. Simply take a photograph of each drawing or papier-mâché castle and then file the pictures in a photo album. You can create one for each child. This way, you can safely dispose of the art itself while retaining the spirit of the artist. By the time your kid is ready for college, you'll have a small but meaningful record of her artistic development.

Scan it. You can eliminate even the photo album if you use a scanner to capture the artwork digitally and then store it on your computer's hard drive. This has the added advantage of making the art more catalogable. And when you store artwork digitally and have the right software, you can manipulate all the images so that they're all the same size. Keep the artwork until high school graduation, then print it all out and present it to your child in a nice album format.

Use it. Turn a few of your kids' smaller pieces of artwork into stationery. Then, when they need to write a letter or thank-you note, they'll have the perfect paper right at hand.

Miscellaneous Paper Clutter

Tiny scraps of paper can invade your home like termites. If you can't stop writing yourself (or others) notes on tiny scraps of paper, take time once a week or so to transfer those notes to a list, then toss the scraps. Here are some more ways to deal with reminder scrap proliferation.

Stick to small Post-its. Can't break the Post-it habit? Then at least steer clear of the big Post-its and go for smaller ones. Why? Because you'll be more likely to remember to jot down only one note per Post-it. Then when you no longer need the information, you can pull off the little Post-it and throw it away. The trouble with the roomier size is that you're going to be tempted to slip new notes into the margins. That's when they really pile up, because you can never throw the old ones away.

Eliminate paper messages. If you don't have enough space to mount a message board near the phone and are tired of paper scraps floating around, consider purchasing an answering machine that has multiple mailboxes. That way, every member of the family can have his own private voice-mail box from which he can retrieve messages. Your callers will hear something like, "To leave a message for Mike, press one; to leave a message for Susan, press two," and so forth. You won't ever miss messages again, and you won't have to find a place to post other family members' messages.

Keep numbers neat and nearby. Don't clutter up your telephone area with paper lists of frequently called and emergency telephone numbers. Instead, tape a typed or handwritten list of the numbers inside the cabinet door closest to your telephone. That

COMBINE YOUR CALENDARS

Keeping track of family members' schedules can make your head spin and clutter your life. Perhaps you're putting your appointments in your electronic organizer, while your spouse keeps track of events in an old-fashioned appointment book, and your kids come home with printed-out sports schedules and lists of after-school activities. How can you keep tabs on all the comings and goings?

Many families have solved the "who needs to be where when" problem by posting everyone's schedule on a huge white board in the kitchen. Here's one way to arrange the information.

1. In a column on the left-hand side of the board write the numbers 1 through 31. These denote the days in any given month. If you're careful when filling in and erasing from the rest of the board, these numbers can stay from month to month.

2. Write each family member's name across the top of the board from left to right. Again, these names won't have to be erased from month to month.

3. Draw vertical lines that run from the top of the board to the bottom, between each name. Draw horizontal lines across the board between each number. You now have a calendar grid.

4. Ask family members to record their schedules in the appropriate spaces. For example, if sister Nicole writes "school dance 8 P.M." in the box under her name and in line with the number 5, that would mean she has a dance on the fifth of the current month. If Nicole isn't yet old enough to drive, that shows Mom and Dad that she needs a ride, and her dance information will also go into Mom or Dad's column.

5. As you work with this scheduling system, you'll create your own methods. You might, for example, want to use different colored markers for each family member, or reserve the red marker for events the entire family will be attending. Some families use large poster board instead of the permanent white board, so they can write in permanent ink and then use highlighters for important events. If you use this method, when the month is done, you can flip over the poster board and use the other side.

A family calendar puts everyone in the picture.

way, the numbers are close at hand, but out of sight.

Dry up. Eliminate paper messages and notes altogether. Instead, hang a dry-erase board near the telephone for jotting down messages and phone numbers. Hang another board on or near the refrigerator to start your grocery list.

Go high tech. Electronics stores sell home message centers. These gadgets are similar to phone answering machines and allow transient family members to leave voice messages for each other. The message center attaches to a refrigerator and records up to four messages in each family member's mailbox. A light flashes if a message awaits.

Use a notebook. To stem the tide of little notes around your house, try this. Hide your scrap paper and Post-it pads for a couple of weeks and replace them with a notebook. Keep it with you at all times to record names, phone numbers, reminders and such that come in via phone and e-mail. This notebook needs to be portable enough to slip into your briefcase and take to meetings where more tasks will be generated, or just into the kitchen to receive notes about domestic tasks. This way, you'll have one set of tasks on one list, and it will be easy to page backward to retrieve old information or check on anything you might have forgotten.

Blizzards of Books

"Out of control" is one way to describe a book lover's passion for the written word. Teetering towers of paperbacks on the bedside table. Imposing stacks of equally imposing nonfiction tomes piled on the floor. Bookshelves that groan with the weight of 20-year-old textbooks. Books never get discarded, and new ones arrive with daunting regularity. Forget finding the time to read them all: The real challenge is knowing where to put them!

If you sometimes feel as though you're running a used-book store, it's time to get organized—and, painful though it may be, to find ways to thin the collection and prevent those much-loved books from taking over your life.

DO YOU HAVE TOO MANY BOOKS?

For some people, more than 100 books in the house feels like clutter. Others have thousands—and would gladly have a few thousand more. If you answer "yes" to any of the following questions, you probably love books a little too much.

☐ Do you rent a storage locker to store extra books?

☐ Does it take more than a few minutes to find a specific book you're looking for?

☐ Do you buy new bookshelves every year?

PUT BOOKS IN THEIR PLACE

If you hang on to every book that comes in the door, you'll quickly come to two conclusions: There will never be enough space to hold them, and it will be very difficult to find a particular book when you want it. You can solve both problems with a little planning and organization. Here's how.

Never leave a room empty handed. Books tend to pile up—beside the couch, on the coffee table, and next to the bed—a lot faster than you put them away. To prevent them from spilling into every corner of your life, get in the habit of always picking up a book when you leave a room. If you immediately set it on the right shelf, you'll save yourself hours of marathon housekeeping.

Buy bookcases with deep shelves. "I live in a small house, so I have to maximize the space I have available," says Richard Levine, a retired librarian in Albuquerque, New Mexico. His trick: bookcases with deep, 14- to 16-inch shelves. "I can shelve books in double rows, which means I can store twice as many books in almost the same amount of space," he explains.

Put in "bonus" shelves. Take a look at your bookcases: Is there a lot of space between the tops of the books and the shelves above? You may want to install extra shelves in between. "I buy laminated or finished boards at Home Depot," Richard says. "They look good

and are easy to attach with screws, and I can fit a lot more books in each bookcase."

Stack 'em high. Don't have room for more bookcases? Consider installing brackets and shelves near the tops of the walls, anywhere from 8 to 10 inches below the ceiling, depending on the size of the books you want to store. The advantage of ceiling shelves is that they can run along almost every wall in the house—even above doorways—without using up floor space.

Stack books flat. The book cops won't arrest you if you stack books flat instead of standing them up. For bookcases with high shelves, this technique allows you to store more books in the same amount of space. Some people alternate books in vertical and horizontal stacks to give the shelves an attractive, parquetlike appearance.

Create a "must-read" spot. New books have a way of disappearing into the forest of old books before you have a chance to read them. Ben Levine, a musician in Los Angeles, California, has solved this problem by always putting new books on a small table next to his favorite reading chair. The books stay in plain sight until he's finished with them, at which point he moves them onto shelves with the rest of his collection.

Shelve books by genre. This is a great way to find books in a hurry. Assign separate shelves to different categories of books. For example, put all nonfiction books on one shelf, mysteries on another, and cookbooks on yet another.

Practice your ABCs. Whether or not you arrange books by category, it's helpful to shelve them alphabetically, either by title or by the author's name. When you want a particular book, you'll be able to put your finger on it in a few seconds.

Create an index. In the days before computers, librarians kept track of books by filling out index cards. It's still a good system. Before any book goes on a shelf, write down the title and author on an index card, along with its location in your bookshelves, then file the card in a small box. It's a lot easier to flip through an index-card file than to wander from bookcase to bookcase trying to find the book you need. Of course, you could use a spreadsheet program and your computer to create an index on your hard drive instead.

CULL THE HERD

Many people get emotionally attached to books. They think of each and every volume as

DO IT LIKE DEWEY

Many libraries organize books according to the Dewey decimal system. You can label the spines of your books the same way, to make it easier to shelve them by category or faster to find what you're looking for. In the Dewey system, books are grouped into 10 main categories, each with its own number.

000 Computers, information, and general
      reference
100 Philosophy and psychology
200 Religion

300 Social sciences
400 Language
500 Science
600 Technology
700 Arts and recreation
800 Literature
900 History and geography

If you're not a number person, you can substitute colored, adhesive dots for the Dewey categories. Put the dot about an inch from the bottom of the spine so it won't obstruct the title.

an old friend that will be with them always. Some books really *are* special—the family Bible, for example, or those life-changing novels you read in high school—but it doesn't make sense to cling to every book you've ever read. The only way to keep the book population in check is to periodically get rid of the ones you haven't read in years and will probably never read again. Don't know where to start? Try these tips.

Identify obvious deadwood. Do you really want to give valuable shelf space to that trashy thriller you read last summer, or a 1948 medical textbook that looked interesting (briefly) when you bought it at a flea market? Madge Van Ness, a physician in Sterling, Virginia, uses the following criteria to weed out unnecessary books:

• Get rid of books about subjects you're no longer interested in. Weed out the ones you don't remember. ("If they aren't memorable, why keep them?" Madge points out.)

• Give up on those books that you've been meaning to read for 20 years. ("If I haven't read them by now, I'm not going to," says Madge—and trust us, you won't, either.)

Do a good deed. Nursing homes, homeless shelters, and other social service agencies are often eager to take used books. They give them to clients or sell them as part of their fund-raising drives. "I never put books in the basement or a storage shed, because they aren't any good after that," says Edith C. Fensom, a former library clerk who runs a small business out of her home in Mechanicsville, Virginia. "It's better to give them to someone who wants them."

Unload at the used-book store. "Two or three times a year, I box all of the books I'm through with and take them to a used-book store near my house," says Jana Murphy, a writer in Olive Branch, Mississippi. "I usually walk away with $20 to $30."

Sell on the Web. On a Web site called Half.com, you can post descriptions of books you'd like to sell, along with the price. The buyer sends a check directly to you, and all you have to do is mail the books. The Web site takes a 15 percent commission, which is charged to your credit card.

Kick back at a yard sale. A yard sale's a great way to unload all of the leftover books

---

THE 1-SECOND RULE

"I go through my books about once a year, and always have a hard time getting rid of them," says Steve Falk, a Philadelphia lawyer. "I've found that the longer I think about each volume, the harder it is to let it go. So I came up with the 1-Second Rule. When I'm sorting books, I decide in 1 second whether they stay or go. It's surprising how many books I've gotten rid of this way—and most of them I've never missed."

ways to stay organized is to limit the books that get onto your shelves in the first place.

Quit the club. Mail-order book clubs are one of the world's primary causes of book clutter. Every 3 weeks, like clockwork, you get a little sheet of paper in the mail asking whether or not you want "this month's featured selection." Forget to send in that paper or miss the deadline, and here come the books. It's a pain to send them back, plus you have to pay the postage, so they lie around the house. The answer? If you already belong to a book club, quit. And if you don't? Don't join.

Use online resources. The failure of the e-book industry suggests that most people won't read novels online—but searching the Web is a great substitute for space-consuming reference books. Rather than buying oversize computer manuals or automotive price guides that you'll consult, at most, a few times a year, look up information you need on the Internet. You'll save on space and reduce clutter, and the information you get will probably be more up-to-date.

Give your library card a workout. Even small libraries have all the latest bestsellers, and bigger libraries, especially those affiliated with universities, carry just about every book you're ever likely to read. Danny Pogue, a retired bookkeeper in Bonita Shores, Florida, finds that browsing library shelves is a great way to discover new authors. And, like millions of other library users, she appreciates the fact that she

that you couldn't sell at secondhand stores or on the Internet. Used books usually go for a quarter or 50 cents—but hey, by then it's time to take whatever you can get.

Lay them to rest. The very idea of destroying books is heresy to book lovers, but books do outlive their usefulness. Do you think, for example, that anyone needs a fondue cookbook, or a craft book that describes how to make orange macramé plant hangers? Books that you can't sell or give away can have a useful second life if you drop them off at a paper recycler.

PUT THE BRAKES ON COLLECTING

For reasons unknown to science, books have the apparent ability to spontaneously regenerate: Put one book on your shelf, and a few days later there will be another . . . and another. Unless you want to spend your entire life organizing and cataloging books, one of the best never has to deal with a house full of books. When she's finished with books, she simply takes them back—and brings a new batch home.

Buy only nonfiction. Reference books, biographies, and books about hobbies and crafts get consulted again and again, so it's worth having them on your shelf. Mysteries or thrillers, on the other hand, usually get read just once. Why accumulate them? "Before buying books, I usually get them from the library to see if I like them and if I'm ever likely to refer to them again," notes Edith Fensom.

Buy one, get rid of one. Here's a great way to make sure your book collection doesn't take over your life. Every time you bring a book home, discard an old one. Think of it as ZBG—zero book growth. It works!

Resources for Clutter Control

FURNITURE AND SHELVING

There are loads of ideas in this book that incorporate specialty furniture and shelving. Here are some of the retailers that carry the items we mention.

COMFORT HOUSE
189-V Frelinghuysen Avenue
Newark, NJ 07114
(800) 359-7701
www.comforthouse.com
Good general source for organizing tools and products.

CREATIVE WOODCRAFT PLANS, LTD.
237 South Dixie Drive, Suite 15
Vandalia, OH 45377
(800) 296-6256
www.woodcraftplans.com
Building plans for bookshelves and benches.

THE HOME DEPOT
2455 Paces Ferry Road
Atlanta, GA 30339
(770) 433-8211
Attention: Consumer affairs
www.homedepot.com
A good general source for everything from hardware to storage devices.

IKEA
Plymouth Meeting Mall
498 West Germantown Pike
Plymouth Meeting, PA 19462
(800) 434-4532
www.ikea-usa.com
Low-cost, functional storage products, including items made especially for small-space living.

OFFICE INNOVATIONS, INC.
3870 Lawrenceville Highway, Suite C101
Lawrenceville, GA 30044
(800) 648-4348
www.officeinnovations.com
Office furniture, supplies, and storage devices.

OFFICE MAX
3605 Warrensville Center Road
Shaker Heights, OH 44122
(800) 283-7674
www.officemax.com
File, magazine, and office supply organizers.

O'SULLIVAN
1900 Gulf Street
Lamar, MO 64759
(800) 327-9782
www.osullivan.com
Computer furniture for home and office.

ROCKLER WOODWORKING AND HARDWARE
4365 Willow Drive
Medina, MN 55340
(800) 279-4441
www.rockler.com
Bookshelf plans.

BEST OF NEW ENGLAND
370 Cedar Avenue
East Greenwich, RI 02818
(800) 891-8644
www.bestofnewengland.com
Good source for free-standing and wall-mounted quilt racks.

SHAKER WORKSHOPS

PO Box 8001
Ashburnham, MA 01430
(800) 840-9121
www.shakerworkshops.com
Reproduction Shaker furniture, baskets, oval boxes, pegs, and pegboards.

SPIEGEL, INC.

Box 9209
Hampton, VA 23670
(800) 527-1577
www.spiegel.com
Good selection of storage benches.

STOREWALL

1699 North Astor
Milwaukee, WI 53202
(414) 224-0878
www.storewall.com
Slatwall storage and organization system.

STOVESDIRECT.COM

3840 West Seltice Way
Post Falls, ID 83854
(800) 395-9509
www.stovesdirect.com
Gas fireplace inserts.

VERMONT CASTINGS, MAJESTIC PRODUCTS

410 Admiral Boulevard
Mississauga, ON, Canada L5T 2N6
(800) 227-8683
www.vermontcastings.com
Gas fireplace inserts.

HARDWARE AND ACCESSORIES

In the preceding pages we've mentioned lots of clever doodads, gadgets, and gizmos that have been designed to help you cut clutter and get organized. Here's where you can get them.

ARTWIRE

7025 Camden Avenue
Pennsauken, NJ 08110
(800) 356-2830
www.artwirecreations.com
Coated wire organizing accessories, including shelves, racks, and baskets.

BED BATH & BEYOND

650 Liberty Avenue
Union, NJ 07083
(800) 462-3966
www.bedbathandbeyond.com
Good general source for organizing accessories.

BUCKETBOSS

Fiskars Brands, Inc.
2537 Daniels Street
Madison, WI 53718
(608) 259-1649
www.bucketboss.com
www.Fiskars.com

CHEF'S CATALOG

PO Box 620048
Dallas, TX 75262
(800) 884-2433
www.chefscatalog.com
High-end kitchenware, including ceiling racks for displaying and storing cookware.

CLOSET MASTERS, INC.

10626 York Road, Suite B
Cockeysville, MD 21030
(800) 548-1868
www.closet-masters.com

THE CONTAINER STORE

Customer Solutions
2000 Valwood Parkway
Dallas, TX 752340
(888) 266-8246
www.containerstore.com
Large, general selection of organizing and storage products.

COOKING.COM

Guest Assistance
2850 Ocean Park Boulevard, Suite 310
Santa Monica, CA 90405
(800) 663-8810
www.cooking.com
Kitchen organizing products.

EXPOSURES

1 Memory Lane
PO Box 3615
Oshkosh, WI 54903-3615
(800) 572-5750
www.exposuresonline.com
Products designed to safely organize, archive, and display photographs.

HOLD EVERYTHING

7720 Northwest 85th Terrace
Oklahoma City, OK 73132
(800) 421-2285
www.holdeverything.com
Functional but attractive storage devices, including bookshelves, baskets, and wardrobes.

LAMPS PLUS

Customer Relations
20250 Plummer Street
Chatsworth, CA 91311
(800) 782-1967
www.lampsplus.com
Lighting fixtures and accessories, including picture lights.

MAGELLAN'S INTERNATIONAL

110 W. Sola Street
Santa Barbara, CA 93101
(800) 962-4943
www.magellans.com
Terrific resource for all kinds of travel products, from maps to jewelry carriers and clothing.

ORGANIZE EVERYTHING/ CLOTHES HANGERS ONLINE

10325 Magnolia Avenue
Riverside, CA 92505
(800) 600-9817
www.hangersonline.com
Hangers and other clothing-storage products.

PETSMART

35 Hugus Alley, Suite 200
Pasadena, CA 91103
(888) 839-9638
www.petsmart.com
Dual-function feeders and products to help you keep your pet's toys and supplies neat and organized.

RADIO SHACK

300 West Third Street, Suite 1400
Fort Worth, TX 76102
(800) 843-7422
www.radioshack.com
Electrical gadgets, including dimmer switches and phone jacks.

RUBBERMAID HOME PRODUCTS DIVISION

Consumer Services
1147 Akron Road
Wooster, OH 44691
(888) 895-2110
www.rubbermaid.com
Food storage and utility products; Web site features a complete product list and a store locator.

SMITH+NOBLE WINDOWARE
PO Box 1387
Corona, CA 92378
(800) 560-0027
www.smithandnoble.com
High-end window treatments, including shades and blinds.

STACKS & STACKS HOMEWARES
1045 Hensley Street
Richmond, CA 94801
(877) 278-2257
www.stacksandstacks.com
Storage and space-saving products including wall-mounting ironing boards and ready-made desktop hutches.

STURBRIDGE YANKEE WORKSHOP
90 Blueberry Road
Portland, ME 04102
(800) 343-1144
www.sturbridgeyankee.com
Traditional accessories and furniture, including mitten trees, quilt racks, and stair baskets.

STYLE-RITE HANGERS AND DISPLAY CO., INC.
1371-7 Church Street
Bohemia, NY 11716
(800) 789-5748
www.styleriteinc.com
Collapsible garment racks and clothing, bedding, and drapery hangers.

ORGANIZATIONS

The following organizations might welcome items you no longer want.

THE ASSOCIATION OF JUNIOR LEAGUES INTERNATIONAL, INC.
132 West 31st Street, 11th Floor
New York, NY 10001
(212) 951-8300
www.ajli.org

BOY SCOUTS OF AMERICA, NATIONAL COUNCIL
PO Box 152079
Irving, TX 75015-2079
www.scouting.org
Check the Yellow Pages under Social Service and Welfare Organizations for the phone number of a council near you.

WORLD COUNCIL OF CHURCHES, U.S. CONFERENCE
475 FDR Drive
New York, NY 10002
(212) 870-2533
www.wcc-coe.org

GOODWILL INDUSTRIES INTERNATIONAL, INC.
9200 Rockville Pike
Bethesda, MD 20814
(800) 664-6577
www.goodwill.org

HABITAT FOR HUMANITY
Partner Service Center
121 Habitat Street
Americus, GA 31709
(229) 924-6935, ext. 2551
www.habitat.org

LIONS CLUBS INTERNATIONAL HEADQUARTERS
300 West 22nd Street
Oak Brook, IL 60523
(630) 571-5466
www.lionsclubs.org

TOYS FOR TOTS
Marine Toys for Tots Foundation
PO Box 1947
Quantico, VA 22134
(703) 640-9433
www.toysfortots.org

YMCA OF THE USA
101 N. Wacker Drive, Suite 1400
Chicago IL 60606
(312) 977-0031
www.ymca.net

YWCA

Empire State Building
350 Fifth Avenue, Suite 301
New York, NY 10118
(212) 273-7800
www.ywca.org

PROFESSIONAL ORGANIZERS AND CONSULTANTS

If you're feeling stuck, maybe it's time for some professional help. The expert organizers listed below can help you at any stage of your decluttering process.

NATIONAL ASSOCIATION OF PROFESSIONAL ORGANIZERS

PO Box 140647
Austin, TX 78714
(512) 206-0151
www.napo.net
Provides referrals to organizing professionals in your area.

CALIFORNIA CLOSETS

1000 Fourth Street
San Rafael, CA 94901
(888) 336-9709
www.californiaclosets.com
Custom-designed and -built home organizing systems.

CLOSETS BY DESIGN

13151 S. Western Avenue
Gardena, CA 90249
(800) 293-3744
www.closets-by-design.com

Recommended Reading

Aronson, Tara, *Simplify Your Household* (Pleasantville, NY: Reader's Digest, 1998).

Aslett, Don, *Don Aslett's Clutter Free! Finally and Forever* (Cincinnati: Betterway Books, 1995).

_____, *Clutter's Last Stand* (Cincinnati: Writer's Digest Books, 1994).

_____, *Not for Packrats Only* (New York: New American Library Trade, 1991).

_____, *The Office Clutter Cure* (Cincinnati: Betterway Books, 1995).

Bredenberg, Jeff, ed., *Clean It Fast, Clean It Right* (Emmaus, PA: Rodale Press, 1998).

Eisenberg, Ronni, and Kelly, Kate, *Organize Your Office!* (New York: Hyperion, 1999).

Gracia, Maria, *Finally Organized, Finally Free* (New York: Avalon, Blue Moon Books, 1999).

Hanby-Robie, Sharon, *My Name Isn't Martha, But I Can Decorate My Home* (New York: Pocket Books, 1998).

Kingston, Karen, *Clear Your Clutter with Feng Shui* (New York: Broadway Books, 1999).

Koopersmith, Linda, *The Beverly Hills Organizer's House Book* (Beverly Hills: Beverly Hills Organizer, 1996).

Lehmkuhl, Dorothy, and Lamping, Dolores Cotter, *Organizing for the Creative Person* (New York: Crown, 1994).

Morgenstern, Julie, *Organizing from the Inside Out* (New York: Henry Holt, 1998).

Proulx, Earl, *Earl Proulx's Yankee Home Hints* (Emmaus, PA: Rodale Press, Yankee Books, 1993).

_____, Yankee *Magazine's Make It Last* (Emmaus, PA: Rodale Press, Yankee Books, 1996).

_____, Yankee *Magazine's Practical Problem Solver* (Emmaus, PA: Rodale Press, Yankee Books, 1998).

_____, Yankee *Magazine's Vinegar, Duct Tape, Milk Jugs & More* (Emmaus, PA: Rodale Press, Yankee Books, 1999).

Yankee Magazine, ed., *Living Well on a Shoestring* (Emmaus, PA: Rodale Press, Yankee Books, 2000).

Yankee Magazine, ed., *Now That's Ingenious!* (Emmaus, PA: Rodale Press, Yankee Books, 2001).

Meet Our Clutter-Cutting Experts

CHAPTER 2 • **Steve Brown** is a family counselor and therapist in Knoxville, Tennessee; **Melanie McGhee** of Maryville, Tennessee, is a longtime therapist, meditator, and personal coach; **Cathy Steever** runs a clutter-controlled household in Medfield, Massachusetts; **Amy Witsil**, a working mom in Chapel Hill, North Carolina, has moved three times in the past 3 years.

CHAPTER 3 • **Steve Brown** is a family counselor and therapist in Knoxville, Tennessee; **Nancy Byrd** is a hard-core neatnik living in Indianapolis, Indiana; Former Peace Corps worker **Bob Grimac**, a veritable recycling guru, has initiated a school system–wide recycling program in Knoxville, Tennessee; **Rose Kennedy** of Knoxville, Tennessee, is a veteran magazine writer, writer for the HGTV cable channel's Web site, and communications consultant. She has reviewed children's books for more than a decade; **Amy Witsil**, a working mom in Chapel Hill, North Carolina, has moved three times in the past 3 years.

CHAPTER 4 • **Evelyn Abbott** is an imaginative clutter-recycling grandmother in Albuquerque, New Mexico; **Judy Van Wyk** of Providence, Rhode Island, is an avid camping mom.

CHAPTER 5 • **Ollie Belcher** is an antiques dealer and avid collector in Corbin, Kentucky; **Nancy Byrd** is a hard-core neatnik living in Indianapolis, Indiana; Graphic designer **Tom Russell** designs the program guide for a house and garden cable network based in Knoxville, Tennessee.

CHAPTER 6 • **Ollie Belcher** is an antiques dealer and avid collector in Corbin, Kentucky;

Joanne Kennedy is a retired reference librarian in Toano, Virginia; **Jim Slate** is a retired electrician in Winnsboro, South Carolina; Art professor **Sam Yates** of Knoxville, Tennessee, also professes a philosophy of clutter control. He is director of the Ewing Gallery at the University of Tennessee.

CHAPTER 7 • **Linda Cavazzini** of Greenville, New York, loves to cook, and maintains an ever-growing but organized collection of recipes and cookbooks; **Ellyn Gellar-Elstein** is president of Creative Closets, Ltd., in Allentown, Pennsylvania; **Beth Hudson**, a professional organizer with 20 years' experience, owns the Philadelphia-based Right@Home; **Rose Kennedy** of Knoxville, Tennessee, is a writer who loves cookbooks but hates clutter; **Kitty Mace** is a graphic designer who lives in the Philadelphia suburbs.

CHAPTER 8 • When he's not docked in East Hampton, New York, **Adrian Algañaraz** spends most of his summers cruising along the East Coast on board his shipshape 36-foot sailboat, *Whistler*; **Ollie Belcher** is an antiques dealer and avid collector in Corbin, Kentucky; **Trudye Connolly** is president of Coco Connolly Company, a PR firm in Chicago that represents numerous design and home-furnishing clients; **Joanne Kennedy** is a retired reference librarian in Toano, Virginia; **Melanie McGhee**, of Maryville, Tennessee, is a longtime therapist, meditator, and personal coach; Art history professor **Amy Neff** lives in Knoxville, Tennessee; **Jim Slate** is a retired electrician in Winnsboro, South Carolina; **Catherine Thimmesh** is a children's book author and former art gallery owner from Minneapolis; Homemaker

Barbara Wilhoit is the mother of four teenagers in Farragut, Tennessee; Joey X (he asked to remain anonymous), of New York City, is an editor at a large comic book publisher and a longtime collector of "stuff" that includes around 15,000 comic books; Art professor Sam Yates of Knoxville, Tennessee, also professes a philosophy of clutter control. He is director of the Ewing Gallery at the University of Tennessee.

CHAPTER 9 • Linda and Boyd Allen of Exeter, New Hampshire, consult their daughter Marjorie in many of their battles with clutter; Volena Askew is an adult home economics teacher and supervisor in Knox County, Tennessee; Retired banker Russell Buchanan of Mendham, New Jersey, has been a clutter buster (and penny pincher) for most of his 70-something years; Nancy Byrd is a hard-core neatnik living in Indianapolis, Indiana; Maureen Cronin of Exeter, New Hampshire, is a community health nurse who specializes in home care; Attorney Addy Eshbach shares her small Boston condominium (about 650 square feet) with a Cairn terrier named Charlotte; Madelyn Gray is a toy-recycling grandmother in Amesbury, Massachusetts; Rose Kennedy is a clutter-cutting mom and writer who lives in Knoxville, Tennessee; Norman (Norm) and Allison MacLean are the owners of The Wingate Collection, an antiques shop in an old farmhouse in Stratham, New Hampshire; Sue Morrill, a wife, retailer, and mother of two now-grown boys, lives in a small but organized house in Amesbury, Massachusetts; Diane O'Halloran is an interior designer from East Kingston, New Hampshire; Cindy Roach is an elementary-school nurse and an educator at a diabetes clinic in Portsmouth, New Hampshire; Interior designer Linda Stone and her husband, Paul, live in an antique farmhouse in Hampton Falls, New Hampshire, where they have owned an interior design business, Paul Stone Interiors, for 20 years; Ann and Bill Winter of Exeter, New Hampshire, work together in clutter management.

CHAPTER 10 • Massage therapist, writer, and reformed clutterer Maryjean Ballner lives with her husband, Roger, in Castro Valley, California; Richard Beaver is owner of Beaver Builders in Knoxville, Tennessee; Margaret Dasso is co-owner of The Clean Sweep, a housekeeping agency in Lafayette, California; Shelly Enos is a first-grade teacher from Loxahatchee, Florida; Bob Farkis is a professional organizer and owner of Clutter Buster in Los Angeles, California; Maria Gracia is the founder of Get Organized Now!, a professional organizing company in Milwaukee, Wisconsin. She is the author of *Finally Organized, Finally Free*; Sharon Hanby-Robie is a professional organizer and interior designer from Lancaster, Pennsylvania. She is the author of *My Name Isn't Martha, But I Can Renovate My Home*; Sewing and craft expert Pamela Hastings is from Wall, New Jersey; Web site designer Paul Hayes of Santa Ana, California, has lived an organized life in a 28- by 70-foot doublewide mobile home for more than 15 years; Californians La Doris "Sam" Heinly, Memories in the Making coordinator for the Orange County chapter of the Alzheimer's Association, and her husband, Daryl, chief executive officer for an electronics firm, enjoy a clutter-controlled life aboard their 48-foot sailboat, *Diversion*; Joely Johnson is a publications editor from Alburtis, Pennsylvania; Karla Jones is a professional organizer from San Mateo, California; For helping people minimize their messes in less than a minute, professional organizer Linda Koopersmith is known as "The Beverly Hills Organizer." She is the author of *The Beverly Hills Organizer's House Book*; Even without a linen closet, Shirley and Howard LaBounty enjoy an organized retirement in Zephyrhills, Florida; Barbara Lee is a family therapist in San Marcos, California; Anne McAlpin is owner of Pack It Up in Jacksonville, Oregon; Debra Moore of Allen, Texas, is an internal auditor for JC Penney; Marcia C. Smith is a newspaper sportswriter from southern California; Courtney Watkins, a former kindergarten teacher and now a professional creativity expert from Los Angeles, has been called the

"Mary Poppins of the New Millennium" by Donny Osmond of the former *Donny & Marie* daytime talk show.

CHAPTER 11 • **Richard Beaver** is owner of Beaver Builders in Knoxville, Tennessee; **Betty Belnoski** is proprietor of Organize 123 in Fogelsville, Pennsylvania; **Tom Cavalieri** of New York City is a reformed and repentant overdue-fine-paying public-library user; **Maria Gracia** is the founder of Get Organized Now!, a professional organizing company in Milwaukee, Wisconsin. She is the author of *Finally Organized, Finally Free*; **Penney Martellaro** of Dovetail Designs is a Missouri crafter of Shaker furniture. Her work is exclusively featured at a store called Simply Elegant in Golden, Colorado; Interior design author **Glenna Morton** is a guide with the Web site About.com (http://interiordec.about.com).

CHAPTER 12 • **Lori Baird** is a writer and book editor who lives in New York City; Organizer **Fifi Ball** is co-owner of Squared Away in Newton, Massachusetts; **Nancy Black** of Organization Plus in Beverly, Massachusetts, has been helping people organize their workspaces for 18 years; **Anne Braudy** is a professional organizer and owner of Before & After in Brookline, Massachusetts; Organizer **Sally Brickell** is co-owner of Squared Away in Newton, Massachusetts; **Barbara Clement** is a professional organizer for OrganizationWorks in Wellesley, Massachusetts; **Carol DaSilva** is a computer expert in Emmaus, Pennsylvania; **Rachel Goldman** is a computer-savvy technical writer in Plano, Texas; **Connie Hatch** is a writer living in New York City; **Paul Hayes** is a Webmaster who lives in Santa Ana, California; **Larry Lachman, Psy.D.,** is a family therapist and dog/cat behavior consultant in Carmel, California; **Richard Nielsen,** of Oceanside, California, owns 24HR Computer Housecalls; **Lynne Silvers** is a professional organizer for Finally (!) Organized in West Roxbury, Massachusetts; **Marcia C. Smith,** of Seal Beach, California, is sportswriter and self-taught computer troubleshooter; **Cheryl Wilhite** is a computer service and support technician in Plano, Texas; **Dexter Van Zile** is a writer living in Brighton, Massachusetts; **Judie Yellin** is a professional organizer for Managing Partner in Newton, Massachusetts.

CHAPTER 13 • **Lori Baird** is a writer and book editor who lives in New York City; **Ollie Belcher** is an antiques dealer and avid collector in Corbin, Kentucky; **Tom Cavalieri** is an artist and art installer living in New York City; **Janet Hall**, a professional organizer, is president of OverHall Consulting in Port Republic, Maryland; **Ed Jensen** lives in Hastings, Nebraska; **Bruce Johnson** is a woodworker and HGTV cable television personality; **Bill Keller** is a longtime home-repair book author and do-it-yourselfer from Lemont, Illinois. He produces videos for the home improvement industry; **Carol Keller** is a personal organizer from Portland, Oregon; **Rose Kennedy** of Knoxville, Tennessee, is a veteran magazine writer, writer for the HGTV cable channel's Web site, and a communications consultant. She has reviewed children's books for more than a decade; **Wade Slate** is a lawn-care professional and avid do-it-yourselfer in Knoxville, Tennessee; **Bill West** of Fort Collins, Colorado, is a professional garage-organizing expert and a real-estate broker with 25 years' experience; Home-improvement enthusiast **T. J. Wilson** is from Monticello, Illinois; **Matt Witsil** lives in Chapel Hill, North Carolina.

CHAPTER 14 • **Chris Bean** of Winchester, Massachusetts, keeps coming up with practical ideas for keeping his workspace tidy; **Nancy Black** of Organization Plus in Beverly, Massachusetts, has been helping people organize their workspaces for 18 years; **Gillian Davies** is a clutter-cutting environmental scientist and mother of two from Acton, Massachusetts; **John Gromek** is the owner of Exeter Cycles in Exeter, New Hampshire; **Pat Moore** is a professional organizer in McKenney, Virginia; **Donald and Nancy Seaton** live in Hastings, Nebraska. Don is a newspaper publisher and an avid collector; **Lynne Silvers** is a professional organizer for Finally (!) Organized in West Roxbury, Massachusetts; **Wade Slate** is a lawn-care professional and avid do-it-yourselfer in Knoxville, Tennessee; Professional organizer **Cherri Smith** is called Dirty Girl by her friends and clients because, as she says, "If you're going to organize a garage or shed, you're going to get dirty." She lives in East Troy, Wisconsin; **Joel Thomas** is the owner of New England Small Craft in Rowley, Massachusetts; **Bill West** of Fort Collins, Colorado, is a professional garage-organizing expert and a real-estate broker with 25 years' experience; Home-improvement enthusiast **T. J. Wilson** is from Monticello, Illinois.

CHAPTER 15 • Tara Aronson, mother of three in Pacific Palisades, California, is author of *Simplify Your Household*. She is also the clutter columnist for the *San Francisco Chronicle*; **Don Aslett** is author of many books about cleaning and clutter busting, including *Don Aslett's Clutter Free! Finally and Forever* and *Clutter's Last Stand*; **Richard Barrale** is the owner and president of All-Star Moving and Storage in Brooklyn, New York; **Richard Beaver** is owner of Beaver Builders in Knoxville, Tennessee; **Betty Belnoski** is proprietor of Organize 123, an organizational training program in Fogelsville, Pennsylvania; **Margaret Dasso** is co-owner of The Clean Sweep, a professional housekeeping agency in Lafayette, California; **Mark Dolar** lives in Los Angeles; **Shelly Enos** is a first-grade teacher from Loxahatchee, Florida; **Maria Gracia** is the founder of Get Organized Now!, a professional organizing company in Milwaukee, Wisconsin. She is the author of *Finally Organized, Finally Free*; **Sharon Hanby-Robie** is a professional organizer and interior designer from Lancaster, Pennsylvania. She is the author of *My Name Isn't Martha, But I Can Renovate My Home*; **Pamela Hastings** is a sewing and craft expert in Wall, New Jersey. **Bernie Kellman** has seen 398 rock concerts, give or take a few, since 1976. His "museum" of concert and rock music memorabilia has been displayed in only two

of the five homes Bernie has lived in over the past 10 years, most recently in Nazareth, Pennsylvania; Feng shui expert **Karen Kingston** explores the symbolism that clutter spaces have for us—and the significance of the stuff we keep there—in her book, *Clear Your Clutter with Feng Shui*; For helping people minimize their messes in less than a minute, professional organizer **Linda Koopersmith** is known as "The Beverly Hills Organizer." She is the author of *The Beverly Hills Organizer's House Book*; **Anne McAlpin**, of Jacksonville, Oregon, lacks the willpower to bypass antiques stores and, especially, items like trunks and tote bags. She has honed her love of travel and packing into a successful business she calls Pack It Up; **Cheryl Ross** is a member of the Minnesota chapter of the National Association of Professional Organizers, and is the founder of Amazing Space, Inc., in River Falls, Wisconsin; **James Sledd** is a personal organizer in Bryn Mawr, Pennsylvania; **Sharon Sobel** is founder of Let's Organize in Haddonfield, New Jersey; **Jack Summerlot** owns Summerlot Home Improvements in Coopersburg, Pennsylvania; **Courtney Watkins** is a creativity expert in Los Angeles; **Lisa Wendt** is a member of the National Association of Professional Organizers and founder of Sort-It-Out in Eagan, Minnesota.

CHAPTER 16 • Sally Brickell is a professional organizer for Squared Away in Newton, Massachusetts; **Barbara Clement** is a professional organizer for OrganizationWorks in Wellesley, Massachusetts; **Steve Falk** is a lawyer who lives in Philadelphia; **Edith C. Fensom** is a former library clerk who runs a small business out of her home in Mechanicsville, Virginia; **Celia Hall** lives in Anchorage, Alaska; **Bob Kennedy** is a retired engineer who lives in Toano, Virginia; **Joanne Kennedy** is a retired reference librarian in Toano, Virginia; **Rose Kennedy** of Knoxville, Tennessee, is a veteran magazine writer, writer for the HGTV cable channel's Web site, and communications consultant. She has reviewed children's books for more than a decade; **Caroline Kirschner** of Jackson, Tennessee, is a scrapbooking consultant for Creative Memories; **Ben Levine** is a book-loving musician in Los Angeles, California; **Richard Levine** is a retired librarian in Albuquerque, New Mexico; **Jana Murphy** is a writer and book lover in Olive Branch, Mississippi; **Danny Pogue** is a retired bookkeeper in Bonita Springs, Florida; **Don Seaton** is a newspaper publisher in Hasting, Nebraska; **Lisa Wendt** is a member of the National Association of Professional Organizers and founder of Sort-It-Out in Eagan, Minnesota; **Madge Van Ness** is a physician in Sterling, Virginia; **Penny Ward** is a computing consultant in Carrboro, North Carolina; **Julie Winters** of Greenville, New York, fights her Concealer nature with effective anticlutter ideas; **Judie Yellin** is a professional organizer for Managing Partner in Newton, Massachusetts.

Index

Boldface page references indicate illustrations. <u>Underscored</u> references indicate boxed text.

Utensils, storing kitchen, 98,
100, <u>100</u>
Utility shelves, using, 304

V

Vertical files, using, 224–25
Vicarious cluttering syndrome,
<u>21</u>

W

Wall mounting. *See also* Hooks
art and collectibles, <u>132</u>, 133
cleaning supplies, 193
kitchen items, 97–98, 115–16
lamps, 148
Wall recesses, 185–86, 199
Wardrobes. *See* Armoire for
storage; Dressers for
storage
Warehouse storage facilities, <u>313</u>
Wastebasket
bucket as, 147
emptying bedroom, <u>141</u>
Wax for cleaning shower tile,
179
Web sites
cooking, 108
saving, 235–36

What Else decluttering strategy,
<u>178</u>
Window covering decluttering,
129–30
Window decluttering, 129–30
Windowsills, decluttering,
129–30
Wine case for toiletries, 147
Wine rack placement, 110,
<u>308</u>
Wire baskets for storage,
188
Wood scraps, storing or
discarding, 255, <u>259</u>
Workbenches, 248–50, <u>249</u>
Work, Clutter Types at, 23–24.
See also Home office
decluttering
Workshop decluttering, 241–42.
See also Tools
benches, 248–50, <u>249</u>
broken items, 244–45
couples and, <u>243</u>
dowels, 255
duplicate items, 245–48, <u>245</u>,
<u>247</u>
fans for ventilating, <u>244</u>
hardware, <u>251</u>
lumber scraps, 255
markers, <u>256</u>
mechanic's chest, avoiding,
<u>257</u>

motivation, <u>242</u>
notebook, <u>246</u>
office supplies and, <u>256</u>
paper pile decluttering, <u>256</u>
Quantify step in, 245
rolling concept, <u>252</u>
safety equipment, <u>244</u>
scissors, hanging, 263
shelves, 250–51
slat board, <u>250</u>
in small area, 260–63
starting, 242–48, <u>242</u>
storage
mechanic's chest, avoiding,
<u>257</u>
tools, 251–56, <u>251</u>, **252**,
<u>252</u>, <u>254</u>, 261
unexpected, 255–56, **255**
tips, 256–60

Y

Yard sales. *See* Garage sales
Yarn, organizing, 138
YMCA/YWCA, 50

Z

Zip computer disks, using, 235